SOLDIERS IN THE
PROLETARIAN DICTATORSHIP

Studies of the Harriman Institute

Columbia University

The W. Averell Harriman Institute for Advanced Study of the Soviet Union, Columbia University, sponsors the Studies of the Harriman Institute in the belief that their publication contributes to scholarly research and public understanding. In this way the Institute, while not necessarily endorsing their conclusions, is pleased to make available the results of some of the research conducted under its auspices. A list of the Studies appears at the back of the book.

SOLDIERS IN THE PROLETARIAN DICTATORSHIP

The Red Army and the
Soviet Socialist State,
1917–1930

Mark von Hagen

Studies of the Harriman Institute

CORNELL UNIVERSITY PRESS

Ithaca and London

First published 1990 by Cornell University Press.

International Standard Book Number 0-8014-2420-8
Library of Congress Catalog Card Number 89-36148
Printed in the United States of America
Librarians: Library of Congress cataloging information
appears on the last page of the book.

⊛ The paper used in this publication meets the minimum requirements of the American National Standard for Permanence of Paper for Printed Library Materials Z39.48–1984.

for my parents

Contents

Illustrations

Preface

In 1924 the Thirteenth Party Congress acclaimed the Red Army as a school of socialism and congratulated officers and political workers for their role in bringing "consciousness" to often illiterate peasant soldiers. A deputy commissar of the army even described the army as a second Commissariat of Enlightenment. By the mid-1920s this positive evaluation of army activities united party leaders of virtually all the contending factions, including, notably, Leon Trotsky, Nadezhda Krupskaia, Joseph Stalin, and Nikolai Bukharin. Only a short time earlier, however, the military had withstood powerful assaults by many influential national leaders. The Mensheviks squarely charged the Bolsheviks with Bonapartist ambitions and denounced Red militarism as a betrayal of the Revolution. During the Civil War and early postwar years, even many prominent Bolsheviks, inspired by Marx's analysis of Bonapartist regimes and recalling the horrors of daily life in the Russian Imperial Army, feared that the officers of a standing army would restore all the worst features of the tsarist officer caste and marshal the reactionary energies of Russia's backward peasantry to destroy the gains of 1917. And, ironically, soldiers' repudiation of the imperial military order had helped bring down both the Romanov autocracy and its successor, the Provisional Government.

The fundamental shift in attitudes toward armies, military service, and soldiers is the central theme of this book. This is not a military history of the early Soviet state; I have investigated rather the political, social, and cultural aspects of the Red Army's development from the revolutions of 1917, when soldiers' status and self-perceptions improved dramatically, to the collectivization campaigns of 1929–1930, when the Soviet leadership learned both the advantages and drawbacks of harnessing soldier power to transform the social and political order of the Russian countryside. In the intervening years, the army gained legitimacy in postrevolutionary society; military careers became respectable avenues of upward mobility; and soldiers came to play an important role in state building. I have limited my focus largely to the Russian population of the Soviet state, though I have occasionally consulted source materials from other national regions. In future investigations I hope to explore the implications of military politics for the evolution of the Soviet federal system and nationality policies.

I have used a modified form of the Library of Congress system of transliteration for Russian words, but familiar names are rendered in their common English form (Trotsky, not Trotskii; Zinoviev, not Zinov'ev). Except where I have indicated otherwise, all translations from the Russian are my own. Dates are given in accordance with the Gregorian calendar.

This book could not have been completed without the generous support of many institutions, including Stanford University; the Mabelle McLeod Lewis Memorial Fund; the International Research and Exchanges Board; the Fulbright-Hays Young Fellows Program; the Kennan Institute for Advanced Russian Studies at the Woodrow Wilson International Center for Scholars; the Lenin Library in Moscow; the Library of the Academy of Sciences in Leningrad; the Library of Congress; the Summer Research Laboratory on Russian and Eastern Europe at the University of Illinois; Indiana University; and the libraries and Councils for Research in the Humanities and Social Sciences at Columbia University. Special thanks go to Galya Dotsenko and Hilja Kukk, librarians at the Hoover Institution; to Edward Kasinec and his staff at the New York Public Library; and to Eugene Beshenkovskii at the Harriman Institute Reading Room.

So many patient men and women have read all or part of this work that one might suspect that I have tried to disqualify in advance all potentially critical reviewers. That was not my intention; rather, I trust that the final product is a far better one than it would have been without them. To those who have read the manuscript or who have heard versions in seminars and lectures I owe a great deal of pleasure and stimulation, which I hope partially to repay with this volume. Among them I thank especially Jonathan Adelman, Seweryn Bialer, Katerina Clark, Frederick Corney, Alexander Dallin, Vera Dunham, Terence Emmons, William Fuller, Richard Hellie, Yanni Kotsonis, Hiroaki Kuromiya, Mikhail Kuz'min, David McDonald, Robert Maguire, Lynn Mally, Michael Melancon, Norman Perreira, Dale Plank, Alexander and Janet Rabinowitch, Thomas

Sanders, Jutta Scherrer, Thomas Sherlock, James Shenton, Wim Smit, Ronald Suny, Isabel Tirado, William Todd, Frank Wcislo, Robert Weinberg, Amir Weiner, Allan Wildman, and Elizabeth Wood. Since coming to Columbia, I have had the privilege of the intellectual and personal friendship of Leo Haimson, Moshe Lewin, Marc Raeff, Alfred Rieber, and Richard Wortman, each of whom has left his substantial mark on my view of Russian history. In Moscow, Mikhail Gefter inspired me with his remarkable perspective on the Soviet period. In Menlo Park, Paul Dotsenko made the Russian Civil War come alive in ways that no book ever could. Other Russian friends, especially Vladislav Kostin, Lev and Natasha Lominago, Mark Pecherskii, Valery Petrochenkov, the late Sergei Shuiskii, Inna Varlamova, and Eugenia Vigilianskaia, have debated passionately with me about the history of their country and people. Sheila Fitzpatrick, Stephen Kotkin, and John Ackerman have read this book in more versions than anyone else except myself and were always generous with helpful insights and advice. Many thanks to Barbara Salazar, who tried valiantly to turn my prose into something others could understand. Finally, without the considerable labors of Dmitry Fedotoff White and John Erickson, historians of the Red Army, including myself, still would be trying to reconstruct the most basic outlines of events.

Because this book deals primarily with education, socialization, and military life, some other influences deserve special mention. The teachers of Thornton High School, especially the late Ivan Ambrose, who infected me with his obsession for things Russian, sent me out into the world with rudimentary knowledge about the politics of education and a thirst for knowledge. My earliest years were spent as an Air Force brat in the warm community of my family's military friends, who taught me a great deal about humanity and generosity of spirit. And as I have pondered how this book came to be, I realize that my parents have been the sustaining inspiration for much of what I believe about the world and its inhabitants. Finally, a word of thanks to Johnny Roldan for sustaining me with his unselfish friendship during the past several months.

My acknowledgments to friends and colleagues should in no way implicate them in my excesses or shortcomings. I alone bear responsibility for this work "in earnest and for a long time."

MARK VON HAGEN

New York City

Terms and Abbreviations

aktivnost'　　independent initiative

batrak　　hired rural laborer

bedniak　　poor peasant

burzhui　　bourgeois; derogatory term for members of formerly privileged classes

Cheka　　Extraordinary Commission for the Struggle with Counterrevolution and Sabotage, the national political police from 1917 to 1922, succeeded by GPU

chony　　special assignment detachments, crack fighting units made up of party members and sympathizers

Council on Labor and Defense (STO)　　superseded Defense Council in April 1920

Defense Council　　Council of Worker-Peasant Defense, formed in November 1918 to coordinate mobilization tasks in civilian economy and military

Democratic Centralists　　a dissident party faction that protested the bureaucratization of the party

dvoenachalie　　dual command, the practice of requiring soldiers to obey an order only if it bore the signatures of both commander and commissar

edinonachalie　　one-man or unified command, in the hands of a commander who had proven his political reliability

fel'dsher　　military medical personnel; orderly

Glavpolitprosvet　　Main Committee for Political Enlightenment

gosudarstvennost'　　stateness, consciousness of state power

GPU　　State Political Administration, national political police and security service from 1922 to 1934, succeeded by NKVD

GUVUZ   Main Administration of Military Educational Institutions

khvostizm   tail-endism, Bolshevik party term applied to members who allowed the popular mood to determine their stance, as opposed to staking out a position in advance of the masses

komandy obsluzhivaniia   service units for disfranchised persons

kombed   committee of the rural (village) poor

Komsomol   Young Communist League

krai   administrative unit

krugovaia poruka   collective responsibility, especially in the village, with specific reference to tax obligations and conscription

kulak   wealthy peasant; often used as a general term of opprobrium for a person who exhibited exploitive or disagreeable behavior

kul'turnichestvo   Russified version of *kulturtregerstvo*, a prerevolutionary movement among the intelligentsia to bring culture to the masses; adjective, *kul'turnicheskii*

kul'turniki   cultural workers attached to army political departments

KVR   L. D. Trotskii, *Kak vooruzhalas' revoliutsiia*, 3 vols. (Moscow, 1923–1925)

mestnichestvo   local patriotism, protection of local interests against central demands

Military Opposition   a dissident party faction that disagreed with Trotsky's policies on the army at the Eighth Party Congress (1919)

Military Organization   Bolshevik party agency to conduct political work in the Imperial Army

military specialists   former officers of the Imperial Army who served in the Red Army

MOPR   International Organization for Aid to Imprisoned Fighters for the Revolution

mushtra, mushtrovka   harsh military discipline

Narkompros   People's Commissariat of Enlightenment

NKVD   People's Commissariat of Internal Affairs

obkom (oblastnoi komitet)   regional committee of Bolshevik party

Osoaviakhim   mass organization to disseminate knowledge about and promote support for military values, aviation, and chemistry

osobyi otdel   special department, an agency of the Cheka operating in the Red Army

partizanshchina   guerrilla warfare

politotdel   political department

politprosvety   departments of political enlightenment, local organs of Glavpolitprosvet

politruk (politicheskii rukovoditel')   instructor in an army political department

politustav   political manual, handbook of minimal required knowledge about political life and party history

PPR I   *Partiino-politicheskaia rabota v Krasnoi Armii (aprel' 1918–fevral' 1919): Dokumenty* (Moscow, 1961)

PPR II   *Partiino-politicheskaia rabota v Krasnoi Armii (mart 1919–1920 gg.): Dokumenty* (Moscow, 1964)

PPR III   *Partiino-politicheskaia rabota v Krasnoi Armii: Dokumenty, 1921–1929* (Moscow, 1981)

PPR IV   *Partiino-politicheskaia rabota v Krasnoi Armii: Dokumenty, iiul' 1929 g.–mai 1941 g.* (Moscow, 1985)

Proletkul't   Proletarian Culture, an organization and movement to bring culture to the working masses, under the aegis of the Commissariat of Enlightenment

Provisional Government   the coalition government that formed after the fall of the Romanov dynasty and claimed power between March and November 1917

PSS   V. I. Lenin, *Polnoe sobranie sochinenii*, 5th ed., 40 vols. (Moscow, 1958–1965)

PUR   Political Administration of the Revolutionary Military Council of the Workers'-Peasants' Red Army

raion   administrative unit

Red commanders   mostly noncommissioned officers of the Imperial Army who were promoted to command rank during the Civil War

Red Guards   urban and worker militias, usually attached to a factory or group of factories

revkom   revolutionary committee, an organ of martial law set up by an army political department after reoccupation of territory that had fallen into White hands

RVS   Revolutionary Military Council of the USSR

RVSR   Revolutionary Military Council of the Republic, supreme organ of martial law during the Civil War, later renamed Revolutionary Military Council of the USSR (RVS)

smychka   worker-peasant alliance or link (the political arrangement of the Soviet constitution)

Sovnarkom   Council of People's Commissars

SP   *Sputnik politrabotnika* (Moscow journal)

SR   Socialist Revolutionary party

TEO   Theater Department, Commissariat of Enlightenment

Tsentrokomdezertir   Central Commission for the Struggle with Desertion

voenkor   military correspondent, part of a mass movement to involve soldiers in newspaper activities

volost'   rural administrative unit

Vsebiurvoenkom   All-Russian Bureau of Military Commissars

Vsevobuch   Universal Military Training Administration

VSNKh   Supreme Council of the National Economy

VTsIK   All-Russian Central Executive Committee, executive organ of
Congress of Soviets

Workers' Opposition   dissident party fraction opposed to state control of trade unions

SOLDIERS IN THE
PROLETARIAN DICTATORSHIP

Introduction

More graphically than anything else, the history of the army demonstrates
the rightness of our views as to the connection between the productive
forces and social relations. . . . All this, moreover, a very striking epitome of
the whole history of civil societies.

—Karl Marx, 1857

In 1917 revolution in Russia brought down first the centuries-old
Romanov dynasty and then the moderate socialist coalition of the
Provisional Government. The demands of the revolutionary constituencies evolved dramatically over the course of the nearly nine
months that separated the two stages of the transfer of power; one
constant thread, however, was the demand for the removal of those
superordinate authorities whose credibility had been eroded by
years of war and economic mismanagement. It was a demand for
greater local autonomy and self-government. Workers, blue- and
white-collar alike, soldiers, peasants, and non-Russians organized
themselves into elected committees, councils, and soviets. They not
only advanced their particular demands but also attempted to coordinate their political actions with those of other national and local
movements. By fall, the Provisional Government's reluctance to resolve the outstanding questions of war, land, and control of the failing economy had polarized society; as a result, the radicalized mass
organizations and their constituencies, in an upsurge of anti-
authoritarian, anti-elitist, and often anti-intellectual sentiment, repudiated the "bourgeois-liberal" political order. On the tide of these
often conflicting and contradictory demands, the Bolsheviks came
to power; soviets of workers' and soldiers' deputies across the country voted for radical platforms associated with the left bloc of the
Social Democratic movement. In the first euphoric weeks after the
fall of the Provisional Government, the deputies proclaimed their
faith in the victory of peace, democracy, equality, social justice, and
the brotherhood of man.

By the 1930s those who spoke on behalf of mass organizations and the Communist Party still paid lip service to most of the ideals of 1917, but their society was a far cry from the one imagined by the men and women who had toppled the old order. The political culture of the Stalin system allowed little or no room for the mass of the population to make the key decisions that affected their daily lives, though those same masses were expected to "volunteer" their services for the center's periodic mobilizations for political campaigns. Stalin and the men who surrounded him insisted on calling their polity socialist while they restored hierarchies in all realms of society, the economy, and culture. The new elites were largely self-selecting oligarchies who combated egalitarianism in the workplace and throughout society in defense of their own privileged status. The most powerful party and state leaders had erected a centralized industrial economy that was planned and managed by an ever-swelling bureaucracy and dominated by defense and heavy industries; the political leadership had assaulted the peasantry to restructure agriculture into collective and state sectors, had driven the remnants of the market economy into the criminal underground, and had introduced a paternalistic welfare state that promised minimum levels of education and health care.

By the mid-1930s political leaders and publicists were celebrating the centralized state authority in an ideology that invoked the heritage of the tsarist past, especially the martial glories of tsars who not many years earlier had been reviled as the most despotic of tyrants. The secret police enlisted the aid of citizens in their constant search for persons of doubtful political reliability and enemies of the people. The state generated a climate of spymania and xenophobia; these conditions encouraged citizens to place a high premium on conformity and a concomitant extreme intolerance of nonconformists.[1] Public culture was marked by a militantly defensive posture toward the outside world, which was perceived as hostile and threatening. The consensus that supported these national security values—the contemporary shorthand was "capitalist encirclement"—was invoked by the leadership to justify the ever-expanding size of the standing army and the large internal security forces, as well as the burgeoning role of the defense industry in the overall national economy. The primacy of national security values permeated nearly all spheres of politics, the economy, and culture.

How is it possible that such a fundamental and long-lasting transformation of society and polity occurred in little more than a decade and a half? Historians generally have argued that the transformation

1. For some very suggestive observations on the nature of the Stalin system and its social structures and political culture, see Moshe Lewin, *The Making of the Soviet System* (New York: Pantheon, 1985), esp. chaps. 9–12.

was either a consequence of the Bolsheviks' drive to implement their brand of socialist ideology or the tragically inevitable by-product of Russia's backwardness. Very often, and not surprisingly, the choice of one or another explanation has seemed to flow from a scholar's political allegiance.[2] Among Bolsheviks, Communists, and many ex-Communists, especially exiled or dissident loyalists, the circumstantial or environmental explanation has held sway. Trotsky-ists and anti-Stalinist Communists have upheld the purity of social-ist doctrine and explained Stalin's triumph as the consequence of the primitive political culture of the largely peasant Russian masses, the "deproletarianization" of Russia's heroic working class, the Ori-ental heritage of despotism, or some variant of these themes.[3] Men-shevik historians, too, have upheld the sanctity of socialist ideals and insisted that Russia was unprepared for the socialist revolution. They argue that Lenin and his party usurped the power that the Mensheviks and other moderate socialists legitimately held in 1917 only by exploiting the nation's economic hardships and pandering to desperate masses. The people who swept the Bolsheviks to power clearly were not the "conscious" proletarians in whose name the revolution was supposed to be made.[4] Still, at least for some Trotskyists and nearly all anti-Stalinist Soviet historians, the Soviet Union, for all its distortions of Leninist and Marxist precepts, re-mained a socialist state.

Anticommunists, from conservative monarchists to radical anar-chists, have blamed socialism itself for the emergence of Stalin's despotism. Leszek Kolakowski argues that totalitarianism unfolded with an iron historical logic from the basic Marxist postulate of a privileged proletarian consciousness and the romantic vision of a perfectly unified humanity of the future.[5] Long before millions had endured the miseries of the Stalin system, anarchist critics of the

2. Daniel Field, in summarizing the current scholarly debate over Stalinism, writes, "What is at issue is socialism. For some, it is a matter of moral urgency to link the victims of Stalinist terror to socialism; for others, it is no less urgent to detach the terror from the socialist cause and show it to be an aberration": "From the Editor: Controversy," *Russian Review* 45 (October 1986): v.

3. For a brief summary of the Trotskyist interpretations of the emergence of Sta-linism, see Robert H. McNeal, "Trotskyist Interpretations of Stalinism," in *Stalinism: Essays in Historical Interpretation,* ed. Robert C. Tucker (New York: Norton, 1977), pp. 30–52.

4. See, e.g., Raphael R. Abramovitch, *The Soviet Revolution* (New York: Interna-tional Universities Press, 1962). For an earlier Social Democratic critique, see Karl Kautsky, *Terrorism and Communism* (Westport, Conn.: Hyperion, 1973), pp. 158–234.

5. See Kolakowski's summary of his views in "Marxist Roots of Stalinism," in Tucker's *Stalinism,* pp. 283–98; and for a full-blown treatment of Soviet history that borrows heavily from Kolakowski's scheme, see Mikhail Heller and Aleksandr M. Nekrich, *Utopia in Power: The History of the Soviet Union from 1917 to the Present,* trans. Phyllis B. Carlos (New York: Summit, 1986).

socialist movement had detected authoritarian, if not dictatorial, tendencies in both Marxism and socialism and had rejected both as merely the latest brands of elite tyranny over the masses.[6]

Of course, the best historians have refused to reduce causality to a result of either ideology or circumstance, but have attempted instead to demonstrate the interplay between objective and subjective factors, or the interaction among structural, conjunctural, and evential aspects of the historical process. For them, the Stalin system is a complex phenomenon explained in part by the social, political, and economic formations the Bolsheviks inherited from the autocracy and the Provisional Government at the end of 1917; in part by the Bolshevik and radical ideological agendas, the exigencies of war and civil war, and the practical responses to wartime emergencies; and in part by the dilemmas that emerged during the NEP years. From 1917 on, every year brought the Soviet leadership new crises that were at once the outcomes (however unwitting) of their own policies and the consequences of domestic and international processes beyond the regime's control—demographic, economic, psychological, cultural.

All these processes converged in a few key institutions of the new political order: the Communist Party, the bureaucracy, the security police, and the military. I have chosen to investigate the multifaceted transformation of Soviet society and politics in the dozen years between 1917 and the early 1930s by focusing on the Red Army as an institution, on soldiers as a social group, and on an important aspect of the soldiers' political culture which I shall refer to as militarism. My aim is to weave together important moments in the institutional history of the Soviet state at the level of "high politics," in the social history of the early postrevolutionary years, and in the far more intangible evolution of political culture and mentalités. I hope that this book will make its most novel contribution to the study of Soviet history in its exploration of the complicated and often elusive relationships between the social history of soldiers and their political attitudes and behavior.

For most of the Civil War years, the army was not only the largest single political institution but the one that occupied the highest rung on the besieged state's ladder of priorities. The fate of the army was at the center of nearly every important controversy during those years because the debates so clearly concerned fundamental matters of power and authority. The first steps in the creation of the armed

---

6. For a contemporary critique of the Russian socialist parties, see the writings of the Polish anarchist Jan Waclaw Machajski: *Bankrotstvo sotsializma XIX stoletiia* (n.p., 1905), and *Umstvennyi rabochii* (Geneva, 1904). Machajski predicted that a new aristocracy of administrators, technical specialists, and politicians would replace the old capitalist class.

forces aroused fierce passions at party congresses and conferences, at congresses of soviets, and within the army itself. Later, as national political leaders attempted to address the Soviet Republic's vulnerability in the international arena and the structural weaknesses of the Soviet economy, their views of the role and function of the Red Army evolved in new directions.

Leon Trotsky, who guided the Red Army through its difficult early years as chairman of the Revolutionary Military Council and army commissar, quipped that "the Army is a copy of society and suffers from all its diseases, usually at a higher temperature."[7] The army's evolution certainly reflected the larger developments that other state institutions were undergoing in those years; by virtue of its special relation to the political order, however—its mission to defend the republic from its foreign and occasionally domestic enemies—the army did more than merely reflect general changes in society. Military institutional imperatives decisively influenced larger processes in the evolution of nonmilitary institutions as well. Moreover, because the Red Army was one of the first institutions created by the Soviet government, the experience that the new political elite gained in building the military apparatus served as a model for state-building activities in other spheres as well.

When I speak of "soldiers," I mean military officers (or commanders, as they were called then, to avoid linking them to the odious heritage of the Imperial Army) and political officers as well as rank-and-file troops.[8] As the role and function of the army changed during those years, the status of soldiers evolved in ways that paralleled the changes in status of other groups in postrevolutionary society. At the same time, soldiers' status was distinctive because they were called to defend the Revolution and the Soviet state; thus they occupied a particularly important place in the social structure. Their evolving status in turn influenced the changes that other social groups were confronting in the realignment of political and economic power during the early years of the Soviet state.

The setting and circumstances of these soldiers' military service and their postservice ties to the army and to the state helped shape their attitudes and behavior. Trotsky later lamented that the military men who returned home after the Civil War "assumed leading posts in the local soviets, in the economy, in education, and they persistently introduced everywhere that regime which had ensured success in the Civil War."[9] Perhaps most important is the prominent

7. Leon Trotsky, *The Revolution Betrayed* (New York: Merit, 1965), p. 222.
8. Sailors and the Red Navy, while having much in common with soldiers and the Red Army, deserve separate treatment and will not receive here the attention they clearly deserve.
9. Trotsky, *Revolution Betrayed*, pp. 89–90.

role played by veterans in the state and party bureaucracies. By the end of the 1920s those bureaucracies, from the Politburo to rural party cells, were populated by hundreds of thousands of men who had undergone the common experience of military service. Increasingly large numbers had performed their service obligations in the peacetime army after 1921. Because army service had become one of the passports to important posts in the postrevolutionary political class, soldiers became part of something akin to a "historical bloc" for the Bolsheviks. The new rulers understood that to establish their party's hegemony over the population, they would have to win assent to their claims that their particular interests were those of society at large.[10] The leaders identified soldiers as key agents in the establishment of that hegemony.

In this area of investigation, the transformation of political attitudes and behavior, I have isolated a component of Soviet political culture of the mid-1930s which I cautiously call militarized socialism. I hesitate to introduce such notions as "militarism" and "militarization" because of the highly ideological charge these terms have acquired and because those who choose to label one or another polity militaristic often fail to define their terms with any satisfactory degree of rigor; furthermore, the charge of militarism was hurled at the Bolsheviks early on by their closest socialist protagonists, the Mensheviks. Of course, the Mensheviks wanted to prevent their former comrades in arms from laying claim to a genuinely proletarian revolution, and some argued that the October Revolution in Petrograd was primarily a rebellion of the soldiers rather than a workers' revolution.[11] Even if the Mensheviks formulated this argument in order to vindicate their own failure, they nonetheless identified an important aspect of the events of 1917 which many Western and Soviet historians have either ignored or downplayed.[12]

All these apprehensions notwithstanding, I am persuaded by Volker Berghahn that militarism, even in the qualified form in which I shall use the term, is a concept that retains its value for describing key aspects of states and societies at certain stages of

10. I have borrowed the concepts "historical bloc" and "hegemony" from Antonio Gramsci, *Selections from the Prison Notebooks of Antonio Gramsci*, trans. and ed. Quinton Hoare and Geoffrey Nowell Smith (New York: International Publishers, 1985), p. 323; for elaboration on Gramsci's concepts, see Walter L. Adamson, *Hegemony and Revolution: A Study of Antonio Gramsci's Political and Cultural Theory* (Berkeley: University of California Press, 1980), pp. 170–79.

11. For a later formulation of the initial Menshevik argument, see Abramovitch, *Soviet Revolution*, pp. 21, 83–84, 88.

12. Notable exceptions to this generalization have been Allan K. Wildman, *The End of the Russian Imperial Army*, 2 vols. (Princeton: Princeton University Press, 1980, 1988); John L. H. Keep, *The Russian Revolution: A Study in Mass Mobilization* (New York: Norton, 1976); and Marc Ferro, *October 1917: A Social History of the Russian Revolution*, trans. Norman Stone (London: Routledge & Kegan Paul, 1980).

their histories, in this case the Soviet polity from at least the mid-1920s until the 1950s.[13] The Soviet state, including the Stalin system, can by no means be reduced to a simple version of the garrison state; it was always much more than that. For several decades socialists identified as components of a genuinely socialist order the centrally planned economy, the national welfare system, the expansion of opportunities for workers, peasants, women, and national minorities, and other aspects of the Soviet state. Still, beginning with the Civil War, Soviet leaders themselves were far more likely to employ martial rhetoric and symbolism and even the word "militarization" (*voenizatsiia*) than foreign socialists in particular might have found appropriate. Moreover, it is noteworthy that much of the critical discussion of the Stalin period in the Soviet Union today focuses on the "administrative-command methods" (*administrativno-komandnye metody*) or "command-order system" (*komandno-prikaznaia sistema*), terms used to characterize the outstanding traits of Soviet politics, economy, and culture bequeathed primarily by Stalin. Its critics oppose the administrative-command style to a political system that takes into consideration the "human factor" (*chelovecheskii faktor*), by which they mean material and moral incentives and greater attention to individuals in Soviet society. Reformers are demanding that personal interests be more carefully weighed against institutional interests in a decidedly nonmilitary way.[14]

The connection I seek to make between the army and the militarized socialism of the Soviet state centers on key aspects of military service: the Civil War experience of millions of men and women, including most of Stalin's closest allies; the emerging professional ethos of the Soviet officer corps; the army's considerable investment in sociopolitical and civic education; and the interpenetration of militarist and socialist values in Soviet political culture. The relationship between army service and political behavior is by no means self-evident. Contemporary sociologists disagree over just how effective military experience is in shaping fundamental attitudes. Many studies of industrial societies suggest that military service only reaffirms values that society ordinarily inculcates in its citizens from early school age. Although these findings may hold true for today's Soviet army, it is less likely that they accurately describe the situation in the immediate postrevolutionary period. In the early Soviet state, the complementary infrastructures of civic

13. For more on the problems that have characterized the debate on militarism, see the excellent historiographical survey by Volker Berghahn, *Militarism: The History of an International Debate, 1861–1979* (New York: St. Martin's, 1982).

14. The historian I. Froianov has decried the importation of military terminology into academic discourse, as in "The Academy of Sciences is the headquarters of scholarship": "Kruglyi stol: Istoricheskaia nauka v usloviiakh perestroiki," *Voprosy istorii* 3 (1988): 15.

training—schools, youth organizations, mass sports movements—
were either absent altogether or only weakly established, so that
conscripts entering Red Army service frequently confronted a "Soviet" setting for the first time in their lives. The overwhelming majority of the conscripts came from the countryside, where the state
had made small inroads at best. For most of these young men, military service was a drastic break with the life they had known.

Sociologists also have found that dramatic generational experiences, especially wars and economic crises, do shape attitudes. One
cannot assume that combat experience instills the sorts of attitudes
or values that incline veterans to support an aggressive foreign policy or military intervention as a first option, that is, a ready resort to
the use of force in international relations. On the contrary, firsthand
experience of battle has been shown to temper youthful enthusiasm
for military adventuring. But combat experience does encourage a
society to coalesce around a leadership that takes a strong stand
against perceived foreign threats.[15] For millions of Soviet citizens in
the 1920s the seven years of war had been such a central common
experience. Moreover, the protracted economic crises that bedeviled
the war years abated only slightly in the mid-1920s and then resumed in new forms. The millions of men who served in the Red
Army even in peacetime shared the experience of economic crisis
with the rest of society, but in a form peculiar to the army setting.
Especially during the 1920s the army seemed to many Russians an
island of security amidst an ocean of poverty and unemployment.
The contrast between the relative security of military service and
subsequent insecurity in the civilian world colored former soldiers'
political attitudes and behavior.

During the 1920s, the political leadership, relying on the experience of the Revolution and Civil War, turned to soldiers to fill its
burgeoning bureaucracies and, most significantly, to reform, if not to
overturn, the established political order in the countryside. The
urban-based Bolshevik revolution was finally brought to the peasants by the collectivization of agriculture at the end of the decade.
Together with militant workers and youths, soldiers and veterans
formed the vanguard that responded to the center's call at the end of
the 1920s to wage a new war on Russia's backwardness and to complete the socialist revolution in the cities and countryside. The soldiers' participation in this momentous assault on the old rural order
influenced both the process and the outcome of collectivization in
important ways.

The Soviet leadership was not unique in looking to the army as an
institution of political socialization for its adult male citizens. At

15. See, e.g., Asher Arian, Ilan Talmud, and Tamar Hermann, *National Security
and Public Opinion in Israel* (Boulder, Colo.: Westview, 1988), pp. 56–67.

least since the nineteenth century, European political leaders, including the ministers of the Russian autocracy, had looked to their armies not only as the primary shield of state borders and the upholders of the domestic social and political order but also as veritable schools of the nation. As Michael Howard has written, "State power, in the intensely competitive atmosphere of the late nineteenth century, was seen more than ever as military power; but military power now involved the effective indoctrination of the entire population in a religion of nationalism."[16] Still, scholars have written relatively little about the success of nation-states in inculcating the new religion in their soldiers.[17] Only a handful of studies about the Russian Imperial Army touch on questions of military service and virtually none touch on the impact of service on postservice careers and political behavior.[18]

The chapters that follow focus on military service—and especially political education—in the new Workers'-Peasants' Red Army as a process through which the new Soviet political leadership and a substantial part of its citizenry improvised and forged a provisional social contract. They describe several key aspects of civil-military relations in the early history of the Soviet state; the origins and evolution of the first socialist army, the dramatic changes in the social and political status of soldiers and officers in postrevolutionary Russian society, and the mutual interpenetration of socialist and military values in an emerging Soviet political culture. Finally, I hope to provide a fresh look at politics and society in the first dozen years of Soviet power by considering the experience of both the men and women who served in this "army of a new type" and the veterans who left military service for civilian political careers.

16. Michael Howard, The Causes of Wars (London: Unwin, 1983), p. 182. Howard writes, "Peasant boys were hauled from remote mountain villages, from the Urals to the Pyrenees, made to pledge allegiance to a flag, taught to sing patriotic songs glorifying their national past and put through a process of training designed at least as much to mould their minds and personalities as to teach them how to handle their weapons."

17. An exception to this generalization is the fascinating study of nineteenth-century France by Eugen Weber, Peasants into Frenchmen: The Modernization of Rural France, 1870–1914 (Stanford: Stanford University Press, 1976), esp. chap. 17.

18. For service conditions in the pre-1874 Imperial Army, see John L. H. Keep's comprehensive Soldiers of the Tsar (Oxford: Clarendon, 1985); D. Beyrau, Militär und Gesellschaft im vorrevolutionären Russland (Cologne: Böhlau, 1984); also John Bushnell, Mutiny amid Repression: Russian Soldiers in the Revolution of 1905–1906 (Bloomington: Indiana University Press, 1985); and Wildman, End of the Russian Imperial Army.

PART ONE

Revolution, Civil War, and Peace

CHAPTER 1

Building a Socialist Army,
February 1917–March 1919

A revolution is certainly the most authoritarian thing there is; it is the act whereby one part of the population imposes its will upon the other part by means of rifles, bayonets and cannon—authoritarian means, if such there be at all . . .

—Friedrich Engels, "On Authority"

Soldiers and Revolution

In March 1917 the atmosphere in the Russian imperial capital of Petrograd was ripe for revolution. The war against Germany and Austria-Hungary dragged into its third disastrous year; food and fuel were in short supply and the prices of all commodities spiraled upward. To make matters worse, several thousand workers were locked out of the Putilov factory. Finally, on 8 March, socialist and democratic groups in the capital celebrated International Women's Day by raising banners to demand an end to the autocracy. In several parts of the city they clashed with police. The next day nearly 200,000 demonstrators joined the citywide strike. They avoided confrontations with soldiers—in fact, they were friendly with them—but were hostile to policemen. Only on 11 March did the tsar act to end the disorders. Police and soldiers fired on demonstrators here and there, but very few of the imperial troops were considered reliable enough to be sent against the swelling ranks of discontented subjects. When military authorities decided to send additional soldiers to the trouble spots, soldiers in one of the key regiments declared that they shared the aims of the demonstrators and mutinied. After this initial break in the ranks, other regiments quickly joined the demonstrators and thereby knocked out from under the tsar's government the most important support it had relied on. The mutiny of the soldiers proved to be the decisive moment of the February Revolution.

Almost immediately after the momentous events of early March, soldiers underwent a dramatic transformation in status. Under the old regime they had carried a moral stigma as the defenders of an oppressive autocratic order and as cannon fodder with even fewer civil rights than the rest of imperial society. Especially after 1905, military authorities tried to "sanitize" and isolate barracks from revolutionary agitators and propaganda. Soldiers were forbidden to visit town parks, taverns, brothels, theaters, wine stores, and teahouses, and were even barred from the sunny side of the street. Officers, noncommissioned officers, and—most embittering for the soldiers—officers' wives had virtually unlimited powers to exploit and abuse them.[1] With the fall of the Romanovs, soldiers attained supreme virtue as defenders of the sacred revolution. No longer moral pariahs, they now became popular heroes. They formed committees and soviets alongside other urban groups and demanded a thoroughgoing democratization of the army. Everywhere soldiers put forward lists of remarkably consistent demands to the new Provisional Government. They wanted improved pay, higher allotments for their families, more disability benefits, and better sanitation and living conditions in general. They also demanded the abolition of both the military salute and the practice of coming to attention, the right to discuss political problems in the army, and the right to perform certain functions by means of elections.[2] The Petrograd Soviet recognized the new government's first contract with the revolutionary soldiers when it issued Order no. 1 on March 14. The soldiers won full civil and political rights, promises of improved living conditions, and the right to elect soldiers' committees that would decide certain matters of military life. The Provisional Government further acknowledged its debt to the soldiers with a Declaration of Soldiers' Rights.[3]

The soldiers' decisive role in the events of early March 1917 was in part the fruit of years of agitation among them by revolutionary parties. After the 1905 Revolution the Bolsheviks and Socialist Revolutionaries (SRs) had recognized soldiers as likely catalysts to advance the radical and democratic movements, even though soldiers had not fitted readily into the plans of earlier Russian and European

1. See Bushnell, Mutiny amid Repression, pp. 1–23.

2. See Marc Ferro, The Russian Revolution of February 1917, trans. J. L. Richards and Nicole Stone (Englewood Cliffs, N.J.: Prentice-Hall, 1972), p. 133. For some suggestive parallels with the French Revolution, see Jean-Paul Bertaud, La Révolution armée (Paris: Laffont, 1979); and John A. Lynn, The Bayonets of the Republic (Urbana: University of Illinois Press, 1984).

3. The best account of soldiers' behavior in the first half of 1917 is Wildman, End of the Russian Imperial Army. See also Mikhail Frenkin, Russkaia armiia i revoliutsiia (Munich: Logos, 1978); and his Zakhvat vlasti bol'shevikami v Rossii i rol' tylovykh garnizonov armii (Jerusalem: Stav, 1982), esp. chaps. 2 and 3.

revolutionaries. For most European radicals, democrats, and socialists, the army was primarily a symbol and instrument of autocratic reaction. In 1848 and again in 1870, regular troops had put down revolutions across Europe.[4] In the Russian Empire itself, civil authorities increasingly summoned soldiers to break up strikes and punish rebellious peasants in the late nineteenth century. In this setting Russian revolutionary theorists, mostly Marxists of one stripe or another who were profoundly influenced by radical European political movements, viewed soldiers as peasants in uniforms; consequently, Russian revolutionaries too had dismissed soldiers as politically unreliable because they lacked the tradition of proletarian solidarity that inclined factory workers toward socialism. Not only were peasants dispersed throughout the countryside, but even their venerable commune was suspect. The commune, allegedly a collectivist institution of rural politics, was in fact rent by bitter class struggles as wealthy peasants (called "kulaks" by some socialist observers) strove to maintain their economic, political, and moral domination over their weaker neighbors. Whatever the accuracy of this rather negative model of peasant politics and society, nearly all the revolutionary parties (Bolsheviks, Mensheviks, and SRs) shared this view. At the very least, they viewed peasants as far less likely to attain a socialist or revolutionary consciousness than their working-class brethren.[5] In accordance with this analysis, the revolutionaries, except the SRs, focused their early efforts on industrial workers, and the parties' theorists paid as little attention to the peasants in the army and navy as they did to those in the villages.

The behavior of soldiers during the 1905 Revolution caught the leaders of the radical parties by surprise.[6] At critical stages during 1905–1906, soldiers and sailors advanced or impeded the political struggle in Russian society. Thousands of soldiers mutinied and pressed demands for justice and reforms in army life; at other times they performed more traditional tasks and bloodily suppressed urban and rural uprisings. Because urban political activists presumed peasants to be incapable of genuinely collective political action, the behavior of peasant soldiers, and for that matter peasants themselves, perplexed them. But in those years at least the Bolsheviks

4. For an interesting summary of Friedrich Engels's writings on military matters, see Martin Berger, *Engels, Armies, and Revolution* (Hamden, Conn.: Archon, 1977). On Marx, see the essay by W. B. Gallie in his *Philosophers of Peace and War: Kant, Clausewitz, Marx, Engels, and Tolstoy* (New York: Cambridge University Press, 1978), chap. 3.

5. See, e.g., Donald Treadgold's characterization of the attitudes of Viktor Chernov, leading spokesman for the Socialist Revolutionaries, and Vladimir Lenin, in *Lenin and His Rivals: The Struggle for Russia's Future, 1898–1908* (New York: Praeger, 1965), pp. 146–47.

6. See Bushnell, *Mutiny amid Repression.*

and the SRs learned that the revolutionary proletariat could look to another ally in a country where the industrial labor force remained a distinct minority. The revolutionaries belatedly discovered that soldiers resembled factory workers more than they resembled the peasant stereotypes held by educated society. After all, soldiers lived together in barracks, forts, and summer camps; like workers, they were used to acting in solidarity. And, like the workers who learned political lessons from the factory managers and inspectors who upheld the tsarist order, the soldiers confronted very tangible representatives of tsarist authority in the drill sergeants and officers who supervised their daily lives. Moreover, the revolutionaries found that, even when the military authorities tried to keep the Revolution out of the barracks, agitators could reach soldiers far more effectively than they could penetrate the countryside. Both the Bolsheviks and the SRs established party departments and combat detachments in the army and navy to win the support of soldiers and sailors for decisive action when the autocratic political order suffered its next crisis. By late 1916 and early 1917, when war-weary soldiers refused to fire on striking workers, those efforts appeared to have been vindicated.

The radical movement among soldiers continued to plague the new dual-authority regime of the Provisional Government and Petrograd Soviet which replaced the autocracy in March. Throughout 1917, against a background of increasing radicalization and polarization in society at large, soldiers' demands too became more strident. Radical soldiers threatened the Provisional Government with several of its most serious crises, notably in April and July 1917.[7] By late summer soldiers' committees were appealing for peace, demobilization, and the power to elect all officers and to vote on all decisions. Because many peasant soldiers were concerned about their relatives and landholdings in the countryside, they also demanded the legal transfer to the toiling peasantry of all lands in the hands of the wealthy classes. Deserting soldiers took active roles in the agrarian revolts, adding their strength to the assaults on landed estates.[8] Soldiers joined workers and peasants in unraveling the fragile polit-

7. In April, Foreign Minister Pavel Miliukov provoked a crisis of confidence in the Provisional Government when his note on Russia's war aims was made public. He was forced to resign his office after soldiers and workers demonstrated for an end to the war. In July Prime Minister Aleksandr Kerensky announced a new offensive against the Germans and Austrians, partly in the hope that renewed fighting would restore discipline and morale in the army. As staff headquarters began sending units from Petrograd to the front, radical armed soldiers demonstrated against the Provisional Government. After 400 or 500 people were killed and wounded in two days of bloody skirmishing with troops called in from outside the capital, the demonstrations, which became known as the July Days, came to an end. The protests indicated the shallowness of popular support for the coalition moderate-socialist government.

8. Keep, Russian Revolution, pp. 159–60, 196–98, 208, 210, 215.

ical settlement of the dual authority. By early November, soviets of soldiers' deputies were electing Bolshevik-dominated coalitions, often acting in advance of workers' soviets; moreover, deserting soldiers carried home to the countryside the news of Bolshevik revolution in the cities and at the fronts. Indeed, soldiers had played critical roles in bringing down two governments in less than a year.[9] They no doubt expected any new government to be more attentive to their needs; and they made no exception for the Bolshevik government proclaimed on 8 November 1917.

On the day after the Military Revolutionary Committee overthrew the Provisional Government in Petrograd, the Bolshevik party's leaders formed a Council of People's Commissars (Sovnarkom), which prominently featured a Committee on Army and Naval Affairs.[10] The first two decrees that Lenin signed as chairman of Sovnarkom, the Decree on Peace and the Decree on Land, directly addressed soldiers' concerns. On the same day, 8 November 1917, the Second Congress of Soviets also abolished capital punishment. The worker, peasant, and soldier deputies hoped that they could end the war quickly, send home the soldiers of the Imperial Army, and begin to build a new political order. The soldiers understood the peace proclamations to be the first step toward the general demobilization they had been awaiting. At front-line and army-level congresses, soldiers' representatives already were demanding partial or complete demobilization. Even before they received official release orders, thousands of soldiers simply departed for home, many to take part in the redistribution of lands in the countryside. On 10 November, Lenin heeded the soldiers' voices and sanctioned the first demobilization of conscripts. To prevent the complete disorganization and demoralization of the 12 million soldiers still serving in the Imperial Army, the Old Bolshevik Mikhail Kedrov was appointed deputy army commissar to oversee demobilization.[11] Kedrov and Army Commissar Nikolai Podvoiskii called a meeting of army representatives to discuss how best to proceed.[12] Soldiers greeted

---

9. Keep argues that historians traditionally have placed the soldiers in the wings of the revolution and that "this is indeed an injustice, for at many of the most critical moments during the revolutionary year their role was decisive and they ought perhaps to be regarded as the principal actors in the drama": ibid., pp. xiv–xv; see also 115–19, 126, 130, 196–98, 240–42, 346, 450–52. See also Abramovitch, *Soviet Revolution*, pp. 21, 83–84, 88.

10. The Committee on Army and Naval Affairs was headed by three party members who had distinguished themselves in the Bolshevik Military Organization: Mikhail Kedrov, Nikolai Krylenko, and Chairman Nikolai Podvoiskii.

11. For an excellent account of the Bolshevik debates about demobilization, see E. N. Gorodetskii, "Demobilizatsiia armii v 1917–1918 gg.," *Istoriia SSSR* 1 (1958): 3–31.

12. The nearly 300 delegates met from 28 December 1917 to 16 January 1918. They

the new government's first actions as a victory for their committees and other mass organizations. The soldiers of the Northern and Western fronts and sailors of the Baltic Fleet rewarded the Bolsheviks with a resounding majority of their votes in the Constituent Assembly elections that began on November 26; Bolsheviks took second place to the SRs in the south and in the Black Sea Fleet.[13]

The war, however, was not yet over. By mid-December none of the warring nations had answered Sovnarkom's appeal for peace; furthermore, opposition parties and former imperial officers had begun to organize armed forces to prevent the further spread of the Bolsheviks' power and to overthrow the workers' and soldiers' soviets that already had seized power. The besieged soviets appealed to Petrograd for protection. Hundreds of workers, soldiers, and sailors left to defend the Revolution, even though the capital could ill afford to part with these makeshift battalions; nearby other anti-Bolshevik forces plotted to overthrow the new coalition government. Just as the Congress on Demobilization was deciding the order in which to release soldiers, Sovnarkom turned to the delegates for help in creating a new people's army and for their opinion about the likelihood of holding together some units of the old army to resist an expected renewal of the German offensive. The delegates expressed grave reservations about the fighting ability of the Imperial Army and a majority called for the government to conclude peace on any terms it could get.

While the congress debated, Podvoiskii convened a separate meeting of the Bolshevik party's Military Organization to discuss how to form a new army of 300,000 soldiers as quickly as possible. The party's representatives met with officials from the former War Ministry, who recommended calling 500 instructors from the front lines. Soldiers' committees would select the instructors to begin training a new army in the rear. Influential delegates expressed concerns about the class composition of the new armed force. Kedrov opposed the initial manifesto on the grounds that it failed to guarantee the "class purity" of the socialist army. If only soldiers from the Imperial Army were recruited, Kedrov argued, the Soviet Republic would be

elected a presidium of five Bolsheviks, three Left SRs, and three nonparty representatives. For more on the initial policies and debates on the creation of a socialist armed force, see E. N. Gorodetskii, *Rozhdenie Sovetskogo gosudarstva* (Moscow, 1965), pp. 353–428.

13. For a comprehensive discussion of the election returns, see Oliver H. Radkey, *Russia Goes to the Polls: The Election to the All-Russian Constituent Assembly, 1917* (Ithaca: Cornell University Press, 1989). When Lenin analyzed the election returns nearly two years later, he concluded that without the support of half the armed forces, "we could not have been victorious": V. I. Lenin, "Vybory v Uchreditel'noe sobranie i diktatura proletariata," *Polnoe sobranie sochinenii*, 5th ed., vol. 40 (Moscow, 1965) (hereafter *PSS*), pp. 8–10.

in the hands of peasants. He insisted that the new state should rely exclusively on industrial workers who had proved their loyalty to the Bolshevik party.[14] The Bolsheviks' early fears betrayed how fundamentally their views of military reliability differed from those of the imperial military establishment, which had always regarded peasants as the most reliable fighters and considered urban conscripts, especially workers and students, as potential revolutionary leaven.[15] After prolonged and heated debate, Podvoiskii submitted to the Congress on Demobilization a proposal agreed upon at the Military Organization's meeting: a socialist army to be made up of "the laboring classes, workers and peasants, with a firm proletarian core." He appealed to all socialists to take part in the creation of an army in order to wage "a sacred war for socialism." The compromise resolution respected the authority of the non-Bolshevik socialist parties and resolved that all citizens who volunteered to serve in the Socialist Guard be required to obtain recommendations from the "revolutionary-socialist parties or workers', soldiers', or peasants' organizations." Nevertheless, the Socialist Guard was approved by only a narrow majority of delegates. The Left SRs abstained from the vote on the grounds that the congress had no authority in the matter, as such decisions should be left to the masses. Menshevik and Right SR delegates voted against the Bolshevik proposal; they recommended partial demobilization and reinforcement of the front line with volunteer detachments and reserve companies.[16]

Sovnarkom persisted in hoping that they could still engage most of the troops who remained in the Imperial Army, and only gradually came to realize how thoroughly the old army had disintegrated. In early January 1918 mass desertion swept through most armies.[17] A report from the Southwestern Front warned that older soldiers were categorically demanding to be sent home. Soldiers' committees were demobilizing entire units on their own authority. In several places where large groups of soldiers were congregating, the situation threatened to erupt into pogroms. Elsewhere soldiers looted

14. Kedrov's proposals are quoted in Iu. I. Korablev, *V. I. Lenin i zashchita zavoevanii Velikogo Oktiabria* (Moscow, 1979), p. 183.

15. See comments by Tsar Nicholas and his army minister, Aleksei Kuropatkin, in Pëtr A. Zaionchkovskii, *Samoderzhavie i russkaia armiia na rubezhe XIX–XX stoletii* (Moscow, 1973), pp. 118, 120. The autocracy ignored military leaders' protests that their units would be subverted by these urban elements and persisted in sentencing convicted revolutionaries to punitive army service.

16. Gorodetskii, "Demobilizatsiia," p. 20.

17. Army Chief of Staff Mikhail Bonch-Bruevich reported to Sovnarkom on 4 January 1918, "The general conclusion from the fronts is such that the army is altogether unsuitable for combat and is in no condition to hold back the enemy, not only at the occupied positions, but even if the line of defense were to be moved far to the rear": *Oktiabr'skaia revoliutsiia i armiia: Sbornik dokumentov* (Moscow, 1973), p. 352.

military storehouses and treasuries. The staff had neither strength
nor resources to halt the disorder. And in spite of a November 1917
decree banning the surrender of arms to demobilizing soldiers, they
held on to their weapons. Soldiers justified their disobedience by
pointing to the danger of counterrevolution. Despite the clear unre-
liability of the surviving imperial units, the military command was
reluctant to release the millions of soldiers because the new government had no other tested means to defend itself and because the already strained rail network could not cope with any further mass
movements of citizens. Kedrov, Podvoiskii, and Efraim Sklianskii—
despite Lenin's objections—ordered a halt to the demobilization of
men called up in 1910, 1911, and 1912. For the first time the new
state acted against the demands that the soldiers most persistently
pressed. The center sent out agitators to persuade the war-weary soldiers that all their revolutionary gains would be lost if they left for
home at such a critical time.

Still, the remaining units were inadequate to defend the cities as
the domestic opposition mounted its first assaults. In desperation
urban soviets turned to the Red Guards. During 1917 factories had
formed Red Guard militias of armed workers, who served in rotation
and elected their commanders from among their own members. By
the end of the year their numbers had reached 200,000 and the general staff of the Red Guards had played a crucial role in the Military
Revolutionary Committee's overthrow of the Provisional Government in Petrograd.[18] In the first battles to defend Petrograd against
the forces organized by General Petr Krasnov and the former
minister-president Aleksandr Kerensky, Red Guard detachments
joined revolutionary soldiers of the capital's garrison. Petrograd and
then Moscow sent Red Guard detachments to aid beleaguered soviets in provincial cities, and initially the militias performed remarkably well.

Among the Red Guards' leaders were men who, like Valentin Trifonov, advocated that the Red Guards be converted into a genuine
people's militia. More than any other revolutionary organization, the
Red Guards embodied the principles of the armed populace which
figured prominently in the later writings of Friedrich Engels and the
French socialist Jean Jaurès.[19] The Russian revolutionary parties, in-

18. For more on the fate of the Red Guards after 1917 and their role in the formation of the Red Army, see the epilogue in Rex Wade, Red Guards and Workers' Militias in the Russian Revolution (Stanford: Stanford University Press, 1984).

19. See Gerhard Ritter, Das Kommunemodell und die Begründung der Roten
Armee im Jahre 1918 (Berlin: Osteuropa-Institut, 1965), chap. 2; also Sigmund Neu-
mann and Mark von Hagen, "Engels and Marx on Revolution, War, and the Army in
Society," in Makers of Modern Strategy from Machiavelli to the Nuclear Age, ed. Peter
Paret (Princeton: Princeton University Press, 1986), pp. 279–80; Jean Jaurès, L'Armée
nouvelle (Paris: Editions Sociales, 1911).

cluding the Bolsheviks, shared with European Social Democracy a preference for a people's militia and an antipathy to standing armies. The officer caste, barracks isolated from civilian influences, and drill-sergeant discipline all bore odious memories of the despotic regimes of absolute monarchies and were incompatible with the principles of a democratic society. In affirmation of the ties of the Red Guard to the militia ideal, Sovnarkom included two representatives from the Guard's general staff, Trifonov and Konstantin Iurenev, when it formed the All-Russian Collegium to Organize a Worker-Peasant Red Army. The other three members, Podvoiskii, Nikolai Krylenko, and Konstantin Mekhonoshin, came from the Bolshevik party's Military Organization and articulated the demands of the soldiers' committees for army reform. In mid-January 1918 the Third Congress of Soviets paid further tribute to the heritage of the European revolutionary movement in its "Declaration of the Rights of the Laboring and Exploited," which sanctioned the arming of all laborers, the formation of a socialist Red Army of workers and peasants, and the complete disarming of the property-holding classes. The congress defined citizenship in the new republic in two articles: first, only people engaged in productive and socially useful labor were eligible to claim the rights of citizens; second, citizens had the exclusive and honorable right to bear arms for the new state. Property holders were not to be trusted with weapons and would be expected to fulfill military duties in the rear—duties that bore a definite moral stigma. Thus the new state made army service integral to its policies of class discrimination.[20]

The Brief Era of the Volunteer Army

When Sovnarkom formed the Collegium to Organize a Worker-Peasant Red Army on 15 January, the new government clearly signaled its intention to centralize military authority in its own hands; nevertheless, the leaders realized that the emergency did not afford them the luxury of waiting until a regular army had taken shape in the center. "Like everything in our revolution," the collegium declared, "the formation of a socialist army cannot await instructions from above. It must be formed from below, by the people themselves; therefore all organizations—factory and *volost'* committees, local party organizations, trade unions, local soviets, and all Red

20. *S''ezdy sovetov Soiuza SSR; soiuznykh i avtonomnykh sovetskikh sotsialisticheskikh respublik: Sbornik dokumentov, 1917–1937 gg.*, vol. 1 (Moscow, 1959), p. 28. For a helpful discussion of Bolshevik policies of discrimination and categories of citizenship, see Elise Kimerling, "Civil Rights and Social Policy in Soviet Russia, 1918–1936," *Russian Review* 41 (January 1982): 24–46.

Guard staff—immediately must set themselves to the task of organizing the Socialist Army."[21] The collegium built the Worker-Peasant Red Army through improvisation and incorporated the diverse traditions and practices of the key constituencies that made up the new fighting force, especially the revolutionary soldiers and urban militias. Yet despite its attempts to appease all the important groups, the collegium's staff faced resistance to every decision. They tried to disarm opponents by arguing that the often disagreeable measures were provisional and temporary and dictated by the national emergency. They assured the skeptics that as soon as the workers of the world, particularly the European proletariat, had overthrown their capitalist masters, the Russian Revolution would no longer require any armed force to defend itself. In the meantime, revolutionaries would have to swallow their scruples and throw their efforts into the struggle against the "imperialists" and the domestic opposition. In the disputes over the army, the new political class was facing its first dilemmas over the emerging contradiction between the goal of popular participation and socialism, on the one hand, and the short-term means—in this case a disciplined fighting force—that were needed to preserve the political order that would usher in full-blown socialism, on the other.[22]

By far the most serious conflicts centered on the issue of authority in the new state, and most troublesome for the collegium were the soldiers' committees. Soldiers called for an end to the old order in the army and the authority to decide their own fates. They demanded the same rights and privileges as all other citizens and refused to obey commands that they deemed unjust or unreasonable. Their committees, which included representatives of all the revolutionary parties, debated matters of army life, removed unpopular officers, and elected new ones.[23] The revolutionary soldiers identified the former officers of the Imperial Army with the reactionary policies of the autocracy and the unpopular Provisional Government and with the imperial system of estates (sosloviia), in which the gentry unjustly occupied the prominent place. Even though the Great War had "democratized" the officer corps, soldiers and antimilitary radicals continued to perceive the corps as a preserve of the aristo-

21. For the early history of the collegium, see S. M. Kliatskin, Na zashchite Oktiabria (Moscow, 1965), chaps. 1–2. The collegium received 20 million rubles from Sovnarkom to begin operations. Volunteers received food, clothing, and shelter plus 50 rubles a month. By the end of April 1918, 200,000 men and women had volunteered, most of them registered with local military commissariats.

22. See Ritter, Kommunemodell, chap. 3; John Erickson, "Some Military and Political Aspects of the 'Militia Army' Controversy, 1919–1920," in Essays in Honour of E. H. Carr, ed. C. Abramsky (London: Archon, 1974), pp. 204–28.

23. On the soldiers' committees in 1917, see Wildman, End of the Russian Imperial Army, 1: chap. 7, 2: chaps. 5–8.

cratic elite.[24] And when, following the Bolshevik victory in Petrograd, large numbers of officers joined anti-Bolshevik forces around the country, all officers became potential targets.

After November 1917, when the soldiers' delegates to the Second Congress of Soviets successfully pressed their demands to ban the death penalty, officers no longer had any formal right to punish soldiers who disobeyed orders or otherwise violated military discipline. Later in November Sovnarkom abolished all special military courts in response to demands for democracy in the army. Newly formed people's courts and revolutionary tribunals tried and sentenced citizen-soldiers. In the army comrades' courts (*tovarishcheskie sudy*) were formed in companies and regiments to investigate infractions. General soldiers' meetings elected the three-man comrades' courts to terms of three months. The courts had the power to reprimand and arrest soldiers, but the most serious sanction they claimed was the right to expel soldiers from their units. Soldiers won further concessions from the new regime when, on 1 December 1917, the Petrograd Military District abolished ranks, insignia, and all privileges for officers and sanctioned the principle of electing officers. Though the Petrograd command had intended its order to apply to that district only, the popular anti-officer measures spread rapidly to other fronts and armies.

Despite the hostility shown toward them, 8,000 generals and officers of the old army volunteered to serve the Soviet state shortly after the collapse of the Provisional Government. Though many distinguished themselves in combat in the Red Army, initially they were received with great suspicion. Radicals in the Bolshevik party, including the Left Communists, warned that the officers would overturn the victories of the revolutionary soldiers in the new army and restore the ethos of the Imperial Army if the opportunity arose.[25] Sovnarkom was reluctant to admit the officers into its service because soldiers often refused to obey them. Soldiers' committees insisted that the imperial officers be replaced by men of their own class.

24. For more on the Imperial Army's officers, see Peter Kenez, "A Profile of the Pre-Revolutionary Officer Corps," *California Slavic Studies* 7 (1973): 121–58; John Bushnell, "The Tsarist Officer Corps, 1881–1914: Customs, Duties, Inefficiency," *American Historical Review* 86 (October 1981): 753–80; and William C. Fuller, Jr., *Civil–Military Conflict in Imperial Russia, 1881–1914* (Princeton: Princeton University Press, 1985), pp. 31–46.

25. See the accounts of the acrimonious debates in the Bolshevik party's Military Organization on the question of admitting former imperial officers to service for the Soviet state, in A. F. Miasnikov, "Moi vstrechi s tovarishchem Leninym," in *Vospominaniia o V. I. Lenine*, vol. 2 (Moscow, 1957), p. 149; S. I. Aralov, *V. I. Lenin i Krasnaia Armiia* (Moscow, 1969), pp. 7–11; see also Ritter, *Kommunemodell*, pp. 130–71.

Once again, moral priorities of class purity and respect for soldiers' sentiments were compromised provisionally in the name of
the need to defeat foreign and domestic enemies on the battleground. Because the revolutionaries had little or no combat experience themselves, Sovnarkom concluded that it had no recourse but
to accept the services offered them.[26] The officers who volunteered
were called "military specialists," both to avoid the opprobrium attached to the word "officer" among the revolutionary soldiers and to
distinguish those officers loyal to the Soviet state from their opposite
numbers who were joining the White cause.[27] At the same time, the
Council on Army and Naval Affairs realized that the number of imperial officers willing to serve probably would remain small and
their loyalties suspect. The collegium authorized local revolutionary
committees to give command positions to experienced and loyal
noncommissioned officers in the old army, men who were likely to
come from more "democratic" class backgrounds than the officers.
In December 1917 the collegium opened the first courses for "Red
commanders" in five cities. The Red commanders were to form the
embryo of a future Soviet officer corps of loyal peasants and proletarians. The collegium, striving hard to maintain the new state's
principles of class discrimination and to provide previously disfranchised groups with opportunities to move into positions of power,
granted workers and peasants who were endorsed by revolutionary
organizations first priority in admission to the courses. Red commanders became an important group of loyal cadres for the new political order. The network of military educational establishments
expanded rapidly and graduated 13,000 Red commanders by the end
of 1918. Though Red commanders generally enjoyed better relations
with soldiers' committees than did the former imperial officers, they
too had to earn the trust of their subordinates. If a Red commander
was poorly trained—as many no doubt were in the crash courses
they completed—soldiers showed little respect for his authority.

The first real test for the improvised socialist armed force came
when the German command resumed its offensive in mid-February
1918. At Narva the German army joined battle with the Red Guards,
who, for all their political attractiveness and their success in skir-

26. For more on the recruitment of officers, see the memoirs of M. D. Bonch-
Bruevich, *Vsia vlast' sovetam* (Moscow, 1957), p. 273. Bonch-Bruevich and another
former general in the Imperial Army, Dmitrii Parskii, used their prestige and army
connections to recruit thousands of officers in the early months of 1918.

27. The new government not only sought to eliminate the word "officer" from its
vocabulary but replaced "soldier" with "Red Army man" (*krasnoarmeets*). Such was
the hostility among revolutionary soldiers toward the old military order that as late as
1925 a writer who used the term "barracks" was condemned for evoking the drill-
sergeant and officer-caste values that no longer could be tolerated in a worker-peasant
Red Army: E. Brunak, " 'Kazarmennoe' stroitel'stvo," *Voennyi vestnik* 35 (1925): 17.

mishes against domestic opponents, proved incapable of resisting a modern mass army. The Germans advanced virtually unimpeded. The Red Guard organization had no central leadership; detachments answered to local soviets, military revolutionary committees, or factories. Red Guardsmen, who considered themselves to be the most class-conscious representatives of the revolutionary proletariat, refused to heed the commands of Red Army officers and obeyed only their elected commanders. When detachments in Petrograd learned that they were likely to be merged with Red Army units, their ranks thinned dramatically.[28] The Narva defeat, the hostility of the Red Guards to the newly forming Red Army units, and the unwillingness of Red Guard detachments to submit to the more traditional authority of army commanders sealed the fate of the urban militias in the eyes of the central military authorities. The military specialists in particular pressed the center to disband the Red Guard and transfer to the Red Army those Red Guardsmen who proved themselves capable of obeying military orders.[29] Units remaining from the Imperial Army also performed miserably against the Germans, undermining the arguments of both those who insisted on using the old army to build the new one and those who defended the volunteer principle. Reports of collapse at the rapidly moving fronts left Lenin's government with little alternative but to sue for immediate peace with Germany. On 3 March 1918, Sovnarkom signed the devastating Brest Treaty. A week later, the Supreme Military Council telegraphed Kedrov that "the Acting Army had ceased to exist."

As long as the Imperial Army had been demobilizing under a temporary cease-fire, the central military authorities could do very little to intervene in soldiers' politics. Soldiers' committees continued to discuss whether or not to obey a commander's order. The Narva defeat had demonstrated clearly that such a state of affairs could continue no longer. The emergency forced an end to the collegium's footdragging on measures to bolster discipline and introduce order in the divergent military and paramilitary forces at its nominal disposal. In mid-March Sovnarkom began a thorough reorganization of the army administration and appointed Lev Trotsky to replace the collegium. Trotsky moved quickly to transform the undisciplined army into a reliable fighting force, but he had to fight determined opposition at every step. Shortly after he took office, Trotsky obtained Sovnarkom's approval to recruit former officers of the Impe-

28. From the intelligence gathered by the Registration Department of the All-Russian Collegium to Organize the Red Army, dated 19 and 26 February 1918, cited in M. A. Molodtsygin, "Krasnaia gvardiia posle Oktiabria," *Voprosy istorii* 10 (1980): 38.

29. For more on the transition from urban militias to Red Army, see Keep, *Russian Revolution*, pp. 276–87.

rial Army. It was one matter to accept the services of officers who volunteered their skills to the new state, but it was quite another actually to recruit them in large numbers. Representatives of soldiers' committees and civilian party leaders condemned Trotsky's

Leon Trotsky, people's commissar of the army and navy, chairman of the Revolutionary Military Council of the Republic, 1918–1925. From Leon Trotsky, *Problems of Life* (London, 1924).

first policies as a betrayal of the Revolution. Trotsky's patience with the defiant soldiers' committees quickly ran out and he provoked further hostility when, at his behest, the Supreme Military Council revoked their right to elect officers and then ordered them to disperse. The committees were not prepared to surrender their authority so readily and disregarded the ban. Trotsky appealed next to the All-Russian Central Executive Committee (VTsIK), which resolved that all commanders in the Red Army were subject to appointment only by higher-ranking commanders. Nevertheless, the committees continued to defy the ban and elected commanders as late as April 1919. For rank-and-file soldiers, the committees symbolized their gains in the Revolution. They were unwilling to surrender those gains even in the name of military expediency.

Even before the Brest Treaty was signed, the collegium had begun to discuss how to bolster commanders' authority over subordinates. In several units, special military tribunals had formed to punish offenders, but the civilian People's Commissariat of Justice, headed by the Left SR Isaak Shteinberg, fought all efforts to grant the ad hoc organs permanent status. In the civilian commissariat the soldiers had found an unexpected ally. Even when the Bolshevik Petr Stuchka replaced Shteinberg in mid-March 1918, the commissariat remained firmly opposed to any separate military tribunals. Despite Trotsky's resolve to bolster commanders' disciplinary powers over soldiers, in May Sovnarkom sided with Stuchka and ordered all military tribunals to disband and hand over their authority to the nearest civilian revolutionary tribunals. The victory of the Justice Commissariat revealed how strongly sentiments ran against the resurrection of any semblance of the military caste of the Imperial Army, with a judicial system free from control by civilian authorities. The political struggles that shaped civil-military relations were waged among professional revolutionaries, many of whom fundamentally distrusted military organizations of any stripe.

The Army Commissariat tried to placate its civilian critics and win some measure of obedience from the soldiers by reforming and expanding the institution of the political commissar. In so doing, Sovnarkom recognized revolutionaries' demands that mass organizations keep tight control over the military apparatus. During 1917 the Provisional Government had sent commissars to army units to forestall counterrevolutionary acts by officers unsympathetic to the new order.[30] After the Bolsheviks proclaimed their power in November 1917, they too dispatched commissars to all government institutions and agencies, including the army. The commissars oversaw the transfer of power and checked the loyalty of the bureaucrats who remained on the job. The commissars in the army, as plenipotentiaries of the Revolution, were meant to discourage the military specialists from acts of treason. Sovnarkom very consciously invested

30. For more on the origins of the commissar, see John Erickson, *The Soviet High Command: A Military-Political History, 1918–1941* (New York: St. Martin's Press, 1962), pp. 41–45; and Ritter, *Kommunemodell*, pp. 171–209.

the institution of the commissar with the solid revolutionary credentials of the workers' militias when it appointed the former Red
Guard commander Konstantin Iurenev as the first director of the
All-Russian Bureau of Military Commissars (Vsebiurvoenkom).
When prominent party spokesmen continued to oppose the recruitment of military specialists, the political leadership devised a compromise principle that became known as dual command
(dvoenachalie); perhaps not suprisingly, it resembled the arrangement known as dual power (dvoevlastie) which had characterized
the political order after the abdication of Nicholas II in March.[31] The
policy of dual command required all commanders' orders to carry
the countersignature of a commissar before soldiers were expected to
obey them. With the new policy the center hoped to secure the dual
imperatives of military expediency and political vigilance.

Each improvised measure the center took to win obedience from
the troops and to satisfy competing civilian political agencies complicated the lines of authority in the army. Above all, the powers of
the military commissar and the practice of dual command remained
at the center of controversy throughout the Civil War and well into
the 1920s. In May 1918 Vsebiurvoenkom convened a meeting of
commissars serving the Moscow Military District to discuss ways to
delineate political authority more effectively in their units. The
commissars identified the soldiers' committees as the primary obsta-
cle to their efforts to consolidate authority. Not surprisingly, the
Moscow commissars, in a rare harmony of interests with Army Commissar Trotsky, demanded the right to disband soldiers' committees
"if their activity was found to be harmful to Soviet power or directed at the undermining of order in the Soviet army." A month
later the All-Russian Congress of Military Commissars adopted a revised version of the Moscow resolution which ostensibly spelled the
end of autonomous soldier organizations.[32] Paper decrees, however,
did not translate into secure powers for the commissars.

As spring 1918 began, still no major foreign power had recognized
the new Soviet Republic. Moreover, foreign representatives were ad-
vising anti-Bolshevik organizations and had landed troops in Vladivostok and in the north. The Bolshevik leaders began to fear that an
all-volunteer army could not withstand the combined forces of domestic resistance and Allied intervention. On 22 April, VTsIK, in a
significant switch from the principle of voluntary service, decreed

31. In its ideal form, dual power was understood as the exercise of state functions
by the Provisional Government and the guarantee of political control by the revolutionary workers, soldiers, and peasants through the Petrograd Soviet.
32. "Polozhenie o voennykh komissariatakh i komissarakh," 6–11 June 1918, in
Partiino-politicheskaia rabota v Krasnoi Armii (aprel' 1918–fevral' 1919): Dokumenty
(hereafter PPR I) (Moscow, 1961), pp. 80–81.

obligatory military training—though not yet obligatory service—for all workers and peasants "who did not exploit others' labor." Eligible citizens between the ages of eighteen and forty were to complete a ninety-six hour program over a period of eight weeks. To coordinate the new program, VTsIK established the Universal Military Training Administration (Vsevobuch) and appointed L. E. Mar'iasin to head it; he was also to form and train volunteer workers' reserve regiments for the Red Army. Indeed, when the government established Vsevobuch, it intended the agency to become the central organization to train volunteers for the new army. Because instructors were in short supply, Mar'iasin turned to former Red Guardsmen, willing soldiers, and loyal former officers and noncommissioned officers to begin training the mostly urban civilians who formed the first reserve regiments.[33] The directorate of Vsevobuch inherited the Red Guards' mantle as the advocates of a people's militia. In urban centers and with a largely decentralized apparatus, the instructors trained workers and other trustworthy urban residents with minimum disruption of their workdays. The Training Administration had neither barracks nor a permanent officer corps; its training program included a broad range of general educational topics.

Because Vsevobuch shared these practices and principles with the Red Guards and because the Training Administration jealously guarded its autonomy, the same military specialists who rejected the Red Guards as a viable armed force also criticized Vsevobuch as a mistaken diversion of precious resources that might have gone more sensibly to the regular army.[34] Vsevobuch countered that the democratic potential of the militia made it ultimately a far more reliable fighting force than any traditional conscript army. The defenders echoed the arguments of Jean Jaurès in favor of the armed people and of Engels's remarks on armies and warfare in *Anti-Duehring*. Sergei Gusev, a Bolshevik military organizer who only later joined the proponents of a regular army, wrote a pro-militia pamphlet titled *How to Build a Soviet Army*, in which he declared that modern military techniques could be learned with relative ease.[35] Vsevobuch could transform even an illiterate muzhik into a "semi-officer," for

33. For statistics on Vsevobuch activity, see *Direktivy komandovaniia frontov Krasnoi Armii, 1917–1922 gg.*, vol. 4 (Moscow, 1978), pp. 323–27; also M. I. Ushakov, "Iz istorii deiatel'nosti partii po organizatsii Vsevobucha," *Voprosy istorii KPSS* 5 (1978): 102–12.

34. For a typical military specialist's hostility toward Vsevobuch, Podvoiskii, and the Red Guards, see Commander Ioakim Vatsetis, "Vospominaniia," in *Pamiat'*, vol. 2 (Moscow, 1977; Paris, 1979), pp. 37, 41–42, 50.

35. Gusev (whose real name was Iakov Drabkin) wrote the pamphlet *Kak stroit' Sovetskuiu Armiiu* in April 1918 for *Petrogradskaia pravda*. It was reprinted in S. I. Gusev, *Grazhdanskaia voina i Krasnaia Armiia: Sbornik statei* (Moscow, 1958), pp. 27–37.

had not Lenin claimed that even a cook could now run the state apparatus? In his defense of the militia principles, Gusev articulated a fundamental distrust of the professional military caste. Such distrust was widespread for years after the Revolution, and was extended to all professional bureaucrats and officials who claimed authority over the masses by virtue of some specialized skill. The revolutionary assaults on established authorities had been fueled in large part by antagonism toward their presumed monopoly on specialized knowledge and skills. The army witnessed similar clashes over the legitimate bases of authority.

Vsevobuch barely had set up its local training centers when full-scale civil war broke out in the east. In late May 1918 the illusory peace of the first months of Soviet rule ended abruptly when a mutiny by Czech soldiers ignited anti-Bolshevik uprisings across the Urals and Siberia. The rapid and sweeping victories of the Czech troops and their allies raised panic in Moscow. The Soviet leaders jettisoned what remained of their commitment to volunteer principles and frantically pushed to expand the army. VTsIK declared all citizens eligible for induction into the Red Army to combat "domestic and foreign counterrevolution and secure the supply of grain to the populace." All males between the ages of twenty-one and twenty-five living in the immediately threatened regions—Siberia, the Urals, and along the Volga—were ordered to report for induction immediately. Within a week's time workers and "nonexploiting peasants" in the major centers of the working-class movement (Petrograd, Moscow, the Don and Kuban regions) were to report as well. As long as Bolshevik authority remained weak in the villages and the supply of workers held out, the Bolshevik leadership was very reluctant to extend its call-up much beyond the urban population and those peasants who maintained close ties with towns; moreover, peasant soldiers, only recently demobilized, were not eager to return to fighting.

Even when the center limited its call-ups to city dwellers, however, it had great difficulty mobilizing the war-weary populace.[36] Local recruiting offices had not had time to complete an inventory of the eligible citizens. The military specialists hired as instructors were at best indifferent and often hostile. More important, a food crisis loomed over the new republic; years of war, a disrupted transport system, and a mismanaged economy had reduced the quantities of food arriving in the cities. Embittered enemies of the new government found fertile soil for their anti-Soviet agitation. The severe food shortages sparked protests against the call-ups in the Mos-

36. The center hoped the call-up would yield 275,000 conscripts, but only 54,000 appeared: Istoriia sovetskogo krest'ianstva, vol. 1 (Moscow, 1986), pp. 131–32; Molodtsygin, "Krasnaia gvardiia," p. 62.

cow region and wreaked havoc with soldiers' discipline. Red Army units in Tula province refused orders to ship out food supplies and engaged in drunken looting.[37] Though Trotsky attributed the often bloody uprisings to the peasants' "senseless and aimless" strivings and to their "confusion and vague dissatisfactions," he admitted that the mutinies had "infected even the most backward part of the workers."[38]

The political leaders in Moscow quickly realized that their ability to mobilize the populace to defend the state from its ever more threatening enemies was inseparable from their success in getting food supplies from the producing regions to the cities and troops. Military imperatives began to intrude on the state's rural policies and its relations with the peasantry. Sovnarkom had declared a food dictatorship in May, and the People's Food Commissariat was dispatching detachments to the villages to seize agricultural surpluses. But the food supplies for the army and the cities continued to dwindle. In June the center escalated "class conflict" in the countryside by ordering local authorities to form committees of the village poor (*kombedy*) and thereby antagonized large sectors of the rural population. Much of the goodwill that the Bolsheviks had earned among the peasantry after the proclamation of the Decree on Land melted away as *kombedy*, acting as agents of the center, redistributed land and enforced the food monopoly by monitoring wealthy peasants' compliance with the order to surrender their surpluses.[39] Significantly, the committees also served as induction agencies for the army in the second half of 1918; because of the hostility they earned among the peasantry, however, they had relatively little success at this task. The Soviet state was learning its first lessons about the inextricable links between its military successes and its rural policies. Reliable food supplies for the army remained at the top of the political agenda during the entire Civil War.

All through June, July, and August the anti-Bolshevik forces toppled local soviets and replaced them with a string of provisional governments. In the face of continuing defeats, the center improvised new institutions and reformed existing ones. Because the ma-

37. See the report to Sovnarkom on the Tula "counterrevolution" in *V. I. Lenin i VChK: Sbornik dokumentov, 1917–1922 gg.* (Moscow, 1975), pp. 66–67. Sovnarkom appointed Vasilii Paniushkin as extraordinary military commissar to Tula province to deal with the defiant soldiers.

38. L. D. Trotskii, "Deviatyi val," 1 June 1919, *V puti*, no. 50; reprinted in Trotskii, *Kak vooruzhalas' revoliutsiia* (Moscow, 1923–1925) (hereafter *KVR*), vol. 2, pt. 1, pp. 187–88.

39. For more details of early Bolshevik food policies, see Sylvana Malle, *The Economic Organization of War Communism, 1918–1921* (Cambridge: Cambridge University Press, 1985), chaps. 7–8; and the excellent study by Lars Lih, *Bread and Authority in Russia* (Berkeley: University of California Press, forthcoming), chaps. 8–9.

jor threats to Bolshevik power initially emerged in Siberia and the Urals, the Eastern Front served as a testing ground for practices and institutions that subsequent fronts copied. On 13 June Sovnarkom created a revolutionary military council to direct operations against the May uprisings. A Left SR and military specialist, Mikhail Murav'ev, was appointed front commander alongside two political commissars, Georgii Blagonravov and Petr Kobozev. Revolutionary military councils also formed at lower levels, often without instructions from above and at the initiative of the political commissars on the scene. Higher councils objected to the grass-roots initiatives of army-level councils and appealed to Sovnarkom to disband them. Sovnarkom rejected the appeals and affirmed the principle of parallel organizations up and down the chain of command. The revolutionary military councils became nerve centers throughout the growing army. The councils were grounded in the principles of collegial decision making and dual command in the persons of the two or more commissars who served alongside the military specialists.

Only gradually did the staffs of the councils work out among themselves even approximate divisions of responsibilities. In theory commanders answered for operational matters, while commissars supervised political affairs. In practice, the broad responsibilities and urgency of decisions made under fire produced constant strains in the day-to-day operations of the councils.[40] However the responsibilities were divided, the military, or political, commissar was quickly becoming the center of the state's efforts to assert its authority over the expanding army. At the first All-Russian Congress of Commissars, called in early June, the delegates declared the commissar to be the direct representative of Soviet power and, as such, to be an inviolable person. Any insult or other act of violence against a commissar while he was executing his official responsibilities was equivalent to the "most serious crime against the Soviet regime." The commissars demanded control over all comrades' courts and "the cultural-enlightment life" of the army.[41] Finally, the commissars also fought for control over the political departments (*politotdely*), which formally answered to the Supreme Military Inspectorate, the agency that had created them. The inspectorate already duplicated much of the work of Vsebiurvoenkom and Vsevobuch, both of which also had been formed in April. The inspectorate trained soldiers with its own staff of instructors and commissars. Headed by Nikolai Podvoiskii, it had broad responsibilities for forming units, organizing supply, and conducting political work among soldiers.

40. For more comments on how collegial principles worked, see S. I. Gusev, *Uroki grazhdanskoi voiny* (Moscow, 1921), pp. 39–40.
41. "Polozhenie o voennykh komissariatakh," in *PPR* I, pp. 79–81.

Political work became increasingly important as the army shed its volunteer principles and became a genuine conscript fighting force. Political workers, who included commissars and their assistants, devoted their efforts to keeping up troop morale with a steady dose of

Nikolai Podvoiskii, chairman of the Universal Military Training Administration (Vsevobuch), 1919–1923

agitational speeches and informational bulletins from the center or front headquarters. Political work was not something altogether new for revolutionaries, especially those like Podvoiskii, whose most recent important post had been in the party's Military Organization. But now, in place of the antiwar and anti-establishment ideas that party agitators had spread among soldiers in the Imperial Army, they found themselves faced with a new situation that must have been strangely familiar if also drastically different from their recent experience. Precisely because it was looming so large among the techniques the new government found useful and necessary for building its armed force, the fierce competition over direction of political work brought Vsevobuch, Vsebiurvoenkom, and the Supreme Military Inspectorate, as well as other organizations that emerged in succeeding months in response to other crises in political control, to loggerheads.

Against the background of the continuing military emergency, the reforms in army service and organization, and the food dictatorship, the Fifth Congress of Soviets convened from 4 to 10 July in Moscow to decide major questions of government policy.[42] The Left SR delegates, whose commissars had left the coalition government with the Bolsheviks after the latter signed the Brest Treaty in March, spoke out against Soviet policies toward the peasantry (especially the committees of village poor); they demanded the abrogation of the shameful Brest Treaty and a renewal of the war with Germany. The Left SRs' politics remained a matter of utmost importance because Left SRs continued to hold high positions in both the army and the Cheka, the national internal police force. The congress's majority defeated the Left SRs' resolutions and voted to remove from the Red Army all "provocateurs and lackeys of imperialism," including Left SRs, who strove to draw the Soviet Republic into renewed conflict with Germany. Sensing that the Revolution was moving decisively against them, a defiant group of Left SRs staged an uprising in Moscow. The mutiny temporarily halted the proceedings of the congress because the delegates rushed to help suppress the rebels.

When the congress reconvened, it reaffirmed the new principles of the Red Army: obligatory service; centralized administration and an end to local autonomy and arbitrary, makeshift structures; the recruitment of military specialists, the death penalty for traitors, and the creation of a cohort of Red commanders eventually to replace the military specialists; and the prominent status of commissars. Immediately after the sessions on military affairs, the congress proceeded to discuss the draft constitution of the Soviet Republic, which was based on the earlier "Declaration of Rights" adopted at the Third Congress of Soviets. Trotsky's deputy army commissar, Efraim Sklianskii, served on the constitutional commission as the army's representative, so it is not surprising that the army's institutional imperatives left their imprint on the constitutional debate

42. Delegates included 745 Bolsheviks; 352 Left SRs; 14 Maximalists; 11 representatives of the anarchists, Social Democratic Internationalists, and others; and 10 who declared themselves nonparty. For a selection of documents from the Fifth Congress, see *S''ezdy sovetov Soiuza SSR,* 1:61–84.

as well.[43] The Constitution reaffirmed the articles on citizenship proclaimed in the "Declaration." Now, however, all citizens shared the honorable duty (no longer just a right) to bear arms in defense of the socialist fatherland. Noncitizens, or those deprived of the franchise (*lishentsy*), were prohibited from bearing arms, but obliged to serve in rear formations in noncombat duty.[44] Notably, the category of disfranchised persons included former policemen, but not former soldiers and officers of the Imperial Army. On the contrary, soldiers in the Red Army were very much citizens of the new state. In the article that delineated suffrage rights, soldiers and sailors were singled out as the second category, after persons engaged in "productive and socially useful labor."[45] In the Red Army oath that each soldier swore upon induction, he affirmed that, "as a son of the laboring people, a citizen of the Soviet republic," he took upon himself the calling of soldier in the workers' and peasants' army.[46]

Another aspect of the new franchise law, however, seemed to be at odds with the special status granted to soldiers: the Constitution established a voting system that discriminated against the rural population by granting urban areas greater representation in the national congresses of soviets.[47] Most soldiers would vote in urban elections, but the fact that their rural relatives suffered this blatant discrimination must have contributed to feelings of confused loyalty toward the Soviet political order. Because of the doubts these constitutional decisions raised, political workers were given special instructions on how to respond to peasant soldiers' questions on these matters. The other important decision that negatively affected state relations with the rural population was the congress's rejection of the Left SRs' demands for a reversal of Soviet policies in the countryside. The majority sanctioned the food dictatorship and the committees of the village poor. The Bolsheviks' commitment to a policy of class warfare among the peasantry held strong even in the face of considerable evidence of its failure. Still, despite the refusal to repudiate the policies of the food dictatorship, the decisions of the Fifth Congress demonstrate that the political leadership was beginning to sense the consequences of its moves toward a conscript army. In future

43. For more on the history of the 1918 Constitution, see G. S. Gurvich, *Istoriia Sovetskoi Konstitutsii* (Moscow, 1923).

44. The congress in fact sanctioned Sovnarkom's earlier emergency decree that all persons not eligible to bear arms had to serve one year of noncombat duty. They faced two years in prison at forced labor and the confiscation of their property if they tried to evade induction.

45. *S''ezdy sovetov Soiuza SSR,* 1:81.

46. The entire text of the oath, adopted by VTsIK on 22 April 1918, is in "Iz knizhki krasnoarmeitsa," in *PPR* I, pp. 47–48.

47. Urban soviets were entitled to send one delegate per 25,000 inhabitants; provincial soviets, representing the rural population, sent one delegate for every 125,000 inhabitants. See art. 25 in *S''ezdy sovetov Soiuza SSR,* 1:74–75.

months, those consequences would make themselves felt more sharply in matters of the social origins of recruits, their political loyalties, and the types of disciplinary policies that could be implemented among them, and in broader questions of the army's relations with other state organizations and the state's relations with various social groups.

The Politics of the Conscript Army

Following the congress, VTsIK decreed more mobilizations to the front. Most new conscripts came from the urban centers and were overwhelmingly workers. From June to August VTsIK ordered fifteen call-ups, eleven of which applied to workers only. Over 500,000 men and women entered the ranks. In addition, despite continued political opposition from anti-Bolshevik parties and a still rudimentary apparatus, Vsevobuch registered remarkable success. The Training Administration instructed 800,000 citizens in military skills by the end of the year. Throughout the summer, Sovnarkom called up more former officers and added new categories of military specialists who were expected to serve the Red Army: military doctors and veterinarians, NCOs, and former ministerial bureaucrats. By the end of the year, 22,295 former officers and 128,168 former NCOs were serving in the Red Army.[48]

Despite the approval Trotsky had won for his policies from the Congress of Soviets, he continued to face resistance within the army and among the party's top leaders. His most vocal opponents criticized him for his decision to recruit large numbers of military specialists and for his attacks on commissars who quarreled with the former imperial officers. In July the commander of the Eastern Front, Mikhail Murav'ev, raised a mutiny against Soviet power under the banner of solidarity with the recent Left SR uprising in Moscow. A Left SR himself, Murav'ev was in favor of renewing hostilities with Germany. Murav'ev had already been arrested once for abusing his authority; Trotsky had arranged not only his release but his promotion to command of the Eastern Front. Murav'ev was killed while resisting his second arrest. His treachery provoked immediate attacks on Trotsky for placing too much faith in the military specialists. Ioakim Vatsetis, the hero of the Latvian infantry division that had just put down the Left SR uprising in Moscow, rushed off to

48. By the end of July 1918, the Red Army counted 725,383 troops and commanders: *Grazhdanskaia voina v SSSR v dvukh tomakh* (Moscow, 1980), p. 171; for figures on Vsevobuch see Ushakov, "Istoriia deiatel'nosti," pp. 107, 108. See also A. G. Kavtaradze, *Voennye spetsialisty na sluzhbe Respubliki Sovetov, 1917–1920 gg.* (Moscow, 1988), pp. 111 (numbers of military specialists); 165–80 (decrees on call-ups of military specialists).

Simbirsk to replace Murav'ev and reorganize the Eastern Front. Vatsetis arrived at headquarters to find bureaucratic chaos; everyone was eager to divert blame from himself for the recent defeats. Vatsetis accused the Supreme Military Council—namely, Trotsky and Chief of Staff Mikhail Bonch-Bruevich—of reducing Soviet Russia to a state of "utter defenselessness."

Trotsky's authority declined markedly in the wake of the Murav'ev incident. He sought to deflect criticism from himself and the military specialists by blaming the commissars for the army's poor performance; but he won the lasting enmity of the commissars after he ordered the court-martial and shooting of one of their number, Commissar Panteleev, for desertion. Though he had warned all commissars a few weeks earlier that they would be the first persons shot if their unit retreated without authorization, still the first execution sent shock waves through the ranks.[49] Trotsky quickly developed a reputation as a commander who placed military expediency over political reliability and who listened too much to the military specialists who surrounded him in increasing numbers. As Trotsky saw matters, he was favoring state imperatives and the requisite military skills of the former officers over the doctrinaire methods that commissars were resorting to in their dealings with the military specialists. As the commissars saw matters, their revolutionary enthusiasm and political credentials were equal if not superior to the narrow skills of the military specialists, especially in such areas as mobilizing troops for battle. Sovnarkom, in response to the vitriolic criticism of the army commissar and the military specialists, sanctioned the formation of a "special department" (*osobyi otdel*) of the Cheka with wide powers to combat espionage, malfeasance, and the "forces of counterrevolution."

The shootings of Murav'ev and Panteleev also signaled that the Soviet government had fundamentally altered its attitude toward the use of force against disloyal or disobedient agents. Shortly after the Revolutionary Military Council was formed on the Eastern Front, it set up field tribunals to try cases of counterrevolutionary activities, including treason, sabotage, desertion, and looting, and, when necessary, to execute the guilty. During the summer and autumn of 1918 military tribunals tried and executed hundreds of soldiers, officers, and commissars.[50] The tribunals offered effective means for officers and political workers to oblige soldiers to obey orders and behave themselves in an appropriately military fashion.

49. Trotskii, "Prikaz Pred RVS i Narkomvoenmora No. 18," 14 August 1918, in *KVR*, 1:235. For a version of the Panteleev incident sympathetic to Trotsky, see Isaac Deutscher, *The Prophet Armed: Trotsky, 1879–1921* (New York: Oxford University Press, 1954), pp. 420, 426.

50. See the statement by Commander Vatsetis in "Vospominaniia," p. 72.

The People's Commissariat of Justice predictably continued to resist the special military tribunals, especially when the latter demanded a separate military punitive policy. In July 1918 a meeting
of local commissars of justice reaffirmed their opposition to special
courts answering exclusively to the military organs. The Justice
Commissariat was determined to keep all judicial activities within
its own jurisdiction.[51] The Justice Commissariat's representatives
were firmly convinced that they were upholding the revolutionary
order by preventing the military from resurrecting its separate caste-
like existence. In open defiance of the civilian commissariat, the
army command introduced a regulation on front-line and regimental
courts and a second one that limited the authority of soldiers' own
comrades' courts. This time the army's arguments for the tribunals
were stronger. The comrades' courts and civilian revolutionary tribunals had left the army at the mercy of endless discussions and
meetings. The authors of the new regulations argued that military
conditions dictated special punitive policies. Soldiers committed
many infractions of discipline that were not serious enough to be
considered crimes, yet if these infractions went unpunished, a unit's
combat ability was threatened. The army won a victory over the civilian commissariat and continued to disregard objections to the
military tribunals during the Civil War.

The treachery of some military specialists and the frequently poor
morale and fighting ability of the conscripts prevented the Red
Army from halting the White advance during the summer months.
The introduction of the death penalty, the field tribunals, and the
special detachments of the Cheka began to turn the tide, but the political leaders increasingly cast about for other solutions to their
manpower problems. Because the proletarian dictatorship had felt it
could not extend its call-ups either to the nontoiling classes or to the
bulk of the peasants, it had relied primarily on the proletariat and a
portion of the peasantry. But workers had little combat experience
and their loyalty to the new order already had wavered in the spring
and summer of 1918. Perhaps the single most important move to bolster fighting strength after the introduction of the new punitive policy was the decision to call up large numbers of Communist Party
members. In a move that would have an enormous impact on the
structure and character of the Communist Party, on 29 July the party's Central Committee announced its first mass mobilization of
members with combat experience for the Eastern Front.[52] Finally in

51. V. P. Portnov and M. M. Slavin, *Pravovye osnovy stroitel'stva Krasnoi Armii,
1917–1920 gg.* (Moscow, 1985), p. 196.

52. On the party mobilizations, see Iu. P. Petrov, *Stroitel'stvo politorganov, partiinykh i komsomol'skikh organizatsii armii i flota (1918–1968)* (Moscow, 1968), pp.
20–22. Petrov reports that the bulk of the Communists were mobilized by the Mos-

September, for the first time Red troops halted the White advance. The Central Committee credited the September victories to the energetic organizing efforts undertaken by the party members sent to the Eastern Front as commissars, commanders, and rank-and-file Red Army men.[53] The call-up not only bolstered the fighting strength but also began to change the structure and character of the party. A political movement to overthrow the old order was being transformed into a reserve for cadres who would defend a new state against its enemies. Military service became a primary test of party members' loyalty.

At the beginning of September 1918 the Soviet government placed the entire country under martial law. After five days of bloody fighting, the Red Army recaptured the city of Kazan on 10 September 1918. Military and political leaders congratulated the victorious troops and VTsIK awarded them the order of the Red Banner for their courage and loyalty to the socialist fatherland.[54] The nation's political and military leaders attributed the welcome victory to their wise and politic decisions in building an army, but they hardly had time to catch their breath when a new threat emerged in the south from the armies of General Anton Denikin. Immediately the center called six new age groups to service. In what was the largest single recruitment drive of the entire Civil War, 1,134,356 men appeared for service between October and December 1918.[55]

On 11 September the Revolutionary Military Council of the Republic (RVSR) created the Southern Front, replicating the model of the Eastern Front with its own revolutionary military council, which included one military specialist, the former general Pavel Sytin, and three commissars, Iosif Stalin, Kliment Voroshilov, and Sergei Minin. Almost at once conflicts erupted between the military specialists and commissars. The new council quickly organized to defend the Soviet frontiers, but the members fell into dispute over the direction of military operations. Sytin declared that he had full authority over military operations and that the other councilmen had no right to interfere with his instructions. The commissars argued that the council should direct operations as a collegium. Sytin threatened to take his case to Trotsky and to the army command. The commissars tried to preempt such a move by ousting Sytin and

cow and Petrograd party organizations, which together sent nearly 3,000 members to the front. At the beginning of 1918, when a voluntary call-up was announced, nearly 106,000 members appeared for service in the Red Army. See Direktivy, 4:247.

53. Leninskii sbornik (Moscow, 1924–1975), 34:44.

54. "Dekret VTsIK ob uchrezhdenii ordena 'Krasnoe znamia,'" 16 September 1918, in Iz istorii grazhdanskoi voiny v SSSR, vol. 1 (Moscow, 1960), pp. 155–56.

55. Those born in 1898 were ordered to show up for induction on 11 September; VTsIK ordered those born between 1893 and 1897 to appear on 22 September: Istoriia sovetskogo krest'ianstva, 1:134.

asking the center to confirm Voroshilov in his place. The RVSR and the party's Orgburo entered the conflict on Sytin's side and demanded that the commissars stop interfering in operational matters. When they refused, the Central Committee transferred Stalin to a job outside the army and Voroshilov and Minin to other commands. Sytin was reinstated with two new commissars.[56] Stalin had voiced the commissar's revolutionary faith in enthusiasm and political reliability against Sytin's specialized training and military expertise.[57] In December Sovnarkom intervened to regulate authority in the revolutionary military councils by issuing a series of instructions, but once again new conditions posed new practical problems. The conflicts between the military specialists and commissars and soldiers continued throughout the Civil War, but they were sharpest in 1918, when 75 percent of all Red Army commanders were former imperial officers and when the number of commissars was still comparatively very small. In 1918 the Red Army employed 165,000 military specialists from the old army. Military specialists far outnumbered the few Red commanders—1,773 in all—who had been rushed through crash training courses or promoted from the ranks of noncommissioned officers from the Imperial Army.[58]

The conflict between commissars and military specialists was only one of several battles over authority in the new army. Both commissars and commanders faced increasing challenges from the mobilized party members. A second mobilization of Communists in November 1918 added another 40,000 members at the Eastern and Southern fronts. Indeed, the center came to regard the percentage of party members in a unit as an index of its fighting ability.[59] By late

56. I. Kolesnichenko, "K voprosu o konflikte v RVS Iuzhnogo fronta (sent.-okt. 1918 g.)," *Voenno-istoricheskii zhurnal* 2 (1962): 39–47. For another version of this conflict, see Deutscher, *Prophet Armed*, pp. 423–25. Stalin joined the Central Committee of the Ukrainian Communist Party; Voroshilov and Minin moved to the command of the Tenth Army.

57. The conflict between Sytin and the commissars at the Southern Front had other lasting repercussions. In general, shared experiences during the Civil War cemented bonds of friendship and political alliances, but they also engendered lasting and very bitter enemies. The clash at the Southern Front united Stalin and Voroshilov against Trotsky in a very critical combat situation. During the intraparty struggles of the 1920s, these alliances worked against Trotsky and in favor of Stalin's rise to power.

58. See *Direktivy*, 4:342–43. In December 1918 Vsebiurvoenkom counted 6,389 commissars for the entire army. See V. G. Kolychev, *Partiino-politicheskaia rabota v Krasnoi Armii v gody grazhdanskoi voiny* (Moscow, 1978), pp. 98–99.

59. Petrov, *Stroitel'stvo politorganov*, pp. 21–22. After the Civil War was over, Sergei Gusev speculated that units that contained only 5 percent or fewer Communists were considered ineffective as regards fighting ability, whereas units with 12 to 15 percent were considered shock troops: Gusev, *Grazhdanskaia voina*, p. 145. Gusev served on several revolutionary military councils and as director of the Political Ad-

1918 the party reinforcements that had been so critical for the September victories were also adding to the tensions in the army's political environment and further complicating lines of command. The influx of large numbers of party members brought into sharp relief the overlapping jurisdictions of agencies claiming to represent the center's interests. The commissars were responsible for their actions to Vsebiurvoenkom, but Communists in the army formally answered to the local civilian party committees that had sent them. Not surprisingly, the civilian committees resisted all attempts by military commissars to usurp their control over the members they had mobilized for the front at such great expense. Moreover, Communists formed their own party cells and committees to decide matters of army life. They claimed special authority because their party, after all, was ruling the country. Although Communists most often appealed to the authority of their local party committees, in fact they acted on their own initiative in defying commissars.

The commissars only recently had won the right, even if they still lacked the power, to curtail the functions of the soldiers' committees. Now the party organizations were contesting commissars' authority in the name of the ruling party. The most decisive factor in explaining the ambiguities in the commissars' relations with party members was the uncertain status of both the commissar as an institution and Vsebiurvoenkom itself, the organization that claimed responsibility for assignments and transfers of commissars. For all the seemingly obvious importance of the commissar, many party members still saw the post as a temporary expedient that would disappear when the army had replaced the military specialists with loyal Red commanders. Fully aware that that time was still very far away, the Northwestern Obkom—only one of many party organizations to do so—nonetheless recommended the abolition of commissars and an increase in the number of rank-and-file party workers to replace them.[60] Because the party itself was so ambivalent about the commissar, Vsebiurvoenkom was never given a clear mandate for its responsibilities and powers. It had no authority as a party organ, nor was its relation to the RVSR very clear. For the moment, powerful local party organizations continued to thwart Vsebiurvoenkom as it tried to implement the center's wishes.

Part of the struggles between party members and commissars must be attributed to the frustrated ambitions of the mobilized Communists. When Communists were sent off by their local committee

---

ministration of the RVSR in 1921. See also the report of Commissar Vladimir Baryshnikov to the party's Moscow District Committee on the role of Communists in strengthening combat readiness in the army: PPR I, p. 116.

60. "Ot severo-zapadnogo oblastnogo komiteta RKP(b)," in Perepiska sekretariata TsK RKP(b) s mestnymi partiinymi organizatsiiami (Moscow, 1957–1972), 5:256–60.

with much fanfare, they expected to be assigned responsible posts, preferably as commissars themselves. In any event, they found it difficult to adjust to a subordinate status in the ranks. This was especially true when the commissar was not a party member himself. Many commissars still were not Communists, though they considered themselves to have respectable revolutionary credentials.[61] Communist Party members felt no obligation to obey these commissars' orders. Even if the commissars were Communists, however, the party members who were mobilized by civilian organizations felt themselves to be perfectly qualified to decide their tasks and resented the military authorities who ordered them about. A leader of a detachment of Moscow workers mobilized for the Eastern Front complained about the commissars' treatment of him and his comrades:

> For me—someone who went to the front not on someone's orders but of my own free will, and furthermore in the detachment of Comrade Ivanov, whom I know, from having witnessed him in battle, to be a dedicated comrade—such orders are demeaning! And I have firmly decided that if any of these people who are strangers to me should want to subordinate me or any of the agitators whom I direct and for whose work I am responsible to a representative of the central government, Comrade Ivanov—I shall refuse and return to Moscow.[62]

Iosif Khodorovskii, director of the political department of the Southern Front, warned party members not to expect to be assigned only responsible work as commissars. "For a Communist any work at the front is honorable and responsible, as long as it contributes to the betterment of the workers and peasants of Russia," he wrote in an instructional pamphlet for party members. "Seek not that work where you will be in a visible position and where your status will distinguish you from the mass of Red Army men."[63] Another head of a political department reported that he was apprehensive about trying to integrate a Moscow workers' division that had recently arrived with his troops. The workers' party organization had been set up in Moscow on strictly collegial principles and "no doubt would

61. Left SRs, anarchists, and nonparty socialists still figured prominently among the commissars. At the first All-Russian Congress of Commissars in June 1918, only 271 of the 359 delegates were Communists: PPR I, p. 78n. As late as December 1918, 40 percent of all political workers were not Communist Party members. By May 1919 this number was down to 11.2 percent: Kolychev, Partiino-politicheskaia rabota, p. 368.

62. "Ot rukovoditelia otriada moskovskikh rabochikh V. Garekolia (Vostochnyi front)," no later than 22 September 1918, in Perepiska, 4:452.

63. "Pamiatka kommunistu na fronte," December 1918, in PPR I, pp. 131–35.

be at odds with the type of organization we have here."[64] Already party organizations in the army had begun to develop along lines that distinguished them from their civilian counterparts. Army conditions did not permit the sort of discussions that characterized party life at home. Party members who were accustomed to questioning decisions, to voting and canvassing for support of alternate positions, and to more generally lax conditions found army life demeaning to their dignity. They were expected to sacrifice far more than they had done at home and to obey unquestioningly.

Many Communists simply refused to demean themselves and went home. The Central Committee learned that many of these Communists were explaining that they had decamped for reasons of principle. With their agitation against "the Soviet regime in general and mobilization in particular," these disgruntled men and women were encouraging desertion. The Central Committee ordered all party organizations to treat as deserters any members who returned from the front without official leave documents. As punishment, they were to be sent to rear units for service.[65] The punitive measures against deserters reaffirmed the important part that military service was to play in party members' career records. Only those men and women who had proved themselves in the heat of battle would be deemed true Communists after the war.

Perhaps equally disturbing for some veteran party members was a tendency among recently enrolled Communists to demand privileges by virtue of the fact that their party was the ruling one in the government.[66] Khodorovskii's pamphlet warned members not to expect an easy life and to forget about comforts while they were serving. They should be examples of self-sacrifice, courage, and discipline. But the center received reports of Communists who occupied the most desirable quarters in town while ordinary soldiers had no roof at all over their heads. The speed with which such practices surfaced after the Revolution is seen in a letter from a Red Army man to the peasant newspaper *Bednota* in November 1918. The soldier, who referred to himself as "a Soviet Red Army man," entered a soviet tearoom for a glass of tea. When a comrade stopped him to ask who he was, he answered with his regimental number.

64. "Iz doklada zaveduiushchego politotdelom VIII armii Iuzhnogo fronta V. Malakhovskogo Revvoensovetu Iuzhnogo fronta o rabote politotdela za noiabr'-dekabr' 1918 g.," in *PPR* I, pp. 272–75.

65. *KPSS o vooruzhennykh silakh Sovetskogo Soiuza: Dokumenty, 1917–1968* (Moscow, 1969), pp. 74–75, 91–92.

66. Party membership expanded rapidly after November 1917, approximately doubling in the first year and a half. The Statistical Department estimated membership in January 1919 at 251,000. By comparison, the party claimed 23,600 at the beginning of 1917. See T. H. Rigby, *Communist Party Membership in the USSR, 1917–1967* (Princeton: Princeton University Press, 1968), pp. 68–74.

"This is not the place for you, comrade, it's for Communists," he was told. He indignantly demanded of the newspaper audience, "How can there be such a difference between a Red Army man and a Communist?"[67]

When political workers attempted to explain to the soldiers how such behavior was possible in the Communist Party, they fell back on a version of class analysis that was becoming a popular means to account for any and all deviations from proper Bolshevik ethics. Early on political departments were ordered to keep close track of their staffs and report regularly to the Central Committee and RVSR. Khodorovskii's report from the Southern Front in early 1919 offers a revealing picture of the categories he deemed vital in evaluating the effectiveness of his political staff. The political department of the Southern Front counted 1,892 staff members, of whom 45 were women. Of the total number, the overwhelming majority were Communists (94.2 percent) and sympathizers (5.2 percent). Four anarchists and eight nonparty workers were also registered. The second important category was age. The staff was remarkably young; one-fifth of the staff was under twenty-one, over three-quarters were younger than thirty-one. Social status was the third matter scrutinized. Though workers (37.2 percent) and peasants (18.5 percent) constituted slightly more than half, the political department relied to an alarming degree on members of what Khodorovskii labeled "vacillating groups": former bureaucrats of tsarist institutions, trade and industry, and intelligentsia professions; in short, white-collar workers. In fact, the only group the author deemed truly reliable were the skilled workers, who made up only 20 percent of the personnel. "Politically backward groups" of unskilled workers and peasants made up 35.3 percent. Khodorovskii next turned his attention to educational background and found 70 percent of his staff to have completed only lower education and 9 percent to be illiterate. Only 9.5 percent had completed middle-level education; another 4.5 percent had had some middle-level education; and 2 percent had higher education. Finally, the report focused on length of party membership, or date of party enrollment. Khodorovskii lamented that the majority of the 1,782 Communists had joined the party only since the October Revolution, a fact that could not help diminishing the initial impression of large numbers. The 61.5 percent who were new to the party had only "begun to adjust themselves to party and political life, it was out of the question to assign them responsible work." A third of the political staff had been sent to work as rank-

67. Bednota, 26 November 1918.

and-file soldiers; the rest occupied more responsible positions in the army administration.[68]

Commissars such as Khodorovskii faced the inevitable dilemmas of the new state's task of forging a new political class in an environment of severe shortages of qualified and tested personnel. Many party members, because they had volunteered for military service, felt that they deserved access to scarce living quarters and commodities, as well as obedience from mere conscripts. They were called by the party to assume greater risks, and they expected greater rewards. Predictably party veterans attributed what they perceived to be a decline in the moral standards of Communists to the "petit bourgeois" attitudes that the new members, especially young ones, brought from civilian life. Here "petit bourgeois" connotes excessive concern with material well-being and unwillingness to sacrifice personal interests and comfort to defend the Revolution. Indeed, with the rapid expansion of the party during 1917, the secretariat had no means to check closely on membership credentials. The weight of "conscious proletarians" declined in the party as it became clear that the Communists were the new arbiters of power. Increasingly "political opportunism" preoccupied the party leadership.

The perceived decline in standards among party members and the charges of opportunism raised concern throughout the party. In the army, however, these phenomena attracted particular attention because of their repercussions on soldiers' morale. After all, soldiers were fighting to preserve a new and just social order; they recognized as legitimate authorities only those persons who acted in accordance with their own revolutionary standards. The troops did not respect party members who assumed privileges; consequently, the Communists had little or no authority outside of their revolvers. In December 1918 Trotsky responded to the vocal criticism of party members from commissars and soldiers alike and proposed that all political departments in the army check up on the behavior of Communists and "take timely measures to expel the bad weeds from the garden."[69] The often overbearing behavior of party members toward soldiers, commissars, and commanders alike was a symptom of the greater political conflicts that grew from the improvised responses to the military and political emergencies and to the breakdown of authority across the country since early 1917. The quarrels among

68. "Kratkii otchet politotdela Iuzhnogo fronta o raspredelenii politicheskikh rabotnikov," 25 February 1919, in *PPR* I, pp. 137–38. Iosif Khodorovskii, as a member of the Revolutionary Military Council of the Southern Front, sent copies of the report to the Central Committee, to VTsIK, to SNK, and to the RVSR.

69. Trotskii, "Rol' kommunistov v Krasnoi Armii: Prikaz Predsedatelia RVSR po Krasnoi Armii i Krasnomu Flotu, 11 dekabria 1918 g., no. 60," in *KVR*, 1:185.

the military and political command staffs also undermined their units' fighting ability. In the absence of a united leadership, soldiers saw little reason to fight. As the war dragged on, initially enthusiastic soldiers lost their zeal. They passed resolutions demanding to be sent home, since they had done what they considered to be their duty. When the fighting did not stop, soldiers simply deserted, especially if their homes were nearby.

The military and civilian authorities struggled to understand why soldiers refused to fight. Initially the center attacked the problem with harshly repressive measures in the name of revolutionary vigilance or against pernicious counterrevolution. Trotsky ordered the arrest of all chairmen of rural soviets and committees of village poor in whose villages deserters were apprehended. Arrested deserters were shot on the spot, but those who returned voluntarily were forgiven. In November a new army policy set returned deserters apart with black collars to alert all those around them of their disgraceful past deeds. In December the Council on Defense set up the Central Commission for the Struggle with Desertion (Tsentrokomdezertir), which included the chairmen of the All-Russian General Staff, Vsebiurvoenkom, and the People's Commissariat for Internal Affairs, and was headed by a member of the Cheka collegium, Sergei Uralov. The council advanced 2 million rubles to the new commission to work out local arrangements and begin a propaganda campaign. The instructions to the commission stipulated that deserters could be executed and people who concealed deserters sentenced to up to five years of hard labor.

When the harsh measures failed to stem the tide of desertion, moderate army spokesmen recommended a combination of firmness and understanding, offering a carrot to go along with the stick. They pointed to a study by the Supreme Military Inspectorate which had concluded that large numbers of soldiers deserted not because they were implacable enemies of the Revolution but simply because they were not receiving their rations. Many of these soldiers would return, after a few days' absence, with a supply of bread.[70] Other soldiers returned home to help their hard-pressed families with farming tasks during the late harvest season. Sovnarkom moved to address the increasingly desperate plight of soldiers' families who were short of hands with various forms of subsidies and exemptions from taxes. Trotsky petitioned Sovnarkom to free all Red Army families from any future emergency taxes. Red Army families in the cities were entitled to free apartments and were exempted from forced

70. Kolychev, Partiino-politicheskaia rabota, p. 253.

labor.[71] The People's Commissariat for Social Welfare had primary responsibility for dispensing the benefits, but the weak network of local administrative offices often delayed deliveries. Still, from all accounts by political workers and many soldiers, the government's commitment in itself was an important gesture that won support from the Red Army men and their families. The welfare measures also distinguished a new category of semiprivileged citizens in the postrevolutionary order. In succeeding legislation, the state consolidated the status of these beneficiaries as part of the social contract it was offering to various social groups. In the case of the Red Army, the soldiers and officers pledged their loyal service in the armed forces in exchange for the state's commitment to guarantee them a decent living standard and to protect their families.

State policies to combat desertion evolved in ways that were roughly parallel to policy changes in other areas, especially rural policies. The changes suggest that much of the political leadership was coming to the conclusion that the initially doctrinaire measures of class warfare were failing to win the state much cooperation from the populace. More immediately, the army command was paying the price for the state's rural policies, which were alienating larger and larger segments of the peasantry. The army's leadership had a special interest in the government's rural policies on at least three grounds. First, the disasters of the fall campaigns had had their roots in part in insufficient supplies, above all food shortages. Hunger weakened morale among troops, but also among the urban populations in Bolshevik strongholds. Better relations with the peasantry promised to improve the food situation, as well as the supply of goods from small-scale peasant artisans and craftworkers.[72] Second, the center realized that its success against the Whites depended increasingly on the attitudes and behavior of peasants. Lenin articulated a hope, which he claimed was based on the actual experience of the center, that the peasants would choose to aid the Reds after they had had a taste of the Whites' dictatorship. But he realized that unless the Red dictatorship could demonstrate that it had something better to offer the peasants, they would be unlikely to give it active support; rather they would sit out the fighting and see who won. The proletarian dictatorship needed at least the neutrality of the bulk of the peasantry and the enthusiastic support of a strategic minority.

71. For measures to aid Red Army families and some problems in delivery of the promised aid, see E. G. Gimpel'son, *Sovety v gody interventsii i grazhdanskoi voiny* (Moscow, 1968), pp. 310–16. Sovnarkom decreed the first cash payments to Red Army families on 24 December 1918.

72. On the role of small-scale industry in supplying the Red Army, see Malle, *Economic Organization of War Communism*, pp. 466–79.

Related to these concerns was the matter of conscription. The initial mobilizations in the spring of 1918 had included peasants only in the most immediately threatened regions; when the center called up former soldiers and NCOs, however, the numbers of peasants—mostly middle peasants, according to Bolshevik categories—rose dramatically. In fact, by the end of 1918 the soldiers were overwhelmingly of peasant origins.[73] Furthermore, by the end of the year, Red intelligence agencies estimated that enemy forces totaled over 700,000.[74] On the basis of field staff recommendations, the RVSR concluded that the Soviet Republic needed an army of 3 million if it were to emerge as the victor in the upcoming struggle. The political and military leaders had by now shed their illusions that victory was around the corner and had reluctantly reconciled themselves to the prospect of a lengthy war. Until very recently, the urban population had contributed the bulk of the new recruits. But as industrial output plummeted, Sovnarkom decreed more and more exemptions from military service for categories of factory workers and administrative personnel. The proletariat could not spare many more cadres if the essential sectors of the economy were to maintain even a bare minimum of activity. There seemed little choice but to turn ever more decisively to the peasantry. But because the political leaders had staked so much on the argument that the Red Army was a class socialist armed force—by which they meant that only loyal toilers served in the ranks—the induction of large numbers of peasants compromised declared principles.

All of these considerations forced the Bolshevik leaders to reevaluate their relations with the population and especially their rural policies. At the center of these reevaluations was the "middle peasantry." Bolsheviks labeled as middle peasants those about whose political attitudes they felt least secure. Poor peasants were assumed to be in favor of class warfare and the Soviet state; wealthy peasants or kulaks were placed in the enemy camp as rural equivalents of the urban bourgeoisie. The middle peasants in a quintessential fashion represented the entire peasantry and in fact made up the overwhelming majority of peasants, according to Bolshevik criteria. These peasants were part proletarian because by and large they worked their own land and lived without exploiting their poorer countrymen. But they were also part bourgeois because they often hired labor or equipment. Because these peasants had a foot in two worlds, their political behavior seemed highly unpredictable to the Bolsheviks.

73. By the end of 1918, volunteers made up only 16.6 percent of army strength; the remaining 83.4 percent had been mobilized: *Istoriia sovetskogo krest'ianstva*, p. 134.
74. *Direktivy*, 4:474.

Beginning in late summer, more and more party leaders argued that the policy of the food dictatorship and village poor committees had lost the government substantial support among the peasantry. The party had aimed during 1918 to "neutralize the peasantry" and ally itself with the poorest peasants against the rural bourgeoisie and petite bourgeoisie in a blatant appeal to class warfare. What this meant in practice was that agents representing the center, usually workers and soldiers, looked for allies among the poorest peasants to confiscate the property of the wealthier peasants and thereby to deprive them of any political role in village life. The bulk of any village, the middle peasants, would have to choose sides. Lenin had already hinted in November that the center was reevaluating its relations with the peasantry. He and other Bolshevik leaders, desperate for new bases of support, couched their discussion in terms similar to those of Khodorovskii at the Southern Front: in a version of class categories, they distinguished those parts of the populace who were likely to be loyal from those who were not and still further from those who vacillated in their sympathies but might yet be won over.[75] Lenin counted on the middle peasantry's support of the proletarian dictatorship after it had tasted White rule. Finally, he concluded that it was politically unwise to dismiss all but the thin layer of poor peasants as sympathetic to the enemy camp and to take the kulaks as the dominant force in the countryside.

At the Sixth Congress of Soviets, in November 1918, the state's spokesmen pressed the delegates to revise the approach toward the majority of the nation's population. As a signal of its more benign attitude toward the rural citizenry, the congress sanctioned the formation of the first all-peasant regiments from the village poor. It was hoped that the committees of the poor would recruit and outfit reliable rural cadres. Ironically, the same congress heard reports of extreme dissatisfaction with the performance of the poor peasant committees and of their conflicts with existing peasant organizations, including rural soviets. In many areas, the committees were manned by returning soldiers and workers from the cities and represented an outside force that had gained little or no local support.[76] The Congress of Soviets sanctioned the merging of the committees of rural poor with local soviets, in what amounted to admission of the failure of this experiment in fomenting class conflict in the countryside. The delegates' resolution acknowledged that the committees, far from establishing Soviet power on a firm footing, had alienated large parts of the peasant population. The decisions of the Sixth Congress opened the door to further revisions of state rural policies and, very critical from the army's perspective, policies of military

75. Lenin, "Tsennye priznaniia Pitirima Sorokina," November 1918, in *PSS*, 28:71.
76. See Keep, *Russian Revolution*, pp. 459–62.

conscription; consequently, the social composition of the army would change drastically and thereby force the state and the army to adopt new techniques in its dealings with soldiers and peasants.

Pressures for Reform

By late 1918 the army was rife with political conflicts, the products of the improvised responses to the military and political emergencies. Commissars, soldiers' committees, party cells, military specialists, and revolutionary tribunals competed for authority to command soldiers' loyalty. Even the agreement won for the center's policies at the Fifth Congress of Soviets threatened to unravel. The September victories temporarily had concealed all these conflicts, but not for very long. As the army grew and its leaders learned from the experiments and reforms, the political conflicts too grew into a seemingly intractable bundle of dilemmas. When the Red Army won victories, Trotsky's critics temporarily lowered their voices. But as soon as Red units suffered defeat, they rushed to denounce the ruthless commander in chief.

Among the burgeoning number of state agencies that competed with the army command over power and resources, the army's major rival during the Civil War was the Cheka. The Cheka now had two military departments, one for each major front. The Cheka's departments contested the power of the political departments that were subordinate to Vsebiurvoenkom on nearly all issues and forced the party's Central Committee to intervene to settle disputes. Frequently the center sent out a commission to investigate the dispute and recommended transferring one of the belligerent sides to another post.[77] Most attempts to regulate the army's relationship with the security forces resulted in increased powers for the Cheka. In February 1919 VTsIK confirmed the authority of the army's Cheka units in a "Regulation on Special Departments," according to which the Cheka claimed an even wider range of powers than it had previously demanded. The Cheka absorbed the staff and responsibilities of the Military Control Section of the RVSR, thereby concentrating in

---

77. A case in point is the conflict between Evgeniia Bosh, head of the political department of the Caspian-Caucasian Front, and K. Grasis, head of the front's Cheka special unit, in January 1919. When the chairman of the front's revolutionary military council, Aleksandr Shliapnikov, was unable to resolve the struggle, Lenin sent several telegrams to Astrakhan; but telegrams—even from Lenin—did not defuse the tense situation. Finally, the Central Committee dispatched a commission to Astrakhan for an investigation. Grasis, the head of the Cheka unit, apparently emerged the victor, for both Bosh and Shliapnikov were recalled from the front. Shliapnikov was replaced by Konstantin Mekhonoshin and Bosh by Sergei Kirov. See S. Ostriakov, *Voennye chekisty* (Moscow, 1979), pp. 24–36; George Leggett, *The Cheka: Lenin's Political Police* (Oxford: Clarendon, 1981), pp. 95–98.

one organization most, but not all, police powers. Mikhail Kedrov, who by now had considerable army experience, was appointed head of a new Special Department of the Cheka with specific responsibility for army affairs.

Vsebiurvoenkom competed also with another authoritative organ that—like the institution of the commissar—embodied one of the most direct claims of the Revolution, the claim that "the people" inspected and controlled the agencies of political power. That agency was Podvoiskii's Supreme Military Inspectorate. The political section of the inspectorate had responsibility for all political work in the units that it formed, and in fact it was the inspectorate and not Vsebiurvoenkom that set up the first political departments at the Eastern and Southern fronts.[78] The inspectorate's control responsibilities also included the investigation of "the moral and political profile of the regular troops and command staff and their relations." This responsibility was clearly part of the charge of Vsebiurvoenkom as well.

The overlapping responsibilities of the Military Inspectorate and Vsebiurvoenkom evolved into a principle of multiple control that became widespread throughout the new state's administration, in part because of the civilians' extreme distrust of large bureaucracies, and especially of the army. But the principle of multiple control agencies also emerged from the center's ever more desperate attempts to bypass regular chains of command in order to get its tasks accomplished. At some point, however, the principle defeated its initial rationale and reduced the army administration to utter chaos. Beginning in the fall of 1918, the center began to reform the control organizations in a series of streamlinings and mergers. The political sections of the RVSR and of the Military Inspectorate were transferred to Vsebiurvoenkom, which in turn was made directly subordinate to the RVSR. Konstantin Iurenev, as head of Vsebiurvoenkom, now had responsibility for all commissars, political departments, and, nominally, all political work and party matters in the army and rear units.[79]

All these measures were intended to reduce the confusion that resulted from overlapping jurisdictions and competing centers of authority in the army. Any improvement in organizational matters still

78. The September 1918 Regulation of the Inspectorate defined it as "the permanent competent organ of the RVSR for the inspection of the army and all its institutions both in the center and locally in all areas of military and political work": "Iz polozheniia o Vysshei Voennoi Inspektsii RKKA," in *PPR* I, pp. 84–85.

79. Vsebiurvoenkom still did not have authority over political work among recruits, who were trained under the auspices of Vsevobuch, the Universal Military Training Administration. Vsevobuch trainees, who were mobilized on a territorial basis, remained under the authority of the local party organizations that had recruited them.

left unresolved the large problem of poor discipline and performance. To remedy this ill, the army leaders undertook to profession-
alize the army—to "militarize" it, as they said—at the level of the
low-ranking commander and common soldier. Not surprisingly, the
state turned to the professional military men, the military specialists, for help in implementing the new order. In turning to the military professionals, the political leadership was retreating from
alternative models of military organization. The first model, the urban militias of the defunct Red Guards, was incorporated in the
principles of Vsevobuch and its network of local training agencies.
A second model that emerged in 1918, rural guerrilla warfare,
proved to be more irksome to the military authorities than the Red
Guard had been. The military specialists and commissars called this
second negative model "partisan warfare." Partisans rejected centralized administration, rigid hierarchies, and the principle of unquestioning obedience. Partisan fighters elected their commanders
and maintained familiar relations with one another and with their
commanders. Because they recognized no central authority that
would have provisioned them, partisans usually lived off the
countryside.[80] Rural partisan warfare was part of a widespread peasant response to the breakdown of central authority which began
with the revolutions in 1917. Peasants everywhere devised methods
of self-defense and self-rule which included a return to the reparti-
tional commune. With no central powers able to defend or control
them, rural communities formed communes to regulate their economic relations and partisan forces to defend themselves from the
depredations of outsiders, be they Red or White recruiters, soldiers,
or food detachments.

In their fierce local loyalties, their attitudes, and their democratic
practices, the partisans were very similar to the Red Guards. In this
sense, the rural partisan forces were inspired by the larger revolutionary repudiation of superordinate authority which had brought
the Bolsheviks to power in 1917; indeed, at first several Red commanders and some commissars, including such influential ones as
Voroshilov, Stalin, and Budennyi, defended the partisans as truly
revolutionary fighting forces. As long as the partisans were waging
their struggle against the German and Austrian occupation forces in
1918 or against the hetman's regime in the Ukraine, especially when
the Red Army was still organizing its first units, the Soviet government welcomed their aid, even if it already looked on their practices
with some misgivings. By late 1918 and early 1919 the attitude of the

80. For a literary account of partisan warfare based on personal experience, see
Dmitrii Furmanov, *Chapaev*, trans. George Kittell and J. Kittell (Moscow: Foreign Language Publishing House, 1959; first published 1923).

center had changed decisively. Most of the major partisan armies formed on the periphery of Soviet power, precisely where the new government's hold was most tenuous; furthermore, the partisans resisted all attempts to integrate them into the Red Army's forces. The fact that the partisans often had anarchist or SR advisers and were ambivalent or hostile toward Soviet power could hardly endear them to Moscow. Worse, very often partisan troops proved to be unreliable when Red Army units tried to coordinate actions with them. And when regular Red Army units fought close to partisans for any length of time, as Trotsky complained, they became "infected" with "the partisan spirit" or with "anarchist moods";[81] consequently Red Army commanders tried, not always successfully, to isolate their units from partisans. After nearly every battle that joined regular army troops and partisans, the local revolutionary military council ordered increased political work and purges of unreliable commissars who had failed to take resolute measures to prevent a breakdown in authority.[82]

Clearly the former imperial officers who served in the Red Army did not look favorably on the unreliable partisans. But many prominent political leaders in the army also rejected partisan warfare as another inevitable consequence of the "petit bourgeois mentality" of the peasantry. Mikhail Frunze, a commander on the Eastern Front and an Old Bolshevik, called the peasantry "the father of *partizanshchina.*" Here *partizanshchina* has a negative connotation, implying backwardness and undesirable political behavior. Frunze explained that because the peasants lived dispersed in isolated corners and were accustomed to acting either as individuals or in small groups, they exhibited corresponding traits in their methods of military operation.[83]

The central military authorities fought against the partisan style with a series of reforms in disciplinary policies. In late November

81. Trotskii, "V Tsentral'nyi Komitet Rossiiskoi Kommunisticheskoi Partii," 1 May 1919, document no. 199, in *The Trotsky Papers, 1917–1922*, 2 vols., ed. Jan M. Meijer (The Hague: Mouton, 1964–1971), 1:388–93.

82. Kolychev, *Partiino-politicheskaia rabota*, pp. 72, 240. White commanders confirmed many of the reports written by Red Army commissars about partisan attitudes. The early Siberian White Army, for example, was founded on democratic principles; it had elected soldiers' committees and abolished epaulettes. In time, more authoritarian former tsarist officers replaced the revolutionary officers and reintroduced traditional discipline. By late July 1919 Kolchak's armies were melting away because of desertion by peasants, who subsequently joined the partisans and fought against both Reds and Whites. See the account of Colonel Viripaev in Paul Dotsenko, *The Struggle for Democracy in Siberia, 1917–1920*, (Stanford: Hoover Institution Press, 1983), p. 79.

83. M. V. Frunze, *Izbrannye proizvedeniia* (Moscow, 1940), p. 45; see also Trotskii, "Vostochnyi front," 6 April 1919, in *KVR*, vol. 2, pt. 1, p. 319.

and December a commission of former imperial officers drafted internal service and garrison service manuals that provided detailed procedures for lower-ranking officers and political workers to regulate troop training and behavior. The RVSR introduced a standardized uniform for all Red Army men, followed by insignia to distinguish types of troops (artillery, infantry, political workers) and to distinguish the command and political staffs from the regular troops. Every measure was designed to make procedures more predictable, so that both soldiers and commanders knew what to expect from one another. The Army Commissariat also persisted in its fight to implement a separate punitive policy for military men and commissioned the drafting of a severe disciplinary manual. It wrested new concessions from the increasingly beleaguered Commissariat of Justice. By January 1919 the chairman of the Revolutionary Military Tribunal of the Republic, Karl Danishevskii, declared in the government's newspaper that "military tribunals are not governed and should not be governed by any juridical norms." In view of the fact that the tribunals were purely punitive organs "created in the course of intense revolutionary combat," they should decide sentences on the basis of political expedience and "the legal sense of communism."[84] Behind the revolutionary bluster can be glimpsed the sense that the army's mission dictated different notions of discipline and infraction than those that guided civilian judicial authorities.

Although these reforms fell far short of restoring the imperial system of rank and privilege, they provoked cries of betrayal and counterrevolution and raised further charges of Trotsky's overreliance on military specialists. The disciplinary manuals in particular were ill received by many lower-ranking commanders, commissars, and soldiers. In early 1919, party members working in the political administration of the Eastern Front passed resolutions against the introduction of insignia and in favor of elections of officers.[85] Elsewhere two members of the revolutionary military council of the Eastern Front's Fifth Army refused to distribute the strict disciplinary regulations because they "absolutely were not in accord with the fundamental principles of army organization." These resolutions and actions clearly resembled the practices of partisan armies. Trotsky, who had as little sympathy for the peasant style of warfare as Frunze, attacked the defiant political workers as "ideologues of

84. Izvestiia VTsIK, 3 January 1919, no. 2; see also Karl Danishevskii, Revoliutsionnye voennye tribunaly (Moscow, 1920), both cited in Portnov and Slavin, Pravovye osnovy, p. 211.

85. Trotskii, "Kommunistam na Vostochnom fronte," 24 March 1919, in KVR, vol. 2, pt. 1, p. 313.

our internal Left SRism [levoeserovshchina]."[86] In so doing, Trotsky conflated the persistent resistance to the military specialists and their attempts to introduce tighter discipline and unquestioning obedience; the "petit bourgeois ideology" of the Left SRs and Left Communists, who had opposed the initial policies of Trotsky as army commissar and advocated the prosecution of a revolutionary war in the spring of 1918; and the peasant partisan forces, who undermined discipline in nearby regular units with their overly democratic principles. After the Left SRs broke with the Bolsheviks, and after their abortive mutiny in July 1918, the Soviet military and political leadership found in them another convenient scapegoat for many of their difficulties with the peasantry. And because Left SRs and anarchists often joined partisan bands, the link between political opposition and alien class elements—that is, peasants—was assured of a central place in Bolshevik political analysis.

Though Trotsky's policies were antagonizing an ever-larger circle of military and political leaders who made their discontent known in coded telegrams to Moscow or in behind-the-scenes intrigues, so far public criticism of the army's performance was deflected to actors and conditions on the scene—exhausted commanders, cowardly troops, poor supply facilities. At the end of November and throughout December the Red Army was still unable to make notable headway in its attempted counteroffensives. Especially at the Southern Front, Red Army units remained unstable and regularly abandoned their positions; their commanders frequently did not carry out combat orders. Staff was still exhausted from the September campaigns, reserves were not arriving, supplies were inadequate, and the administration of the units was deficient. Enemy agents on the staffs of the front and individual armies regularly betrayed vital information to the White general Petr Krasnov. The Central Committee concluded that the Red Terror was more crucial now than ever before and should be ruthlessly applied not only "against outright traitors and saboteurs, but against all cowards, self-seekers, connivers, and concealers."[87]

At the end of December, the city of Perm fell to Kolchak's armies and threatened the Bolshevik stronghold of Viatka. This time the response to the military defeat was different; the string of failures had emboldened Trotsky's critics to attack him directly. The day after the Whites' victory, two articles appeared in Pravda, penned by two

86. One of the two "ideologues" was Vladimir Smirnov, who led the Military Opposition at the Eighth Party Congress. Smirnov was relieved of his military posts after the congress on orders from Lenin. See Trotsky, Trotsky Papers, p. 398; Kolychev, Partiino-politicheskaia rabota, p. 241; Leninskii sbornik, 38:135–40.

87. "Postanovlenie TsK RKP(b) ob ukreplenii Iuzhnogo fronta," 26 November 1918, in PPR I, pp. 36–37; see also n. 67 on pp. 350–51 for further analysis and recommended measures.

army political workers, A. Kamenskii and V. Sorin. The authors attacked the policies of the Army Commissariat from the platform of
the Left Communist faction of the party. Sorin opposed what he perceived as the steady move away from collegial decision making toward one-man command in operational and tactical matters, the
continued presence of military specialists, and the weak authority of
party members. Kamenskii, in an article headed "Long Overdue,"
repeated Sorin's charges and called the military specialists "Niko-
laevan counterrevolutionaries." The Central Committee struck back
at the opposition with a special resolution, "On the Policies of the
Army Administration," in which it declared that any attack on the
policies of the Army Commissariat was equivalent to an attack on
the Central Committee.[88]

In the wake of the Perm defeat, however, the left opposition's critique was impossible to dismiss so easily; moreover, the Ural party
obkom, the most influential party organization at the site of the recent defeat, also criticized the center for its lack of effective coordination and for its shoddy organization. According to the blistering
report from the Urals, everything had been done in the most hap-
hazard fashion. The political staff had even warned the military
command that their troops would go over to the enemy's side because they had had insufficient time to prepare them for battle. The
Ural committee drew alarmed attention to "the predominance of me-
diocre old officers or outright White Guardists." The authors concluded that their experience in the Urals had demonstrated "the
total unsuitability of the old officers for drill or front-line service in
the Red Army." These officers unfailingly reintroduced their old
style of command, which Red Army men were justifiably unwilling
to countenance. The command headquarters had acquired all the
worst features of staff life in the old army, including drinking bouts
and debauchery with women, and they maintained close ties with
White Guard organizations. The *obkom* demanded that the Central
Committee immediately appoint an authoritative commission "to locate and punish the individuals responsible for the shameful defeat, . . . to account for the bitter experience of the defeats suffered,
and to facilitate a radical reevaluation by the party on an all-Russian
scale of the methods of building the Red Army."[89] Nearly a year after
the first steps were taken to organize the Red Army, vocal party
leaders still were disputing Trotsky's leadership.

The Central Committee heeded the Ural committee's recommendations. The commission it appointed, headed by Stalin and Feliks

88. *Pravda*, 25 and 26 December 1918.
89. "Doklad Ural'skogo oblastnogo komiteta RKP(b) v TsK RKP(b) o prichinakh
padeniia Permi i neobkhodomosti rassledovaniia obstoiastel'stv porazheniia 3 armii,"
not later than 30 December 1918, in *Perepiska*, 5:312–18.

Dzerzhinsky, the Cheka chairman, was clearly stacked against Trotsky: both Stalin and Dzerzhinsky had considerable scores to settle with him. Their findings predictably confirmed the conclusions of the Ural *obkom.* Harsh criticism was leveled against Trotsky's overreliance on military specialists, not surprisingly, since Stalin earlier had represented the commissars' position. The commission agreed that party members and commissars exerted little or no influence over military specialists. Officers not only interfered with party work but had been known to arrest chairmen of party committees and comrades' courts.[90]

A second major focus was conscription policies. The commission once again charged the military specialists who sat on the local military commissariats of placing military imperatives higher than political considerations. The commissariats were recruiting citizens without any attention to their property holdings, so that "what resulted was not so much a Red as a people's army." A people's army, according to Bolshevik rhetoric, included alien social groups; it did not restrict its conscripts to "class-conscious" workers and poor peasants. By definition such an army must be unreliable in combat.[91]

The charges added up to a powerful indictment of the military and political leadership at the Eastern Front, but more especially of the politics of Trotsky and the center. The indictment was repeated in reports that were arriving from other fronts by the end of 1918 and persisted into the first months of 1919.[92] It was clear that major issues of authority in the new army were far from a satisfactory resolution. The party scheduled its Eighth Congress for mid-March and the belligerent factions prepared for a political battle while the hostilities continued at the front lines.

The Eighth Congress opened in Moscow on 18 March 1919. Of the 403 delegates in attendance, 40 represented the more than 31,000 party members serving in the army. In addition to the expected debates about the army itself, many discussions touched on issues of direct importance for the army—a new policy in the countryside, a new party program, and party organization and membership.[93]

90. "Otchet komissii TsK partii i Soveta Oborony tovarishchu Leninu o prichinakh padeniia Permi v dek. 1918 g.," in I. V. Stalin, *Sochineniia,* 13 vols. (Moscow, 1946–1951), 4:197–224.

91. "People's army" was, significantly, the slogan of moderate socialists, especially Mensheviks and SRs, during the post-1917 years. The moderate socialists hoped to avoid the brutal civil war they predicted would occur if the proletariat and poor peasantry were to seize power by means of a minority dictatorship. Hence the slogan "people's army" paralleled the still often-heard calls for an all-socialist government.

92. See, for example, "Zaiavlenie Kommunisticheskoi iacheiki batal'ona sviazi Ural'skoi divizii (Iuzhnyi front)," 2 January 1919, in *Perepiska,* 6:448–49.

93. The decisions on party organization and membership are addressed in chap. 2.

Speaking for the absent Trotsky, Grigorii Sokol'nikov presented the commissariat's theses on the military question to the congress.[94] Sokol'nikov declared that it was time to eliminate all vestiges of the volunteer army and "partisan warfare" and to complete the transition to a regular Workers'-Peasants' Red Army with "iron discipline." Sokol'nikov defended the use of military specialists under the vigilance of military commissars as the Army Commissariat's carefully considered policy, but he promised to step up the schooling of workers and peasants to prepare them for command positions. The ideal of a people's militia had lost its relevance, he argued, just as the slogan of democratic parliamentarism had become a weapon of the reaction. Those who persisted in defending the ideal of a people's militia were as blind as the despicable German Social-Democrat Karl Kautsky; nevertheless, he persisted in referring to the new army as a "class militia army." Speaking for Trotsky, Sokol'nikov also rejected outright the arguments in favor of "partisan detachments" as inspired by Left SRs and the petit bourgeois intelligentsia. "Preaching partisan warfare as a military program is equivalent to recommending returning from large-scale industry to handicrafts." Trotsky's use of the industrial example tells much about the mentality of the Bolshevik leadership. It was held to be self-evident that bigger was better and that central authority in the hands of the conscious proletarian dictatorship was better than local autonomy in the hands of backward Russian peasants or even unconscious Russian workers. History was moving toward an industrial urban future, away from the idiocy of rural life. By implication, partisans and partisan warfare were vestiges of an incorrect and backward world view, and anyone who advocated such views was aiding the enemy.[95]

Nearly every thesis provoked impassioned debate from the emerging Military Opposition. Vladimir Smirnov presented the counter-theses of the Military Opposition and charged that Sokol'nikov had misrepresented the opposition's criticisms. The Military Opposition contended that the commissars deserved more than a narrow control function, because they already had more combat experience than many military specialists. Two new regulations issued by Sovnarkom in December 1918 had practically reduced political departments to bureaucratic chancelleries and deprived them of any

94. Trotskii, "Nasha politika v dele sozdaniia armii," in KVR, 1:186–95.

95. See Sokol'nikov's address in *Vos'moi s''ezd RKP(b), Mart 1919 goda: Protokoly*, (Moscow, 1959), pp. 144–53. Before Sokol'nikov began his address, Rozaliia Samoilova, a delegate from the Eighth Army, moved that the congress hear him in a special closed session because "many delegates have certain opinions that can be expressed only in a closed session if this matter is to be considered by us in a comprehensive way"; Sokol'nikov declared that he wanted to report to the entire congress (ibid., p. 143).

real political role in the military.[96] Smirnov reminded the congress's delegates of their revolutionary scruples and warned that Communists needed to persuade peasants that "our army is not an army of the old type." He attacked the new disciplinary code, which revived the practice of saluting an officer and introduced obligatory forms of address. Smirnov charged that the code also allowed commanders a whole series of privileges and exemptions, including special conditions if they were arrested, the right to live in separate quarters, and the right to maintain orderlies.[97]

After Smirnov's address, the Central Committee resolved to move the discussion of military affairs to a special closed session. The discussion revealed a wide array of platforms in opposition to a permanent conscript army. Widespread sentiment for an eventual transition to a socialist militia persisted, sentiments more in accord with the earlier platforms of the party, the Social Democratic Erfurt Program, and the ideology of Vsevobuch. What united nearly all the dissenters was their objection to the growing role of the suspect military specialists. During the turbulent closed session, a majority of the voting delegates actually supported the Military Opposition.

A special committee, consisting of three spokesmen in the Central committee and two for the Military Opposition, was appointed to resolve the outstanding differences.[98] The congress's eventual compromise resolution represented a victory for most of Trotsky's theses, but the military delegates were assured that some of the practices they most detested would be corrected. Most important, the army command promised not to place excessive trust in the military specialists to the detriment of the commissars. The congress revealed its sensitivity to criticism from Mensheviks and SRs abroad by rejecting it as "an expression of their political ignorance or charlatanry or a mixture of both." The émigrés were charging the Bolsheviks with militarism and Bonapartism. The congress argued that

96. The two regulations were "Postanovlenie Sovnarkoma RSFSR o komanduiush-chem armiiami fronta," 15 December 1918, in *PPR* I, pp. 40–41; and "O komanduiush-chem armiei, vkhodiashchei v sostav armii fronta," *Izvestiia Narkomvoen*, 14 December 1918, cited in Portnov and Slavin, *Pravovye osnovy stroitel'stva Krasnoi Armii*, pp. 153–54. The regulations markedly limited the powers of commissars to intervene in operational matters and were received among political officers as an attempt to demote them at the expense of the military specialists.

97. See the text of Smirnov's speech in *Vos'moi s''ezd*, pp. 153–58.

98. Stalin, Grigorii Zinoviev, and Boris Pozern, the military commissar of the Petrograd Labor Commune, defended the Central Committee's position; Emel'ian Iaroslavskii and G. I. Safarov represented the opposition's views. Stalin, in a dramatic turnabout, by now had become a fervent supporter of strict discipline, despite his recent defense of the principles of "partisan warfare" in his conflict with Sytin at the Southern Front. For an excerpted version of Stalin's speech to the closed session of the military section, see "Iz rechi po voennomu voprosu na VIII s''ezde RKP(b)," 21 March 1919, in Stalin, *Sochineniia*, 4:248–49. Stalin points to the presence of "non-working-class elements" (peasants) in the army as justification for "iron discipline."

"Bonapartism was not a product of a military organization as such, but a product of certain social relations," in particular the predominance of the petite bourgeoisie. "Since the most likely candidates to lead a petit bourgeois counterrevolution, the kulaks, are excluded from civic life, military service, and all genuine political power in the Soviet Republic, and since the proletarian dictatorship is pursuing a policy directly opposed to the counterrevolutionary forces that might install a Bonapartist regime, the potential for Bonapartism is excluded."[99] The most important guarantee that the Red Army would not fall prey to Bonapartist dangers was the work of the party and the political departments. The congress resolved to create an authoritative and effective body to coordinate commissars and political workers in the army, and to dismantle Vsebiurvoenkom and transfer its functions and apparatus to a new political department directly subordinate to the RVSR and headed by a full member of the Central Committee.[100] The reform made clear the importance the party attached to political control in the army and the urgency of keeping a vigilant eye on the military specialists. The Central Committee passed over the logical candidate to head the new Political Administration (PUR), Chairman Iurenev of Vsebiurvoenkom, and appointed Ivar Smilga as first director in May. Smilga began an immediate reorganization of the political staff and structure.

The second fundamental issue that would affect the future of the army was the "peasant question," or rural policies. The party congress reaffirmed the measures adopted at the Sixth Congress of Soviets in November 1918 and went even further in revising the center's policies in the countryside. The party congress recognized the "middle peasantry," by which was meant the overwhelming majority of peasants, as a social group that would persist for a long period after the Revolution and without whose support the Revolution could not survive. The congress declared a new slogan—a retreat from "neutralization of the middle peasantry" to "alliance with the poor and middle peasantry against the kulaks." In practical measures the center instructed its agents in the countryside to take a more cautious attitude in requisitioning food and to distinguish more precisely between enemies and allies of the Soviet state. The congress went even further in proposing forms of agricultural aid to poor and middle peasants, including land surveying, household consolidation, improvement in livestock, repair of machinery, irrigation, and aid to cooperatives. Finally, in a special resolution on political propaganda and "cultural-enlightment work" in the coun-

99. Vos'moi s''ezd, pp. 419–20.
100. For the countertheses presented by the Military Opposition, see the speech by Vladimir Smirnov in ibid., pp. 153–58. For the congress's resolution on the military question, see ibid., pp. 412–23.

tryside, the congress demanded greater attention to rural matters in party propaganda efforts, including expanded publication of literature aimed directly at a peasant audience.[101]

By extension, the more conciliatory attitude toward the middle peasantry meant improved relations with the families of increasingly large numbers of soldiers and former NCOs. More important, the state was gradually moving toward conscription of middle peasants; the week preceding the Eighth Congress, in fact, Sovnarkom had ordered another mobilization of workers and peasants in Petrograd, Moscow, and several nonagricultural provinces. The government once again was seriously considering extending the call-up to primarily agricultural provinces and finally resolved to do so after the Eighth Party Congress.[102] The predicted expansion of peasant conscripts and the concomitant threats to the army's "class purity" continued to trouble not only prominent political figures but rank-and-file party members in the army as well. At party conferences convened in preparation for the Eighth Congress in March, delegates argued heatedly and at length about proposals to extend general mobilization beyond "toilers" (workers and poor peasants). In the Eighth Army the delegates rejected as "entirely out of the question" the possibility of admitting to the army's ranks "the urban grande or petite bourgeoisie and the rural kulak."[103]

Trotsky recognized that the majority of the peasantry would have to be subject to conscription, but he too warned of the risks posed by expansion of the conscript pool and pointed to the serious problems the army already faced. He attributed soldiers' poor discipline and performance to the careless recruiting practices of local military commissariats. He insisted on the exclusion of "class-alien elements" from the army, especially in the wake of the Menshevik charges of Bonapartism. After all, Bolsheviks too believed that kulaks were dangerous. "Kulaks, together with the sons of the bourgeoisie, belong in the rear units." But he admitted that determining the line that separated the middle peasant from the kulak was very difficult. Local economic conditions required the problem to be resolved in different ways in different provinces. Kulaks were more numerous in Siberia and the Ukraine than in the Central Industrial Region (CIR), Trotsky explained, and this disparity accounted for the widespread resistance to military conscription outside the Bolshevik

101. "Ob otnoshenii k srednemu krest'ianstvu," and "O politicheskoi propagande i kul'turno-prosvetitel'noi rabote v derevne," in ibid., pp. 429–35.

102. Earlier in the year, the government decided not to call up peasants in the central provinces after an experimental recruitment drive, announced for June in Tambov province, had to be called off because it failed miserably: *Istoriia sovetskogo krest'ianstva*, 1:131–32.

103. *Zvezda krasnoarmeitsa* (February 28, 1919), quoted in N. Tsvetaev, *Voennye voprosy v resheniiakh VIII s"ezda RKP(b)* (Moscow, 1960), pp. 20–21.

stronghold, the CIR. "The military commissariats cannot resolve this matter on their own," and here the proletarian dictatorship faced what Trotsky described as "the fundamental issue of our politics— our relationship with the middle peasant."[104] Other leading Bolsheviks were coming to similar conclusions. After his first year's experience in the army, Vladimir Zatonskii, who was a member of several revolutionary military councils on the Southern Front and the son of a rural clerk, concluded that the behavior of the peasantry in the Ukraine was a reflection of "the peasant soul, for centuries downtrodden and ignorant, unexpectedly aroused, eternally vacillating, at once revolutionary and reactionary, frightening in its cruelty, and, in the end, childishly naive and childishly helpless." For Zatonskii everything about the peasants had "a certain mix of revolutionary sentiment, adventurism, selfless valor, and cowardly greed."[105]

The Eighth Party Congress marked a transition in the histories of both the Red Army and the Soviet state. In the course of the more than two years that separated the congress from the fall of the Romanov dynasty, a new political elite had begun to take shape. Painfully but surprisingly quickly they had learned fundamental lessons about state power and the techniques necessary to secure it. Beginning in February 1917, previously disfranchised social groups formed soviets, workers' militias, front councils, and other bodies of direct democracy as means to restructure political authority so that they might claim some measure of the immense power that the central state had monopolized under the tsar. Almost immediately the Bolshevik party, under Lenin's guidance, embraced the soviet as the Russian version of the revolutionary commune that Marx had celebrated as a means to abolish the despotic power of the bourgeois state. For Marx the model of the commune entailed decentralized authority and local self-rule by small-scale administrative units in

---

104. Trotskii, "Izdykhaiushchaia kontrrevoliutsiia," 27 March 1919, in *KVR*, vol. 2, pt. 2, p. 245; "Interview to ROSTA correspondent," 29 March 1919, in ibid., pt. 1, p. 51. Trotsky reserved his harshest judgments for Ukrainian peasants. "A mobilized Ukrainian," he warned, "with his shattered psychology . . . will pass through the barracks for no other reason than to receive a rifle and return home with it." He not only ruled out the possibility of a general mobilization in the Ukraine, but even toyed with the idea of disarming the entire Ukrainian population: "Nashi ocherednye voprosy," in ibid., pt. 1, p. 80.

105. S. I. Aralov, "Spokoinoe muzhestvo," in *Revoliutsiia nas v boi zovet* (Moscow, 1967), p. 216. Zatonskii, a former Menshevik who joined the Bolshevik party in March 1917, graduated from Kiev University in 1912. He was one of the leaders of the October uprising in Kiev. After extensive military service during the Civil War, Zatonskii served in high-level posts in both the Ukrainian and central Soviet governments. He was people's commissar for enlightenment in the government of the Soviet Ukraine.

the name of freedom and an end to alienation.[106] Lenin believed the imperialist state would dissolve in a sea of self-governing bodies that would involve all of society in a noncoercive resolution of its social and economic problems.

This naively optimistic expectation foundered on the rocks of continuing war, famine, and industrial chaos. By the spring of 1918 the top leadership was gradually abandoning its utopian faith in the commune and changing its own mission from liberation of the downtrodden masses to organization of their productive capacities to defend and feed the nation. Although Lenin, Trotsky, and Bukharin, among others, wrote theoretical works about this transformation only in 1920, the actions of the Bolshevik party's Central Committee and Sovnarkom beginning in mid-1918 revealed a new set of social and political attitudes that have had a decisive impact on the Soviet state ever since. Instead of the commune, the leadership increasingly invoked the authority of the dictatorship of the proletariat. In place of a decentralized republic of soviets that strove to maximize participation and freedom, the still inchoate elite tried to erect a highly centralized, coercive production.[107] Of course, the dictatorship of the proletariat had a Marxian pedigree too; in fact, the mature Marx rarely mentioned the commune because he became more concerned with the problem of transforming property relations than with restructuring patterns of authority. Moreover, as Neil Harding points out, "the Commune model was tarred with the anarchist brush and smacked too much of asceticism and anti-industrialism."[108] Marx warned against those who wanted to abolish authority in large-scale industry, for that was "tantamount to wanting to abolish industry itself, to destroy the power loom in order to return to the spinning wheel." Marx could not imagine maintaining the productive capacity of the modern factory system in conditions of free uncoerced labor. Following the October Revolution, the central leadership quickly found that local soviets were helpless to stop the advancing Germany army, to feed the hungry cities, and to restore industrial production in the factories. In response to the crises, the center claimed more and more authority for itself and backed up its claims with its new instruments of coercion, the Red Army and

106. I borrow much of the succeeding analysis from a very insightful argument about the Bolsheviks and the dualism in Marx's view of the state by Neil Harding, "Socialism, Society, and the Organic Labour State," in The State in Socialist Society, ed. Harding, pp. 1–50 (Albany: State University of New York Press, 1984). See also his more comprehensive discussion in Lenin's Political Thought, vol. 2 (New York: St. Martin's Press, 1981), chaps. 5, 6, 8–10.

107. Harding also calls the new form of state power "the organic labor state." For the purposes of my argument, however, a key defense element is lacking in this formulation, as I shall discuss below.

108. Harding, "Socialism," p. 14.

the Cheka. The new political elite appropriated the attributes of "stateness," or *gosudarstvennost'*, which had informed the ideology of the imperial bureaucracy and of the political parties that most actively articulated that ideology, especially the Kadets.[109] In the process of these state-building activities, local soviets changed from autonomous organs of self-rule to administrative bodies implementing central directives.[110] Factory discipline and one-man managerial authority supplanted industrial democracy as the state's primary goals.[111] Political rivalries and party debates came to be viewed as symptoms of ill health as the wartime emergency was used to justify increasing intolerance toward dissent.[112] The party membership, just like the population at large, was viewed as a reservoir of necessary labor and soldier power.

The history of the armed forces runs parallel to that of the state, but it also forms a very integral part of the larger process of state building.[113] In the general enthusiasm of 1917, the small group of revolutionaries who declared themselves to be the new rulers of the former Russian empire hoped to dissolve the army and police and turn over all coercive authority to the armed populace, much as the citizens of Paris had tried to do in 1871 when they proclaimed the Commune. However, the urban factory militias and the soldiers who had performed so well against the "forces of counterrevolution" in the final months of 1917 proved no match for the German army and suffered a crushing defeat at Narva. The Narva defeat marked the first retreat from the principles of the commune in matters of defense. Shortly after the defeat, the Red Guards, the improvised defense organizations that most closely embodied those principles, were ordered to merge with the new Workers'-Peasants' Red Army. The center also stepped up its efforts to recruit former officers of the Imperial Army, thereby abandoning the elective principle that had formed a crucial part of soldiers' demands a year before. The outbreak of civil war in Siberia and the Urals in May 1918 compelled

109. For some suggestive observations about the Bolsheviks' similarities to the Kadets on the matter of state authority, see Leopold Haimson, "The Parties and the State: The Evolution of Political Attitudes," in *The Transformation of Russian Society*, ed. Cyril E. Black (Cambridge: Harvard University Press, 1969), esp. secs. VI–VII.

110. See Keep, *Russian Revolution*, chaps. 24–27, 32–33; Oskar Anweiler, *The Soviets: The Russian Workers, Peasants, and Soldiers Councils, 1905–1921* (New York: Pantheon, 1974), chap. 5.

111. On the politics of Civil War industry and transformation of attitudes among the Bolshevik leadership, see Thomas Remington, *Building Socialism in Bolshevik Russia: Ideology and Industrial Organization, 1917–1921* (Pittsburgh: University of Pittsburgh Press, 1984).

112. On changes in the Bolshevik party during the Civil War, see the excellent study by Robert Service, *The Bolshevik Party in Revolution: A Study in Organizational Change, 1917–1923* (New York: Macmillan, 1979).

113. I found Gerhard Ritter's *Kommunemodell* very helpful in formulating the remarks that follow.

Sovnarkom to abandon one more element of the commune model of defense forces with the transition from service by largely urban volunteers to a universal military obligation for the proletariat.

With the introduction of conscription, the state faced the problem of how best to discipline its citizen-soldiers so that the new fighting force could defeat the growing ranks of the White Armies. Very early the Bolsheviks showed relatively few inhibitions about employing coercion against disloyal military specialists. Next Trotsky ordered commissars shot, and then, with his secret orders to the Eighth Army in November 1918, sanctioned the execution of regular soldiers for indiscipline and succumbing to panic. In another important action to reconstitute genuine state authority, Trotsky commissioned a group of military specialists to draft new service and disciplinary manuals. Just as the party's leaders had abandoned industrial democracy in the name of the greater goal of maximizing productivity, so army spokesmen combated soldiers' democracy as a dangerous form of syndicalism in the name of military expedience. In abandoning the commune model of army building, the Bolsheviks could appeal to Friedrich Engels's writings about military affairs in 1851, in which he warned future revolutionary states that they would have to fight powerful regular armies with disciplined centralized forces of their own.[114] Even with Engels's authority, however, the center's every step toward the creation of a regular army during 1918 provoked opposition and required Trotsky's considerable debating skills to win over more of the crucial party leadership to his and Lenin's position. The defeat of the Military Opposition at the Eighth Party Congress was the definitive defeat of the commune model in the Soviet Republic until the end of the Civil War.

The principles of state authority, the new form of *gosudarstvennost'* that embraced the dictatorship of the proletariat, found fervent advocates among several groups of new state servitors, including former white-collar workers, or lower-middle strata, and, in the army, the military specialists and commissars.[115] Especially the commissars, with their black leather jackets and working-class caps, came to represent the Soviet state for millions of citizens and certainly for the soldiers of the Red Army; indeed, the state's enemies often referred to it as a "commissarocracy." For the commissars, as for the Cheka agents, the Civil War was a course in state

114. Ibid., pp. 93–101.

115. On the lower-middle strata, see Daniel Orlovsky, *Russia's Democratic Revolution: The Provisional Government of 1917 and the Origin of the Soviet State* (Berkeley: University of California Press, forthcoming), chap. 9. On the military specialists, see Ritter, *Kommunemodell*, pp. 150, 209. Ritter attributes certain features of the later Soviet system, including the militarization of Soviet society and the nationalism of the 1930s and 1940s, to the fateful employment of the military specialists.

administration.[116] By the end of 1918 both commissars and military specialists were repudiating the principles of partisan warfare and the militia in the struggle to build a centralized regular army. They justified their efforts by pointing to the "self-evident" advantages of large-scale industry over cottage industry; moreover, they saw themselves as defenders of the national state interest against the upholders of local autonomy, which the commissars demeaned as *mestnichestvo* (localism).

Finally, the state and party defined their relations with society in policies and actions that also bore the heavy imprint of the army's prominent role during the first two years since the fall of the Romanovs. The new state and its agents saw their tasks as the organization of resources for labor and defense. In accordance with the mobilizational goals, Soviet laws and, significantly, the first constitution virtually eliminated not only "the distinctions between citizen and workers, republic and mode of production,"[117] as Harding has said, but also the distinctions between worker and soldier, republic and armed camp. Citizenship and noncitizenship were fixed by military service.[118] The most important political organization in the postrevolutionary order, the Communist Party, also redefined its mission and membership in wartime conditions. Admission to party membership was made nearly as simple for soldiers and officers as it had been earlier for workers; military service during the Civil War became a primary test of loyalty and virtually a ticket for promotion to a high party post. For tens of thousands of men and women, the army was their school of politics. Not all of them learned the same lessons; but the lessons they learned shaped the political culture of later years in fundamental ways.

116. See Ritter, *Kommunemodel*, pp. 196–209. On the Cheka, see Leggett, *Cheka*.

117. Harding, "Socialism," p. 27.

118. Neil Harding contends that these early definitions were crucial for shaping the "attitudes and institutions of later Soviet-type regimes." He further argues, "In both constitutional theory and in actual practice, . . . individuals and groups are only conferred such rights as tend to promote and enhance *the state's* objectives. Their exercise of those rights is expressly limited by that very large condition. The distribution of awards, honours, and social prestige is, likewise, directly linked to functional contribution to the goals set by the state. Even the definition of citizenship is determined by the same criteria": ibid., pp. 2–3.

CHAPTER 2

War and the Soviet State, April 1919–November 1920

The army must reflect that regime which we are building in all areas of social and political life.

— Leon Trotsky, 1919

Desertion and the Peasant Question

By the spring of 1919 the proletarian dictatorship had entered a new period in its relations with key sectors of the nation's population. By mid-1918 the situation and the economic collapse left the government little choice but to turn to those citizens who had the skills needed to administer the state and keep foodstuffs and supplies flowing to the soldiers and the factory workers. The turn away from the utopian policies of the spring and summer of 1918 had begun at the Sixth Congress of Soviets in November and was consolidated at the Eighth Party Congress. State and party spokesmen spoke less often of class warfare when they referred to peasants and white-collar workers; now they appealed to all "conscious" citizens in the struggle against the foreign and domestic counterrevolution.[1] Despite persistent opposition to the employment of military specialists in the army, the party leadership had backed Trotsky's policies in this critical matter. The center also seemed fully aware that in "turning to the middle peasantry," it had chosen a course that was full of ambiguities and that would significantly alter relations of authority in the Red Army. Again, despite the apprehensions of considerable segments of the party, in April the center announced two new mobilizations.

The immediate cause for alarm was a new assault by the White armies of Admiral Kolchak in late March 1919. By April enemy

1. On the question of Bolshevik policies toward the intelligentsia and "bourgeois specialists," see S. A. Fediukin, *Sovetskaia vlast' i burzhuaznye spetsialisty* (Moscow, 1965); and his *Velikii Oktiabr' i intelligentsiia* (Moscow, 1972).

troops had reached the Volga and were planning an attack on Moscow. Sovnarkom finally resolved to call up workers and peasants in both nonagricultural and agricultural provinces.[2] The Central Committee declared that supplying the Red Army was the populace's first priority. Accordingly, it instructed trade unions, factory committees, party organizations, and cooperatives to set up aid bureaus (biuro pomoshchi) and assistance committees (komitety sodeistviia) to mobilize the labor and resources needed to meet the latest emergency. As further evidence of the party's repudiation of class warfare, the Central Committee instructed trade unions to draw peasants, especially peasant youths in the nonagricultural provinces, into the Red Army and for service in food detachments and food armies in the Ukraine and the Don region.[3]

The Commissariat of Internal Affairs (NKVD), in response to the Eighth Party Congress's recent decisions, was responsible for the first call-up—formally on a voluntary basis—of the middle peasantry. On 26 April the NKVD instructed each volost' executive committee to recruit and outfit ten to twenty poor and middle peasants. After two months of anxious waiting the Central Committee declared the mobilization a failure.[4] According to reports from outlying regions, peasants claimed that they favored the mobilization in principle, but they refused induction because they considered the system of random recruitment unfair. In fact, the center had treated the peasants the same way they had treated Communists and trade union members in earlier call-ups, by requesting a percentage of all available citizens. The peasants insisted that call-up by age groups was far more fair. In fact, the general mobilization by age groups, although it too fell short of expectations, was far more successful than the volost' recruitment drive.[5] Perhaps equally important, however, was the timing of the call-up. Late April was the height of the spring plowing season, and every pair of male hands was indispensable.[6]

2. "O prizyve srednego i bedneishego krest'ianstva k bor'be s kontrrevoliutsiei," in Dekrety Sovetskoi vlasti, 12 vols. (Moscow, 1957–1986), 5:107–8. On 11 April Sovnarkom had called up all men born between 1886 and 1890 in nine nonagricultural provinces: ibid., pp. 63–65.

3. "Tezisy TsK RKP (b) v sviazi s polozheniem Vostochnogo fronta," 11 April 1919, in PSS, 33:271–74.

4. "Otchet TsK RKP(b)," 4 July 1919, in Perepiska, 8:96. Instead of the anticipated 140,000 "volunteers," only 24,661 appeared: Istoriia sovetskogo krest'ianstva, 1:136; Direktivy, 4:274.

5. During the first half of 1919 more than 523,000 men were inducted for military service: Istoriia sovetskogo krest'ianstva, 1:137.

6. This was the conclusion of the Nizhnii Novgorod provincial party organization in a report to the Central Committee: V. M. Andreev, Pod znamenem proletariata (Moscow, 1981), p. 168.

In short, the peasants behaved as skeptical Bolsheviks had expected them to. The leading Red Army specialist on desertion, S.
Olikov, described the rear in June 1919 as "a boiling volcano." By
mid-1919 the number of deserters had already reached 917,000; by
the end of the year, official statistics had recorded 1,761,104 deserters who had either been arrested or finally appeared voluntarily.[7]
The category of desertion also covered the illegal flight of soldiers
from their units, but citizens who failed to appear for call-up constituted 75 percent of the deserters. Another 18 to 20 percent included
runaways from conscription centers, from rear units, and from detachments en route to the front. Actual deserters from front-line
combat units made up only 5 to 7 percent.[8]

Clearly front-line commanders suffered from the high rates of desertion when desperately needed reinforcements failed to appear at
critical moments in the fighting; however, local and central authorities were alarmed by other political consequences as well, for when
deserters fled home, they often spoke out against conscription, the
war, and the Soviet state (or sovdepiia, in its more popular form)
that had brought them all these ills. Other armed deserters fled the
fronts and conscription centers and joined "bandit" groups and an-
tigovernment uprisings. Their paths were strewn with corpses and
terrorized villagers.[9] Local authorities called in Cheka units to restore order, but the mutinous troops were no more intimidated by
the Chekists than they had been by the local police. Commissars reported that the deserters did not just strike out randomly at their
enemies, but had rather clearly defined political goals and targets.
After one of the Red Army regiments sent against Ataman Nikolai
Grigor'ev mutinied, they smashed the Cheka units in Berdichev, Ka-
satin, and Fastov. Then they convened meetings to decide whether
to continue toward Belaia Tserkov against Grigor'ev, whom they still
recognized as an enemy, or to turn toward Kiev and "have done

7. S. Olikov, Dezertirstvo v Krasnoi armii i bor'ba s nim (Leningrad, 1926), p. 31.
Provincial statistics give a fuller picture of the magnitude of the problem. In July 1919
Ivanovo-Voznesensk alone reported 3,000 deserters. Borisoglebsk district in Tambov
province reported 4,000, the Krapivensk district of Tula province not fewer than
6,000. Mogilevsk district counted as deserters 25 percent of the total eligible cohort,
while another district in Tver province counted 75 percent of the total. See N. I. Kizilov, NKVD RSFSR, 1917–1930 gg. (Moscow, 1969), p. 75.

8. For a discussion of categories of desertion, see N. Movchin, Komplektovanie
Krasnoi Armii (Moscow, 1928), chap. 6.

9. Desertion did not begin with the 26 April mobilization, but its scale changed
dramatically in the late spring. See the report dated 17 March 1919 from Simbirsk
province, "Ot Syzranskogo revoliutsonnogo komiteta," in Perepiska, 6:399–400;
Olikov, Dezertirstvo, pp. 27, 69; Document 174 in V. I. Lenin i VChK, p. 197; also pp.
193, 194n.

there with the Cheka and the *kommuniia*."[10] The local revolutionary military council sent one of its members, Vladimir Zatonskii, to the mutinying regiment to dissuade them from their plans. After an hour and a half of discussion, Zatonskii persuaded the soldiers to rejoin their army and promise not "to touch the Cheka."[11]

Local and central authorities alike concluded that the cause of most of the army's current troubles was the presence of large numbers of middle peasants in the ranks. Although occasionally Bolshevik analysts admitted that poor military leadership and especially the center's chronic inability to deliver needed military supplies also added to the waves of desertion, they preferred the strangely more comforting class analysis that pointed clearly to the vexing "peasant problem." Political workers on the scene sensed a change in their units very shortly after the first call-up. One commissar observed that "very few of the old, conscientious, and developed Red Army men" remained in his regiment by May, and that the physiognomy of the regiment was changing perceptibly. "I remember in the winter that workers made up 65 percent of our regiment, and peasants 30 percent," Kiriukhin recalled, "but now, it appears, that has reversed."[12] Communists, including those in the army, viewed the preponderance of peasants among the troops and the entire policy of the state toward the peasantry with considerable misgivings. In local meetings speakers criticized the "wager on the middle peasant," arguing that peasants were property holders by nature, that they were clever and crafty.[13]

The center responded to the problem posed by the "peasantization" of the army with several practices. First, it continued and expanded its mobilizations of mostly urban citizens from loyal Bolshevik strongholds and stepped up recruitment among former soldiers, NCOs, and officers with combat experience. Second, it reformed its policies on deserters by expanding the army's coercive apparatus at the same time that it tried to make the application of force more discriminating and thereby more effective. Third, it promoted workers and peasants from the ranks to positions of authority

10. S. I. Aralov, "Spokoinoe muzhestvo," in *Revoliutsiia nas v boi zovet*, p. 216. Ironically, Ataman Grigor'ev himself had only recently served the Red Army in the south of the Ukraine. At the beginning of May 1919 he refused to transfer his troops to Bessarabia and raised a mutiny in the rear of the Red Army. Grigor'ev commanded 20,000 men and was defeated only after several months of fighting. Soviet historians rather uncritically adopt the Civil War rhetoric of the Soviet state and call Grigor'ev's armed opposition "an anti-Soviet kulak-SR bourgeois nationalist mutiny" that had the support of Makhno; more concretely, Grigor'ev's forces proclaimed the slogans of Ukrainian independence, soviets without Communists, and free trade.

11. Ibid.

12. N. I. Kiriukhin, *Iz dnevnika voennogo komissara* (Moscow, 1928), p. 113.

13. See, e.g., the report from a civilian committee dated 28 May 1919, "Ot Ivanovo-Voznesenskogo gubernskogo komiteta RKP(b)," in *Perepiska*, 7:483.

as commanders and political workers. Fourth, it promised more material aid to soldiers and their families and tried to fulfill its promises. Finally, it reformed and expanded its political education and cultural programs targeted at largely peasant soldier audiences.

In May 1919, even before the Central Committee had declared the *volost'* peasant call-up a failure, both the party and the Young Communist League ordered yet another mass mobilization for the Eastern Front. The appeals garnered 10,000 Komsomol members and 20,000 party members (the figures are somewhat inflated because many Komsomol members also belonged to the party) by 1 July.[14] In addition to outright mobilization, and in response to the poor performance of regular army units in late 1918 and early 1919, the Central Committee sanctioned the formation of special-assignment units (*chasti osobogo naznacheniia*, or *chony*) to concentrate party loyalists in crack fighting outfits. Local factory committees, party cells, and other mostly urban organizations formed the first *chony* of party members and sympathizers, members of Komsomol, and trade union members aged seventeen to fifty-five. The crack units were trained and outfitted outside of regular army channels by Vsevobuch; consequently, Podvoiskii gained a new constituency in his agency's persistent campaign to replace the regular army with militia-like formations. The local organizations that recruited them provided them with emergency supplies. Once they arrived at the front, they were not integrated into the regular formations, but instead operated in close cooperation with the special departments of the Cheka.

The *chony* preserved a large measure of autonomy in order to maintain their combat readiness. No doubt because the crack detachments appeared to be favored by the center, military staff workers resented them and frequently protested their ineffectiveness. A member of the Western Front's revolutionary military council, Andrei Potiaev, complained to Lenin that "the special units, with very few exceptions, were exceedingly capricious and demanding (that they always get everything left in the supplies)" as long as they were still in the rear, but that as soon as they moved closer to the lines of battle, they "quickly lost their snappy fighting appearance."[15] Opposition to the special detachments united the commissars, the Red commanders, and the military specialists. Despite the antagonisms the *chony* engendered, however, the party center felt them to be effective and upheld its commitment to them throughout the Civil War. Only in 1921 were they formally transferred to the jurisdiction of the RVSR.

14. Reinforcements sent to the Eastern Front totaled 55,000, including 15,000 Communists, 3,000 Komsomol members, and 25,000 trade union members.

15. "Ot Potiaeva, Chl. RVS Zap.," 18 December 1919, Document 432, in Trotsky, *Trotsky Papers*, 1:796.

The mobilizations and the generally good performance of the special assignment units saved the proletarian dictatorship during some of its darkest months in the spring and summer of 1919. But increasing numbers of peasants failed to show up for induction. "Desertion" reached its highest point during the summer of 1919; though two more waves of desertion followed in the fall of 1919 and in 1920, it never reached such a peak again. The shortage of soldiers hit the state just when it needed them most, when the center was being threatened from three sides: by Nikolai Iudenich from the north, Anton Denikin from the south, and Aleksandr Kolchak from the east. To counter the continuing unwillingness of peasants to heed the mobilization calls, the center bolstered its coercive apparatus. An interagency Central Commission for the Struggle with Desertion (Tsentrokomdezertir) experimented with a wide range of measures. During the fall and winter of 1918–1919 the center had learned that Trotsky's declared policy of shooting all apprehended deserters was counterproductive, though exemplary shootings for particularly notorious "deserter-bandits" continued throughout the Civil War. Threats to local officials, whether urban bureaucrats and factory managers or rural soviet authorities, also had made little dent in the mounting numbers because the center was too weak and short of personnel to back up its threats with real force.[16]

The party began sending plenipotentiaries into especially uncooperative areas to round up deserters. Out of this practice, and as an outgrowth of the center's new rural orientation, emerged a June 1919 decree designed "to convince the populace that the struggle against desertion was the responsibility of the entire populace." In tune with the center's new approach, the rhetoric of class warfare had been replaced by an appeal to all the people. The decree introduced collective responsibility (*krugovaia poruka*) for families and villages whose members concealed deserters. Desertion commissions had the authority to fine offenders, confiscate their property, and sentence them to work for Red Army families; they could execute guilty soviet officials. Sovnarkom paid special attention to the composition of the committees, so the provisions are particularly revealing about the center's views of whom it could trust in the countryside. The committees were to include representatives of the local military commissariat, the agricultural department, and, most notably, families of Red Army men "in order better to ascertain and satisfy the

16. In a March decree the RVSR threatened to expel from service for three years any official guilty of concealment of deserters. Later, local soviets were ordered to publish lists of the names of all deserters. In May 1919 the Central Committee received reports that rural soviets, most of them dominated by noncommunists, were refusing to implement the more comprehensive conscription laws. See "Ot upolnomochennogo TsK RKP(b) i VTsIK po tambovskoi gubernii V. N. Podbel'skogo," 13 May 1919, in *Perepiska*, 7:381.

needs of those serving in the Red Army." Confiscated property was to be turned over to the families of Red Army men for their temporary use. The decree thus recognized a new category of villager that was playing a growing role in rural politics—the Red Army family. Soldiers' families were singled out once again, as they had been in earlier Sovnarkom legislation, for special protection and welfare benefits.[17]

Shortly after the decree was issued, Olikov led a detachment of men to a "well-to-do" *volost'* in Orel province. They arrived in a deserted village to find all the huts locked and the livestock driven into the forest and fields. Only the chairman of the local executive committee had stayed behind, and he confessed that the population had firmly resolved not to hand over the considerable number of men evading the call-up. The detachment immediately posted an announcement warning the villagers that all their property would be inventoried and confiscated if the deserters did not appear within four hours. A few soldiers were dispatched to the fields to retrieve the horses. In an hour the entire village was present, minus the deserters. The detachment leader made no attempt to bargain with them, but merely repeated his warning. True to his word, when the four hours were up, the detachment began loading property onto wagons. After another hour had passed, the village assembly invited the detachment leader to a meeting and presented him with their resolution to turn over all deserters for the front. Immediately the detachment began to unload the wagons. Eventually thousands of deserters turned up, and Olikov noted later that "this news spread faster than telegraph wires across the district and beyond."[18]

After the Civil War, Olikov concluded that desertion was a complex phenomenon that went to the heart of the state's relationship with the bulk of its population. He stressed that the army had learned a great deal about the psychology of soldiers and peasants. The staff of the commission abandoned its initially indiscriminate violence and established categories of deserters and corresponding categories of punishment in order to fulfill their mandate more effectively. Deserters in the first category were considered to be genuinely hostile to the proletarian dictatorship; they included soldiers who had fled their units two or more times or carried off uniforms, ammunition, or arms. These men were to be punished to the full extent of the law, but Olikov warned that even here execution must

17. "Postanovlenie Soveta Oborony o merakh po iskoreneniiu dezertirstva," in *Dekrety Sovetskoi vlasti*, 5:264–67.

18. Olikov, *Dezertirstvo*, p. 73. A later account of a visit by a desertion committee was reported in *Bednota*, 18 August 1920, p. 4. The Vitebsk District Committee for the Struggle against Desertion captured ninety-five deserters. The committee confiscated from the deserters and their concealers twenty-four cows, seven horses, and one pig. All this livestock was handed over to the families of honest soldiers.

Woe to the deserter! Courtesy of Poster Collection, Hoover Institution Archives, Stanford University.

The deserter's nightmare. Courtesy of Poster Collection, Hoover Institution Archives, Stanford University.

be applied very selectively and only after a meeting had been called to try the offender, for maximum propaganda value. The second category of deserters, by far the overwhelming majority, evaded service "out of weak wills." The desertion commissions must treat these men not as enemies but as "spiritually sick or forlorn." Olikov advised commission workers to approach these men "with heart. We can go even further: you have to love the deserter as you would an ignorant and downtrodden slave, in order to begin his reeducation."[19] This attitude of a forgiving father or perhaps priest was certainly the one that dominated agitational trials and the public confessions made by contrite former deserters.[20]

Olikov's relatively compassionate approach was reflected in the state's practice of declaring frequent amnesties for deserters. Olikov insisted, however, that amnesties must not be proclaimed too often and must be limited to soldiers who had committed only minor offenses or to deserters who had not fled more than once, that is, the deserters "of weak will." He stressed too that great attention had to be paid to the men appointed to the desertion detachments. Preferably, at least half should be party members and either local men who were eligible for service or soldiers from nearby units. Under no circumstances should the detachment include former deserters or any villagers who had bad local reputations. "By all means it was necessary to exclude well-to-do peasants."[21] Most peasants, according to this view, were not intrinsically anti-Soviet, but resisted army service because they were ill informed or unaware of the issues involved in the fighting. Patience, caution, and constant agitation and propaganda went a long way toward winning peasants' cooperation.

Other measures were taken to ensure that conscripts would not desert on the way to the front and would stay with their units once they arrived. First, local military commissariats organized party members into patrols to escort recruits from induction centers to dispatching points. Second, and in explicit response to uprisings of

19. Olikov, Dezertirstvo, pp. 82, 83.
20. Bednota published the confession of a soldier on 24 August 1920:
I can't find any rest. Dear comrades across the entire Soviet Republic, through the newspaper Bednota accept my heartfelt penance for my past unconscious deeds. Because of my ignorance I fought with the traitor Petliura against the Red Army. For nearly a year I helped the murderer of toilers. When I at last realized who was my friend and the friend of all of you, I went over to the Reds' side and into the ranks of the Workers' and Peasants' Army, where I have been fighting for nearly a year. But my conscience torments me for my past errors. I am ashamed that I betrayed my brothers. That is why I appeal for advice for my sick soul. What can I do to redeem myself before all toiling people? And is it enough only to be at the Red Front and to give my life for the triumph of the proletariat?
21. Olikov, Dezertirstvo, p. 74. The ideal size of the detachments was 50 men, but some of them had as many as 200.

deserters and the "Greens," the Defense Council increased the budget and expanded the ranks of the Cheka to keep closer watch on the loyalty of troops already at the front and serving in the rear.[22]

While the state shored up its coercive apparatus to combat desertion, the army and Sovnarkom also took several practical measures to assure the peasants that the Red Army was indeed a workers' and peasants' institution. A very visible reminder of the new power of the previously disfranchised classes was the growing numbers of officers and political workers who were themselves former workers and peasants. Although the officer ranks of the Imperial Army certainly had become more open to nonnoble subjects by the end of the Romanov dynasty, and the Great War had tended to democratize the officer corps, still the military elite continued to be viewed as a preserve of the privileged classes of imperial Russian society. Very early the Soviet state determined to create its own Red officer corps by promoting former NCOs of the Imperial Army and commissioning graduates of the intensive military courses organized in major cities. By the end of the Civil War, the military specialists constituted only 34 percent of the total officer corps; the intensive military courses turned out nearly 65,000 Red commanders, whose class origins testified to the policy of favoring workers and peasants for admission. Of the new commanders, 12.0 percent claimed working-class origin, 67.3 percent peasant origin; 20.7 percent were still from the intelligentsia (mostly Old Bolsheviks).[23] The opportunities for promotion made military service an increasingly attractive career for many men and women of lower-class origin, especially when most of the country lay in economic ruin and the army promised a better chance of survival.

To make military service more attractive or at least tolerable for rank-and-file troops as well, the center tried to keep up with inflation by increasing soldiers' pay and rations, although the chaotic supply situation rendered many of these efforts stillborn. Because many soldiers deserted to help their families with farm responsibilities, the Agriculture and Social Welfare commissariats cooperated with Internal Affairs to provide subsidies and labor assistance to

22. KPSS o vooruzhennykh silakh (1981), p. 74; "Postanovlenie Soveta Oborony o priniatii mer k uvelicheniiu voisk VChK," 11 July 1919, in V. I. Lenin I VChK, pp. 230–31. The Greens were detachments of men who fled to the forests and the mountains to evade military service. They fought against Reds and Whites in central Russia, the northern Caucasus, and the Crimea.

23. P. N. Dmitriev, "Organizatsionnye printsipy sovetskogo voennogo stroitel'stva i ikh vliianie na sposoby vooruzhennoi bor'by," in Iz istorii grazhdanskoi voiny i interventsii, 1917–1922 (Moscow, 1974), p. 196. The educational backgrounds of the new officers give further evidence of the consequences of the discriminatory policies. Only 395 had completed middle and higher education, while 61 percent claimed only lower education.

Red Army families. The Central Committee ordered rural soviets to guarantee that the land of serving soldiers would be plowed and seeded, and to do everything else they could to ease the plight of families whose letters to their soldiers complained about forced requisitioning and land seizures. A leaflet from the Smolensk party committee summarized the entitlement program in a pamphlet:

> The Red Army man's family is the highest priority of the Soviet Republic; his family is exempted from all direct taxes; his family keeps its right to the land; his family can receive a subsidy to maintain his household; his family members who are no longer able to work are exempted from paying apartment rent; his family has the right to the "Red Star" ration card and to receive bonus groceries; in case of death, [the Red Army man's family] receives his pension.[24]

The welfare measures further reinforced the soldiers' perceptions of themselves and their families as a new privileged stratum in the postrevolutionary social order. The state awarded soldiers' families welfare benefits because they had earned them by their loyalty; furthermore, the state stepped in as a surrogate breadwinner and guardian for the family to release soldiers from personal concerns so that they might fulfill their military obligatons with selfless devotion and obedience. From the beginning military leaders and political workers encouraged soldiers to look on the army as their family; subsequently, the family motif figured prominently in army symbolism. Finally, to win the sympathies of peasants both in and out of the army, but also to relieve the desperate food situation, revolutionary military councils often sent units to the fields to help nearby villagers with plowing, seeding, and harvesting.

All these measures helped to break the first and most serious wave of desertion. By the end of July, seven military districts reported that 380,500 deserters had returned. These successes allowed the army to cancel its planned August call-up of men born in 1901.[25] The state viewed its promotion policies and welfare measures as part of an emerging social contract with its soldiers and their families. The terms of the contract were specific to wartime conditions, and they were frequently successful in maintaining good morale among troops. Kiriukhin reported that a large group of Cossacks came over to the Reds' side after they heard that the Reds took good care of soldiers' families. Kiriukhin makes it clear that these commitments to the Red Army man and his family were important for his own morale as well and for his sense that he was fighting for the morally superior side. He reported finding the diary of an officer, a Socialist Revolutionary, who was serving in Kolchak's army.

24. Olikov, Dezertirstvo, pp. 57–58.
25. Istoriia sovetskogo krest'ianstva, 1:138.

Kiriukhin copied out long passages into his own diary and expressed great sympathy for his SR counterpart. The officer claimed that he himself was insulted regularly by nondemocratic officers, who called him a socialist with the greatest contempt in their voices. What troubled the SR officer most, however, was the brutal way the other officers treated the soldiers. The SR wrote that he awaited the day when all these oppressive tyrants and their ilk would be thrown out.[26]

The Kiriukhins and Olikovs in the army were not naive believers in the goodwill of the peasants and their natural socialist tendencies, nor did they brand all peasants as implacable enemies of the new regime. Rather, they, and large numbers of other political workers, advocated a program of "political enlightenment" that presumed that peasants were more susceptible than proletarians to political errors and undesirable "moods" and "tendencies," but also presumed that most of them would come to see the relative advantages of the dictatorship of the proletariat and help fight the forces that threatened to restore the old regime. Despite the party's leaders' misgivings about the reliability of peasants, the republic, as the Eighth Party Congress had apprehensively concluded, simply could not do without them. "The crushing of counterrevolution cannot be entrusted to the working class alone," wrote Ivar Smilga, director of PUR, in the Red Army's mass weekly paper *Krasnoarmeets*, of 1 June 1919. In the same issue, the editor, Dmitrii Poluian, declared that "we see in the middle peasant not an enemy but a friend and ally."

Though the desertion figures remained high, the army grew from 800,000 to nearly 3 million during 1919.[27] The successful mobilizations in July and August reversed the tide of losses for the Red Army through the end of the summer. The major victories were against Kolchak's forces in the east. In mid-1919 Kolchak's forces numbered 400,000 men, including nearly 30,000 officers. By the fall, however, desertion had decimated Kolchak's armies and the partisan movement gained strength throughout Siberia. The Red Army launched its last offensive against Kolchak and reoccupied the Urals by the beginning of August. From August through December combined Red Army and partisan forces chased Kolchak from Siberia, and thereby eliminated the major threat from the east. Iudenich finally was defeated in the north in December. Heavy fighting was still ahead in the south and the Ukraine. Denikin's White armies blocked an attempted counteroffensive in August and in fact launched an assault that once again threw the Moscow leadership into panic. But at the end of November Denikin's forces were retreat-

26. Kiriukhin, *Iz dnevnika*, pp. 77, 115.
27. *Direktivy*, 4:54–55, 112.

ing in the face of a determined Red counterattack. With Denikin's temporary retreat, Soviet Russia gained a brief breathing space before hostilities broke out with Poland in the spring of 1920.

The Army and the Party

Denikin's assault had called forth yet another round of appeals to the nation to gird itself for disaster, but the center now had a considerable arsenal of tried practices and a large and more experienced army at its disposal. In fact, the Central Committee's theses on the struggle against Denikin forbade any further organizational improvisations and urged all personnel to work through existing agencies. At the end of September the Central Committee had sent a group of high-level party workers to the Southern Front and transferred there some of the best commanders from other fronts. But for the first time the party did not order a general mobilization of party members. Instead, the center restricted itself to "personal mobilizations"—that is, individual orders to report for duty—and some local mobilizations. Even with this scaled-down appeal, 40,000 party members were sent to the Southern Front.[28].

The immediate cause of the reluctance to call a general mobilization was a steady stream of distress calls from local organizations. In the summer of 1919 the Ivanovo-Voznesensk city committee reported that mobilizations for the army, the party, and the food detachments had "literally sucked dry the life forces of our Manchester, and the center's view that our city is an inexhaustible reservoir of proletarians is incorrect."[29] The army had bled the country dry with its insatiable appetite for dedicated party and trade union members. Since Communists were exhorted to serve as examples of bravery and self-sacrifice, their losses were usually very high.[30] The center not only demanded more cadres but assigned more and more responsibilities to the local party committees. Not surprisingly, local

28. The Central Committee assigned Communists to posts as commissars, commanders, and administrative and economic agents: 438 in July, 432 in August, and 1,027 in September. In September some local organizations conducted mobilizations: Moscow, Ivanovo-Voznesensk, Vladimir, Tver, Petrograd, and Penza.

29. "Ot Ivanovo-Voznesenskogo gorodskogo komiteta RKP(b)," 14 June 1919, in *Perepiska*, 8:307. In September 1918 the city organization counted 1,000 members; that number had declined to 833 by 1 April 1919 and to 709 by 1 June. A provincial committee wrote that after the fifth mobilization in one year, "all that was left were old men and cripples": "Iz pis'ma Severo-Dvinskogo gubernskogo komiteta RKP(b)," 10 June 1919, in ibid., p. 263. For earlier complaints, see "Ot Iukhnovskogo komiteta RKP(b)," 26 September 1918, in ibid., 4:285.

30. Typically 50 percent of the political staff were put out of action by death, wounds, or sickness after major battles: "Iz svedenii politotdela Iuzhnogo fronta," 20 December 1918, in *PPR* I, pp. 256–61; see also Kolychev, *Partiino-politicheskaia rabota*, p. 120.

organizations became very reluctant to let go of their few remaining experienced members.

At first the Central Committee had ignored the warnings. When large numbers of members simply refused to go to the front, the Central Committee harshly ordered the expulsion of weak spirits to eliminate their "demoralizing influence on the masses in the countryside." But the center was quick to come to its senses and realize that it could hardly spare any experienced members. Now the Central Committee could no longer ignore the signs of trouble.

The desperate cries coming from local organizations explain only part of the Central Committee's reluctance to call further general mobilizations of party members. Although the center continued to look upon these largely urban cadres as vital "injections" of "proletarian spirit" into an increasingly peasant-dominated army, both the center and the army complained that each mobilization brought ever poorer and poorer cadres—the very young, the very old, and invalids. Furthermore, the complaints were not limited to party members who were being sent to the army; similar complaints were heard throughout the party. The Eighth Party Congress had deplored the poor quality of party members in the recent mass recruitment and had demanded a "cleaning up of the ranks." The congress adopted a new party statute and several resolutions on organization and membership.[31] Because the party had expanded so rapidly after 1917, the new members who left for the army were inexperienced and often could not win authority among the troops for whom they were supposed to serve as models of revolutionary fervor and dedication. The records departments in the capital and regional centers were short of competent personnel, so admission to party membership often was a matter of men and women simply declaring themselves to be Communists because they lived in an agricultural commune or "simply because they wanted to call themselves so."[32]

---

31. Vos'moi s''ezd, pp. 369–411, 423–27.

32. "Iz otcheta zaveduiushchego politotdelom IV armii o sozdanii iacheek RKP(b) i sostoianii partiino-politicheskoi raboty v armii," 24 December 1918, in PPR I, p. 203. The political department chief complained that party cells took upon themselves all imaginable functions: party tribunal, comrades' court, administrative control commission, and, "in a word, everything they wanted to assume. They admitted, expelled, and even arrested members, and collected money." They acquired official seals and handed out documents left and right, including mandates to requisition hay from the local populace. A party committee in another infantry regiment begged forgiveness from the center for the inexperience of its members, since "everyone has been a member for all of a few months or even weeks." Registered comrades came mainly from organizations in provincial towns, where "they simply showed up at the party committee, registered as members, and received a party card, i.e., they became party members without the slightest preparation": "Ot komiteta RKP(b) 162 strelkovogo polka," 24 April 1919, in Perepiska, 7:527.

Many of these self-declared Communists fell prey to the "demoralizing influences" they were expected to combat among the rank and file. A commissar complained that political workers in his unit had "fallen completely under the influence of Makhno and Grigor'ev and altogether refused to recognize the center." This was his explanation for the soldiers' actions in shooting Communists and shouting such slogans as "Beat the kikes, chase away the commissars, save the Revolution!"[33] In other units, Communists exercised little or no authority among the troops and tolerated drunkenness, card playing, arbitrary searches and seizures, and unauthorized requisitioning raids. Kiriukhin complained that, despite a full staff of political workers in his unit, no one except himself and one assistant did any political work at all. He had the impression that all the Communists in his unit were afraid of the soldiers.[34]

The head of the recently organized Political Administration (PUR), Ivar Smilga, had a mandate from the Eighth Party Congress and the Central Committee to reform the political life of the army. Immediately after he assumed his new office, Smilga began a vigorous campaign of promotions, demotions, and transfers in the Political Administration. Tested Bolsheviks replaced nonparty commissars and political workers. In December 1918, 40 percent of all political workers were not members of the Communist Party; by May 1919 Smilga's purge had reduced their numbers to 11.2 percent.[35]

The Central Committee also turned its attention to its own rank and file and tried to reform several widespread practices that applied to civilian as well as army organizations. Local committees were fining comrades found guilty of a variety of offenses: drunkenness, card playing, failure to attend meetings, refusal to travel on assignment. The center forbade the fining of delinquent members and encouraged local committees instead to draw public attention to such offenders, publish their names in the press, temporarily exclude them from party activities, and, as a last resort, expel them from the party.[36] The center announced its first membership purge, the "general reregistration," scheduled for completion by 1 July. All members were required to return their party cards, pay up all outstanding membership dues, fill out individual questionnaires, and

33. "Ot politicheskogo komissara 1 Zadneprovskoi divizii (Iuzhnyi front)," 11 July 1919, in ibid., 8:697–99.

34. Kiriukhin, *Iz dnevnika*, pp. 65–66.

35. "Iz otcheta Politupravleniia pri Revvoensovete Respubliki o partiino-politicheskoi rabote v Krasnoi armii s nachala ee reorganizatsii po 1 oktiabria 1920 g.," in PPR I, p. 74; Kolychev, *Partiino-politicheskaia rabota*, p. 368.

36. "Tsirkuliarnoe pis'mo TsK RKP(b) gubernskim komitetam partii," 29 May 1919, in *Perepiska*, 7:146–47.

present recommendations from two party members.[37] Smilga supervised the reregistration campaign in the army. The campaign was
delayed by the difficulties of collecting recommendations at the
front and confusion about the roles of the political departments and
party committees.[38] Heavy fighting in June and July also slowed the
clean-up operation.

The army's bitter accusations that civilian party organizations
were sending them unacceptable personnel and the civilians'
equally resentful charges that the army was draining them of their
lifeblood were symptoms of a larger crisis that was looming in army-
civilian relations in 1919. As PUR and the political departments
gained experience and authority, they usurped more and more powers of the civilian party organizations that had sent their members
and that claimed full authority over their activities. Party committees, both inside and outside the army, demanded that the center
disband the appointed political departments and restore authority to
elected civilian organizations. Initially the Central Committee sided
with the military and formally abolished all elected party committees in the army, but it did so in a way that only confused matters
because it refused to turn over complete authority for party affairs to
the political departments. Civilian organizations retained nominal
control over the party committees, which continued to function in
violation of the Central Committee's orders.[39] Responsibility for
units stationed in the rear was assigned directly to civilian party
organizations, but with a stipulation that they not interfere in the
army's administrative affairs. The military commissars predictably
took this stipulation as a license to exercise their own untrammeled
authority, but civilian party organs jealously guarded their autonomy and fiercely resisted any encroachments by the army's Communists. Local party officials persisted in transferring commissars and
agitation workers without the permission of military authorities and
frequently even refused to release files for the mobilization

---

37. The Central Committee authorized expulsion from the party for the following
offenses: acts unworthy of Communists (drunkenness, debauchery, disorderly conduct, cruel or excessively crude treatment of subordinates, exploitation of position in
soviet service for personal gain); desertion; violation of party resolutions; failure to
attend party meetings without a valid excuse; and failure to pay membership dues:
"Tsirkuliarnoe pis'mo TsK RKP(b) partiinym organizatsiiam," 24 April 1919, in
Perepiska, 7:44–46. The instruction defined the purge as "the cleansing of the party
of noncommunist elements, particularly people who have attached themselves to it
because of its ruling position and who are using the title of party member in their
personal interests."

38. Rigby, *Communist Party Membership*, p. 71. The party shrank between March
and August 1919 from 350,000 to about 150,000 (ibid., p. 77).

39. "Postanovlenie TsK RKP(b) o partiinoi rabote v armii," 25 October 1918, in
Perepiska, 4:74.

campaigns.[40] From Moscow came vitriolic charges of localism and insubordination, or *mestnichestvo*, as the party's center gradually forged an alliance with the political workers in the army against its own local civilian affiliates. Military men would later claim that only they understood state interests, in large measure because of their Civil War experience in a wide array of administrative fields and geographical areas.

Wartime conditions inevitably eroded the authority of civilian party organizations. Front lines moved rapidly, and invading enemy armies regularly executed or chased underground members of civilian soviet and party organs. Local party organizations had little contact with their members serving in the army, let alone significant control over them. The political departments stepped in to fill the political vacuum and decided questions of committee membership, set agendas for meetings, assigned members tasks, and intervened in internal party disputes. In reoccupied territories they set up new party and soviet administrations. In effect, political departments replaced local governments and party committees in the territories they oversaw. The authority of political departments and revolutionary military councils was wide-ranging in a country that lived under perpetual martial law. To settle the frequent disputes between civilian and military organizations, the Central Committee's Orgburo served as a court of appeal. In September the Orgburo issued a new instruction outlining its right to approve all appointments to both political departments and revolutionary military councils,[41] but, as usual, an instruction from Moscow was little guarantee that the situation in the field would change.

Although the civilian organizations had little chance to increase their clout as long as the war raged, they continued to resist what they deemed to be the inordinate demands of army political workers. The center tried to resolve these disputes by resort to other tactics. One measure that was not new but that was considered essential in the face of the party organizations' inability to provide ever larger numbers of men and women was a mass mobilization of Komsomol members. The Young Communist League's Central Com-

40. The Central Committee correspondence is full of charges from both sides, the civilians complaining about military officials' heavy-handedness and insensitivity, the military complaining about parochialism and insubordination bordering on counterrevolution. See *Perepiska*, 3:287; 4:467; 6:517–18; 8:645, 649.

41. Any transfer from army to army required a report to the Orgburo. In the event of a conflict over a transfer, the minority in the revolutionary military council had the right to delay the command until the Orgburo had conducted its own investigation: "Vypiska iz protokola zasedaniia Orgbiuro TSK RKP(b) o poriadke naznacheniia v revvoensovety i politotdely," 22 September 1919, in *Partiino-politicheskaia rabota v Krasnoi Armii (mart 1919–1920 gg.): Dokumenty* (hereafter PPR II) (Moscow, 1964), pp. 46–47.

mittee advised against this step because they too felt that their numbers were being perilously depleted, but the party overrode their objections and ordered the mobilization for October. The successful campaign yielded 38,000 members for the Southern Front.[42]

A second measure to combat the resistance of the civilian party organizations was to encourage soldiers to join the party. The Eighth Party Congress had recommended throwing open the doors to "healthy proletarian and peasant elements" to replace the members—their numbers eventually reached 200,000—who would be expelled during the summer reregistration. At the end of September the Central Committee finally decided on a "Party Week," during which workers, peasants, and Red Army men were to be recruited without the usual requirement of two written recommendations.[43] The results fell wide of the million-member goal; nevertheless, the drive was declared a success. The party added approximately 200,000 members to its ranks, 40 percent of them military personnel. Rank-and-file soldiers made up between one-half and three-quarters of the new military members; the remainder were commanders, commissars, and administrative personnel.[44] In the towns, 47 percent of the new recruits were workers and 53 percent Red Army men, while in the rural districts, the breakdown was 69 percent workers, 10 percent Red Army men, and 20 percent peasants.[45]

From now on, at least for the remainder of the Civil War, army organizations grew at a faster pace than the party as a whole; moreover, their growth came mainly from within the army itself rather than from civilian mobilizations. Beginning in the fall of 1919, party membership in the army shot up dramatically. As might be ex-

42. For more on the Civil War history of the Komsomol, and particularly on the dilemmas of recurrent mobilizations, see Isabel Tirado, *Young Guard! The Communist Youth League, Petrograd 1917–1920* (Westport, Conn.: Greenwood, 1988), esp. chaps. 3 and 6.

43. After the purges in the army, only 60,000 members and 70,000 candidate members and sympathizers remained. See the leaflet printed by PUR for distribution in the army, "Tsel' 'Partiinoi nedeli,' " after 12 October 1919, in *PPR* II, pp. 47–49. The Petrograd and Baltic Fleet organizations had already conducted their own crash recruitment campaigns earlier in the month; their success prompted the announcement of the army-wide campaign. See also the original Central Committee letter on Party Week, "Iz tsirkuliarnogo pis'ma TsK RKP(b) ko vsem partiinym organizatsiiam o provedenii partiinoi nedeli," 30 September 1919, in *Iz istorii grazhdanskoi voiny v SSSR*, 2:466–67.

44. For a discussion of Party Week in the army, see Petrov, *Stroitel'stvo politorganov*, pp. 91–93. Rigby, *Communist Party Membership*, p. 78, prefers a lower figure of 160,000 for the recruitment drive.

45. Rigby, *Communist Party Membership*, p. 85. A detailed summary of the recruitment drive by province is found in "Svedeniia informatsionno-statisticheskogo otdela TsK RKP(b) o rezul'tatakh provedeniia partiinoi nedeli v oktiabre-dekabre 1919 g.," in *Iz istorii grazhdanskoi voiny v SSSR*, 2:804–7.

pected, however, the increase in numbers brought new problems. Because the mass recruitment occurred during some of the heaviest fighting of the Civil War, procedures were often slipshod; political workers violated even the lenient admission requirements sanctioned by the center's instructions. As thousands of soldiers and commanders insisted on becoming party members before going into battle, political departments and commissars issued temporary documents that attested to the new members' acceptance at a fictional party meeting. The documents stipulated that the temporary papers were to be exchanged for permanent party cards in the future, but in combat conditions such formalities were often forgotten. Political departments never had adequate supplies of membership cards, cameras, or photographic paper.[46]

One consequence of the dramatic growth in numbers—perhaps one that was even anticipated—was a decisive shift in power away from the party's civilian organization toward PUR and its political departments. This change was registered in the amendments to the party rules adopted at the December conference and in a new instruction for party organizations in the army published after the first assembly of political-enlightenment workers met. Army cells were put on an equal footing with factory and city cells, no longer answering to outsiders but regulating all their own affairs.[47] This recognition of the equal rights and autonomy of party organizations in the army registered a temporary defeat for the civilian organizations. Even though such a defeat was only logical in a nation at war for its very survival, the civilian organizations carried grudges against their military counterparts and their particular style of political organization. The discontent simmered just below the surface of political debates for most of the Civil War; but during every lull in the fighting, when the nation might reasonably have expected an end to the hostilities, the resentments burst into the open in vitriolic charges and countercharges.

A major bone of contention was the changing profile of the party's membership. Here, too, practices in the army were fundamentally changing matters. The success of the army's recruitment drive was in part a consequence of the changed policy on admission of new members. The amended party rules stipulated that workers and peasants must undergo a two-month probation period as candidates before they could be admitted to membership; others had to wait six

46. M. Rudakov, I. Kolesnichenko, and V. Lunin, "Nekotorye voprosy raboty politorganov v gody inostrannoi interventsii i grazhdanskoi voiny," *Voenno-istoricheskii zhurnal* 8 (1962): 8.
47. "Instruktsiia organizatsiiam RKP(b) krasnoarmeiskikh chastei v tylu i na fronte," 13 February 1920, in PPR II, pp. 74–84. The controversial nature of the instruction delayed its release in the army itself until 2 July 1920.

months. For Red Army men, however, the probation period was reduced to one month. The Central Committee justified this departure from its regular procedures on the grounds that a candidate's desirability could be more readily tested in battle conditions than in civilian life. The party's leaders thus accepted army service as a primary criterion for political reliability. More important, however, the amendment signaled that the proletarian dictatorship, in its search for pillars of social support, had identified the army again, as it had done in 1917 and early 1918 and as it was affirming in its social welfare policies. Behind the slogan of a "workers' and peasants' government" stood a firm reliance on workers and soldiers of peasant background. Workers and military men made up the two largest categories of new entrants during the recruitment drive, 52.5 and 40.0 percent, respectively. Even though many party members were soldiers of peasant background, peasants plain and simple—that is, nonsoldier peasants—still accounted for only 7 percent of the new group. Peasants in uniform clearly stood apart from their fellow villagers back home. The party, without acknowledging any major change in its ideological pronouncements, nonetheless recognized in its membership practice that when it sought to identify men and women loyal to the state, "Red Army personnel" carried more weight than the class categories of "peasant" and "white-collar worker" and the professional label of "military specialist." The fall Party Week marked the first time the party made significant inroads among the peasantry, and the increase in membership among commanders, commissars, and army administrative personnel certainly increased the representation of the white-collar workers and intelligentsia.[48]

Before and during the Revolution, the Bolsheviks maintained a somewhat clear notion of the most crucial social support for their party's cause: the proletariat. In the ensuing years, however, the proletariat became increasingly difficult to identify. All along, many party members could not have claimed proletarian origins. Even before 1917 the party's leaders and theorists had included as "proletarians" many intellectuals who lacked working-class origins. Later, when the Bolsheviks tried to identify potential allies for their revo-

48. According to Rigby, *Communist Party Membership*, p. 85, the party's official class analysis reveals that percentages changed as follows: workers went from 60.2 percent (1917) to 56.9 (1918) to 47.8 (1919) to 43.8 (1920); peasants from 7.5 (1917) to 14.5 (1918) to 21.8 (1919) to 25.1 (1920); white-collar workers and others from 32.3 (1917) to 28.6 (1918) to 30.4 (1919) to 31.1 (1920). Rigby cautions (p. 36) that these figures "purport to represent neither current occupation nor the occupation of one's father ('social origin') but basic occupation on the eve of the Revolution." Furthermore, "their precision should not be exaggerated," especially because the "advantages of proletarian status and suspicion of 'class alien elements' prompted many recruits to conceal or distort their prerevolutionary background."

lutionary struggle, they looked for ways to justify the inclusion of peasants, or at least some peasants, in their political strategy. Lenin, among others, argued that only an alliance of workers and poor peasants—the rural proletariat—could topple the old regime.[49]

When complications arose as the Bolsheviks tried to match their analysis with changing circumstances, rather than abandon troubled or problematical categories of social structure, they adapted these categories to the circumstances they found. From the beginning the new government insisted on calling itself a dictatorship of the proletariat, but the Bolshevik party and its most loyal sympathizers increasingly accepted a revised definition of the category of proletarian. During the first years of Soviet power, the still evolving Soviet political class discovered that not all factory workers were reliable, not to mention whole categories of workers who earned their livings outside factories. The economic hardships that years of war had brought to all city dwellers, the continued loyalties of large parts of the working class for Menshevik and SR politicians and platforms, and the frequent repressions of strikes and of workers' social organizations turned many working people against the state's policies.

At the same time, the proletarian dictatorship identified other sources of relatively loyal support in unexpected places, especially among white-collar workers, former imperial officers and NCOs, and the predominantly peasant Red Army men. Since these groups offered their support and services to the self-styled dictatorship of the proletariat, the political class clearly but unconsciously redefined the category of "proletarian" to embrace the loyal cadres, whatever their social background, and to exclude those "genuine" proletarians—that is, factory workers—who succumbed to anti-Soviet "moods" and "mentalities," or "petit bourgeois" and "degenerate" workers. True, the proletariat was composed of trustworthy (to some extent) industrial workers, but it now included not only peasants (albeit in the army), but even (ironically, in Bolshevik eyes) civil servants![50]

49. For a discussion of Lenin's writings on peasants and revolution before November 1917, see Esther Kingston-Mann, Lenin and the Problem of Marxist Peasant Revolution (New York: Oxford University Press, 1985).

50. For provocative discussions of social support for the Bolsheviks during the Civil War and definitions of the concept "proletariat," see the following contributions to Slavic Review 44 (Summer 1985): 213–56: William G. Rosenberg, "Russian Labor and Bolshevik Power after October"; Moshe Lewin, "More than One Piece Is Missing in the Puzzle"; Vladimir Brovkin, "Politics, Not Economics, Was the Key." Orlovsky, in the final chapter of his Russia's Democratic Revolution, suggests that in many important senses the white-collar working class can be considered a genuine victor in the Revolution. See also Sheila Fitzpatrick, "The Bolsheviks' Dilemma: Class, Culture, and Politics in Early Soviet Years," with replies by Ronald Grigor Suny and Daniel Orlovsky, Slavic Review 47 (Winter 1988): 599–626.

By the end of the Civil War the army had left its considerable imprint on the Communist Party. Army imperatives affected recruitment policies, techniques of party purge, and, by extension, the social and occupational profile of party membership. In general, the party in the army quickly became a career path that promised a high degree of upward mobility. Military service was recognized as an important, if not the most important, test of political loyalty and effectiveness in the new state; alternatively, desertion, refusal to serve in the army, or military failure was branded the most serious offense a party member could commit and certainly constituted grounds for expulsion. These considerations also shaped the relationship of the party to the Young Communist League, which came to be viewed as a perpetual full reserve supply of working-class youths and students for military service. The Komsomol lost much of its autonomy and had to subordinate its personnel and resources to the Communist Party. For Communists and Komsomol members, wartime conditions reinforced the earlier party ethos of sacrifice and obedience and effectively split the party into civilian and military organizations that waged their own civil war over resources, personnel, and political authority. Finally, the military emergency served to justify the Bolshevik leadership's moves to circumscribe the activities of all non-Bolshevik political parties and organizations. Those who were closest in sympathies to the Bolsheviks, the Left SRs and some anarchists, frequently represented the gravest threats because they served in key military positions on revolutionary military councils, as commissars, and in the Cheka. When party members disputed Bolshevik policies or, even worse, mutinied against Bolshevik-dominated Soviet organs, they condemned themselves to the harsh retaliations of "revolutionary legality." Even within the party, wartime imperatives restricted debate in the name of "defense of the Revolution." The Central Committee struck back at the Left Communists, the Military Oppositionists, and the Democratic Centralists in large measure because they contested the center's military policies. The opposing sides would play out one more episode in the drama at the Tenth Party Congress, which would formalize the one-party system and make challenges to the central leadership increasingly difficult even within that party.

Soldiers' Culture and Political Work

Despite the implicit redefinition of the all-important political category of proletarian, that redefinition did not sit altogether well with the party's top strata. Those with the most uneasy consciences could find some consolation in their constant insistence that the party's organizations devote heightened attention to political work, especially agitation and propaganda. After all, social origin in and of itself had never been considered a surefire guarantee of loyal political behavior and attitudes, or "consciousness," as the Social Democrats had been calling it. Without a vanguard party to direct and shape mass consciousness, Lenin had argued, even the proletariat could achieve at best a "trade union consciousness." Accordingly, the early careers of all party members who had joined before 1917 were biographies of organization building, speech making, and pamphlet writing.

The dramatic surge in party membership following the October Revolution brought the Bolsheviks tens of thousands of untested men and women. When the new members' behavior ran counter to the old party elite's expectations, the veteran revolutionaries quickly concluded that a good number of these people were either opportunists or well-meaning but unconscious cadres. For the opportunists the party organization devised purges and regular membership reviews. But for the far larger numbers of unconscious cadres, the veterans turned to what they knew best—political work. Political work, like the category of proletarian, quickly and imperceptibly changed its primary focus: where once political workers had concentrated on winning new members to the revolutionary cause, they now sought to remake the mentalities, or at least to alter the objectionable behavior, of the new members who already were invested with considerable state authority. Even as the Bolsheviks had identified the proletariat as the class with a historic mission, they felt it necessary to help the proletariat define and express that mission. In short, the Bolsheviks had all along assumed that the vanguard party would have to act for the proletariat. Now, with the redefinition of the proletariat, the imperative of shaping the consciousness of that proletariat was felt even more strongly.

In several important senses, the political workers in the army were direct successors to the combat organizations of the Bolshevik and SR parties before the Revolution. Not only did the political workers themselves claim a revolutionary precedent for their work, but many of the Red Army's personnel were the same men and women who had been active in the Imperial Army only a few years earlier. Until the February Revolution, party members had been assigned to conduct propaganda and agitation among troops in the Imperial Army and to organize clandestine revolutionary cells that promoted social and political change. During 1917 Bolshevik agitators tried to win soldiers over to a defeatist platform in order to bring down the Provisional Government. Once the Bolsheviks achieved power, however, they sought to bolster soldiers' morale.

Admittedly, the content of their work had changed drastically, but many of their techniques were remarkably similar to those they had used in the recent past. The Eighth Party Congress had acknowledged the shift in purpose of political work and had demanded that party organizations raise the quality of members, by which it meant their ability to articulate and implement state and party policies, by increasing their efforts in political education.

In the Red Army the fundamental rationale for political work was to maintain combat readiness, good troop morale, and good relations with the nearby civilian population. By the end of 1919 every revolutionary military council had formed its own political departments down to the levels of individual armies and divisions.[51] Departments bore responsibility for organizing and coordinating the political work of all organs representing or claiming authority from central Soviet power for the populations of front-line areas.[52] In accordance with that important charge, the political departments acted as the key military agencies in the matter of regulating civil-military relations. In order to ensure the army's representative a voice in local politics, the heads of political departments had voting rights in the party committees located in those areas where their army units were stationed. Because the Red Army depended for supplies and recruits on the goodwill of the nearby population, political departments had special responsibilities to maintain close ties with the rural population. In 1919 most departments established special "peasant sections" for political work outside the army. A year later the RVSR formally approved the peasant sections, but their name was changed to "soviet sections." By means of the peasant, or soviet, sections the Red Army served as a major organizer of the new type of power that came to be called "soviet" and took the form of revolutionary committees (revkomy). The committees were temporary organs of martial law that combined civil and military authority. If the revolutionary committees determined that conditions were propitious for calling elections for local soviets, they would do so and hand over their authority to the soviet's executive

51. During the Civil War the Red Army comprised very irregular formations. An army usually united anywhere from 30,000 to 100,000 men. Artillery divisions comprised two to five batteries, each made up of 80 to 100 men.

52. To divide these responsibilities, each department had several sections, typically including agitation, organization, information, culture and enlightenment, registration and assignment, chancellery, literary and publication, theater and club, and library: "Iz polozheniia o politicheskikh otdelakh armii," 22 January 1920, in PPR II, pp. 61–63; "Polozhenie o politicheskikh otdelakh divizii," 22 January 1920, in ibid., pp. 63–71.

committee after it formed itself. Political workers also frequently helped organize committees of poor peasants and rural soviets.[53]

Within the army itself, the responsibilities of political departments grew phenomenally. Because of their broad mission, the departments intervened in nearly every aspect of the daily life of a unit. They had a wide range of functions and responsibilities, most important of which were organization, personnel management, and intelligence. As personnel officers, political workers kept inventories of party members and supervised their assignments to critical tasks. The political department awarded party cards to members, appointed party commissions to decide questions of admission and expulsion of members, and convened party conferences and assemblies. In this capacity the departments functioned as the equivalents of the executive committees of civilian party organs. As a means for the center to exercise some control over all outlying organs, every political worker had to file regular reports with his superiors. The reports summarized the work accomplished and provided intelligence about conditions among soldiers and commanders.

The task next in importance was the "general organization of agitational, propaganda, and enlightenment work." This task included publishing and distributing brochures, pamphlets, and newspapers, conducting meetings and assemblies, staging plays, managing libraries, teaching various courses, and maintaining the unit's Red Army club. Especially in an army continually plagued by shortages of high-quality weaponry and operating in conditions of severe material deprivation in a protracted civil war, agitation played a far greater role than it had in previous European wars. All the major belligerent armies in the Great War had discovered the benefits of propaganda for mobilizing soldier and civilian populations.[54] But the Soviet state's commitment to education and culture in the army during the Civil War was extraordinary, especially given that the new leaders faced competing priorities of defending and feeding the nation. That sizable commitment stemmed as much from the successful innovations of wartime propaganda as it did from longstanding values of the Russian democratic intelligentsia and the rise of a genuine popular culture in the prerevolutionary period. On the

53. In March 1919 the Southern Front's revolutionary military council created a department of civil administration, which coordinated the activity of revolutionary committees. In October this improvisation by the Southern Front was sanctioned and regulated in a "Statute on Revolutionary Committees." See PPR II, pp. 17–18. For more on the *revkomy*, see N. F. Bugai, *Revkomy* (Moscow, 1981).

54. See Harold D. Lasswell, *Propaganda Technique in World War I* (Cambridge: MIT Press, 1971), esp. chap. 9 for Lasswell's conclusions on the results of propaganda.

one hand, a large number of Old Bolsheviks shared with the broader democratic intelligentsia conceptions of a mission to impart the benefits of enlightenment to the formerly disfranchised and benighted toiling masses in order to transform backward Russia into a modern urban nation-state. On the other hand, workers and peasants wished to better their lots in life and sensed that they would remain shut out from real political power as long as education remained a monopoly of their traditional social "betters." As a consequence, during the years of the Revolution diverse groups put forward not only social and economic demands but an agenda of cultural reform as well.

The Red Army was inescapably part of the cultural revolution. Its leaders—Trotsky, Bubnov, Frunze, Gusev, Sklianskii, and Tukhachevsky, to name only a few—were orators, writers, newspapers editors, teachers, doctors, and musicians. Commissars and most of the army's first political workers had similar professional and educational backgrounds. The early Red Army elite shared a vision of a new type of army that contrasted sharply with its tsarist predecessor in educating soldiers to be not only able and courageous fighters but enlightened citizens. Trotsky reminded graduating Red commanders in September 1918 that theirs was not only a combat mission but also "a great cultural and moral mission."[55] The Red Army leadership inherited the vision of an army as a genuine force for the dissemination of enlightened values in part from the militia ideal of progressive European political thinkers.

The institution that deemed itself to be the carrier of that progressive ideal to the emerging Soviet political culture was Vsevobuch, whose director, Nikolai Podvoiskii, was the most consistent and fervent advocate of a comprehensive general educational program for all conscripts.[56] Podvoiskii had close ties with the People's Commissariat of Enlightenment, especially with the organizations of Proletkul't.[57] In the cities where Vsevobuch administrations had large staffs, their ambitious programs in natural history, the arts, and physical culture employed hundreds of members of the intelligent-

55. Trotskii, "Krasnye ofitsery," in KVR, 1:327. In March 1919 the Eighth Party Congress resolved that "all efforts of the military are directed at transforming the barracks as nearly as possible into a military school and to make them a center not only of purely military training but also of general education and political instruction": Vos'moi s''ezd, p. 415.

56. Originally Vsevobuch was intended as the primary agency for military training, but by the end of the Civil War the army itself was training most of the conscripts. Podvoiskii replaced the original director of Vsevobuch, Mar'iasin, in November 1918 and remained in that position until Vsevobuch was disbanded in 1923.

57. See the memoirs of Aleksandr Fevral'skii, Zapiski rovesnika veka (Moscow, 1976), pp. 54, 288; and a recent study of Proletkul't by Lynn Mally, Culture of the Future: The Proletkult Movement in Revolutionary Russia (Berkeley: University of California Press, forthcoming.)

sia, providing them work and income after many of their former patrons and institutions had either disappeared or been destroyed. As
a result of these and similar projects, the army and its affiliated
agencies assumed much of the role of cultural patrons that traditionally had been played by the now dispossessed and impoverished aristocracy and bourgeoisie. From the beginning, however, the new
patrons—soviet and party institutions, including the army—viewed
their cultural enterprises as part of a political transformation that
would be won only after decisive struggle with the heritage of the
backward past and by winning the loyalty of the populace to the
Soviet state. These were not necessarily the goals of the members of
the intelligentsia who collaborated with the new government. Many
members of the intelligentsia were confident that in imparting the
best of the old cultural heritage they would awaken the vast potential of the Russian people. They assumed that they could avoid forc-
ing an overtly political content upon their audience. Nor were the
aims of the party and state patrons necessarily the goals of the soldiers, workers, and peasants, who wanted more immediate practical
benefits from what they learned—skills to empower them to maneuver more effectively in the new world that was emerging in the wake
of the Revolution. The army served as one of several environments
in which competing groups fought to define the contours of a new
culture.

A letter from Emel'ian Iaroslavskii, Moscow District commissar, to
the Socialist Academy of Sciences illustrates the nature of early utopian experiments in political work. Iaroslavskii asked the academy
to send him outlines and lecture notes on "socialist theory" for distribution to Red Army political workers.[58] The Central Committee
proposed simply to reproduce the classics of radical political
thought and leave it to political workers on the scene to organize the
appropriate lectures and discussions. Political workers on the job
immediately judged such efforts to be insufficient and naive. The
reports filed by political departments on "political enlightenment
work" reveal how the army organized culture and education in the
first years after the Revolution. Only at the end of 1918 and the beginning of 1919 did enlightenment activities warrant a separate sub-
heading in the reports; formerly they were subsumed under
recruitment, processing, and military instruction. Vsebiurvoenkom,
the organization that had been responsible for commissars before the
Eighth Party Congress directed the Central Committee to organize
PUR, issued a "scheme for the organization of cultural and enlightenment matters in Red Army units at the front," according to which

58. "Pis'mo TsK RKP(b) Sotsialisticheskoi akademii nauk o neobkhodimosti
podgotovki konspektov lektsii dlia politrabotnikov Krasnoi Armii," 2 October 1918, in
Iz istorii grazhdanskoi voiny v SSSR, 1:157.

company, battalion, and regimental "culture and enlightenment commissions" would execute the instructions of the political departments.[59] The commissions' first task was to compile a list of illiterate Red Army soldiers and set up schools to instruct them. During the first months of 1918, illiteracy was not considered an urgent problem because the bulk of the soldiers were either town dwellers or peasant soldiers who had served in the Imperial Army and were minimally literate. That situation quickly changed as the state conscripted large numbers of peasants who had rudimentary literacy or were altogether illiterate.

At first the commissions focused most of their energies on general education courses and series of lectures, organized in such a way that "they contributed to the formation of an integrated and harmonious socialist world outlook." A soldiers' club was the center for all these activities and was expected to house a mobile library, a reading room, a stage for performances by invited theatrical companies, and an area for playing such games as chess and checkers. According to the same scheme, the commissions should organize the following sections: (1) political literacy, where "every genuine Communist" should register; (2) literature, because "consciousness [soznatel'nost'] is the best bulwark of the Revolution," and political workers should strive to introduce the world of enlightenment among soldiers by means of books and the "live" word; (3) theater and music, to organize "rational entertainment" for soldiers and develop in them "an aesthetic taste and fortify their courage and faith"; and (4) physical culture, remembering that only in a healthy body can there be a healthy mind. PUR allocated a large operating budget to its political departments; in the second half of 1919 alone, 450 million rubles were earmarked for the needs of the political enlightenment staff.[60]

59. "Skhema organizatsii kul'turno-prosvetitel'nogo dela v krasnoarmeiskikh chastiakh, nakhodiashchikhsia na fronte," 12 December 1918, in PPR I, pp. 93–96. One of the co-authors of the "scheme" was the director of the agitation and enlightenment department of Vsebiurvoenkom and later of PUR, Valentina Suzdal'tseva (Tagunova). She was one of the organizers of the political department of the Sixth Army on the Northern Front and later served in high-level positions on other fronts. In the first two years of the Civil War women played a large and significant role in the army, not only in enlightenment work but also as commissars and soldiers.

60. See the budget report in "Iz otcheta Politupravleniia Revvoensoveta Respubliki o deiatel'nosti za 1919 g.," in Iz istorii grazhdanskoi voiny v SSSR, 2:816–18, 821. For the second half of 1919 PUR's overall budget was 664,217,243 rubles. Of the total, 215 million rubles were assigned to the political departments of the fronts and military districts. Another 106.25 million rubles went for the maintenance of the staff of political and agitation-enlightenment organizations, the organization and maintenance of literacy schools, clubs, mobile theaters, and libraries, printing equipment and supplies, and many more activities. To put these astronomical figures in the perspective of the inflationary economy of the Civil War years, see the summary of the state budget compiled by R. W. Davies, The Development of the Soviet Budgetary Sys-

At the end of 1919 PUR convened the First All-Russian Congress of Political Workers to summarize their experience to date, to exchange advice among themselves and with the center, and to propose improvements and reforms. The congress was important for the delegates' attempts to define their mission and status within the army and their relationship with the state. The delegates reached a consensus that what they were engaged in was "political enlightenment," and they described that enterprise as "an extension of political agitation that must be strictly adapted to the combat mission of the Red Army." The foundation of enlightenment for Red Army men must be the principles of "revolutionary Marxism, which will awaken and organize the class consciousness and creative initiative of the armed toiling masses."[61] It was assumed, apparently, that "the creative initiative" that Marxism would awaken would be in harmony with the "combat mission" of the army, even though that mission depended on unquestioning obedience to commands. Not all political workers in the army, however, let alone the members of the civilian intelligentsia who volunteered or were mobilized by the Commissariat of Enlightenment, shared the optimistic vision of harmony between initiative and obedience. Very soon, hard choices had to be made between encouraging soldiers' initiative and securing their unquestioning obedience. Under the pressure of battle political workers came down on the side of obedience, but even then they referred to it euphemistically as "conscious" or "revolutionary" discipline, in order to distinguish their enlightenment programs from the drill-sergeant discipline of their tsarist predecessors.

Underlying the consensus at the congress and the instructions on political enlightenment were several attitudes that were made explicit by Director of Agitation and Enlightenment Valentina Suzdal'-tseva and her fellow workers in the political administration. Above all, she insisted that enlightenment work be intertwined with political work because the goal of the army in this area was the formation of a loyal Soviet citizen who was skilled in the fundamental practices of power in the new political system. Because so much of the modern conception of political authority rests on printed documents, literacy occupied a prominent place in all army plans. Suzdal'tseva argued in her first report on party and political work that "an illiterate and benighted person is incapable of apprehending with any depth, processing, or consciously mastering the high ideals of Communist morality." Furthermore, an illiterate person

tem (Cambridge: Cambridge University Press, 1958), pp. 42–43. Davies calculated total defense expenditures for the first half of 1919 at 5.122 billion rubles, for the second half of 1919 at 10.74 billion rubles.
    61. Politrabotnik 1 (1920): 15.

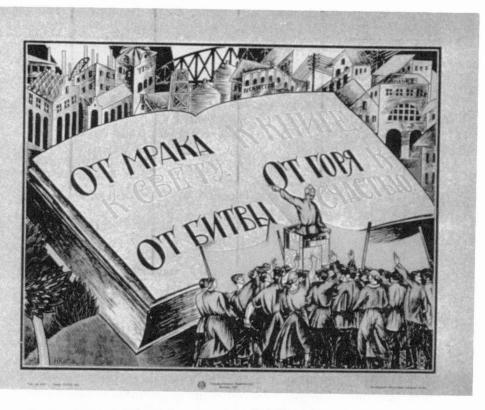

Literacy campaign. Courtesy of Poster Collection, Hoover Institution Archives, Stanford University.

"cannot understand the complicated tasks of socialist construction, nor can he respond to the undertakings of Soviet power with any understanding of their profoundly vital and moral significance."[62]

PUR also believed that soldiers wanted enlightenment and would look kindly on the government that provided it. An illiterate or semiliterate soldier who returned home literate "would never forget that the workers' and peasants' government had provided him with the most powerful weapon for the defense of his interests— enlightenment."[63] Of course, the political workers wanted more than

62. "Iz otcheta Politupravleniia pri Revvoensovete Respubliki o partiino-politicheskoi rabote v Krasnoi Armii s nachala ee organizatsii po 1 oktiabria 1920 g.," 8 October 1920, in PPR I, p. 70.

63. Ibid., p. 821. Roger Pethybridge, The Social Prelude to Stalinism (New York: St. Martin's Press, 1974), pp. 161–62, confirms PUR's optimistic self-image and compares the demobilization of "tens of thousands of young peasants who had become both literate and party members while serving the Red Army" with the military de-

a citizen's gratitude; they wanted a change in his loyalties, or "consciousness." And they believed that literacy would enable them to win those loyalties, because they had faith in the power of words to transform behavior.

Eyewitnesses of the revolutionary struggle confidently believed that speeches and slogans had indeed changed the country by mobilizing large masses of the populace to take political power into their own hands. Vsevobuch director Podvoiskii declared that revolutionary warfare depended on the skillful use of words, for "our word is our best weapon." Words blow up and scatter the ranks of the enemy, "disintegrate his soul, paralyze his nerves, split him into warring camps and class factions."[64] Even for a soldier less prone to hyperbole than Podvoiskii, words held a transformative power. After one group of Red Army men had completed their six-week literacy course, they reported that their lives had changed remarkably. Whereas before they had wasted their time in "card games, swearing, and often drunkenness," now their eyes were opened. They no longer needed their former amusements; instead, they demanded newspapers, set up a reading room, and collected a small library.[65] Illiterate soldiers concluded that learning to read and write words, and thereby gaining a sense of control over the world of written documents, gave them access to new levers of influence over the events that were shaping their lives. With the enthusiasm of the newly literate, soldiers supported literacy programs back home in the countryside. *Bednota*, the most popular newspaper among soldiers, and other journals received frequent inquiries from soldiers about the progress of literacy and enlightenment campaigns in their home villages.

Primarily because of the perceived close ties between literacy and a soldier's capacity to form correct political opinions, the Red Army made a substantial commitment to the eradication of illiteracy. In the fall of 1918 the Moscow Military District had required all illiterate soldiers to enroll in reading courses. Other districts established volunteer literacy programs, in which already literate soldiers were to be released from drill duties in order to teach their illiterate fellow soldiers. Finally in September 1919 the RVSR declared literacy an urgent priority; by this time the army was overwhelmingly peasant in makeup, and the peasants could no longer be counted on to

---

serters and demobilized men toward the close of 1917. Both groups acted as cultural and political leaven in the countryside. The post-Civil War soldiers "played a valuable role in spreading literacy and with it the prestige of the party."

64. Nikolai Podvoiskii, "Osnovy revoliutsionnoi voiny i taktiki v internatsional'noi mezhduklassovoi bor'be," in *Revoliutsionnaia voina*, ed. Podvoiskii and M. Pavlovich (Moscow, 1919), p. 66.

65. A letter reprinted from the army newspaper *V ruzh'e*, 25 November 1919, in A. Vyrvich, *Krasnaia armiia v bor'be s negramotnost'iu* (Moscow, 1925), p. 72.

have the minimal reading and writing abilities of a veteran of the Imperial Army. The deputy chairman of the RVSR, Efraim Sklianskii, charged political commissars and culture and enlightenment commissions to compile lists of all illiterates and semiliterates and appoint "cultural workers" (*kul'turniki*)— preferably soldiers, but if necessary civilians—to teach reading and writing every day at times least disruptive to military training. The decree established standardized definitions of literacy for the first time.[66]

The high priority that the RVSR assigned to literacy was symbolized in the Red Army's first emblem, which depicted a hammer and sickle for the workers and peasants, a rifle, and a book.[67] PUR proudly proclaimed that no government in the world had done so much for the struggle against illiteracy and ignorance as the worker-peasant state had done in the first two years of its existence. In the second half of 1919 PUR reported that its literature and publishing department—despite paper shortages that had cut planned output by nearly half—sent to the army more than 6 million items, including a special journal for soldiers, *Krasnoarmeets*, brochures, leaflets, posters, and *lubok* pictures (popular prints and booklets).[68]

When Sklianskii announced mandatory enrollment in literacy classes for soldiers, he commanded that the illiterates not be excused from regular instruction in "political literacy" (*politicheskaia gramota*, or *gramotnost'*), but that special programs be devised for them. As texts *kul'turniki* might use the brochures and speeches of the leaders of Soviet Russia.[69] "Political literacy," or the rudiments of political knowledge, carried the assumption that a political concept could be taught to the politically naive, much as reading and writing could be taught to illiterates. Something of the same conception of politics was inherent in the title of the political department's new instructor (as of October 1919), the *politruk*. The full title, *politicheskii rukovoditel'*, suggests a political leader or guide for those uninitiated in the appropriate ways of understanding the world and acting in it.[70]

66. Illiterates were expected to be able to read and write their full name, their unit, their address, and a letter of a few words, and to count to 1,000. Semiliterates (*malogramotnye*) must be able to read and write a letter or official dispatch and paraphrase it in their own words, and to add and subtract to 1,000.

67. M. M. Lisenkov, *Kul'turnaia revoliutsiia v SSSR i armii* (Moscow, 1977), p. 99.

68. "Iz otcheta," in *Iz istorii grazhdanskoi voiny v SSSR*, 2:822–23. A fuller listing of PUR's organizations appears in ibid., pp. 820–22. By the end of the year, PUR counted nearly 4,000 schools, three Red universities, numerous movie projection teams, more than 1,000 clubs, and other organizations.

69. "Prikaz Revvoensoveta Respubliki o likvidatsii negramotnosti sredi krasnoarmeitsev," 4 September 1919, in *PPR* II, pp. 42–45.

70. Because commissars focused most of their attention on the primary task of maintaining the fighting ability of their units, organizational matters and enlightenment programs often suffered from neglect. Only after October 1919, when PUR intro-

The "schools of political literacy" were the cornerstone of an impressive edifice of educational and cultural institutions that evolved
during the Civil War from the practices of political workers in the
army. The Red Army inherited some of these practices from the final
days of the Imperial Army—meetings, brochures, special soldiers'
newspapers, even literacy programs. The fundamental task of the
political workers in the new army was to win over as many soldiers
and officers as possible to a type of politics that was characterized as
broadly revolutionary and socialist and particularly Bolshevik; in
other words, to render them "politically literate." The new type of
politics included the versions of class analysis and social categories
that activists of all the revolutionary parties had used—a specific
rhetoric that emerged from the inter- and intraparty polemics of the
revolutionary years starting as early as the end of the nineteenth
century. The meanings of many of these terms changed—often imperceptibly to the men and women who employed them—during
that revolutionary period and in the early years of the post-1917 order. The terms were presumed to apply to a world that preceded the
Revolution, and even then they often fitted uneasily. In the new conditions of the postrevolutionary world, however, they came to mean
very different things. The new politics also included specific forms
of action: meetings, speeches, formal agendas; forming committees,
electing representatives, and voting for resolutions; and newspaper
and pamphlet writing. This kind of politics was somewhat familiar
to factory and white-collar workers who had experience in revolutionary politics; it was considerably less familiar to most peasants
and soldiers. Rural politics operated according to different rules and
by means of different institutions and practices. And until 1917 the
political order of the Imperial Army strictly excluded soldiers from
any form of political participation in matters that affected their
lives.

The encounter of these diverse kinds of politics made up the stuff
of political work in the Red Army. The memoirs of commissars and
political instructors (politruki) abound in lively descriptions of
highly charged debates about state policies. Andrei Kuchkin, a commissar who served on the Eastern Front in 1919, described a characteristic confrontation. A party member reported in despair to
Kuchkin that a certain Semenov was attracting a large crowd of soldiers by railing against "the Communists," declaring that they forced
peasants into communes, took away their grain, and offered nothing

duced the politruk as a deputy to the commissar responsible for political education,
did political education assume any systematic or sustained character. See "Prikaz
Revvoensoveta Respubliki o vvedenii dolzhnosti politicheskogo rukovoditelia," 14
October 1919, in PPR II, pp. 50–52. Soviet historians frequently give Stalin credit for
this innovation, but the evidence is dubious.

in return. Kuchkin braced himself to face the angry crowd. Semenov was not intimidated by the appearance of the divisional commissar; the attention he was attracting only fueled his audacity.

First, Semenov declared that the Bolsheviks and Communists were two different parties. The Bolsheviks had opposed war, tsarist epaulettes, and the old regime. It was they who had ended the war with the Germans and distributed land to the peasants. According to Semenov, the Bolsheviks were for "all the people. They make the burzhui work, and when they don't work, they give them no bread." Semenov approved of these measures, but acknowledged nevertheless that the Bolsheviks were "semicommunists." Soldiers seated nearby shouted, "That's the way, Leontii! Give it to him!" When Kuchkin asked Semenov to explain why he felt that Communists had a different program, Semenov spat on the ground, pushed back his cap, and presented his case: "Communists are only for the workers. They are against factory owners. They want to give all factories to the workers. But the peasants they want to force into communes, which means everyone ends up in one kettle, like in a factory. That's Communists for you!" When Kuchkin declared that he was both a Communist and a Bolshevik, Semenov smiled sarcastically and accused him of deceiving them. "That cannot be! You're a Bolshevik, but not a Communist." Kuchkin recounted a brief history of the party, and for a moment it seemed to him that Semenov believed him. Suddenly Semenov asked, "So why then does the Soviet regime shoot burzhui?" One of the soldiers joked, "Say, what's got into you? Are you for the burzhui now?" Semenov menacingly retorted, "Lay off!" The commissar explained that the Soviet regime shot only those who raised arms against it. Peaceful burzhui were not touched. He went on to explain that the Communists had not started the current war, that the workers and peasants were fighting only because the landowners, capitalists, generals, and foreign bourgeoisie refused to give up their power without a struggle. Semenov proposed that the war be ended so that the peasants could return home for spring sowing; if necessary, they could return to the fighting after the fieldwork was done. He complained about the forced grain requisitioning. Kuchkin persisted until Semenov finally conceded that he couldn't win the argument. "That's why you're a commissar, after all." Later Semenov admitted that he found the talk interesting and suggested that they talk further in the future. Kuchkin reports that he and Semenov grew to be close; he even took on Semenov as his orderly and he proved to be reliable and precise.[71]

Though Kuchkin's self-serving account of his confrontation with Semenov clearly corresponds to a certain idealized narrative that

71. A. P. Kuchkin, V boiakh i pokhodakh ot Volgi do Eniseia: Zapiski voennogo komissara (Moscow, 1969), pp. 92–96.

shapes most memoirs of these years, it is nonetheless revealing about fundamental Bolshevik attitudes toward the peasantry and about techniques of political work in the army. The first explanation that Kuchkin offers for Semenov's "muddle" (which, he asserts, was typical of peasants during the Civil War) is Semenov's class background. Semenov was a middle peasant from Simbirsk province, whose father had two horses, one cow, several head of sheep, and an iron plow.[72] Semenov's views, according to Kuchkin, reflected the "mood" of middle peasants, a characterization that suggests that peasants really had no firm ideas about politics, but were susceptible to influences from either side. Their vacillating moods reflected their ambiguous social character, neither property holder nor proletarian in a real sense, both exploited and exploiter at the same time. Indeed, Kuchkin blames the enemies of the Revolution for sowing the confusion that reigned in the minds of the peasants.

Some of Semenov's arguments revealed elements of a world view that Kuchkin could use to appeal to his sympathies. The commissar started by highlighting the grounds they shared—their antagonism toward the *burzhui* (the pejorative term connoting a town dweller who derived income from the work of others' hands). It was the same old elite, Kuchkin argued, that was waging the war against the Soviet state. Kuchkin evaded a ticklish issue when Semenov suggested that the Communists favored the workers over the peasants. Political workers later identified this motif as "peasant envy of the worker" and devised lectures and excursions to factories to dispel these purportedly unjustified and inaccurate impressions. Kuchkin claimed that Communists did not force peasants into communes, but peasant experience in several regions suggested otherwise. Semenov displayed plenty of attitudes that could have been based on peasants' experiences and that appeared perfectly reasonable from their perspective. But it was Kuchkin's mission to replace those confused "moods" with a proper political understanding, one that accorded with the Bolsheviks' goal of forging a strong modern state.

Kuchkin described the "school of political literacy" that his political department organized in response to the soldiers' perceived misunderstandings about Soviet and party policies. The department employed not only commissars, commanders, and political instructors but also literate and "developed" soldiers and members of the local civilian intelligentsia. The program was targeted at a peasant audience and sought to impart the army's views of the current war and how it differed from previous wars (the current war was the confrontation of capitalism and socialism); the gains of the peas-

72. Ibid., p. 92.

antry from the Revolution and the threat from the enemy to those gains; the nature of the new Soviet government and its relations with peasants and workers; the church and the school; and the politically very important differences between the principles of the Red Army and those of partisan warfare.[73]

The principles of political literacy quickly came to dominate the cultural life and educational programs of army units. But political workers faced a major problem in locating suitable materials to use. They found the content of available literature highly suspect, and they lacked suitable primers for an adult male, mostly rural audience. Here, too, improvisation became the rule. An enlightenment worker on the Southern Front claims that she composed the first text that had a content politically acceptable for a postrevolutionary audience. Dora El'kina recounts that in 1919 she wrote on the board a phrase that would have been fine for a group of schoolchildren but that elicited only snickers from the soldiers: "Masha ate the kasha." After some frustrating moments that brought her close to tears, she hit upon the idea of turning the lesson into a political discussion and explained to the soldiers why they could not be with their Mashas and why the country was experiencing a shortage of kasha. Following this small triumph, she returned to the board and wrote a new sentence: "We are not slaves, slaves we are not" (*"My ne raby, raby ne my"*). This was an even more resounding success. On the basis of her initial experience, El'kina wrote a primer that taught reading and writing by slogans.[74]

El'kina's experience suggests that soldiers had a very instrumental approach to education. They wanted knowledge that could be put to use, if possible immediately, and were not interested in knowledge for knowledge's sake, an attitude they attributed to many of the civilian *kul'turniki* who were entering army service in increasing numbers. Literacy gained in importance during the war because soldiers were often far from home and could no longer rely so exclusively for their information on oral sources. They wanted to know how the Red Army was faring on other fronts and the fate of their relatives back home. Political workers quickly realized that such news had an immediate impact on troop morale and combated rumors, which they attributed to "kulak agitation," that nearby cities

73. Ibid., pp. 277–79.

74. D. Iu. El'kina, "Likvidatsiia negramotnosti v Krasnoi Armii na frontakh grazhdanskoi voiny," *Narodnoe obrazovanie* 12 (1957): 52–56. El'kina was a Socialist Revolutionary before she joined the Communist Party in 1919. The poet Vladimir Maiakovskii composed another popular primer that he illustrated himself, *Sovetskaia azbuka* (Moscow, 1919), in which each letter of the alphabet was accompanied by a political lesson written in humorous two-line rhymes.

had already fallen and that the Whites were approaching rapidly.[75] Soldiers trusted written documents more than they trusted their political workers. They had great incentive to learn to read so that they could dispense with the mediation of political workers.

Precisely because many soldiers had so instrumentalist an attitude toward knowledge, they quickly learned to distinguish what was essential from what was alien to their needs. Political content that served no ostensible purpose but to trumpet the state's achievements and advantages turned soldiers away from lectures and club activities. Enlightenment workers complained that initially most soldiers avoided the "rational and organized leisure" activities and nearly all forms of political education. Typically, not more than 30 to 40 percent of the soldiers attended any classes at all, despite all the circulars and commands decreeing attendance.[76] The political workers attributed the soldiers' poor attendance to their "lack of consciousness," but soldiers were no doubt quite conscious of what they considered worth hearing. To entice soldiers into clubs, kul'turniki set up cafeterias, buffets, or tearooms and organized dances. One lecturer reprimanded soldiers for wanting to be rewarded for attending educational meetings. He refused to give out the sugar, jam, and slices of bread on the table until the soldiers had sat through the entire lecture. "Aren't you ashamed, comrades?" he asked his audience: "Must you really be enticed like small children with candies? After all, these lectures are organized for you and for your general welfare. You should come running to them and not wait for a reward for doing so."[77] Soldiers lacked "voluntary school discipline" or manifested "sleepiness in their revolutionary mood," according to reports. Kul'turniki constantly appealed to commissars to enforce the mandatory attendance provisions.[78]

The soldiers had their own explanations for their "apathy" toward enlightenment programs. First of all, they found little of practical value in what they were taught. The content of lessons was too abstract and removed from their day-to-day concerns. Second, political workers were often inexperienced and their propaganda materials

75. Olikov, Dezertirstvo, pp. 84, 96; Kolychev, Partiino-politicheskaia rabota, pp. 183, 214–15; V. I. Suzdal'tseva, Partiinaia rabota na Severnom Fronte (Archangel, 1926), p. 40. Kiriukhin, Iz dnevnika, p. 103, reported that when news reached soldiers that their families had been arrested or shot as sympathizers by White forces, they demanded to be returned home to take revenge.

76. Kratkii ocherk kul'turno-politicheskoi raboty v Krasnoi Armii za 1918 god (Moscow, 1919), p. 69.

77. Bednota, 20 April 1920.

78. "Ot komiteta RKP(b) 162 strelkovogo polka," 24 April 1919, in Perepiska, 7: 527; Kratkii ocherk, pp. 20, 56; Kiriukhin, Iz dnevnika, pp. 30–31.

КЛУБ НЕ БУРЖУАЗНАЯ
ГОСТИННАЯ ДЛЯ ЛЕГКОГО
ВРЕМЯПРЕПРОВОЖДЕНИЯ, А ГОРН,
НА ОГНЕ КОТОРОГО ВЫКОВЫВАЮТСЯ И
ЗАКАЛЯЮТСЯ СТОЙКИЕ БОРЦЫ
РЕВОЛЮЦИИ,
ДОСТОИНЫЕ ВЫСОКОГО ЗВАНЬЯ
СОЛДАТА
КРАСНОЙ АРМИИ.

Description of a Red Army club. Courtesy of Poster Collection, Hoover Institution Archives, Stanford University.

were quickly outdated.[79] The soldiers also complained that the political workers' language was unintelligible. They explained the language problem by a form of class analysis: the class backgrounds of more and more of the *kul'turniki* made their concerns alien to the soldiers. Not only did the *kul'turniki* teach material irrelevant to them, but the soldiers resented the "privileged" lifestyle that the smooth-skinned intellectuals enjoyed in a workers' and peasants' army.[80] Though many of the educators mobilized from civilian life were men, the soldiers' most pointed criticisms were directed at young women and suggest that especially young women of petit bourgeois backgrounds enjoyed little or no authority among the troops.

79. In the April 1919 report of one infantry unit, the party committee admitted that much of their trouble in holding soldiers' attention stemmed from their inexperience and that the literature they had available dated from mid-1918, when the Czech insurrection was still the dominant theme: *Perepiska*, 7:527–528.

80. See soldiers' complaints in *Krasnoarmeets*, 1 May 1919. See also similar complaints and rationalizations among peasants in the late nineteenth century in A. Benoit Eklof, "Reconsidering Peasant Sloth: Strategies of Education and Learning in Rural Russia before the Revolution," *Journal of Social History* (Spring 1981): 335–85.

When the army's political workers convened at the end of 1919, they too criticized PUR for recruiting too exclusively from "intelligentsia and semi-intelligentsia social elites," and they pledged to promote "the Red Army masses into political enlightenment work." Despite the resistance to female teachers, however, PUR insisted that it had to continue recruiting educators from civilian institutions, "by no means excluding women."[81] In fact, in the face of a continuing shortage of teachers who shared the soldiers' working-class or peasant origins, the Council on Defense ordered the Commissariat of Enlightenment to conduct a mass mobilization of "school workers" (shkraby) in February 1920. One month later the Red Army had swallowed up so many teachers that Sovnarkom decreed that several thousand be released "to save the cause of the people's education."[82] At the same time, PUR acknowledged the soldiers' complaints about the class-alien kul'turniki and issued a new regulation that guaranteed soldiers and political workers a voice in the personnel decisions of the army's culture and enlightenment commissions. In order to "encourage creative initiative from below," political workers and party cells had the right to veto candidates nominated for membership on these commissions.[83]

When Dora El'kina's students snickered at sentences devised for schoolchildren, she improvised a political lesson and proclaimed her efforts a great success. But not all political lessons were as acceptable to the soldiers, especially those of the agitators sent from urban trade union and party organizations. Much of what the soldiers heard had little of immediate value for them or their families. Soldiers' resolutions continued to rail against inadequate supplies, abusive superiors, and inadequate attention to the needs of their relatives. Lecturers responded with lessons on The Communist Manifesto and the history of the workers' movement. When soldiers reacted with indifference, political workers concluded that what really bothered them was the foreign and abstract terminology that filled the lectures.[84] Kiriukhin recounted the experience of a

---

81. "Rezoliutsiia I s"ezda politrabotnikov Krasnoi Armii o merakh po obespecheniiu fronta politprosvetrabotnikami," 11–15 December 1919, in PPR II, pp. 57–58.

82. "Postanovlenie Soveta Oborony o vvedenii trudovoi povinnosti dlia rabotnikov prosveshcheniia po likvidatsii negramotnosti v Krasnoi Armii," in Dekrety Sovetskoi vlasti, 7:215–19. The decree instituted a personal data card for each mobilized teacher, which included an entry for experience in rural schools, with working-class audiences, or in Red Army clubs. "Postanovlenie SNK ob uvol'nenii iz Krasnoi Armii rabotnikov prosveshcheniia," in ibid., pp. 409–10.

83. "Iz polozheniia o kul'turno-prosvetitel'nykh komissiakh v chastiakh i uchrezhdeniiakh Krasnoi Armii i Flota RSFSR," in PPR II, pp. 73–74.

84. Trotsky exhorted the authors and printers of brochures and newspapers to keep their work comprehensible to the Red Army masses. "Instead of simple picture-like explanations, they speak in abstract, high-flown, bookish sentences": "Tovarishcham pechatnikam s fronta," 19 April 1919, in KVR, vol. 2, pt. 2, p. 255. In early 1920

politruk who organized a reading of *The Communist Manifesto*. As soon as he began, one soldier stood up and asked that he first explain what the words "Communist" and "manifesto" meant. Kiriukhin was glad that the soldiers in this company were at least interested in foreign words; he could recall other occasions when nobody asked a single question about the material, though "certainly there were some unfamiliar phrases and words."[85] When soldiers complained that they did not understand the agitators' language or refused to attend lessons, however, they were often expressing their unwillingness to accept the ideas they were hearing.

The language of Russian urban socialist political culture, which was the initial language of political literacy in the army, had imbibed much of the vocabulary of European left-wing movements and parties. In the army the rhetoric of the new political elite underwent something of a nativization as enlightenment workers attempted to adapt their message to their audience. Whenever possible they replaced words of foreign derivation with Russian words that had religious overtones or invoked nature. In their brochures educators made transparent efforts to appeal to what they thought were peasant sensibilities. A cartoon in *Bednota* depicted a stocky, round-faced Russian peasant lad with spiders and leeches crawling over his torso. The parasites were labeled "landowner," "priest," and "interventionist."[86] Thus the state linked its enemies with the predators and parasites that plagued peasants in their daily struggle for survival. Elsewhere, a Red Army man was depicted astride a white horse slaying the dragon of counterrevolution, a direct appeal to the traditional iconographic representation of St. George.[87]

The military press became a forum for the continual redefinition of the proletarian dictatorship: the center and the soldiers defended their own revolutionary agendas while political workers translated the frequently divergent agendas into language understandable to

---

PUR instructed all editorial staffs to publish newspapers that were "popular, striking, short, and clear. Nothing superfluous, boring, or incomprehensible should have a place in them. A revolutionary and businesslike temperament, colorful and lively language, force and urgency in slogans are more imperative for army newspapers than they are for general proletarian ones": *Politrabotnik* 2 (1920): 16; see also the complaints about shabby printing work that rendered even *Pravda* illegible, "Ot Politotdela revvoensoveta 5 armii Vostochnogo fronta," 11 October 1918, in *Perepiska*, 4:462.

85. Kiriukhin, *Iz dnevnika*, p. 162.

86. *Bednota*, 1 May 1919. Examples of these creative adaptations to the imagery of the rural world are numerous in the poster art and leaflets. Another example of the "peasantization" of political discussion appeared in *Krasnoarmeets*, 11 June 1920. The involvement of the Entente powers in the Civil War was recounted by way of a fairy tale in which a rapacious old woman (the foreign interventionists) was about to gobble up a tantalizing nut (Soviet Russia).

87. See the cover of *Krasnoarmeets*, October 1919 and again February 1920.

A military correspondent checks the daily press. From *Raboche-krest'ianskaia Krasnaia Armiia* (Moscow, 1938), courtesy of Division of Art, Prints, and Photographs,
The New York Public Library, Astor, Lenox, and Tilden Foundations.

both parties. The soldiers, political workers, and Moscow leadership
communicated with one another in the hundreds of army and peasant newspapers and journals that PUR and local political departments published.[88] Even though Red Army men themselves began
writing for the military press and eventually became known as
voenkory, short for "military correspondents,"[89] it was the political

88. In 1919, according to PUR statistics, 520,674 copies of newspapers were sent
daily to the army for distribution among soldiers and the front-line populace. This
figure includes 383,130 copies of *Bednota*, 73,673 of *Pravda*, and 40,567 copies of
Izvestiia. By the end of 1919 the army itself published 25 newspapers with a total
circulation of 250,000: *Politrabotnik* 1 (1920): 11. In April 1919 PUR centralized military publishing activities in the press bureau of its literary-publishing department.
89. On 10 April 1919 the political department of the Eleventh Army convened the
first assembly of Red Army men who were writing for the newspaper *Krasnyi voin*. In
1921 the first army-wide assembly of *voenkory* met and elected as chairman the So-

A Red Army man points to his article in a wall newspaper. From the journal *Krasnoarmeets*, courtesy of Hoover Institution, Stanford University.

workers, specifically the section in every political department charged with literary and publishing activities, who selected and edited the contents of each issue.

On 1 May, 1919 PUR's literature and publishing department released the first issue of *Krasnoarmeets (The Red Army Man)*, a weekly journal intended for a mass soldier readership. *Krasnoarmeets* quickly became the most popular army-wide journal.[90]

viet writer Dmitrii Furmanov, a commissar with the legendary units of Commander Vasilii Chapaev. The military correspondents had an analogue in the workers' and peasants' correspondent movement *rabsel'kory*. See Stephen Cohen, *Bukharin and the Bolshevik Revolution* (New York: Knopf, 1973), pp. 207–8; also V. N. Alferov, *Vozniknovenie i razvitie rabsel'korovskogo dvizheniia v SSSR* (Moscow, 1970).

90. By its third issue, *Krasnoarmeets* was circulating 150,000 copies. PUR's literature and publishing department reported that between 1 June and 1 November 1919 over a million copies of *Krasnoarmeets* reached soldiers: "Iz otcheta Politupravleniia

Its first editor was Dmitrii Poluian, a former teacher whose father, a Cossack, had been shot by the Whites. Leading artists and writers contributed material to the journal; political and military leaders explained official policies; and commissars and soldiers wrote articles and letters to the editor. The journal featured regular accounts of the deaths of heroes and martyrs in the Red Army and published important government decrees with commentary, particularly those affecting the welfare of soldiers and their families. At the same time the editors worked to build new loyalties among the soldiers, as when they identified Moscow and the Kremlin as "the heart of Soviet Russia" and printed biographies of Soviet leaders and heroes of the world proletarian and socialist movement.

The first editors of Krasnoarmeets tried to make their journal responsive to soldiers' needs and concerns while at the same time transmitting a version of official positions on important issues. The journal regularly solicited readers' opinions about topics of interest to them. The most interesting dialogue between the government and its soldiers appeared in the letters to the editors and in the editors' responses. Here a clearer picture of soldier politics emerges, even if it is filtered through the editors' prejudices. Soldiers' letters expressed virtually the same complaints they voiced in the meetings that commissars recorded in their memoirs.

The major concern of the soldiers was why they still had to fight, why an army was needed, why they could not go home for religious holidays or to care for sick parents. The editors explained about the dangers of counterrevolution and gave bloodcurdling accounts of life in a White prison camp. They waged antireligious campaigns with the help of Dem'ian Bednyi, the poet laureate of the Red Army, who portrayed village priests as skirt-chasers, lazy hypocrites, and money grubbers in his viciously satiric poems. The soldiers complained about citizens who bought their way out of military service and about speculators and saboteurs in the rear. The editors explained that many citizens continued to exhibit little "consciousness" and, knowingly and unknowingly, abetted the forces of counterrevolution. One letter writer was reprimanded for excoriating the Jews for bringing ruin upon Russia. Soldiers asked for advice on domestic affairs, such as the propriety of marrying a "politically condemned" woman.[91]

The soldiers also complained about injustices in the army, especially the privileges of the military specialists and civilian employees and the inadequate rations of rank-and-file troops. As far as they

---

Revvoensoveta Republiki o deiatel'nosti za 1919 g.," in Iz istorii grazhdanskoi voiny v SSSR, 2:822. In April 1919 PUR also created a weekly journal for political workers, Politrabotnik (The political worker).

91. The preceding summary is based on the 1919 issues of Krasnoarmeets.

could see, the Red Army differed little from the tsarist army. Soldiers constantly complained of abuses. "Officers were playing out their love intrigues with elegantly dressed ladies" in first-class trains reserved for the command staff, a committee of soldiers complained to *Bednota* on 6 June 1920. Indignant letter writers demanded an end to this "bureaucratic state of affairs." The editors pleaded with soldiers to understand inequality and hardship as a temporary but inevitable injustice that was part of the scandalous heritage of backwardness left by the Russian autocracy. Trotsky warned officers and commissars that "blatant excesses in privilege" were a crime and that "the Red Army masses generally understand perfectly well where necessary privileges end and abuse of privileges begins."[92] At the same time, he continued to defend the military specialists and to transfer political workers to other posts when they interfered too much in military matters.

Further opportunities for cultural interaction were found in theatrical performances. Because so many soldiers were illiterate, political departments embraced the theater as an effective forum for enlightenment work, especially some of the experimental varieties of theater that had appeared before the Revolution, which involved audience participation. The army sponsored a whole range of theatrical and dramatic activities: traditional performances of plays by touring companies; free tickets provided by the Union of Cultural Workers (Rabis) to productions in garrison towns; amateur productions by soldiers; agitational skits (*agitki*), "live newspapers" (*zhivogazetnyi teatr*), and dramatized trials of real and fictional culprits (*agitsudy*) staged by amateur civilian and army groups in the soldiers' clubs.

The Theater Department of the Commissariat of Enlightenment (TEO) sent the first troupe to tour the front lines in the fall of 1919 with a performance of Aleksandr Vermishev's *Red Truth (Krasnaia pravda,* or *Krasnye i belye).* Vermishev was a political commissar who had recently been killed after falling into enemy hands. His play dramatized the political lessons learned by the poor peasantry during the Civil War.[93] Aleksandr Serafimovich's play *Mar'iana,* about the transformation of a peasant girl under the guidance of a Bolshevik Red Army soldier, was banned in Moscow, but it played in provincial and front-line theaters throughout the Civil War.[94] The new plays and short stories gave Red Army men and their families

92. Trotskii, "Bol'she ravenstva! Pis'mo k revvoensovetam frontov, armii i ko vsem otvetstvennym rabotnikam Krasnoi Armii i Krasnogo Flota," 31 October 1920, in *KVR,* vol. 2, pt. 1, p. 84.
93. David Zolotnitskii, *Zori teatral'nogo Oktiabria* (Leningrad, 1976), p. 340.
94. For an account of the fate of *Mar'iana* and Serafimovich's struggles with Proletkul't censors, see ibid., pp. 341–43.

leading roles in a genuine political drama. When the plays were successful, soldiers responded to familiar situations and characters in
ways that made some sense to them. Most of the playwrights were
political workers, and they passed up no opportunities to infuse
their works with topical political themes.

Another early star of the Soviet theater, Vsevolod Meyerhold, also
fell into the Whites' hands. He was captured by Denikin's counter-
intelligence agents in Novorossiisk in the summer of 1919. Upon his
release he swore to give everything he had to the victory of the Red
Army. Meyerhold, a close friend of Nikolai Podvoiskii, declared that
he would first militarize the theater and then "theatricalize" his
friend's Military Training Administration. He also helped create the
first Red Army amateur theater in the fall. The new troupe performed a proletarian mass spectacle and a contemporary comedy.[95]
With the cooperation of the Commissariat of Enlightenment, PUR ordered political departments to organize sixty amateur theaters, one
per army, and fifteen studios for instruction. Amateur theater, "in
essence proletarian theater," PUR explained, "serves as a powerful
means in the cause of raising class consciousness and developing
the cultural level of the Red Army masses."[96]

The amateur theaters organized by soldiers dramatized many of
the same themes that preoccupied the writers of letters to *Krasnoarmeets*: desertion, life in the village, women, religion, specula-
tion, and privilege. In the agitational trials they staged, soldiers split
into two camps, one for and one against the defendant. When a deserter was "tried," for example, one group of soldiers improvised
what they deemed to be a convincing argument for his motives,
while their opponents took the role of political workers and attempted to explain the official arguments against desertion. Soldiers
clearly preferred these lively debates to the dry lectures read on political themes, but on occasion the political staff lost control over
the "theater" and had to call a stop to the spontaneous activity.

95. Lunacharsky appointed Meyerhold director of Proletkul't's TEO in September
and Meyerhold set about his program of "militarization" of theater. See the biography
by Konstantin Rudnitsky, *Meyerhold the Director*, trans. George Petrov, ed. Sydney
Schultze (Ann Arbor, Mich.: Ardis, 1981), pp. 247–81; and Iurii Elagin, *Temnyi genii
(Vsevolod Meierkhol'd)*, 2d ed. (London: Overseas Publications Interchange, 1982),
pp. 220–23. The Red Army Amateur Theater was renamed RSFSR Theater No. 2 in
November. For more on the relationship between Meyerhold and Podvoiskii, see
Fevral'skii, *Zapiski rovesnika veka*, pp. 54, 288.

96. "Prikaz Revvoensoveta Respubliki o sozdanii samodeiatel'nykh krasnoarmeiskikh teatrov i studii," 20 December 1919, in *PPR* II, pp. 58–59. According to
PUR's report of its activity in 1919, by 1 October the Culture and Enlightenment Department counted 250 theaters in the army: "Iz otcheta Politupravleniia Revvoensoveta Respubliki o deiatel'nosti za 1919 g.," in *Iz istorii grazhdanskoi voiny v SSSR*,
2:821. Also in 1919 the Political Enlightenment Department of the Petrograd Military
District established a Theater of Political Dramatizations (Teatr politicheskikh instse-
nirovok).

Throughout these enlightenment activities ran a dialogue between the government, which was trying to win the loyalties of some of its key constituencies, and previously disfranchised workers and peasants, who now felt themselves empowered and demanded a large measure of accountability from a government that proclaimed itself to be of and for the workers and peasants. By the end of 1919 each side had learned techniques and rhetoric that made its claims clearer to the other. The key figure in the exchanges was the political worker, especially the *politruk*, who mediated the discussions in a variety of improvised forums: newspapers and journals, soldiers' clubs, party cells, and others. Political workers concluded after nearly two years of work in the army that soldiers did respond to efforts to reach them, but that soldiers, as complicated human beings, demanded caution and patience if those efforts were to have any lasting or, more important, immediate impact. Kiriukhin spoke for many when he entered in his diary the following mixture of optimism and challenge: "A great deal has been done, but how much more remains to do to raise the cultural, intellectual, and moral level of the Red Army masses! How much we need to work to reveal to them their class consciousness, to explain to them the aims of the struggle in which they are the major participants."[97] And Trotsky, who would later have second thoughts about the role that demobilized soldiers played in the transformation of the Revolution, promised in a speech to VTsIK that the soldiers would return home after demobilization "not quite the same as they left." They would have changed for the better, and "wherever we assign our cadets and Red Army men in the future, they will do their job."[98]

In the end, however, the ultimate test for agitation was its effectiveness in maintaining soldiers' morale and the cohesion of units. Not only Bolshevik observers credit political work with a major role in the ultimate victory of their party and state. A sober account of the contribution made by political workers to the Bolsheviks' military successes also came from a White officer, who grudgingly admitted that the role of the commissars in moving the units forward was immense. "They conduct unceasing agitation," he reported, "taking advantage of every available opportunity and exploiting even the most trivial fact to highlight the benefits that the Bolshevik regime has brought to their lives."[99] When soldiers were first mobi-

97. Kiriukhin, *Iz dnevnika*, p. 176.
98. Trotskii, "Oborona Petrograda: Doklad vo VTsIKe," 7 November 1919, in KVR, vol. 2, pt. 1, pp. 442–43.
99. Trotsky quotes from a White officer's report in "Krasnaia armiia v osveshchenii belogvardeitsa," in KVR, vol. 2, pt. 1, p. 192. See also the tribute paid to Bolshevik political workers by a prominent French commander, Bertaud Serrigny, in his *Reflexions sur l'art de guerre* (Paris: Charles-La Vauzelle, 1921), p. 150n; translated into

lized they hated the commissar, but they grew to look upon him as their intercessor and even as the defender of their interests. The White officer was willing to attribute a large part of the commissar's success to his skills as an orator, agitator, and advocate.

A Breathing Space and Civilian–Military Conflicts

By the end of 1919 Red Army forces on the Eastern Front had dealt decisive blows to Kolchak's armies between Krasnoiarsk and Irkutsk. On the Southern Front they had reoccupied the Don region and were chasing Denikin's volunteer army to the Black and Azov seas. In the north they had lifted Iudenich's siege of Petrograd. During the short breathing space of fewer than three months Sovnarkom announced a series of new peace proposals to the nations still aiding the Whites, and the Soviet Republic turned its attention to domestic affairs. The costly victories had reduced the nation to a state of economic crisis. A drastic fuel shortage compounded the desperate situation in transportation. Martial law was proclaimed on all railroads; passenger traffic was banned. Food shortages undermined the populace's health; epidemics of typhus swept through the land.

Despite determined efforts to maintain a steady channel of supplies to the front, the center was unable to isolate the army from the nationwide near-collapse. The director of the army's mobilization staff confessed that he could not guarantee delivery of more than two-thirds of the expected footstuffs for the army, and that armies and districts in grain-producing provinces should make up the shortfall on their own.[100] Even this estimate probably was overly optimistic. Clothing and medicines were in alarmingly short supply. Red Army men passed endless resolutions demanding measures to improve the situation.[101] Wherever food and clothing were scarce, disease followed. Army doctors worked round the clock to combat rashes, mange, eczema, and more serious diseases, especially typhus. During 1920, 30 percent of the Red Army contracted typhus.[102] The army had called up thousands of doctors, *fel'dshery*

Russian as *Razmyshleniia o voennom iskusstve* (Leningrad, 1924). Serrigny wrote, "The Bolsheviks were masters at the art of combining moral and military actions. . . . The results that followed were amazing and deserve a profound study."

100. "Spravka nachal'nika mobotdela mobilizatsionnogo upravleniia Vserosglavshtaba o chislennosti Krasnoi Armii, ustanovlennoi postoiannoi mezhduvedomstvennoi komissiei pri Revvoensovete Respubliki k 1 dekabria 1919 g.," 27 November 1919, in *Direktivy*, 4:112.

101. Kiriukhin, *Iz dnevnika*, pp. 166, 169.

102. *Tyl Sovetskoi Armii za 40 let* (Moscow, 1958), p. 30. According to a typical report from these months, a theater troupe of forty departed for the Southern Front on 30 October 1919; by the beginning of March, thirty-two had contracted typhus and two of that number had died: Zolotnitskii, *Zori*, p. 341.

(medics), and nurses, but medical personnel fell even faster than the soldiers themselves.[103]

The epidemics undermined unit morale and absorbed the energies of the political staff in the winter of 1919–1920. When typhus broke out in his brigade, Kiriukhin organized a "health commission, to include the regimental commissar, the supply director, and the senior doctor." The commission isolated the sick and ordered baths and the steaming of underwear for all soldiers.[104] The Defense Council created a Special All-Russian Commission for the Improvement of the Health Situation of the Republic. Mikhail Kedrov stepped down from his office as head of the Special Department of the Cheka to take charge of the new interagency administration. PUR had a permanent representative both on the central commission and in all local branches.[105] Among its important and innovative actions, the Special Commission organized a mass vaccination campaign against typhus for the military and civilian populace. After an outbreak of typhus the year before, a meeting of hygiene directors in the army had proposed a program of "sanitary enlightenment," but the suggestion went largely unheeded in the confusion of the fierce fighting and reorganization of the army's political administration. Only when the weather improved did the epidemics begin to abate.

In the temporary lull in the fighting the nation's leaders dared to hope that they might be able to begin planning for peacetime rule. The Mobilization Staff drafted a plan to demobilize a large part of the army. The still vocal proponents of the militia army seized the opportunity to renew their campaign to repudiate the decidedly unrevolutionary way in which the Red Army had been organized. Criticism of Trotsky and of the state's military policy surfaced as soon as the immediate military danger had passed. In response to the critics' persistent claims, the RVSR devised a plan for restructuring the Red Army along territorial lines. The advantage of the plan was that local communities could have more control over the military apparatus, and, in accordance with antimilitarist convictions, wars would be waged exclusively for defense.

103. Pierre Sorlin, *The Soviet People and Their Society,* trans. Daniel Weissbart (New York: Praeger, 1968), p. 78, estimates that nearly 10,000 members of the medical profession lost their lives between 1914 and 1920.

104. Kiriukhin, *Iz dnevnika,* pp. 169–70.

105. "Postanovlenie Soveta Oborony ob obrazovanii Osoboi Vserossiisskoi Komissii po uluchsheniiu sanitarnogo sostoianiia Respubliki," 8 November 1919, in *V. I. Lenin i VChK,* pp. 285–86. Another measure intended to stem the spread of disease and relieve the victims of the war was the official approval extended to a network of locally organized committees to coordinate efforts to help the wounded and sick in the army (*komitet pomoshchi ranenym i bol'nym*). The committees' work seems to have been very similar to that of the Zemgor committees during the Great War.

Comrades! Fight infection! Wipe out lice! Courtesy of Poster Collection, Hoover Institution Archives, Stanford University.

What do "health groups" do in the Red Army? Courtesy of Poster Collection, Hoover Institution Archives, Stanford University.

The politics of the transition to peacetime dominated the debates at the Ninth Party Congress in March and April 1920.[106] Trotsky, this time in person, delivered one of the keynote addresses on the transition to a militia system. While granting his critics a rhetorical concession, he in fact made the promised transition contingent upon his scheme of "labor militarization." Prominent government spokesmen, especially Trotsky, proposed that soldiers not be released to return home but be converted instead into conscripted laborers in "labor armies." They pointed to the successful experience with the Third Army, which had been put to work repairing the devastated rail network in the Urals.[107] The armies provisionally erased all status markers that distinguished workers from soldiers; furthermore, they applied military methods to traditionally civilian economic tasks by

106. The congress was attended by 554 voting delegates, including 103 from the Red Army.

107. In the spring of 1920 nearly 2.5 million soldiers fulfilled their military obligation by work in labor armies. In May 1921 the remaining labor armies—constituting about one-quarter of the Red Army—were transferred to the "economic front" and to the jurisdiction of the Commissariat of Labor.

stressing discipline and sacrifice at the expense of material incentives. Finally, Trotsky recommended the labor armies as vehicles to introduce socialist planning into the devastated economy. He recognized the high degree of bureaucratization that such a scheme would entail, but, typically, defended the militarization of labor as the only means to build socialism in a backward country.[108] Trotsky's writings on the labor armies indicate the degree to which influential statesmen had begun to look upon labor and military service as key civic obligations.

The proposals to militarize labor and to expand the experiment of the labor armies provoked opposition from many trade union leaders and the party opposition group of Democratic Centralists.[109] Vladimir Smirnov, the spokesman for the Military Opposition at the Eighth Party Congress, now led the attack on Trotsky's proposals in defense of trade union autonomy and worker's democracy. But the trade unions and Democratic Centralists were not the only centers of opposition to Trotsky's policies. Civilian bureaucracies tried to grab hold of whatever they could from the military's jurisdiction in the fluid situation of the breathing space. Both Vsevobuch, where Director Podvoiskii led the forces for transition to a genuine militia army along the lines of the prewar Social Democrats' platform, and the Commissariat of Enlightenment, whose extramural department had some role in army enlightenment programs, made claims against the broad powers and privileges of the army and its political administration.

At the Party Congress the Commissariat of Enlightenment introduced a proposal to unify all political enlightenment in the country within its own organization. The military delegates swiftly passed a resolution opposing the proposed merger and won a temporary halt to the expansionist designs of Narkompros.[110] The delegates argued that it was too early to declare the tasks of the Red Army already

108. For an exposition of Trotsky's views on the militia and labor armies, see KVR, vol. 2, pt. 1, pp. 115, 118–21; pt. 2, pp. 43–50.

109. For a discussion of the trade union opposition to labor militarization, see Robert V. Daniels, The Conscience of the Revolution: Communist Opposition in Soviet Russia (Cambridge: Harvard University Press, 1960), pp. 119–36.

110. In 1919 Lunacharsky's commissariat already had begun to battle with PUR over the boundaries that separated civilian from military programs. Lunacharsky insisted that the army needed strong civilian influences on its enlightenment programs if it were to counter the pernicious effects of traditional military settings. His long battle with PUR was an extension of the greater struggle to define civil-military relations for the new society. For example, Narkompros claimed authority over the network of "reading room-cottages" (izby-chital'ni), and in May 1919 they were nominally transferred to civilian control. Soon thereafter, however, they were returned to PUR, which held onto the rural literacy centers until the next round of battle with Narkompros in late 1920. For another version of the fight between Narkompros and PUR, see Sheila Fitzpatrick, The Commissariat of Enlightenment (New York: Cambridge University Press, 1970), pp. 243–45, 250, 252.

accomplished; on the contrary, the envisioned transition to a militia army and the formation of labor armies currently under way only complicated the work of the Political Administration, which, after all, had accumulated extensive experience during the past two years. What Narkompros was demanding in effect was the dismantling of the army's political apparatus, evoking charges of "liquidationism" from the military delegates.[111] The army's spokesmen responded defensively with a call to strengthen their own organization, beginning with the top, where the leadership changed hands too often and where no firm hand was felt to be in control.[112]

The battle was just beginning, and both the military and civilian sides defended their organizational claims with increasingly well-articulated arguments. In the course of the struggles, especially Vsevobuch and various agencies in the Commissariat of Enlightenment insisted that a standing army was incompatible with the ideals of a socialist society because it threatened to revive the militarist values of the tsarist army and the European military establishment. The moral bankruptcy of those traditional political orders had been clearly demonstrated. The major powers had still not extricated themselves from the suicidal struggles of the recent world war. The advocates of the militia alternative unceasingly reminded their military protagonists that every party resolution to date had sanctioned any transition to a regular cadre army as a strictly temporary policy dictated by the emergency conditions of the Civil War and foreign intervention. On purely practical grounds, they argued that the economic devastation of the country made the demobilization, or at least partial demobilization, of the army imperative: the nation simply could not afford to support a vast military machine.

The army's military specialists and political workers in turn argued that it was too early to think about an all-people's militia or even the decentralized version of the Red Army that some of their moderate critics advocated. With some justification they insisted that the European proponents of the militia had presumed that their more democratic form of military organization was feasible only within the context of an urbanized educated populace with a socialist political culture. Russian conditions were a far cry from any of the accepted prerequisites. On purely practical grounds, they re-

---

111. Despite the fundamentally different contexts of the debates, these charges too dated back to the prerevolutionary struggles among the Social Democrats. The Menshevik Paul Axelrod had proposed "liquidating" the underground party in 1907, interestingly, because it had become too degenerate to reform. Lenin considered the proposal outrageous and branded Axelrod's supporters thenceforth as "liquidators" and "opportunists."

112. "Rezoliutsiia soveshchaniia voennykh delegatov IX s''ezda RKP(b) ob usilenii politiko-prosvetitel'noi raboty v Krasnoi Armii i na flote," 6 April 1920, in *PPR* II, pp. 86–87.

minded their civilian counterparts that the military administration had gained valuable experience in forging relations with the nation's peasant majority and, after all, the country had withstood two years of sustained external threats thanks to the techniques and policies of the army. In other words, their successes in state building should not be dismissed so cavalierly.

Although the army's delegates argued their case with passion and won a temporary delay in the reformists' schemes, the advocates of some measure of demilitarization nevertheless were gaining strength. The Ninth Party Congress resolved to begin a very gradual transition to a militia army, while it cautioned that any change in the international situation that threatened the security of Soviet Russia would suspend the implementation of the reform. The militia army was to be organized on a territorial principle, with major units stationed in areas where large industrial work forces were concentrated. Each militia unit should have as its core tested elements of the local proletariat.[113] Significantly, however, the advocates of militarization won several victories. The congress accepted the principle of mass mobilizations of conscripted labor along the lines "by which we proceeded in the building of the Red Army." It also authorized the formation of labor armies.[114] An earlier draft of the Central Committee's theses on the mobilization of labor went much further than the final resolutions adopted. There the party leaders recommended building the system of labor conscription in accordance with the organizational principles of the Red Army and the Soviet state overall; in other words, "to provide for the less conscious and more backward peasant masses natural leaders and organizers in the persons of the most conscious proletarians, the overwhelming majority of whom would be professional skilled workers." The army was, the theses continued, the most important experiment in mass Soviet organization; its methods ought to be transferred to the sphere of labor conscription, admittedly with all necessary adjustments.[115] From the center's perspective, the proletarian dictatorship's fundamental charge was to mobilize the nation's human resources for economic and military tasks. Indeed, in recognition of the primacy of these mobilization tasks, the streamlined inner cabinet of Lenin's government took the name Council on Labor and De-

113. "O perekhode k militsionnoi sisteme," in Deviatyi s''ezd RKP(b), mart-aprel' 1920 goda: Protokoly (Moscow, 1960), pp. 428–30. See Trotsky's report to the congress, pp. 384–96.
114. Deviatyi s''ezd, p. 407.
115. "Tezisy TsK RKP o mobilizatsii industrial'nogo proletariata, trudovoi povinnosti, militarizatsii khoziaistva i primenenii voinskikh chastei dlia khoziaistvennykh nuzhd," in ibid., pp. 556–57. For another, even more enthusiastic endorsement of these principles, see Trotsky's theses, pp. 533–38.

fense (STO) in April 1920, replacing the Council of Worker and Peasant Defense that had been formed in November 1918 in response to the fall emergencies.[116]

The Final Struggle

The army was saved from the schemes of its enemies by an invasion from Poland in late April 1920. The Polish army amassed forces totaling 738,000 men and, together with the guerrilla forces of the Ukrainian hetman Simon Petliura, struck on the Red Army's southwestern front. The exhausted Soviet leadership once again called its citizens to postpone their peacetime plans and direct all their efforts to the struggle for national independence. A mobilization order went out to men born in 1901; the recruitment drive proceeded in a relatively organized fashion and yielded more than 300,000 troops.[117] Several labor armies were reconverted to regular combat status; the party mobilized 4,600 executive personnel and the Komsomol and trade unions several thousand members; and armies and political workers were transferred from other fronts and the rear to the Western Front. The Defense Council and the party's Central Committee organized endless "weeks for aid to the front," aid to wounded Red Army men, weeks of the Red soldier, more sign-ups of volunteers, collections of winter clothing, and yet another mobilization of medical personnel.[118]

Just as the Red Army was beginning a successful offensive against Poland, General Petr Wrangel attacked from the south and reoccupied the northern Tauride with the remaining forces of the Volunteer Army. Though the renewal of a two-front war strained the resources of the Red Army, by the end of July Soviet forces were advancing on Warsaw. Within weeks, however, they were retreating in the face of a Polish counterattack. In October Poland agreed to a cease-fire and began peace negotiations. With the end of hostilities

116. The Council on Labor and Defense included the commissars of the army, labor, communication and transportation, agriculture, food, and worker-peasant inspection; the chairman of the Supreme Economic Council; and one representative of the National Trade Union Council.

117. In addition, a second call-up for several age cohorts brought more than a million men into the ranks: Direktivy, 4:278–79. By the end of the Civil War, the Red Army stood at 5,317,159, including more than 4 million peasants: ibid., p. 227.

118. Among others, see "Vozzvanie TsK RKP(b) i VTsSPS ko vsem partiinym, komsomol'skim i profsoiuznym organizatsiiam ob okazanii pomoshchi bol'nym i ranenym krasnoarmeitsam," not earlier than 25 April 1920, pp. 174–75; "Postanovleniia Soveta Truda i Oborony," 30 April 1920, pp. 179–80; "Postanovlenie Soveta Narodnykh Komissarov ob okazanii narkomatami pomoshchi Zapadnomu frontu," 4 May 1920, pp. 183–84; "Dekret VTsIK 'O merakh bor'by s pol'skim nastupleniem,' " 11 May 1920, pp. 119–20; "Tezisy TsK RKP(b) 'Pol'skii front i nashi zadachi,' " 23 May 1920, pp. 200–203; all in Iz istorii grazhdanskoi voiny v SSSR, vol. 3.

on the Western Front, attention was shifted to a counteroffensive in the south. After only a few weeks of fierce fighting, Wrangel evacuated his forces from the Crimea.

During the summer and fall of 1920 the campaigns gave the army and its political apparatus a new lease on life. PUR's highest-ranking officials were sent to the Southern and Southwestern fronts, leaving the direction of the political campaigns to local military authorities. By this time, however, the local political departments had a familiar routine. Still, the absence of influential spokesmen for PUR left the army without any adequate political defense from the leaders of hostile civilian organizations, who did not give up their recently won concessions without a fight. In the struggle over resources and personnel, military and civilian agencies frequently came to blows. Also because the fighting had less of a sense of emergency in 1920 than it had had a year earlier, tensions that had been evident before the Polish invasion refused to go away.

At the Ninth Party Conference, in September 1920, the army again came under attack for its privileged status in governmental considerations. Delegates complained that the constant campaigns to aid the army drained them of resources and that military officials had no sympathy for their difficulties. They protested against the frequent transfers that the central party agencies ordered. More pointedly they criticized the institution of the political department because, they claimed, it splintered party work and created a separate party life in the army. A senior member of PUR, Sergei Anuchin, described the fundamental principles underlying the organization of political departments and defended them as essential for the conduct of party and political work in the army. While he admitted that political departments could be more effective if they had a more standardized form and if they were more subordinate to the center, he rejected the proposition that radically new organizational schemes were needed. In response to the criticism, however, PUR's spokesmen promised to convene regular assemblies of senior political workers to keep better track of the activities of its local agencies.[119]

Podvoiskii, as head of Vsevobuch, continued his struggle to persuade his fellow political leaders to be true to their socialist ideals and abandon Trotsky's regular cadre army in favor of one closer to the militia ideal that his Universal Military Training Administration advocated. Since the Ninth Congress had committed the nation to a gradual transition to a militia, Podvoiskii saw himself as the creator

---

119. "Iz doklada chlena revvoensoveta IX armii S. A. Anuchina na soveshchanii voennykh predstavitelei na IX Vserossiiskoi partiinoi konferentsii o merakh po dal' neishemu usovershenstvovaniiu partiino-politicheskogo apparata v Krasnoi armii," 26 September 1920, in PPR II, pp. 95–101.

of the new army. His hegemonic ambitions grew in proportion to his sense that the war was winding down. Much like the Red Army's leaders themselves, Podvoiskii saw a great threat to his plans in the persistent power of local civilian party committees, which already had a network of territorial formations in the special assignment detachments (*chony*). The army's Political Administration found itself an unexpected ally in its own struggle with the civilian party organizations when Podvoiskii demanded that the local committees surrender their armed forces to his organization. In September the Central Committee acceded to Podvoiskii's demands and ordered local party committees to transfer the authority of their detachments to Vsevobuch. The Central Committee defended its measures as an attempt to reduce unnecessary parallelism and pointed to the success of Vsevobuch during the Civil War in upholding the principles of the militia army.[120] In decreeing the merger of the special units with Vsevobuch's administration, the center made Podvoiskii an ever more formidable contender in the postwar settlement of the struggle over the military. Podvoiskii's new strength, however, remained largely on paper for the moment because local party committees were no more eager to turn over their powers to his organization than they had been to surrender their authority to the Red Army.

The army's political leadership was also attacked from within its own ranks. The charges of the military critics resembled those made in the civilian organizations by various opposition groups, especially the Democratic Centralists, and can be summarized as resentment against the privileges accumulated by a new Soviet elite. Rank-and-file soldiers joined with lower-level political workers in charging their superiors with "bureaucratism" and being "out of touch with the masses." The military specialists were still distrusted by many in the army, but disgruntled Red Army men also complained that too many petit bourgeois elements had crept into positions of authority, or that Jews or Latvians failed to treat native Russians and Ukrainians with appropriate tact. The party discussed the conflict as the problem of "the upper and lower strata" (*verkhi i nizy*).[121]

The Ninth Party Conference passed resolutions to attack the problems from several angles. The delegates critical of the army's mode of operating won assurances that the party's leaders would reverse the trends that were creating a party organization in the army whose style was distinct from that of the party in general. The Central

120. "Vsem gubkomam RKP(b)," 23 September 1920, in *KPSS o vooruzhennykh silakh* (1981), pp. 147–48.
121. See also the discussion in an earlier section of this chapter, "Soldiers' Culture and Political Work," for details on the specific charges that soldiers brought against their superiors and against party members.

Committee, by means of its Orgburo and Secretariat, would keep closer watch over party matters in the army and convene regular meetings of executive personnel to hear their reports. The conference demanded that the reregistration campaigns be undertaken more carefully than they had been to date, as delegates complained that workers and peasants were being discriminated against, and that a control commission be created with local affiliates as a permanent review board for all members. The local control commissions had the authority to investigate any complaint originating from party members and to take disciplinary actions against those deemed guilty after the investigation. Furthermore, all executive political workers were ordered to spend as much time as possible among Red Army men and not to contrive excuses to avoid such contact. Party cells should meet regularly and political workers must attend the meetings. In what was a victory for the various oppositions that emerged within the party, political workers were ordered to stop transferring party members out of their units for expressing dissident views.

The conference acknowledged that the army had been operating in ways that earned it the legitimate resentment of the working class, especially in its arbitrary seizure of living quarters without concern for the displaced inhabitants. Provincial party committees were empowered to conduct surveys of local housing and to reach agreement with the military authorities on evacuating all nonessential living space for the civilian population. The center promised to limit its campaigns of "weeks" and "days" so as not to drain local organizations entirely. Finally, the Central Committee promised that by its next conference or congress it would propose a plan for "the unification of all party work" and put an end to the tension-ridden splintering of decision making between civilian and military authorities.[122] Together with the commitment to make Vsevobuch responsible for the creation of the new militia army, this final plan for the unification of all party work posed the greatest potential threat to the Political Administration in the army. The party opened itself up to a fierce struggle between its military and civilian organizations. That struggle was just around the corner.

The military defeat of the White armies marked the Bolshevik victory in the Civil War. Certainly the Bolshevik's good fortune in occupying the working-class stronghold of the Central Industrial

---

122. "Ob ocherednykh zadachakh partiinogo stroitel'stva," in *Deviataia konferentsiia RKP(b), sentiabr' 1920 goda: Protokoly* (Moscow, 1972), pp. 276–82. The future evolution of the party's organization was the major topic of discussion at the conference. Delegates representing military agencies played a large role in these formative debates. See, e.g., the testimony by Khataevich, Degtiarev, Khodorovskii, Stalin, Poluian, Minin, and Smirnov.

Region, the Russian heartland and communication nexus of the former empire, was critical to their success. By contrast, the Whites' base was in the borderlands and on the peripheries, where they antagonized non-Russian populations with their nationalist politics and were forced to rely on foreign suppliers for their arms. Foreign governments' support for the Whites was more helpful to the Bolsheviks, who portrayed the Soviet leadership as leaders of a national liberation struggle against foreign imperialists than to the Whites, who failed to secure any lasting military advantage from it.[123] The military victory, however, was equally a political triumph, for what most distinguished the Reds from the Whites was their approach to civil-military relations. The Bolsheviks understood far better than their protagonists the political aspects of civil war and adapted available organizations and techniques to those peculiar circumstances. In the Red Army the commissars and revolutionary military councils guaranteed the Communist Party a relatively large measure of control over the military professionals who served the dictatorship of the proletariat. Trotsky, the ruthless chairman of the Revolutionary Military Council, antagonized both military professionals and political officers, but ensured that both groups executed the will of the Moscow leadership, even when the center's control was far less than historians have claimed. The commissars and their extensive political staffs set up civilian administrations in recaptured territory, often employing former imperial civil servants, but in new institutions, most notably the network of soviets and *revkomy*, which bore the stamp of revolutionary legitimacy. The Whites' military men had undisputed power over the civilian politicians who chased after their mobile headquarters. With virtually no civilian influence over the military's activities, the White military campaign deteriorated into warlordism, accompanied by arbitrary terror, looting, and brigandage.[124] When civilians had some say in White politics, they appealed to anachronistic slogans and resurrected discredited institutions, such as the dumas and zemstvos.[125] Of course, the Bolsheviks too employed coercion, unashamedly so under the slogan of Red Terror, but their coercive organs, however merciless, acted in more predictable, less random ways; consequently, their violence alienated the populace less than did the Whites'. In the Civil War, such relative advantages were decisive. Moreover, the

123. For a comprehensive summary of the factors contributing to the Bolsheviks' victory in the Civil War, see Evan Mawdsley, *The Russian Civil War* (Boston: Allen & Unwin, 1987), pp. 272–90.

124. See the memoirs of Anton Denikin, *Ocherki Russkoi Smuty* (Paris, n.d.), 5: 154, 261n, 294.

125. See William G. Rosenberg, "The Zemstvo in 1917 and under Bolshevik Rule," in *The Zemstvo in Russia*, ed. Terence Emmons and Wayne S. Vucinich, pp. 410–16 (Cambridge: Cambridge University Press, 1982).

Bolsheviks appealed to formerly disfranchised social groups with blatantly discriminatory policies against members of the old imperial elites and in favor of workers, soldiers, and peasants, who moved into positions of authority for the first time in their lives. The Whites' social base remained confined to the property-owning minority (tsenzovoe obshchestvo); their civilian politicians occupied the nationalist right and center of the Russian political spectrum. Finally, the Bolsheviks learned the advantages of wartime propaganda very early in the Civil War. Here too their understanding of the conflict as a political as well as a military campaign set them apart from the military men who headed the White movement, who disdained most forms of mass political activity and had little use for the members of the moderate socialist parties who reluctantly volunteered their services to them. Finally, programs of political enlightenment in the Red Army served as testing grounds for the propaganda campaigns aimed at a broader civilian audience. Though the Bolsheviks' promises were vague and utopian, the new Soviet citizens derived some measure of psychological satisfaction from them.

During the years of the Civil War the Bolsheviks proved far better at state building than their enemies; through a combination of terror, promises, and the creation of a new political elite, they achieved a "primitive accumulation of legitimacy"[126] that eluded the Whites. In a period when political authority was transferred from one elite to another, still inchoate elite, military skills alone were inadequate to win ultimate victory over the enemy. The White movement never became much more than its armies. By contrast, the Red Army, in addition to fulfilling more traditional military roles, helped to build the new state order.

126. I borrow this phrase from Alfred G. Meyer, "The Functions of Ideology in the Soviet Political System," Soviet Studies 17 (January 1966): 279.

CHAPTER 3

From War to Peace,
November 1920–December 1922

*Except for the period of the Brest negotiations, it is unlikely that our army
was ever again as weak, in spite of its large numbers, as it was in 1921.*
—Lev Degtiarev, 1924

The Dilemmas of Demobilization

The defeat of Wrangel's forces in November 1920 opened a new
era for the Red Army, though hostilities continued well into 1922.
The major White armies were on the retreat everywhere and foreign
aid to the opposition forces had dried up. Even before Wrangel's
armies had fled the Crimea, the party's Central Committee appointed a commission to study possible cuts in the Red Army's
numbers.[1] The study commission recommended substantial immediate cuts to a second commission that was appointed to organize
the demobilization itself. At its largest the Red Army numbered
nearly 5 million men in the fall of 1920. The Defense Council (STO)
hoped to have half the soldiers home in time for spring sowing in
1921, "if the international situation and the transport system allowed." In October 1921 a Central Committee plenum further reduced the size of the army to 1.5 million.[2] The army's propaganda
cautioned Soviet citizens that the current apparent peace was only
temporary because world capitalism could not tolerate the existence
of the Soviet state much longer. The themes of capitalist encirclement and the isolation of a vulnerable and besieged Soviet Republic
gradually became the focus of all discussions of the "international

1. The commission was headed by Field Staff Director Aleksandr Samoilo and
included Feliks Dzerzhinsky and Deputy Army Commissar Efraim Sklianskii. For a
discussion of the study and early demobilization plans, see Oleg F. Suvenirov, *Kommunisticheskaia partiia—organizator politicheskogo vospitaniia Krasnoi Armii i
Flota, 1921–1928* (Moscow, 1976), pp. 48–49.
2. Ibid.

Comrades, to work! (demobilization poster). Courtesy of Poster Collection, Hoover Institution Archives, Stanford University.

question," as party and state spokesmen referred to the foreign policy component of their political analyses. Still, the economic devastation wrought by the years of war was straining the state's relations with workers, soldiers, and, above all, peasants. The nation could not afford a large standing army; consequently, the Eighth Congress of Soviets, which met in December 1920, resolved to free the republic from the crippling expense of maintaining the large Civil War army without jeopardizing the defense of the nation against those enemies who continued to threaten it. Because every diplomatic crisis provoked fears of a new intervention, however, the congress urged all local organs of Soviet power to ensure that the army receive all necessary aid and attention during its partial demobilization.[3]

The demobilization triggered new crises and threatened the very fragile hold the proletarian dictatorship had on its populace. Despite the strict schedule for demobilization, this first peacetime test caught the government unprepared. Train pile-ups in the center stranded demobilizing troops during the bitter cold of December and January. Excessive red tape, coupled with the indifference of station officials, so fueled resentment among the troops that commissars feared even to try to calm them down. By mid-February the transportation network had so deteriorated that the Central Committee recommended that the RVSR authorize units in Petrograd and Moscow to leave on foot.[4] Units began to demobilize themselves. Troops refused their sanitary processing before release and spread disease along the way home. Soap and linens were in short supply. To make matters worse, overzealous food detachments tried to seize the rations that the soldiers were permitted to take home with them.

The economic collapse and the chaotic demobilization created a situation that was neither war nor genuine peace. The army reported 170,000 battle casualties in 1921.[5] Soldiers returned to pillaged homes and farms, and many could not find employment. Tens of thousands of men joined the remnants of partisan bands and roaming marauders who fed on the seething discontent left by the years of deprivation. Armed insurrection swept Tambov and Orel provinces, the Ukraine, Turkestan, the Crimea, the Caucasus, the entire Western Front, the Chinese border, and Mongolia. In the confusion of the demobilization, the army often proved useless in combating "banditry," as the party called the domestic uprisings.[6] Morale deterio-

---

3. "Pravitel'stvennoe soobshchenie o sokrashchenii armii (utverzhdeno VIII s''ezdom Sovetov)," in *S''ezdy sovetov Soiuza SSR*, 1:156–58. The RVSR decreed the release of all soldiers and sailors according to a strict schedule: first all men aged thirty-five and older, then men aged thirty-two to thirty-four, followed by the next three age groups. The center would then study the feasibility of further cuts, but hoped to be able to release even twenty-five-year-olds beginning in late spring 1921.

4. Suvenirov, *Kommunisticheskaia partiia*, p. 38n, citing Central Party Archives at the Institute of Marxism-Leninism.

5. *Narodnoe khoziaistvo Soiuza SSR v tsifrakh: Statisticheskii spravochnik* (Moscow, 1925), p. 11, cited in ibid., p. 50. Even in 1922, the Red Army reported 21,000 combat losses.

6. S. Olikov, in his exhaustive study of desertion, distinguishes among various forms of collective peasant behavior. Mass banditry he defines as "an elemental protest of the not very conscious masses against authority. Mass banditry in the Civil

rated and regular army units went over to the enemy's side.[7] The Cheka's Special Department formed a new section for "the direction of the struggle with political banditry." In many regions Cheka forces were the only reliable military or quasi-military organizations available to combat the rebels.

Army units could not be relied on in part because life was harsh for the soldiers who remained on duty. Indeed, soldiers mutinied across the country in protest against the intolerable conditions in which they lived by the end of the war.[8] The army faced a dramatic reversal in its fate as the party turned its attention from military priorities to the "economic front." No longer were the needs of the army at the center of the regime's attention. The rapid shift in fortunes affected all aspects of the army's organization. During the first twenty days of demobilization the army fell from second to sixth place in priority for food rationing. (Workers in the defense industry were first.) In May the rations of all basic foodstuffs were cut for front-line troops. Political departments received instructions to prepare explanations for the cutbacks before "certain elements try to use the reductions for their own low-minded and sinister agitation among the tired, unconscious Red Army men."[9] Both regular soldiers and the command staff began to "starve and feel the shortage in consumer and domestic goods" when a lack of funds shut down the Central Administration of Red Army Shops.[10]

Once the army lost its privileged position, it became less immune to the hardships that plagued the rest of the country. The fuel shortage left barracks cold. No repairs could be afforded. A reporter complained that the barracks had become "uninhabitable accommodations, cold and dirty, where a man becomes wild, dull-witted, and embittered."[11] Chronically underfed soldiers suffered prolonged

---

War was a simple protest against war. It was a product of mass desertion, began with it, and ended with it." A second category of banditry was outright criminal behavior. Finally, Olikov identifies "partisan" or "principled" (*ideinyi*) banditry, which "exploited mass banditry as a reserve, albeit for a short while": Olikov, *Dezertirstvo*, p. 69. Even Olikov confuses the categories of partisans and bandits in this definition, but the important thing is that he recognizes the phenomenon as a type of political protest, albeit "not very conscious," against policies of the Soviet regime or the army.

7. See the Central Committee's coded telegram sent to all provincial committees in March 1921, cited in *V. I. Lenin i VChK*, p. 435n.

8. See the memoirs of Anastas Mikoyan, who was sent to Nizhnii Novgorod in November 1920 to combat mutinous soldiers and party oppositionists, *V nachale dvadtsatykh* . . . (Moscow, 1975), pp. 34–44.

9. "Ob agitatsionnoi rabote v sviazi s sokrashcheniem paika," in *Tsirkuliary i instruktsii Politupravleniia Turkestanskogo Fronta* (Tashkent, 1921), p. 11.

10. I. P. Tishchenko, *Istoriia organizatsii i praktiki voennoi kooperatsii Sibiri* (Novonikolaevsk, 1922), pp. 5–6.

11. *Krasnoarmeets* 33–35 (1921): 44.

bouts of typhus, scurvy, and night blindness. In many units sick soldiers far outnumbered the wounded.[12]

Civilian organizations simply left the army to fend for itself, perhaps, in some cases, exacting revenge for the army's abusive treatment of them in the recent past. "Even considering our devastation, our poverty, the shortages of everything," charged a bitter official in PUR, "still it must be said that in this case the Red Army soldier was not shown the attention he deserved."[13] The Central Committee reminded party organizations that they were still obliged to see to the needs of the military. Demobilization did not mean that the army was being dismantled entirely.[14]

At the very time when the army most needed competent and experienced personnel to bring the nightmarish situation under control, it found itself desperately short of political workers. Even before the general demobilization had been announced, PUR and the Central Committee responded to the anxious demands of party and state organs for cadres.[15] Within weeks, political departments found themselves stripped bare of commissars and politruki. In mid-February the center ordered a halt to the demobilization of Communists and denied all requests for leaves, but the center proved powerless to reverse the flow. Again in May the directors of political departments demanded the return to the army of illegally demobilized Communists. "Such a situation," warned the officials, "threatens to thoroughly disrupt political work in the Red Army."

It was strange for political workers to conclude that conditions could actually be worse than they had been during the Civil War, but many in fact began to recall the recent past with nostalgia and itched for a new fight. Instead of throwing themselves into the heat of battle, now political departments devoted most of their time to "stopping up economic holes," one commissar reported. "Teaching and political education were, for the most part, conducted formally, rather than in substance. We literally lost heart." Many political

12. Rezoliutsii partkonferentsii chastei Petrukraiona i spetschastei P.V.O. proiskhodivshei s 15–18 dek. 1921 g. (Petrograd, 1922), p. 7; see also Voennoe znanie 11–12 (1921): 32; A. S. Kulish-Amirkhanova, Rol' Krasnoi Armii v khoziaistvennom i kul'turnom stroitel'stve v Dagestane (1920–1923 gg.) (Makhachkala, 1964), p. 88.

13. N. Gorlov, "Agitatsiia sredi otpusknikov," Politrabotnik 2 (1921): 3. Lenin admitted to the Tenth Party Congress that the Central Committee had erred in not taking into account the difficulties associated with the demobilization: PSS, 43:9–10. See also the speech by G. I. Mashatov, a military delegate to the Tenth Congress, in Desiatyi s"ezd RKP(b), mart 1921 goda: Stenograficheskii otchet (Moscow, 1963), p. 303.

14. "O Krasnoi Armii," 12 January 1921, in KPSS o vooruzhennykh silakh Sovetskogo Soiuza: Dokumenty, 1917–1981 (Moscow, 1981), pp. 153–54.

15. From November 1920 to 15 February 1921 the Central Committee returned 2,082 executive personnel to civilian work. PUR released 385 Communists. For a breakdown of the transfers, see A. Iurkov, Ekonomicheskaia politika partii v derevne, 1917–1920 (Moscow, 1980), p. 157.

workers wanted out of the army because they could see no important role for them in peacetime. They asked, "Why are we here? What are we going to do—twiddle our thumbs?"[16]

The Army under Siege

Political workers' sense that they lacked any prospects (which they referred to as *besperspektivnost'*) had its roots in the regime's uncertainty about the future of the army as an institution. The expected political assault on the army—both from its civilian critics and within its own ranks—materialized as soon as the major fighting abated. Both the Ninth Party Conference and the Eighth Congress of Soviets committed the republic to the creation of a militia army without resolving the issue of what to do with the existing Red Army. If the army's future were up for grabs, so was the fate of its Political Administration, which symbolized a distinctive party "style" that a large sector of the civilian organization had come to loathe. An army inspector confessed that "civilian organizations look upon us as an invasion of Huns or barbarians."[17] Rather than attack the army directly, its critics could attack PUR and be certain of powerful support.

The Commissariat of Enlightenment signaled the start of a new fight when, in November 1920, it stepped up its campaign to unify all political work in its hands by forming a new Main Political Enlightenment Committee (Glavpolitprosvet), headed by Lenin's wife, Nadezhda Krupskaia, and subordinated directly to the party's Central Committee. Lunacharsky received the party's imprimatur for Glavpolitprosvet to direct all work tied to literacy campaigns, schools and courses for adults, reading room–cottages, clubs, libraries, agitational trains and ships, and all soviet and party schools. If Glavpolitprosvet succeeded in gaining control over all these activities, it would cut significantly into the army's powers.

The army's political workers had won a delay in April 1920 when the Ninth Party Congress considered transferring all educational activities to the extramural department of the Commissariat of Enlightenment. The Polish campaign and Wrangel's last offensive also temporarily checked the commissariat's ambitions, but now the situation was different. The war was over, Glavpolitprosvet had the Central Committee's authority behind it, and PUR was undergoing its own political turmoil.

16. "M. V. Frunze na Ukraine," *Sputnik politrabotnika* (hereafter SP) 27–28 (1925): 35.

17. "Politinspektsiia PURUkrkryma v Kh. V. O.," *Put' politrabotnika* 8 (1921): 60.

In December 1920 at their second national assembly, political workers in the army hammered out a defense of their position and took measures they hoped would guarantee their security in the face of increasing threats from the army's critics. For most of the meeting,

Sergei Gusev, director, Political Administration of the Revolutionary Military Council of the Republic (PUR), 1921–1922. From S. I. Gusev, *Grazhdanskaia voina i Krasnaia Armiia: Sbornik statei* (Moscow, 1958).

the delegates excoriated their director, Ivar Smilga, for his lack of leadership and for his failure to defend their interests in conflicts with civilian authorities. They demanded a thorough overhaul of the organization and a reduction in the size of the central apparatus. To improve the quality of the central apparatus, they recommended promoting personnel from within the ranks of the political departments to central positions.[18]

Smilga conceded that PUR had of late been "dying out," but he blamed the Central Committee for failing to give him the support he needed to hold on to reliable assistants. Though he had been appointed director of PUR in April 1919, he claimed that he had held that post in fact for only a little more than a month because he was sent to one front after another as a member of revolutionary councils and even as a front-line commander. In his absence assistant directors filled in for him, and as soon as an assistant director proved his mettle, he too was sent off to the front.[19] Two weeks after he heard the devastating critique of his directorship, Smilga was replaced by Sergei Gusev.[20]

On the second issue discussed at the assembly, the future of the militia army, the leadership once again found common ground with the political workers and, ironically, also with the military specialists. Smilga delivered a bristling attack on Trotsky's latest schemes for a militia army. Trotsky's reversal on the militia—recently he had argued that conditions were premature for a transition—took many commanders and commissars by surprise. Smilga's arguments restated the objections that every party and soviet meeting had raised, but whereas earlier resolutions had always spoken of the military emergency dictating a temporary compromise with the principles of a militia army, Smilga claimed that the experience of the Civil War had demonstrated that a very long time would elapse before conditions were suitable for abandoning the regular army. The major shortcoming was Russia's backwardness, meaning the preponderance of small-scale peasant agriculture in the nation's economy, and all the political consequences that flowed from that fact. The militia army could not guarantee "proletarian hegemony" in the military. "Militia forces can be bought only at the price of losing the fundamental principles of the dictatorship of the working class in the army," he declared. His opposition to the militia was vindicated not only by the Red Army's experience with units formed primarily of peasants who were natives of the territory where the fighting was taking place, but in all other armies, including those of the

18. "Rezoliutsiia 2-go Vserossiiskogo soveshchaniia politrabotnikov Krasnoi Armii i Flota po dokladu o rabote Politupravleniia Respubliki," 21 December 1920, *Politrabotnik* 1 (1921): 17–18. Smilga's report, "Otchet o deiatel'nosti Politupravleniia Respubliki za 1920 g.," 19 December 1920, appeared in the same issue, pp. 2–5.

19. *Politrabotnik* 2 (1921): 1, 32.

20. Smilga had been Trotsky's candidate for the post in April 1919, but subsequently came to blows with him over many military decisions. Gusev, however, was appointed to replace Smilga over Trotsky's objection.

Whites.[21] Finally, Smilga argued that in time of war, Russia's rail network would hinder the rapid mobilization of an army that was territorially organized.

The future director of PUR, Sergei Gusev, shared Smilga's opposition to the militia plan. He too raised the "peasant question" as the major objection to a premature abandonment of the regular Red Army. He contended that the militia army could well become "the organized armed form for the petit bourgeois and anarchist counter-revolution."[22] The army's current campaigns against "banditry" around the country gave persuasive evidence of the fragility of the regime's support in the countryside. Besides, Gusev argued a militia army was suitable only for a defensive war. In the recent Polish campaign, when the prospect of bringing the Revolution to the Polish proletariat on the bayonets of the Red Army seemed likely, a large number of influential commanders, including Mikhail Tukhachevsky, favored a very active role for the new army. If the revolutionary regime looked forward to promoting revolution abroad, then a militia army was entirely inappropriate.

The delegates who heard these addresses affirmed the leadership of PUR in its wholehearted opposition to any transition to a militia army. On the basis of their recent experience in the Civil War, the political workers declared that "in a peasant Russia the implementation of a militia system for the entire country would meet with insurmountable political and strategic difficulties." A militia system would deliver the army into the hands of the peasantry, and in the event of war would doom the country to military defeat because of the poorly developed rail network. They advocated instead "a permanent army, not necessarily large, but well trained in the military sense and politically prepared, made up of young age groups." The delegates repeated the by now ritual insistence that the barracks become a military and political school for young citizens, and, accordingly, that the miserable condition of the existing barracks be rectified immediately. Finally, if the nation were to experiment with a militia system, the formation of new units should not be entrusted to Vsevobuch, but should be left in the hands of the army itself. According to the delegates, the appropriate role for Vsevobuch was to direct pre-induction training and sports activities for toilers.[23]

Once they had formulated a position on the future of the army and their political administration, the delegates turned to the major threat from outside, Glavpolitprosvet. They conceded that with the

21. "Rech' tov. Smilga," *Politrabotnik* 1 (1921): 10–11.

22. Gusev, *Uroki grazhdanskoi voiny*, pp. 15, 34.

23. "Rezoliutsii 2 Vserossiiskogo soveshchaniia politrabotnikov Krasnoi Armii i Flota," 21 December 1920, in *Vsearmeiskie soveshchaniia politrabotnikov, 1918–1940 (rezoliutsii)* (Moscow, 1984), pp. 31–32.

end of the war a period in the history of the Russian Revolution and
Red Army had also come to an end. Clearly the economic tasks facing the country demanded a shift in society's attention away from
the tremendous privileges the army had grown accustomed to. But it
was precisely at this time, in conditions of peace, that the Red Army
finally had an opportunity to bring order to its own house, and
therefore the Red Army "should be able to meet the difficulties that
lie ahead not in a weaker condition, but ten times stronger and more
powerful than before." The political workers certainly were sensitive
to the criticisms of their organization, and sought to reassure their
critics that they would remedy the admitted ills. They defended the
military system of political control as one inextricably tied to the
effectiveness of command and administration. The delegates conceded that many of the organs now within the military's jurisdiction
should be transferred to civilian control and that some of the army's
cultural and educational activities (the military publishing house,
library buildings, and museum and film organizations, for instance)
might even more appropriately be handed over to the Commissariat
of Enlightenment; however, in no circumstances should PUR be
dismantled, nor should it be excluded from the work of Glavpolitprosvet. PUR should maintain the right to direct any work that Glavpolitprosvet might undertake in the army in the future.[24]

The consensus that the delegates were able to reach testifies to a
set of common attitudes and approaches that were forged on the basis of similar experiences in the recent war. For a large group of
commanders, commissars, and political workers, the army was their
fundamental identification with the new regime and with the Revolution. They were accustomed to an army with political controls
from the Communist Party and to practices that gave more power to
soldiers to intervene in army politics than had been characteristic of
the tsarist army, but they had also grown accustomed to many features of the Red Army that were characteristic of all modern
armies—an appointed officer corps, strict discipline with punishments for infractions, and obligatory service. Gusev, when he reflected on the lessons that other revolutionary parties might have
learned from the Russian Civil War, summarized the chastened view
of a man who once wrote eloquently about the democratic potential
of a militia army but had since changed his mind:

> The issues of voluntarism, of the elective principle and of voluntary
> discipline all in essence boil down to the question: Is the proletariat
> disciplined and conscious enough on the day after the "social revolu-
> tion," after the seizure of power, to show up at the first call in the
> ranks of the army without any external compulsion and to implicitly

24. "Rezoliutsii 2 Vserossiiskogo," in ibid., pp. 32–33.

obey all commands and to elect not those commanders who will indulge all their weaknesses, but those who will wage an unrelenting
and harsh struggle against those weaknesses which undermine combat
readiness of the army? The answer to this question is clear: even in
countries with a conscious and disciplined proletariat, only a small
minority will satisfy these requirements.[25]

Gusev nevertheless assured European revolutionaries that they
would probably be able to spare themselves the vast commitment
that the Red Army had had to make in political education because
European conditions were better than Russian ones. "It is entirely
possible," he explained, "that the tremendous scale of political work
in the Red Army is a Russian peculiarity."[26] Gusev was referring
again to the peasant problem. The delegates to the December assembly shared Gusev's commitment to the peculiar hybrid form of army
that emerged from the first three years of revolutionary improvisation under fire. The real test of their political clout in the party was
just ahead at the Tenth Party Congress, scheduled for the beginning
of February and delayed until March 6.

The Tenth Party Congress

In anticipation of the congress's discussion of a whole series of
issues directly affecting the army, the interested parties began to
make public statements of their positions. Local party meetings
elected delegates to the congress and voted on the agenda fixed by
the party's Central Committee.[27] Podvoiskii drafted a proposal for a
"resolution on the question of the reorganization of the armed forces
of the Republic." As he had done earlier, Podvoiskii defended the
militia as the only genuinely socialist form of military organization
because only a militia gave the party "the opportunity to involve
the masses in the creation of the army." The current system of organization had proven itself a complete failure in the areas of troop
preparedness and political education, he said. Of course, his organization, Vsevobuch, had a better record. It had managed to instruct 5
million citizens without resort to harsh discipline and had a more
extensive and enlightened training program, which included physical education and cultural activities.[28]

25. Gusev, *Uroki grazhdanskoi voiny*, p. 18. Trotsky makes a similar statement in
his introduction to KVR, 1:8–9.
26. Gusev, *Uroki grazhdanskoi voiny*, p. 42.
27. See Gusev's instruction, dated 19 February 1921, to all political departments
about the congress's agenda and the procedures for electing delegates: Suvenirov, *Kommunisticheskaia partiia*, p. 67.
28. "Rech' tov. Podvoiskogo," *Politrabotnik* 1 (1921): 12–13.

Trotsky seconded Podvoiskii's resolution favoring a transition to
the militia system in an address titled "The Involvement of the
Masses in the Creation of the Army." Trotsky still entertained hopes
that the territorial militia would be the vehicle for his pet project of
"labor militarization," which had been inspired by the labor armies
at the beginning of 1920. A year later, however, enthusiasm for the
labor armies had dwindled. Nevertheless, Trotsky proposed the immediate creation of experimental militia units in three military districts.

Smilga restated his opposition to any form of militia as premature,
and he advised the army's political workers to temper their criticism
of their own organization because "it would be a crime to conceal
the fact that the army has come upon difficult times" and that there
are "comrades who would like nothing better than to take apart the
entire military administration."[29] The Moscow Party Committee
adopted Smilga's theses, arguing that as long as capitalist countries
existed, the RSFSR could not consider itself safe and therefore must
maintain a permanent army. Vsevobuch should be entrusted only
with pre-induction training and a few experimental formations of
militia units.[30]

At the first session of the Tenth Party Congress, the session that
was to set the congress's agenda, military and civilian delegates confronted one another in a struggle over how best to reorganize the
army and to guarantee the party's influence in army life. Speaking
on behalf of an assembly of military delegates that had convened
before the opening of the congress, Vasilii Solov'ev an assistant director of PUR, moved to refer the discussion of military matters to a
special commission. The congress had too full an agenda to spend
time on what promised to be a rancorous discussion, he argued; as
the contending parties had already made their positions clear, he
recommended that in the interests of the appearance of party unity,
a commission be entrusted to work out a set of resolutions that
would be acceptable to a majority of the congress's delegates. Another delegate immediately argued that the reorganization of the
army and navy was an issue that concerned *all* Communists and not
only army workers. "Comrade Solov'ev speaks as if this were a
purely military matter," the unidentified delegate declared. "It has to
be considered as a general agenda item."[31] A majority of the delegates agreed that the military issues were too grave a concern to be

29. *Politrabotnik* 1 (1921): 1–2.

30. Elsewhere the Caucasian Labor Army passed a resolution in support of
Smilga, and the national Conference of Communist Cells in Higher Military Educational Institutions voted for an extremely gradual transfer to the militia system: *Politrabotnik* 3 (1921): 8.

31. *Desiatyi s"ezd*, pp. 10–11.

left to a commission, so the congress set aside three closed sessions for the discussion.

Even before the discussion began, the delegates clashed over who was to control political enlightenment. Again, it was far easier to attack the system of political control and education in the army than it was to attack the army directly. In support of Glavpolitprosvet, Evgenii Preobrazhenskii delivered the Central Committee's address, which focused on the critical need to adapt "the psychology of the masses . . . to the Communist economy that was under construction and to the new Communist relationships" by means of a state apparatus for the propagandizing of communism.[32] Preobrazhenskii strove to impart to Glavpolitprosvet an aura of revolutionary legitimacy by claiming as its ancestors not only the extracurricular department of the Commissariat of Enlightenment, but also many of the same organizations that PUR claimed as its ancestors, including the party in 1917 and the sailors and soldiers who returned from the front to the countryside and the factories. The major political question that Preobrazhenskii raised was the proper sphere of Glavpolitprosvet's activities and how to differentiate its responsibilities from those of other organizations that conducted agitational or propaganda work, in particular the party organizations. As far as the army was concerned, Preobrazhenskii proposed, in the interests of reducing parallelism and waste of resources, that PUR either be replaced entirely by branches of Glavpolitprosvet or be demoted to "something like an inspection administration for the RVSR, attached to Glavpolitprosvet and responsible for keeping track of how well Glavpolitprosvet was fulfilling its functions."

Preobrazhenskii anticipated the critics of the Commissariat of Enlightenment, including a large number in PUR, who considered the commissariat to be not "Communist" enough; that is, it was dominated by the intelligentsia, people of nonproletarian social backgrounds, and accordingly of suspect loyalty. He promised to increase efforts to recruit more Communists and to expand the influence of Communists already serving in Glavpolitprosvet. Lunacharsky defended the interests and mission of his Commissariat of Enlightenment in what was quickly becoming a desperate struggle for resources with other commissariats that were responsible for sectors of the economy. Lunacharsky tried to turn his commissariat's sponsorship of the propaganda apparatus into a lever for more influence in the competition. He demanded a more complete transfer of all agitation and propaganda functions to Glavpolitprosvet than Preobrazhenskii had done. Several delegates noted the opposition of the military's representatives to the proposed reassignment of PUR's

32. For the debate over Glavpolitprosvet see ibid., pp. 139–80.

functions to the Commissariat of Enlightenment. Nadezhda Krupskaia reported that many political workers in the army, fearing an imminent merger of their departments with Glavpolitprosvet, were
transferring to other types of work. The consolidation of the propaganda apparatus ought to be speeded up, she argued, before the situation in the army deteriorated further.

Indeed, the army was vehemently opposed to the schemes of
Glavpolitprosvet and especially to Lunacharsky's policies at Narkompros. The representative of the party organization of the Kiev Military District accused Narkompros of "too lighthearted" an approach
to propaganda. "It released Futurist and all sorts of literature, but
none that was for agitation and propaganda." He proposed removing
all responsibility for propaganda from Narkompros because the commissariat had subordinated tasks of propaganda to purely artistic
considerations. Sergei Gusev sensibly proposed that the future of
Glavpolitprosvet, especially its role in the army, could not be resolved until a more important matter was addressed, the future of
the army itself. But he also reminded both Preobrazhenskii and
Krupskaia that the Eighth Congress of Soviets had acceded to the
military delegates' insistence that PUR not be merged with Glavpolitprosvet but only be required to enter into closer contact with
local organs. Gusev also reminded the delegates that the republic
was not quite yet enjoying genuine peace. After all, were not Red
soldiers now fighting against guerrilla forces? He cautioned them
not to treat the matter of PUR too lightly because "the issue of the
political apparatus of the Red Army is the issue of the existence of
the Red Army itself."

More to the point, Gusev objected to Preobrazhenskii's proposal
that in the event of war Glavpolitprosvet could quickly and
smoothly transform itself into an equivalent of the current PUR.
There cannot be two separate organizations in the army, one for
peacetime and one for wartime, just as there cannot be two different
types of discipline in the army, he argued. An army is an instrument
of warfare and even in peacetime must prepare itself for war. This
argument cut to the heart of the problem that the army posed for the
party as it tried to adjust to peacetime. How could an army be an
army if it were not to some degree distinct from the normal life of
civilian society? How could military preparedness be guaranteed if
elections were not banned and if strict discipline were not enforced?
Gusev put it bluntly: an army can have only one boss and "not ten
nannies who will order it about." Once again he defended the
uniqueness of political work in the army. The work PUR performed
did not resemble that of local civilian party organizations, or the
type of propaganda that was conducted among the peasantry or
among the trade unions or among youth. "These are altogether dif-

ferent conditions, altogether different goals." Just as each set of conditions dictated a particular type of political work, so military
imperatives demanded that political institutions adapt their practices to the army's unique conditions. In the end, the congress took
no decisive action, but left the details of a compromise to be worked
out between PUR and Glavpolitprosvet. PUR was kept intact, Glavpolitprosvet was given responsibility for propaganda, but the working out of procedures to regulate the relationship was postponed.
For the moment, Gusev seemed to have won.

Another assault was being prepared in the corridors. This time the
forum was the debate over the appropriate form for the Communist
Party's organization in the future.[33] Nikolai Bukharin delivered the
Central Committee's official theses. He attacked the two factional
groups that had challenged the party's organizational style, the
Democratic Centralists and the Workers' Opposition, and he singled
out the army's party organization as the least democratic of any
party organization in the country, though he conceded that conditions in the army partly justified a different style of political life. It
was also the party organization with the largest percentage of "nonproletarian elements."

The Democratic Centralists attacked the principles of party organization in the army, especially because "military methods" were so
frequently carried over into civilian political life, even after the
fighting had stopped in most of the country. They emerged as the
most consistent and thoroughgoing opponents of "militarization" in
all its forms, which they understood variously as certain formal, bureaucratic approaches to problems, hierarchies sustained by excessive privileges, and a general decrease in elections and in
meaningful participation by citizens in political life. One spokesman
for the Democratic Centralists, Vladimir Maksimovskii, characterized the military method in party affairs for the congress: "On the
front it's all right, instead of a discussion of some question at a party
meeting, to simply deliver a fiery militant speech, then vote through
a resolution, sing the 'Internationale,' and rush into battle."[34] But in
peacetime such practices were a mockery of party life. The oppositionists admitted that the special conditions in the army demanded
certain limitations on the principles of democratic centralism prev-
alent in the rest of the party. For example, they were not in favor of
restoring the elective principle to army politics; nevertheless, the
situation in the army had gone too far in the direction of complete
elimination of criticism and control from below, and had estranged

33. For the prolonged debate over the party's organizational principles, actually a
continuation of the debates waged at the Ninth Party Conference and earlier, see ibid.,
pp. 217–336.
34. Ibid., p. 244.

the party's elite in the army from the concerns of its larger membership. The Democratic Centralists demanded that party conferences have the right both to propose disciplinary action against directors of political departments and to organize party commissions, elected by rank-and-file members at their regular conferences, with the power to review the work of political departments.

Ivar Smilga, only recently head of PUR, defended the army's special character and criticized Bukharin's proposals—that is, those of the Central Committee—as "liberal rose-colored politics." He denounced those of the Democratic Centralists and Workers' Opposition as "incorrect, syndicalist, petit bourgeois, and anarchist." Communists in several army units currently were electing political staffs, he warned, and soldiers were again demanding the right to elect officers. "If the army turns into a political club—and this has happened—then we will have entered a period of a Soviet Kerensky regime [period sovetskoi kerenshchiny]." Smilga reminded the delegates that he had experience both in destroying the tsarist army and in creating the Red Army, and he warned that the radical proposals being put forward to reintroduce "democracy" in the army would destroy what little fighting ability Red Army units had managed to preserve. He made several pointed references to the fighting under way against "banditry" and the Kronstadt mutiny near Petrograd, to which several delegates had been sent from the congress. Smilga ended with a ringing endorsement of strict unity in the party "as it faced the threats ahead" and demanded the expulsion of any party members forming factions. He enthusiastically endorsed the ban on party factions which the congress eventually adopted.[35]

Smilga made the most violent assault on the two opposition groups at the Tenth Congress. He articulated the fears and concerns of hundreds of senior political officers who had considerable experience in military affairs. But the views of these men did not sit well with many other delegates. D. B. Riazanov, representing the Moscow provincial organization and recently appointed to head the Institute of Marx and Engels, bitingly referred to Smilga as "our Prishibeev," an allusion to the main character in a Chekhov short story of the same name, "Sergeant Prishibeev." Prishibeev, an army veteran, interfered in village life by ordering peasants and officials about. He went strictly by the book, demanding fawning respect for all superiors and displaying no imagination or initiative in solving problems.[36]

35. For Smilga's speech, see ibid., pp. 252–61. In anticipation of the congress's debates on the "organizational question," Smilga also wrote a brochure, Na povorote (At the turning point).

36. Anton Chekhov, "Sergeant Prishibeev," in The Portable Chekhov, trans. and ed. Avrahm Yarmolinsky, pp. 97–103 (New York: Viking, 1968).

The other delegate who most fully shared Smilga's hostility to the two oppositions was Karl Danishevskii, a military commissar, member of several revolutionary military councils, and the chairman of the Revolutionary Military Tribunal of the Republic. He accused the oppositionists of *mestnichestvo*, the autonomy that local organizations so jealously guarded from the central authorities, using terminology that was popular among the army's political workers, who had met frequent and determined resistance from local civilian party organizations.[37] Earlier Danishevskii had earned a reputation as a fierce fighter for the army's style of justice in the fight against the Commissariat of Justice.[38]

All final decisions on the future of PUR and its relation to Glavpolitprosvet and the other civilian party organizations were postponed until the congress had discussed the army's future role and profile. Gusev and Mikhail Frunze, a decorated Civil War commander and Old Bolshevik, drafted a series of "theses on the reorganization of the Workers'-Peasants' Red Army" for distribution to the delegates. The theses summarized the views of an influential majority of the political staff, Red commanders, and military specialists. They also represented one of the first attempts to present the "lessons of the Civil War," as Gusev's earlier pamphlet had been titled. When political and military authorities discussed the lessons of the Civil War, they were obviously debating the most important factors in the Bolshevik victory, the type of war that had just been fought, and the nature of future wars. But it was clear to all the participants that this was above all a debate about the future of the army in Soviet society, the nature of political organization and life, and the shape of the socialist order to come.

The Civil War, Gusev said, had been shaped by the wavering loyalties of the peasant masses between the dictatorship of the bourgeoisie and the dictatorship of the proletariat. But he did not dwell long on the Civil War, because, in his opinion, wars of the future would be different. The Soviet Republic would not again face an army like the Whites', made up of elements variously "shaky, hostile, or neutral to the proletarian dictatorship, poorly trained and armed, hastily formed," and unreliable because of the soldiers' hostility toward the officers. Instead, the Red Army would confront a more or less "chauvinistically inclined" imperialist army, well

37. See Danishevskii's statement in *Desiatyi s"ezd*, pp. 283–86.
38. He had stated in January 1919 that military tribunals "are not governed and should not be governed by any juridical norms. They are punitive organs created in the course of intense revolutionary combat and [they] decide sentences according to the principles of political expedience and by means of the legal sense of communism": *Izvestiia VTsIK*, no. 2 (3 January 1919), in Portnov and Slavin, *Pravovye osnovy*, p. 211.

armed and well trained. During the recent war, the Red Army was trained and armed more poorly than the Whites', had a very weakly prepared command staff, and was organized hastily in conditions of incessant civil war. The Reds won only by virtue of their numerical superiority and greater internal cohesion, achieved by the unceasing efforts of the political departments, commissars, and Communist cells, in an atmosphere of "the toiling masses' broad sympathies for the Soviet regime and their revolutionary enthusiasm." In other words, PUR had won the war by its political work and its improvised civil–military relations. Gusev was not merely justifying the existence and mission of the organization he now headed but articulating a view that corresponded to the experience of a by now rather substantial body of political workers and "proletarian commanders." The White generals simply had proved to be incapable of understanding the special requirements of civil war and viewed the conflict as a purely military one.

From Gusev's characterization of the Civil War as a conflict between two shaky and improvised peasant armies and from his expectation that future wars would be waged against more formidable foes—traditional European standing armies—flowed a series of conclusions about the future army which appealed to the military specialists. Gusev concluded that the Red Army, "in the form that it has currently taken, is altogether powerless against mighty imperialist armies." Therefore, the Soviet state must undertake to make the Red Army equal to its imperialist counterparts. This goal ruled out any wide-scale resort to a militia army as too great a risk to countenance for the foreseeable future. Gusev did, however, preserve an important role for Vsevobuch in the military instruction of civilian youths. First, he reaffirmed the state's long-term commitment to a militia and an armed Communist people; but even though Podvoiskii, Trotsky, and their allies had proposed only a few militia armies in provinces that had no foreign borders, this minimal proposal was still too great a risk for Gusev. These armies he argued, would form the bulwark for "local particularistic strivings to the detriment of the interests of the Workers'-Peasants' Republic." Gusev viewed the currently existing centralized army organization as embodying state interests, as opposed to the regional loyalties that a militia would appeal to. If the party and government insisted on shifting to a militia system, Gusev demanded that it be strictly limited to proletarian and semiproletarian cities and villages, and that the new units maintain close ties with the special assignment detachments and with trade unions. In primarily agricultural areas, Gusev concluded, the "particularistic strivings" of the peasantry would reinforce the local authorities in their inclinations toward autonomy.

Second, Gusev discussed the sensitive matter of the Political Administration, tying the peasant question to the future of political work as well. He warned that the persistence of an overwhelmingly "petit bourgeois peasant" majority that remained fully capable of spontaneously reviving capitalism in the Soviet Republic, combined with the delay of revolution in the West and the economic devastation of the country, created a situation particularly ripe for "Bonapartist attempts to overthrow Soviet power."[39] Gusev argued that only by preserving its political apparatus could the Red Army manage the peasants' political energies effectively enough to make a peasant-based counterrevolution impossible. PUR should take an inventory of its political workers, establish a network of special schools and courses to improve their background, and promote lower-ranking political workers who had proven themselves in the recent war to positions of authority in the army organization. In proposing the promotion of the lower-level political workers, Gusev was meeting one of the key demands made by the December 1920 assembly that had denounced Smilga for his poor leadership.

Third, Gusev argued for the training of a highly qualified officer corps, beginning with the reeducation of the Red commanders, who had learned their trade while fighting in the recent wars. The formation of an adequate officer corps would require a long period of training, and only "a workers'-peasants' government" was capable of producing a cohort that was not only militarily competent but also "politically conscious." The Red Army, with an officer corps that was both proficient in military matters and politically conscious, would present a clear threat to any "bourgeois" government that kept its soldiers in a state of ignorance, "scarcely conscious unskilled workers of war, capable only of marching, shooting, and digging trenches." In order to ensure the state of a steady supply of "conscious" Red Army men, Gusev repeated the Eighth Party Congress's injunction to transform the barracks into a military and political school, but he added a thesis that revealed his endorsement of Trotsky's labor militarization schemes: the barracks should also become a "labor school" that would tie the Red Army man to the general "working life of the nation." Soldiers would participate in the economic recovery in ways that would not detract from their military training. They could help repair, rebuild, and expand the network of barracks in such a way as to "accommodate the tasks of

39. Here Gusev was following Marx's analysis of the revolutions of 1848 in *The Eighteenth Brumaire of Louis Bonaparte* (New York: International Publishers, 1963). Marx located the social support for the "bourgeois monarchy" of Louis-Philippe in the conservative small peasants, who resembled "a sackful of potatoes." Moreover, Marx attributed many of the worst features of the Napoleonic despotism to the preponderance of the army, the *point d'honneur* of the peasants.

political, military, and labor training." Gusev also referred to the experience of soldiers in helping peasants with agricultural work. The
only sure means both to train a reliable and conscious officer corps
and to produce the desired type of soldier was through political
work, that is, by preserving the Political Administration in the form
that it had taken during the Civil War.

Frunze developed several of Gusev's themes. He proposed that
the party reach a firm agreement on the nature of the army and its
role in society, and that the agreement be based on Marxist teachings, which he called a "unified proletarian military doctrine" or
"proletarian scientific theory of warfare." Like Gusev, Frunze called
for such a doctrine to be created through the combined efforts of
experienced political workers and military specialists. He too challenged Trotsky's policy of letting high-ranking former imperial officers alone determine strategy and doctrine, and proposed that the
General Staff be transformed into a "military and political headquarters of the proletarian state," mainly by the addition of the army's
most senior political workers.[40] If political and military leadership
could be unified in one central state institution, Frunze argued, then
the defense needs of the state would be ensured. Specifically Frunze
had in mind the assignment of a high priority to defense industry.
Gusev too demanded that the government plan a major investment
in modern weaponry. The Gusev-Frunze theses on the defense economy and military planning are the first public statements by high-
ranking Communist Party officials of what eventually became an
informal defense industry lobby. The closest model for Gusev and
Frunze as they envisioned their "military and political headquarters
of the proletarian state" was the Defense Council, which served as a
virtual unified government or cabinet during the Civil War and the
first years of the 1920s.[41] The council was the major state forum
with the power to consider and decide various questions of domestic and foreign policy. It was assigned primary responsibility for
drafting a unified plan for economic reconstruction, but later, especially after Lenin's death, its influence declined.

Despite the ambitious scope of the Gusev-Frunze theses and their
wide appeal in the army and the party, they were not published in

40. "Reorganizatsiia Raboche-Krest'ianskoi Krasnoi Armii (Materialy k X s''ezdu
RKP)," in Desiatyi s''ezd, pp. 710–14. Podvoiskii's countertheses are in his "Rezoliutsiia X s''ezda partii po voprosu o reorganizatsii vooruzhennykh sil Respubliki,"
in ibid., pp. 708–9.
41. For more on the concept of "unified government," in this case in connection
with late imperial foreign policy decision making, see David MacLaren McDonald,
"Autocracy, Bureaucracy, and Change in the Formation of Russian Foreign Policy
(1895–1914): 'United Government' and Russian Diplomacy during the 'Crisis of Autocracy' " (Ph.D. diss., Columbia University, 1987), esp. the Introduction.

the official account of the congress's proceedings. According to Gusev, Trotsky attacked them fiercely at the closed session devoted to military discussion and won Lenin's approval to keep them out. Because of the extremely volatile discussions on the military issue, even the congress's resolution was labeled "absolutely confidential" and not included in the first edition of the proceedings. The congress resolved to continue the demobilization of the army's oldest soldiers, to slow the release of workers, and to stop altogether the release of Communists. Because the government had decreed a reduction in the size of the army with no loss of its combat and political effectiveness, the congress resolved that, as far as possible, the army should be freed from labor assignments in the civilian economy. At the same time, it ordered the creation of transitional militia units in industrial regions, combining the principles of workers' participation in industry with their service in militia forces. In an affront directed at the most enthusiastic proponents of the militia army, the congress also declared as "incorrect and practically dangerous at the present moment" the agitation of several comrades for the liquidation of the Red Army and an immediate transition to a militia system. For the immediate future, the basis of the Soviet armed forces would remain the existing Red Army. The militia system would be introduced only in those areas with a highly concentrated proletarian population, the regions of Petrograd, Moscow, and the Urals, which had contributed the first volunteers and the most proletarian conscripts to the Red Army. The militia units were to be formed only of experienced troops and whenever possible were to include members of the special assignment detachments and "healthy elements of territorial cadres of Vsevobuch." Furthermore, the congress declared as "politically dangerous, and likely to provoke and intensify the breakdown of the Red Army," the agitation of several groups and individual comrades who sought to alter the current organizational principles of the Red Army by introducing the elective principle and by making commissars subordinate to party cells. The congress proposed that the Central Committee "take exhaustive measures to eliminate all such disorganizing agitation."

PUR was instructed to clean up the ranks of its staff, to prosecute as deserters party members who had left their units without permission, and to keep strict track of all army personnel who had been assigned to civilian positions so that they could be called back to service immediately in the event of war. PUR was further instructed to "renew" the commissar staff by recruiting new personnel and reassigning those still on duty to different environments. The army was ordered to conduct a thorough inventory of its command personnel, in particular their social background and "political groupings," and to increase political and enlightenment work among them. Whenever possible the army command was to promote deserving commissars and Red commanders, and to improve the material conditions of the command staff, especially the lower ranks, to encourage loyal cadres to remain in army service as a long-term career. On the most controversial question of the future of PUR itself, the congress agreed "to preserve the political apparatus of the Red Army in the form it took during the three years of war." The congress made a concession to the local party organizations by enjoining PUR to strengthen its ties with local organizations; however, the qualification that followed the concession rendered it practically meaningless: PUR was to maintain full autonomy as an apparatus. The final resolution did not represent a clear victory for any side; the delegates chose to postpone indefinitely any final decisions on the military question. Nevertheless, PUR, and much of what it stood for in attitudes and techniques, emerged from the fray intact, albeit somewhat battered.

The party convened an assembly of senior political staff members in May 1921 to work out the details of the compromise settlement over the division of responsibilities between PUR and Glavpolitprosvet. After Gusev replaced Smilga, he continued to assert the special conditions of political work in the Red Army and the urgent need to maintain the autonomy of PUR. Since he had no choice now but to concede that the civilian enlightenment and party organizations had a role to play in the army, he adopted a new tactic: he would grant the organizations a place in the army as long as they functioned under the "ideological direction" of PUR. Vladimir Maksimovskii, Smilga's major opponent at the recent Tenth Party Congress and a spokesman for the Democratic Centralists, now defended the interests of Glavpolitprosvet as its deputy chairman. He demanded direct supervision by Glavpolitprosvet of all political enlightenment work through political enlightenment departments (*politprosvetotdely* or *politprosvety*), which would have the authority to assign and transfer all political workers. Maksimovskii's proposal was rebuffed by the assembly, which voted instead for Gusev's theses and appointed a new commission, to include Gusev, Maksimovskii, and a senior army political worker, Leonid Degtiarev, to hammer out the final agreement. The compromise solved practically nothing because neither side conceded any substantial ground. "Autonomous" *politprosvety* would be subordinate to Glavpolitprosvet but through PUR! PUR was to be converted into "an inspection and organization apparatus," which meant that it would serve as a liaison between Glavpolitprosvet and the Revolutionary Military Council. PUR's inspection responsibilities required it to monitor the activities of Glavpolitprosvet to make certain that it was operating in accordance with the "orders and directives of the RVSR and the party's Central

Committee."[42] The vague and often contradictory description of the crisscrossing lines of control reflected the deep-seated suspicions that the army and Glavpolitprosvet felt toward each other and the reluctance of the party's leadership to intervene decisively in favor of either organization. Still, PUR had lost some decisive ground since the end of 1920.[43]

In the wake of the reorganizations and transfers of personnel, many political workers threw up their hands in despair as they saw the organizations they had so painstakingly built dismantled before their eyes. They lost faith in their leadership and often resigned themselves to the civilian takeovers, in what was called a wave of "liquidationism." Especially in those areas where civilian organizations were relatively stronger than the army's party organizations and political departments, the central military districts of Moscow, the Volga, and parts of Petrograd, political departments virtually collapsed. Their staffs fled into other sectors of the army or into civilian life. To make matters worse, army political departments frequently tried to sabotage the takeover operations of their civilian antagonists by giving up to Glavpolitprosvet those personnel they most wanted to be rid of, keeping the best specialists in other army work.[44] The opposition to Glavpolitprosvet and to the ever more intrusive civilian party organizations was strongest in the outlying military districts. There the army's own party organizations were stronger than their civilian counterparts because the transition to civilian rule had been more recent or was still incomplete: the Ukraine, the Trans-Volga district, the Western and Southern fronts, and parts of the Petrograd district.[45]

42. The instruction that spelled out the details of the compromise introduced an ill-defined division of labor which seemed almost certain to produce more conflict in the future. Glavpolitprosvet was responsible for developing plans and programs of "military and political courses for commissars and lower-ranking political workers," and for organizing its own higher schools for political enlightenment workers. "Under no circumstances" should Glavpolitprosvet publish any agitational literature, but "only issue directives to local [agencies] concerning the need for publication." PUR retained responsibility for "the consolidation and regulation of party work in army units" and won the right to "assign special tasks to Glavpolitprosvet which were dictated by military necessity." Finally, PUR had the exclusive right to implement all Glavpolitprosvet orders in the army's administrative bodies. See Put' politrabotnika 3 (1921): 2–3; Politrabotnik 2 (1921): 1, and 6–7 (1921): 36.

43. Glavpolitprosvet received PUR's political enlightenment department and the special subdepartment for political work among the nationalities troops. The party's Central Committee took over the other PUR agencies that handled programs for the nationalities. The Enlightenment Commissariat's supply divisions annexed PUR's supply section, and the Commissariat of Internal Affairs inherited the Polish section. See Politrabotnik 2 (1921): 1.

44. Vil' Khripunov, "Kul'turnaia rabota v Krasnoi Armii v 20-e gody (po materialam Sibirskogo voennogo okruga)" (doctoral diss., Novosibirsk State University, 1977), pp. 46–47.

45. Put' politrabotnika 3 (1921): 4.

The army suffered from the continuing precipitous drop in the number of political workers and party members. By the end of 1921, only 86,000 Communists remained in the army, down from the peak of 278,040 in August 1920.[46] Many party members were resigning, some in protest over the New Economic Policy (NEP) and other decisions taken at the recent congress. Arguably the most important decision made by the Tenth Congress was to restore a limited legal market economy and abandon the forced grain requisitions for a food tax. Not only in the army but in the party at large, thousands of Communists and Young Communists resigned or committed suicide out of a sense that the Revolution had been betrayed to the peasantry.[47] Others left because they were exhausted from the years of fighting; still others resigned when the party announced a purge to rid the organization of class-alien elements, particularly those of bourgeois, white-collar, or intelligentsia origin, but also "kulak elements." The purge instructions had identified the army as one of the organizations through which "kulak propertyholders and philistine [*meshchanskie*] elements of the peasantry" had succeeded in "bogging down" party organizations.[48] Party members of long standing, those with no less than three years' membership and preferably those with pre-October standing, formed commissions to organize the purge. The older members seized the opportunity to rid the organization of the many men and women who had entered during the Civil War and who in the veterans' eyes were deficient in "proletarian consciousness."[49]

In August 1921 Gusev reported to a plenum of the Central Committee that the political condition of the army was grave. He once again demanded that the Central Committee take more decisive measures to stop Communists and senior political workers from leaving the army and to return as soon as possible those who had already left. In December, when that measure too had failed to improve conditions in the army, the Central Committee ordered its first peacetime party mobilization: all members between the ages of twenty and twenty-two were to enlist for military service.[50] Though the sit-

46. *Desiat' let Krasnoi Armii: Al'bom diagramm* (Moscow, 1928), p. 42.

47. Merle Fainsod, *How Russia Is Ruled* (Cambridge: Harvard University Press, 1962), p. 244.

48. "Pis'mo TsK RKP(b) vsem partiinym organizatsiiam o provedenii chistki partii," 27 July 1921, in *KPSS v rezoliutsiiakh i resheniiakh s"ezdov, konferentsii i plenumov TsK* (Moscow, 1970), 2:274–75. The party declared the major danger to be the "elemental forces of the petite bourgeoisie."

49. For a semifictional account of the purges in an army unit, see Iurii Libedinskii, *Komissary* (Moscow/Leningrad, 1927), pp. 464ff. The novel was written between April 1924 and October 1925. Libedinskii served as a political commissar in the Urals Military District; his brother worked in Moscow for the Cheka.

uation in the army improved slightly when the party reinforcements arrived, PUR was not prepared for the influx. In the confusion of the purges, resignations, and ongoing demobilization of the older soldiers and Communists, PUR tried desperately to find out who was staying and who was leaving. The registration and assignment sectors of the political departments fell into complete disarray, so PUR had little real control over its own dwindling staff.[51]

The contested and disorderly transfer of resources and staff to Glavpolitprosvet had disastrous consequences for political and educational work in most military districts. Within months after the reorganization, educational work in the Red Army had halted so completely that *politprosvety* were now begging the military political administrations to take back responsibility for their former activities.[52] Glavpolitprosvet proved unable to handle the tasks of political work in the army. Even officials in the Commissariat of Enlightenment were conceding defeat. The director of the Siberian People's Education Administration, D. K. Chudinov, admitted that *politprosvety* had been unable to get work moving in military units.[53] In the fall of 1921, Glavpolitprosvet finally organized a special Military Section to coordinate its work in the army. Before the fall, *politprosvety* had not separated military programs from their programs for the populace at large and treated soldiers the same as any civilian citizen of the Soviet Republic. As soon as Glavpolitprosvet officially conceded that it could not handle educational and cultural activities in the army entirely on its own, PUR struck to win back jurisdiction over organizational and administrative matters and the right to veto appointments to all senior positions in the new Military Section. PUR's victory on appointments to the Military Section marked the beginning of the end for Glavpolitprosvet's claims to authority in the army.[54] In nearly every military district, confer-

---

50. A. Gromakov, "Deiatel'nost' Kommunisticheskoi partii po ukrepleniiu Krasnoi Armii v 1921–1923 gg.," *Voenno-istoricheskii zhurnal* 2 (1973): 87. Between the Tenth and Eleventh (March 1922) party congresses, the Central Committee sent 2,785 high-ranking Communists to the army, 75 percent of its mobilization target. In addition, the call-up of young party members yielded 16,000 men by the beginning of March 1922. See *Sbornik materialov III Vsesoiuznogo soveshchaniia po politrabote v Krasnoi Armii i Flote* (Moscow, 1924), p. 80.

51. For a biting critique of the sectors' performance, see Chervenka, "Raspredelenie partsil v Krasnoi Armii," *Politrabotnik* 11–12 (1921): 16–17.

52. The political administrations of the Ural and Petrograd districts reached agreements with the provincial party organizations to restore army control over educational and party affairs. See *Put' politrabotnika* 3 (1921): 4.

53. Khripunov, "Kul'turnaia rabota," pp. 46–47.

54. The RVSR, on the recommendation of an assembly of supply directors for Red Army and Navy political departments, also appointed a commissioner with instructions to set up a secretariat to restore normal supply operations. See *Politrabotnik* 8–10 (1921): 45–46, 49. Formally, Glavpolitprosvet continued to direct the army's

ences and assemblies of political workers were demanding reforms
to restore army staff control over army programs. They called for the
abolition of civilian enlightenment organs in the army, the subordination of the *politprosvety* to regimental party bureaus, and an end
to electing staff members of the *politprosvety*.[55] In all of their demands, the army's political workers were seeking to restore the practices and structures they knew best from the Civil War years, when
civilians knew their place and the army had had virtually free rein
over its own affairs.

Defining Culture and Politics

Civilian enlightenment workers failed to win the leading role in
army programs in large part because the fortunes of Glavpolitprosvet itself declined rapidly in the very first months of its existence.
Budget cutbacks in the postwar economy forced all government
agencies to part with personnel and resources. At the beginning of
1921 Glavpolitprosvet listed 475,000 employees. A year later, barely
one-tenth survived, 53,000.[56] More important than the decline in
Glavpolitprosvet's fortunes, however, was the continued and determined, although diminished, resistance from the army's political departments to the civilian "intruders." The political workers asserted
that civilian personnel had a distinct style of work that was entirely
inappropriate to military conditions. Their disagreements centered
on what was the proper mixture of culture and politics and, in fact,
over how to define culture and politics. Discussions about the character and role of culture in a socialist society raged throughout the
party and the intelligentsia, and in every setting where men and
women were engaged in the arts or education. The Bolshevik leadership turned for guidance to the Marxist philosophical heritage, but
found only ambiguous answers to their questions.[57]

In the army, the conflict over the new culture dated back at least
to the fall of 1920, when civilian *politprosvety* were working side by
side with army political departments. A political department reported that the civilian agency concentrated all its attention on erad-
icating illiteracy and "had given up on specifically political

enlightenment programs for another year. Finally, a December 1922 order of the RVSR
stripped Glavpolitprosvet of its military section and returned all political enlightenment activity to PUR.

55. See, e.g., I. Petukhov, "Ko organizatsionnomu voprosu," *Politrabotnik Sibiri* 6
(1921): 4.

56. In June 1921 that figure sank further to 20,000, followed by the release of another 10,000 personnel within months.

57. For an excellent study of these early discussions, see Boris Thomson, *Lot's
Wife and the Venus of Milo* (Cambridge: Cambridge University Press, 1978).

work."[58] In 1921 a senior political worker complained that the masses remained politically uneducated and without a "military revolutionary spirit" because most of the department's enlightenment resources during the recent past had gone to *politprosvety*, "with a deeply entrenched *Kulturträger* content, to drama, music, and choral circles, and to clubs with similar orientations."[59] At a conference of political workers convened by the Siberian Political Administration which called for the abolition of civilian enlightenment agencies, yet another senior staff member, I. Petukhov, demanded that PUR "eradicate *kulturtregerstvo* and establish a firm hold on army education for the proletarian dictatorship."[60] *Kulturtregerstvo*, and its more Russified variant *kul'turnichestvo*, was a clearly pejorative term from the pre-1917 vocabulary of the revolutionary parties. Radicals and socialists used the term to disparage a movement among Populist-inspired, liberal, educated members of society to bring the treasures of elite culture to uneducated workers and peasants. For a working-class militant, *kul'turnichestvo* was associated with the bourgeois intelligentsia, who endeavored to replace genuine class struggle with the palliative of "abstract enlightenment activity."[61]

When military men used the term *kul'turnichestvo*, they referred to the orientation of the civilian enlightenment personnel, whose slogan, according to their critics, was "culture for culture's sake." What exactly the army's commissars and *politruki* meant by these accusations was not always clear. Sometimes they appeared to mean that civilians subordinated the mission of genuine agitation to some suspect aesthetic considerations. This suspicion lay at the heart of the charges made by a delegate at the Tenth Party Congress who complained that the Commissariat of Enlightenment indulged in all sorts of Futurist excesses and had no idea how to conduct good agitation. At other times, they meant that the civilian enlightenment workers had abandoned any attempt to conduct serious agitation in favor of the easier task of organizing entertainment for the soldiers. A political worker in Kherson complained that he now saw a bifurcation of educational activities in the army. Army personnel organized meetings and discussions "of a military character," while civilians stuck on to these meetings "various entertainments having nothing in common with the aims of the agitation either in content

58. Report of the political department of the Fourth Army, dated September 1920, cited in E. L. Evdokimov, *Politicheskie zaniatiia v Krasnoi Armii* (Leningrad, 1933), p. 5.

59. *Politvestnik* 5–6 (1921): 3.

60. Petukhov, "Ko organizatsionnomu voprosu," p. 4.

61. Earlier references to *kul'turnichestvo*—or "culturism," as Jeffrey Brooks translates it—are discussed in his *When Russia Learned to Read* (Princeton: Princeton University Press, 1985), p. 318.

or in spirit." He reported that political enlightenment work was characterized by "purely *kul'turnicheskie* amusements." More concretely, the political workers who used the term were charging that their civilian counterparts had no interest in instilling loyalty to the Revolution and the new state in the soldiers, most likely because the civilian personnel did not have very strong loyalties themselves and were performing their jobs out of suspect careerist motives.[62] At a deeper level, the conflict was based to a very large extent on the insistence of military authorities that armies operated with a particular type of discipline and political life and, accordingly, required a distinct cultural life.

The fact that Vladimir Maksimovskii, a spokesman for the Democratic Centralists, was now deputy chairman of Glavpolitprosvet illustrates how organizational and ideological struggles overlapped and reinforced one another. The Democratic Centralists, at the Tenth Party Congress and afterward, opposed what they saw as manifestations of a military spirit in the country's political life. Of course, the source of all that they saw as pernicious was the army, with its habits of unthinking obedience, hierarchy, and undemocratic principles. The civilian-staffed *politprosvety* were elected, not appointed, in sharp distinction to the political departments of the army proper. The civilian workers, and some army workers who also sympathized with their aims, tried to organize their educational activities in ways that would offset the military practices and structures that denied soldiers an opportunity to shape their own fates. They argued that they were trying to encourage a psychology of independent initiative, which they called *aktivnost'*. The advocates of *aktivnost'* understood the Revolution as a cataclysmic event that had unleashed the creative energies of the masses, who could now create a just society. These ideas were an important part of the rhetoric of the Democratic Centralists and Glavpolitprosvet and Proletkul't, but they were also popular among the advocates of the militia, especially the leaders of Vsevobuch.

A Congress on People's Education, for example, hoped to restore health to the arts by organizing theater circles in the countryside. The circles would be "an inexhaustible source of living creative forces."[63] The men and women who viewed the Revolution as the

62. Actors and theater directors, for example, received Red Army rations if they performed at least four times a month. According to an army political worker, many, but certainly not all, actors grew accustomed to looking on the army as a philanthropic institution and were quite content to perform any tasteless and poorly rehearsed play in order to receive their ration. See A. Gavronskii, "O teatral'no-muzykal'noi rabote Kul'tprosveta," *Voennoe znanie* 3–4 (1920): 18.

63. Resolution of Congress cited in R. P. Makeikina, "Kul'turnoe stroitel'stvo v Novgorodskoi gubernii v 1921–1927 gg." (candidate's diss., Hertsen Pedagogical Institute, Leningrad, 1972), pp. 146–47.

release of creative energies looked upon theater as an especially promising arena to awaken the genuine personalities of the masses, including soldiers, who had lived for centuries under tsarist despotism. Indeed, except for literacy programs, theater clearly was the dominant activity in Red Army clubs and enlightenment circles.[64] A theatrical instructor reminded his army colleagues that "the goal of their work above all is to draw the masses into creativity. The task of theater is to instill healthy, strong feelings in the souls of performers and audience, to unite them in one transport of joy and courage, or indignation and resentment." He recommended that theater directors throw away the old plays and rely on improvisation, because only then would Red Army theater stop being "a feeble copy of a bad professional theater" and become "a genuinely conscious proletarian art."[65] The advocates of aktivnost' preferred theatricalized political trials and agitational skits, but even more important, they preferred improvisation to performing plays from an already established repertoire.

Indeed, many other experiments that Glavpolitprosvet staff members introduced into the army were designed to replace authoritarian structures with settings that would allow soldiers to participate more actively in their own education. The advocates of aktivnost' assailed the classroom and the lecture for reinforcing a self-image of soldiers as pupils (uchenicheskii kharakter), expected to memorize material assigned by a teacher. Teachers ought instead to encourage independent and creative thinking based on soldiers' own assessments of what was an appropriate lesson. Educators in the Ukraine proposed an alternative, labeled talgenizm, which aimed to reduce the role of the teacher to a minimum. A student was to be thrown together with "universal human experience and theory, recorded in the best sources," and given the opportunity to analyze these materials and to share experiences with others like himself. All this would be sufficient to awaken in each student his talent and genius, hence talgenizm. A teacher was not needed; the students would select, ideally from among their own ranks, an "organizer of the learning process," who could master the same knowledge as the students. The enthusiasts of talgenizm claimed that in a short time a literate soldier could be made into a man with a higher education in any discipline.[66]

---

64. Gavronskii, "O teatral'no-muzykal'noi," p. 17.
65. A., "Teatr i improvizatsiia," Politrabotnik 6–7 (1921): 31–32. See also Vestnik poarma-5 5–6 (1921): 17, cited in Khripunov, "Kul'turnaia rabota," p. 135.
66. Evdokimov, Politicheskie zaniatiia, p. 24; for other descriptions of some of these experiments, see also I. Kuznetsov, Metodika politzaniatii v Krasnoi Armii (Moscow, 1927), pp. 38, 46.

The accusations by the army's political workers that their counterparts in Glavpolitprosvet were interested only in entertainment, amusement, or "art for art's sake" was unfair. No doubt many of the actors and directors who looked on the army only as a source of charity and who performed tired versions of old classics did not share the loyalties of the political staff; but the same could not be said of the Glavpolitprosvet activists, who denounced apolitical views on art with a vehemence that certainly matched that of their military co-workers. Glavpolitprosvet employees were as firmly convinced as the army personnel that what they were doing was political.[67] When the army's defenders charged Glavpolitprosvet with apoliticism, they meant that the advocates of *aktivnost'* were abdicating their proper role as political guides or mentors and exhibiting too great a faith in the political instincts of the masses. The military personnel adopted another pejorative label from the pre-1917 discourse when they referred to the apoliticism of their civilian counterparts as "tail-endism" (*khvostizm*), a charge that Bolsheviks made against the Mensheviks for having too much faith in the spontaneous political will of the masses and disregarding the need for a determined and well-organized vanguard organization. All the experiments in anti-authoritarian or participatory educational and cultural activities did not sit easily with the army's political workers, who were quite content with their Civil War style of command and methods of agitation, and who felt they knew better how to treat soldiers of peasant background than the various well-intentioned civilians whose main experience was with "more conscious" urban blue- and white-collar workers.

Their resistance to civilian influences had other roots as well. Many of the army's staff suffered from a version of the "demobilization moods" that also afflicted the soldiers and officers and were having a difficult time understanding their place in a peacetime society. The peace had knocked out from under them any sense of their old mission, and they vented their frustrations on the civilian intruders. Gusev reminisced in 1924 that "political work posed the greatest difficulties for the Red Army not during the Civil War but after it was over."[68] A perceptive political worker from Kherson described the situation he and his colleagues faced as "a dead end." They had been accustomed to having their tasks assigned them by the presence of "a concrete, palpable enemy." Now the party de-

---

67. See, e.g., the resolution of the Third Provincial Congress on People's Education in Novgorod, January 1921: "Art is not an aim in itself, but a mighty means for conducting systematic political and educational work among the working-class masses." The congress went on to demand the nationalization of the "entire theatrical business" in order to establish a "unified theatrical front": Makeikina, "Kul'turnoe stroitel'stvo," pp. 146–47.

68. Gusev, *Grazhdanskaia voina i Krasnaia Armiia*, p. 178.

clared the enemy to be Russia's economic collapse, but such an enemy demanded altogether different battle plans.[69] Just at the time when PUR and its staff began a search for new techniques and organizational forms, the civilians descended upon them and threatened further their already tenuous sense of security. One of PUR's greatest weaknesses was its internal splits and factions. During the Civil War many firm political alliances had formed among men who together faced danger in the heat of battle. But the Civil War also left a highly poisoned atmosphere of lasting enmities as well. Still, it was easier to blame the outsiders, the civilians, than to fault fellow military men for the army's disastrous condition.

Relations remained especially strained between PUR's leaders and lower-level local political workers. Despite Gusev's pledges to strengthen the ties between the center and the political departments, he too proved unable to remedy the situation. A commissar in the Ukraine complained that his staff was at a loss as to how to conduct political work. "The periphery, as never before, needs and eagerly waits for leadership from the center," he wrote. "The periphery requests and demands inspections, instructions, and substantive ties with the center." The commissar cited resolutions and reports from several departments that attested to the seriousness of his appeal and the "near revulsion toward the cottage-industry work methods."[70] PUR did convene two assemblies of senior political workers in 1921, one in May and a second in December, in an attempt to make some response to the crisis in its organization. In addition, army delegates attended an October congress of political enlightenment departments (*politprosvety*) convened by Glavpolitprosvet. The May meeting mainly addressed the problems of the outflow of Communists from the army and the relationship with Glavpolitprosvet.

At the December meeting Gusev raised more substantive issues of political education when he proposed that political workers "proletarianize the peasant Red Army man by educating him in the spirit of internationalism, large-scale industry, and antagonism to religion." In the two years that a peasant served, his psychology should be transformed from "that of a proponent of small-scale economy into that of a passionate agent of large-scale production in industry and agriculture."[71] The delegates endorsed Gusev's ambi-

---

69. *Otchet o deiatel'nosti Politicheskogo otdela RVS 6-i armii s 1 ianv. po 1 apr. 1921 g.* (Kherson, 1921), p. 15. Libedinskii's novel *Komissary* provides an excellent characterization of the daily lives of the political staff and officers in the post–Civil War army.

70. A. Orlinskii, "Zhizn' Krasnykh chastei i politrabota v nikh," *Put' politrabotnika* 3 (1921): 13–14.

71. S. Gusev, "Na piatyi god," *Krasnoarmeiskaia pechat'* 3–4 (1922): 2.

tious program: the political staff should use the peasant's two years in the barracks to "clear up his petit bourgeois psychology and lay firm foundations for a Communist world view."[72] A Red Army man would leave the barracks with a background "not inferior to that of a graduate of a provincial party school."[73] They also managed to snipe at their civilian protagonists by declaring that most of the resolutions passed at their last conference had been implemented except those entrusted to Glavpolitprosvet.

Gusev and his allies advocated these apparently extremist or utopian schemes because they shared fundamental attitudes toward the social and political problems facing Soviet Russia and the measures necessary to resolve them. First, Gusev and like-minded military men felt strong attachments to the practices and slogans of the Civil War years. The Red Army emerged victorious, in their understanding, because of the political work that PUR had improvised during the heroic years of struggle. Second, all institutions that survived the Civil War years found themselves competing desperately for moral and material support from a beleaguered central leadership. The army suffered in the disastrous economic situation as it endured its own troubled demobilization. Because many commissars, political workers, and Red commanders perceived a lack of wholehearted commitment to the army's future on the part of influential party leaders, they promised what amounted to a quick-fix solution to the nation's outstanding problems: a rapid transformation of the attitudes and behavior of the peasant masses. The promise smacked of voluntarism. Circumstances were secondary; a will to act and change would overcome all difficulties. Not only did PUR feel itself in competition with existing bureaucracies for a role in shaping society, but new institutions such as Glavpolitprosvet now aimed to move in on PUR's traditional territory with hegemonic designs to consolidate all political work in a civilian organization. Indeed, the designs of Glavpolitprosvet and other civilian organizations came to symbolize for men such as Gusev the disagreeable post–Civil War political orientation that was known as NEP. NEP had distinctly negative consequences for the stability and security of the military apparatus and, by extension, for a particular vision of the Revolution that was tied to the Red Army's fate.

Gusev conceived of the army as a permanent revolutionary force. He shared the view of many in the party, often called revolutionary

72. "Rezoliutsii Vserossiiskogo soveshchaniia nachal'nikov politupravlenii okrugov," 16–18 December 1921, in Vsearmeiskie soveshchaniia, p. 41.
73. "Rezoliutsiia dekabr'skoi 1921 g. konferentsii RKP po voprosu ob ukreplenii partii, v sviazi s uchetom opyta proverki lichnogo sostava ee," affirmed by the Eleventh Party Congress, in Odinnadtsatyi s''ezd RKP(b), mart–aprel' 1922 goda: Stenograficheskii otchet (Moscow, 1961), pp. 554–58.

romantics by their detractors, that the chances for world revolution had not died entirely and that a war with the armies of the imperialist world was certain to occur in the near future. His convictions about the Red Army's active role in promoting the world revolution were bolstered by his ally at the Tenth Party Congress and fellow combatant during the Civil War, Mikhail Frunze, as well as by other military leaders, such as Mikhail Tukhachevsky. Since the Tenth Congress, when Gusev and Frunze were persuaded to withdraw their theses in the face of Trotsky's opposition, Frunze had been developing his ideas on a "unified military doctrine." The doctrine started from an assumption that any future war would be a mass war, and the state would have to mobilize all its resources, as in the Great War and the Civil War. Frunze was confident that the socialist state would triumph because it could rely on its working class far more than could the ruling bourgeoisie of the capitalist states. But the victorious army would have to rely largely on the proletariat, for it alone had the capacity to wage offensive warfare; a peasant army, as the recent experience with the partisan units and in the Polish war had demonstrated, was suitable only for defensive purposes. Finally, Frunze conceded that a mass army, even with the high degree of proletarian solidarity that he posited, was not quite enough to defeat world capitalism. The army of the future would have to attain a level of technological superiority over its imperialist rivals.[74] In order to achieve the technological revolution that Frunze deemed crucial for success, a majority of the nation's political elite would have to be won over to a program of industrialization that assigned a high priority to the defense industry. The army Frunze was proposing demanded nothing less than a large-scale and ambitious program of education, coupled with structural changes in the national economy, which would transform peasant soldiers into something closer to a proletariat. Frunze's conception of the Red Army as an offensive force and his call for industrialization tied directly in to Gusev's educational program, focused on internationalism and large-scale production.

Trotsky continued to combat Gusev's and Frunze's ambitious proposals as unrealistic and premature. First, Trotsky did not see any immediate reason to hope for a new outbreak of world revolution; the bourgeoisie had temporarily abandoned its initial plans for military overthrow of the Bolsheviks and settled into a strategy of long-term siege of the proletarian revolution. Second, Trotsky repudiated

---

74. M. V. Frunze, "Edinaia voennaia doktrina i Krasnaia armiia," *Armiia i revoliutsiia* 1 (1921), reprinted in *Izbrannye proizvedeniia* (1957), 2:4–22. An account of the debates between Frunze and Trotsky may be found in Walter Darnell Jacobs, *Frunze: The Soviet Clausewitz, 1885–1925* (The Hague: Martinus Nijhoff, 1969), pp. 17–88.

the methods of the Civil War as a guide to current practice. He disputed his opponents' interpretation of the Civil War as an offensive
war; it had been "overwhelmingly a war of defense and retreat." He
dismissed the need for a proletarian doctrine and charged the proponents of the new science with diverting attention from the most
important tasks, which were to persuade the nation's populace and
the conscripts that an army was still necessary in peacetime and to
make them understand why, in a considerably reduced peacetime
Red Army, only certain age groups now had to serve and not the
entire nation. Trotsky argued that political work should "emerge
from military propaganda." A soldier ought to know why, against
whom, and in defense of what interests he was fighting. In other
words, the contemporary political environment should provide the
material for political education, and not abstract Marxist schemes
about industrialization and internationalism. Simply stated, the Soviet Republic needed a reliable army because it could expect future
military interventions by its enemies.[75]

Trotsky went further in his critique of Gusev and Frunze to dismiss most of their ideas about transforming the peasant conscript as
well. Trotsky went over Gusev's head and signed a command in
which he unsparingly criticized political life in the Red Army as
"falling behind life's demands." The staff was content, he charged,
with "clichés, routine, and repetition of the same old phrases that
no longer stick in anyone's head." What was needed, according to
Trotsky, was more attention to the details of everyday army life; "the
essence of political instruction is in adaptation to people and
conditions."[76] And adaptation meant a reform of political work for a
new target audience, the young men of twenty and twenty-one years
who now accounted for the overwhelming majority of new recruits.
Older soldiers were quickly disappearing from the ranks. In some
units barely 10 percent of the remaining soldiers had any Civil War
experience, so political workers could no longer count on the old
slogans to have any serious effect. Trotsky's command to revise and
scale down political education clearly undermined Gusev's ambitious schemes. Trotsky demanded that "political instruction begin
with a correct polishing of boots and end only with the highest matters of the Communist International." If the political staff would
worry more about soldiers' boots and less about electrification, the
army might be in far better condition than it was. Many people perceived Trotsky's open fight with Gusev and Frunze as an assault on
the commissars and Red commanders, on whose behalf the two men

75. Trotsky, "Voennaia doktrina ili mnimo-voennoe doktrinerstvo," 22 November–
5 December 1921, in *KVR*, vol. 3, pt. 2, pp. 210–40. See also Condoleezza Rice, "The
Making of Soviet Strategy," in *Makers of Modern Strategy*, ed. Paret, pp. 653–59.
76. Trotskii, "Prikaz No. 254," 5 August 1921, in *KVR*, vol. 3, pt. 1, pp. 154–56.

claimed to speak. Every attack Trotsky made on the Red commanders and the commissars linked him in their eyes more closely to the
military specialists who continued to dominate the General Staff.

Trotsky's continued alliance with the military specialists and his
often vitriolic attacks on the Red commanders and commissars
earned him a reputation as a defender of the old order. Such a
charge no doubt sounds ironic in the light of Trotsky's later associa-
tion with the slogan of "permanent revolution," but in fact Trotsky's
views of warfare and of the army's proper educational role came
much closer to those of traditional military thinkers. Despite his earlier enthusiasm for the future roles that Red Army men would play
after they were demobilized, he now seemed to be very disillu-
sioned about the contribution that the army could make to the creation of a new political class. Trotsky did not dismiss altogether the
chances for influencing a peasant during his army service, but he
doubted that two years of service would permanently change a peasant conscript's world view and attitudes. Certainly the army setting
could provide "a propitious arena for Communist influence" by
bringing peasants into close contact with working-class Communists, but not much more than that, he concluded.[77]

Trotsky and Gusev battled again at the Ninth Congress of Soviets
in December 1921. At an assembly of military delegates to the congress, Trotsky delivered one more attack against the current practices of PUR. Assigning soldiers to read Bukharin's ABC of
Communism, he charged, was inappropriate for young peasants who
had only the barest knowledge of the world outside their village.[78]
The military delegates adopted resolutions very close to Trotsky's
proposals, demanding "a decisive change in the content and tone of
political agitation by adapting it entirely to the interests and com-
prehension of a young, inexperienced peasant audience."[79] A few
days after the congress closed, Trotsky dismissed the now defeated
Gusev as head of PUR, sent him off to the Turkestan front, and replaced him with a more amenable commissar, Leonid Serebriakov.

The battle was far from over. The next battleground was the Eleventh Party Congress, in March 1922. Because Gusev was far away in
Central Asia, he did not attend the congress; moreover, Frunze was
very ill during most of its sessions. Trotsky tried to recoup his
losses from the previous year. No debate on the army was included
in the general agenda. Initially several delegates proposed that the

77. Trotskii, "Rech' na II Vserossiiskom S"ezde Politprosvetov," 20 October 1921,
in KVR, vol. 3, pt. 1, pp. 24–37.

78. Trotskii, "Soveshchanie voennykh delegatov S"ezda Sovetov," 4 January 1922
(date of publication), in KVR, vol. 3, pt. 1, pp. 106–8.

79. "Rezoliutsii Vserossiiskogo soveshchaniia voennykh delegatov IX S"ezda
Sovetov," 21–23 December 1921, in Vsearmeiskie soveshchaniia, pp. 43–47.

congress at least hear an informational report on the Red Army at a plenary session, and the motion was carried. When Trotsky demanded a revote, probably to avoid having to face criticism for his policies, the congress denied his request. Trotsky delivered an official report as the army commissar, but the chairman closed the session without allowing a discussion. The congress's proceedings signaled a clear defeat for the army's civilian critics, who now were increasingly excluded from any debates on military matters. The military delegates hammered out a set of resolutions at their own meeting and presented them at the final session. They were adopted with only minor revisions from the floor.

At the meeting of the military delegates, Frunze and another Civil War Red commander, Klim Voroshilov, raised the question of military doctrine in connection with a discussion about military instruction and training. Trotsky delivered a lengthy report repeating most of his earlier criticisms of the unified military doctrine. He again rejected offensive warfare and argued that peasants and workers must be trained in a spirit of defense because nothing else could be expected of them.[80] Frunze answered that his analysis of the lessons of the Civil War was not an idealization of the army's experiences; on the contrary, Trotsky's dismissal of that experience was not only inappropriate but psychologically harmful. Frunze's positive evaluation of some aspects of the recent experience was clearly more likely to appeal to an audience of Civil War veterans than Trotsky's arrogant and condescending tone. Frunze declared that "we are the party of the class that has embarked on the conquest of the world," and that a revolutionary offensive was an entirely honorable orientation. The debate with Trotsky ended on an inconclusive note. Frunze delivered the report of the military delegates' separate assembly, which reflected none of the acrimonious polemics they had just witnessed. The delegates called for the government to fix a firm number for the army, to budget a suitable sum for the number of military men decided upon, and to reduce the army's role in the civilian economy during the current tight fiscal situation. They appealed to local party and soviet organs to devote "the most serious attention" to the support of Red Army households so that "the Red fighter, at peace about his family, might devote himself wholeheartedly to the matter of his military preparedness." The delegates repeated the warnings they had been making all year long about the dangers posed by the exodus of Communists from the army and the insufficient mobilization of party members of regular recruits' age cohort. They objected to the exemption granted to students because it would deprive the army of the "most progressive

80. Trotskii, "Doklad i zakliuchitel'noe slovo na soveshchanii voennykh delegatov XI s"ezda RKP," 1 April 1922, in KVR, vol. 3, pt. 2, pp. 242–70.

and conscious element" of Communist youth. Finally, the congress approved new categories and procedures for recruitment to party membership, which formalized the already widespread practice of granting far easier access to soldiers. The amended party rules equated workers and soldiers of working-class and peasant origins.[81]

Political Work in the Peacetime Army

Before Gusev was replaced by Serebriakov as director of PUR, he introduced several measures to turn his much-maligned institution into an effective one that could be defended against civilian critics. Of course, given the conditions facing the army, many of the well-intentioned efforts were stillborn; nevertheless, they provided a framework for further reform once army numbers became more stable and the country settled into peace. Beginning in the fall of 1921 PUR issued a series of regulations on its local organizations and personnel. Many addressed the confusion produced by the interminable tug-of-war between the civilian and military organs; others attempted to sort out the responsibilities of party organizations and the command staff and commissars; still others established firmer hierarchies among political departments and their staffs.[82] Especially important was a regulation that introduced a new power-sharing arrangement between commanders and commissars in those units and agencies where the commanders had been members of the Communist Party for at least two years. In these cases, an "assistant for the political section" (pomoshchnik po politchasti) could replace the commissar in charge of political enlightenment and administrative matters. PUR declared that its long-term policy was one-man command, a concept not yet clearly defined and certainly not overwhelmingly accepted by the political staff. At this time, the principle of one-man command was put forward as a means to eliminate the parallelism and tension that continued to plague the relations between commanders and commissars under dual command by restoring to a Communist commander all military, political, administrative, and enlightenment functions. In order to soften the

81. See the congress's resolutions formally amending the party statute, "Ob ukreplenii i novykh zadachakh partii," in Odinnadtsatyi s"ezd, pp. 546, 549. The second category for membership priority was peasants (other than Red Army men) and craftworkers who did not exploit others' labor; in third place were "others" (white-collar workers, etc.).

82. "Polozhenie o politiko-prosvetitel'nykh komissiakh v chastiakh Krasnoi Armii i Flota," 16 November 1921, in Partiino-politicheskaia rabota v Krasnoi Armii: Dokumenty, 1921–1929 gg. (Moscow, 1981) (hereafter PPR III), pp. 33–37; "Instruktsiia komiacheikam voenno-uchebnykh zavedenii," 20 November 1921, in ibid., pp. 37–42; "Polozhenie o politicheskikh rukovoditeliakh rot, eskadronov, batarei i komand," 25 November 1921, in ibid., pp. 43–44; "Polozhenie o klubakh Krasnoi armii i flota RSFSR," 12 December 1921, in ibid., pp. 47–51.

blow to the political staff, which now seemed marked for extinction, the commissar was given the grave responsibilities both of drawing the commander into "the sphere of Communist ideas" and of educating himself in military matters so that "with time he might occupy a command or administrative post." The commissar still had authority to veto commanders' transfers and promotions, and, in the event of disagreement between commander and commissar in an emergency, the commissar had the right to sanction personnel changes provided that he immediately informed the next higher-ranking commissar and commander. The commissar also retained a very substantial role in all promotions of commanders by means of personnel files (*kharakteristiki*) in which he recorded the commanders' work habits, political activities, and other information that entered into consideration for promotion. The new regulation still preserved a large measure of distrust for the command staff, so the commissar's control function continued to occupy a prominent place in his responsibilities. The commissar bore final responsibility for all political enlightenment work and, as a member of the party cell, directed party activities as well. He alone "answered for the political condition of the unit or institution entrusted to him."[83]

PUR also tried to raise professional standards among its personnel and to tighten control over its local agents by instituting a new system of "political certification commissions" (*politicheskie attestatsionnye komissii*) to monitor the views and behavior of the entire political staff and all party members. In September 1921 political departments created temporary commissions in response to party directives to improve the quality of the political staff. In January 1922 the now permanent commissions played a prominent role in the appointment, transfer, and promotion of party members to responsible positions. The commissions had representatives from all the important control agencies most directly concerned with the security of the army: senior political officers, Special Section heads (Cheka), the registration and information sector chiefs, and the chairman of the party purge commission.[84] Finally, to upgrade the skills of the political staff PUR consolidated the Red Army University and the Tolmachev Instructors' Institute into the Tolmachev Higher Military-Political Courses.[85]

83. "Polozhenie o komissarakh Krasnoi Armii i Flota," 3 January 1922, in *PPR* III, pp. 56–65.

84. "Polozhenie o postoiannykh politicheskikh attestatsionnykh komissiakh," 16 January 1922, in *PPR* III, pp. 66–67.

85. "Prikaz PURa o sozdanii Vysshikh voenno-politicheskikh kursov imeni N. G. Tolmacheva," 3 March 1922, in *PPR* III, pp. 69–70. The Red Army University (Krasnoarmeiskii Universitet, or Krunt) was attached to the Sixteenth Army in Mogilev. It opened 1 July 1920 after a reorganization of the party school of the army's political department. Its branches included instructors, pedagogy, library, general education,

All these measures were intended to introduce more accountability on the part of local political departments and more control by the center over its widely scattered staff; however, the lower-level political workers continued to appeal for more direction from the center because they were lost in the confusion of the ongoing demobilization. The leadership changed frequently at all levels. Serebriakov remained in office less than seven months before he was replaced by Vladimir Antonov-Ovseenko, in August 1922. Between January 1921 and January 1923, the Siberian Political Administration had six directors, while the Eastern Siberian Political Administration had five.[86] The lack of personal continuity in the PUR hierarchy strained the center's ability to enforce its wishes. Serebriakov severely reprimanded the directors of the Siberian and Ukrainian political administrations for failing to deliver their obligatory reports to him. In the same month, January, he reprimanded the directors of the political administrations of Moscow, Orel, Petrograd, and the Western Front for failing to send representatives to an assembly of senior political officers he had convened. Serebriakov noted that the Moscow Political Administration had shown "particular negligence" because it was located in the same city as PUR, and, "despite two separate appeals, sent its representatives on the 18th instead of the 15th." The exasperated Serebriakov threatened to turn all the guilty parties over to the revolutionary military tribunal if they ever repeated their behavior.[87] The center's desperate response, punitive transfers and demotions, only exacerbated the situation. Communications between center and periphery so deteriorated that political workers typically bypassed the established chain of command and sent envoys directly to Moscow for counsel and aid. The frequent journeys of political workers to the center not only disrupted work in their units but placed inordinate demands on the already strained transport system. PUR responded with a ban on all travel by representatives of political departments except in cases of "particularly urgent matters," and only after permission had been granted by the district-level political administration.[88]

---

and drama studios. During 1920 the university graduated 431 political workers. The Tolmachev Institute, or the Petrograd Red Army University, opened on 14 April 1920, with the following departments: political, rural culture, technical, arts (*PPR* II, p. 515n). The Tolmachev Institute is the predecessor of today's Lenin Military-Political Academy. Nikolai Tolmachev (1895–1919) was a political worker and Bolshevik, member of the Military Opposition, and senior official in the Petrograd Military District political administration. He shot himself rather than be taken prisoner in the battle of Krasnaia Gora and was buried in the Field of Mars in Petrograd.

86. Khripunov, "Kul'turnaia rabota," pp. 239–41.

87. "Prikaz PURa No. 15," *Biulleten' PUR* 1–4 (1922): 32, 39; "Prikaz PURa No. 54," *Biulleten' PUR* 7 (1922): 7.

88. "Prikaz No. 133 (PURa)," *Biulleten' PUR* 12 (1922): 22.

The chaos of demobilization and constant military reorganizations, the struggles with civilian institutions over control of army life, and the instability and near impotence of PUR provided the background against which the first peacetime programs of political education were formulated. When soldiers had faced an armed enemy in the field, political workers had found it far simpler to explain why soldiers should obey orders to march in formation or perform endless duty assignments. The party's leaders complicated the political staff's tasks by sending very mixed signals about the post–Civil War political order. On the one hand, new party guidelines on propaganda and the media stressed that the nation's economic ruin was a much greater threat than Kolchak's armies had been, but this message failed to inspire troops who were ordered to repair barracks and dilapidated weaponry. On the other hand, party members were being exhorted to learn how to trade, ostensibly to prevent hostile bourgeois and petit bourgeois classes from reasserting their control over the economy. Propaganda and agitation workers also reminded citizens that the nation was still encircled by hostile capitalist powers, ready at the first opportunity to renew hostilities; however, this message too was undercut by the concessionary agreements and peace treaties that the Soviet state was signing with its former enemies. Most party members sensed and feared that the peacetime political compromise of the NEP was fraught with severe contradictions.

The party, with its New Economic Policy, ended forced grain requisitioning, legalized private trade, and denationalized many industries. The new policies produced considerable confusion among the army's political workers. Many party members inside and outside the army disagreed with the policies of economic liberalization, especially once they witnessed the return of merchants and petty traders. The lifting of trade restrictions quickly revived the private economy. In the towns, shops and stores reopened with large supplies of products that had not been seen for years. Elsewhere millions starved to death during the famine that swept the country in the late summer, fall, and winter of 1921–1922. To many people the tragic contrasts seemed a new injustice visited upon the citizens with the state's sanction. The American anarchist Emma Goldman recalled overhearing a Red Soldier ask, "Is this what we made the Revolution for? For this our comrades had to die?" For this soldier and many like him, the revolutionary slogan "Rob the robbers" had now been replaced by "Respect the robbers" as the center's policies in effect proclaimed the sanctity of private property once again.[89]

89. Emma Goldman, *My Disillusionment in Russia* (Gloucester, Mass.: Peter Smith, 1983), pp. 201–2.

Political workers confirmed Goldman's observations. Like the rank-and-file soldiers, they "could not look with indifference at store window displays, at the pubs" and other signs of new wealth; their reaction to the NEP was negative.[90] Not only among the soldiers but among the populace at large the most vivid symbol of the new policies were the NEPmen, the private traders who were seen as a new "bourgeoisie" of self-seeking profiteers.[91] In the fall of 1921 the party's Central Committee defended its controversial policy reversals and complained that many of its members had failed to master "our new economic course." The leadership urged them to study the relevant speeches and brochures in order to equip themselves with the knowledge they needed to explain the center's policies to the nonparty populace.[92]

According to a senior PUR spokesman at the national assembly on agitation work, the objections to the NEP stemmed from the immediate consequences of loosening the wartime economic controls. "The Red Army experiences NEP in its most negative aspects and expresses dissatisfaction with this NEP," he declared.[93] The denationalization of industry and legalization of private trade put army supply officials at the mercy of a chaotic market, where they had to compete with civilian agencies and individual citizens for often scarce goods. As the army's budget was slashed and inflation spiraled, life in the army deteriorated markedly. Dire economic straits forced many soldiers and officers into the marketplace to make business deals with NEPmen. These practices provoked an assembly of military delegates to the Tenth Congress of Soviets to demand that PUR ban all private occupations among servicemen.[94] The delegates feared the erosion of unit morale and discipline if servicemen's attention was distracted, especially by so disreputable an occupation as trade. Petty trading was deemed entirely inappropriate for a military man, not to mention a soldier in a socialist army. After all, soldiers did not live by a code of material interest, but rather obeyed a higher ethos of self-sacrifice. Political workers were troubled by the demoralizing effects of the New Economic Policy. They applied a variety of labels to the syndrome that was afflicting the army, but, as one political worker put it in an article titled "Down with the Rust and Mold," "the fundamental one, of course, is NEP, 'peacetime con-

90. Evdokimov, "Soveshchanie," *Krasnaia prisiaga* 15 (1923): 59.
91. For some observations on evaluations of the NEP and NEPmen in the language of the 1920s, see A. Selishchev, *Iazyk revoliutsionnoi epokhi* (Moscow, 1926), p. 196.
92. "Tsirkuliar TsK RKP(b) o populiarizatsii osnov novoi ekonomicheskoi politiki," 10 September 1921, in *PPR* III, pp. 32–33.
93. Moisei Rafes, in *Vserossiiskoe soveshchanie po agitproprabote v Krasnoi Armii i Flote* (Moscow, 1922), p. 22.
94. A. O., "Soveshchanie voennykh delegatov X S''ezda sovetov," *Politrabotnik* 1–2 (1923): 75–76.

ditions,' material well-being."[95] They also applied the version of class analysis that had guided them during the Civil War; they attributed a large part of the current malaise to the social composition of the army, now more than ever made up of young peasants. Because so many of the urban and proletarian cadres had returned to civilian life, the army was being transformed into "an exceedingly sensitive organism, very receptive to and painfully experiencing all manifestations of petit bourgeois ideology." The introduction of NEP had only served to create a base for the further "demoralizing influence of bourgeois ideology."[96] The political workers called for an ideological counteroffensive.

The demands for an ideological assault on bourgeois influences reflected a larger party unease with the consequences of the NEP arrangement. In particular, delegates to the Eleventh Party Congress in 1922 expressed alarm at the revival of pernicious intellectual currents among the intelligentsia.[97] Military delegates criticized the omnipresent "primitive cottage-industry work" (kustarnym metodam), the tinkering and amateurism, and rejected a proposal to encourage local initiative.[98] Fears of excessive local autonomy reinforced a prejudice in favor of central control and large-scale enterprise to discourage innovation.

At several meetings in 1922, political workers throughout the army demanded a more systematic approach to peacetime political education. By the end of the Civil War most political departments had instituted daily political lessons (politchasy), but the content and form of the lessons varied widely.[99] Despite an impressive number of hours that political workers claimed their troops had attended, the staff knew that soldiers' political knowledge was very thin. Even soldiers who had been through the recommended cycle

95. R. Shaposhnikov, "Doloi rzhavchinu i gnil'," Krasnyi boets 10 (1922): 1–2. Among the images of decay and degeneration that prevailed in the discourse of the 1920s, the metaphor of rust was especially popular in capturing the sense that the Revolution had lost its will and that society was threatened by the restoration of many of its prerevolutionary features. See in particular the play by Vladimir Kirshon, Rzhavchina, translated as Red Rust, adapted by Virginia and Frank Vernon (New York: Brentano's, 1930).
96. "Tsirkuliar PURa ob ukreplenii partiinogo apparata Krasnoi armii," 14 October 1922, in PPR III, pp. 99–100. See also Rezoliutsii partkonferentsii chastei Petrukraiona i spetschastei P.V.O., p. 1.
97. See Roger Pethybridge, "Concern for Bolshevik Ideological Predominance at the Start of the NEP," Russian Review 41 (October 1982): 445–53; and S. A. Fediukin, Bor'ba s burzhuaznoi ideologiei v usloviiakh perekhoda k NEPu (Moscow, 1977).
98. Politrabotnik 4–5 (1922): 92.
99. PUR conducted an army-wide survey to determine the condition of political education in 1922 and found that practically every unit had devised its own variant: Politrabotnik 10–11 (1922): 41.

A political worker distributes literature in a Red Army club. From *Raboche-krest'ianskaia Krasnaia Armiia* (Moscow, 1938), courtesy of Division of Art, Prints, and Photographs, The New York Public Library, Astor, Lenox, and Tilden Foundations.

of conversations could not explain who Lenin, Trotsky, and Kalinin were or what a soviet was.[100] Soldiers received a certificate of political literacy after formally completing a six-week course of daily lessons,[101] though attendance was now irregular—even poorer than it had been during the Civil War. Because so many units were chronically under strength, soldiers were assigned an extraordinary number of duty details and had little time to spare for political lessons. Aleksandr Shifres, a senior political worker, warned that "if we don't eat up the duty details, they will eat us up."[102]

At a September 1922 meeting the army's specialists in agitation and propaganda work proposed a "political manual" to systematize

100. N. Rabichev, "Utochniaite formulirovki," *Politrabotnik* 12 (1922): 29; L. Geiman, "Blizhe k zhizni," *Krasnyi strelok* 3 (1922): 29; S. Golubev, "Politrabota v Krasnoi Armii," *Put' politrabotnika* 9 (1922): 29–30; *Krasnyi boets* 11 (1922): 32.
101. See PUR's order, dated 30 November 1920, in *Politrabotnik* 11 (1920): 16.
102. *Voennyi vestnik* 14 (1923): 54.

A political lesson during summer maneuvers. From *Raboche-krest'ianskaia Krasnaia Armiia* (Moscow, 1938), courtesy of Division of Art, Prints, and Photographs, The New York Public Library, Astor, Lenox, and Tilden Foundations.

all the "political knowledge" that was deemed crucial for the creation of a "conscious citizen-soldier." The manual was modeled both on the party's statute and on the army's other internal manuals on discipline, service regulations, field duty, and the whole gamut of army life. The assembly suggested that PUR work out "short, precise, and clear formulations of primary political concepts" and that the manual focus on the following topics: the Red Army, the Soviet state, its friends and enemies, and the rights and obligations of a Red Army soldier.[103] PUR quickly devised a provisional political manual based on the version proposed by the Ukrainian-Crimean Political Administration and distributed 1,000 copies of it for review by party, soviet, trade union, and military organizations. In October it

103. *Vserossiiskoe soveshchanie po agitrabote*, pp. 36, 44, 46. A party conference on the Western Front had proposed something like a political manual in December 1921 and the military delegates to the Eleventh Party Congress had also noted the experiments in several districts. See *Politrabotnik* 3 (1922): 113; 4–5 (1922): 82; 6–7 (1922): 64.

was approved and published for distribution in all political departments.[104]

The manual summarized an image of the army that the Political Administration wanted to project to soldiers and also set about answering some of the most frequent and troubling questions that soldiers had been asking. It defined the Red Army as the friend of all oppressed people who were fighting for their liberation and as the defender of workers and peasants against the landowners and capitalists of the world. It explained the military service obligation as based on class categories: the bourgeoisie was forbidden to bear arms, but was required to perform nonmilitary work in the rear. The manual reminded the soldiers that as citizens of the Soviet Republic they enjoyed the right to elect deputies to the soviets and serve in the soviets themselves; furthermore, because soldiers were expected to take an active part in political life after military service, the barracks had been transformed into a school that would help them raise their cultural level and fight for the advancement of their own and the state's interests. The first chapter ended with a condemnation of all who tried to evade military service as deserters, subject to the severest measures of the Soviet penal code.

Chapter 2 provided basic civics lessons about the Soviet state, including the nature of workers' and peasants' power, the federal system and information on each republic, the Constitution, the commissariat system, the powers of and election procedures for soviets, and the symbolism of the Soviet seal. Chapter 3 quickly explained the origins and meaning of the October Revolution. The fourth chapter outlined the organization of the Red Army and its early history, emphasizing the Red Guard as its revolutionary predecessor. By choosing the Red Guard, the authors of the manual intended to tie the Red Army to its "proletarian roots," though those roots were receding into the realm of political mythology. The manual explained who the military commissars and the Red commanders were (but not the military specialists) and the purpose of political departments, military tribunals, and the special departments. Finally, it explained the symbolism of the red star: its five points designated the union of the working class in all parts of the world against their common enemy, capital. Soldiers wore the red star because the Red Army served as the armed force committed to the liberation of all toilers. Chapter 5 warned of the continuing threats to peace and instructed soldiers about the enemies of the Soviet Republic. The manual insisted that the Soviet state pursued a

104. For a summary of the contents of the manual and a detailed description of the first chapter, "The Workers'-Peasants' Red Army," see "Iz Politicheskogo ustava Krasnoi Armii i Flota," October 1922, in *PPR* III, pp. 112–16. The complete text is in *Politicheskii ustav Krasnoi Armii i Flota*, 2d ed. (Petrograd, n.d.).

peace-loving policy, and that any threat to the international order would come from foreign capitalists, who acted in league with tsarist generals, bandits, and counterrevolutionary political parties. Chapter 6 listed as friends of the Soviet Republic the international working class, the Communist parties, especially the Russian Communist Party, and Karl Marx. Chapter 7 explained fundamental Soviet policies, including the land laws, taxation, labor protection, trade unions, social security, benefits and exemptions for military men, courts, the separation of church and state, education, nationalities, and the "path to communism." Upon completion of the entire program, the soldiers were to swear a Red oath, affirming their loyalty to the Soviet state. According to the authors of the political manual, the political staff should prepare a soldier "consciously" to take the oath, by which they meant that a soldier ought to understand what he was called to defend and why his service was so necessary. When the oath was introduced earlier in the year, it had provoked criticism from party members for evoking the practices of the tsarist army. Soldiers in the Civil War army had not needed any oath to die valiantly in battle, so why, the critics asked, did they need one now? Mikhail Landa, deputy director of PUR, defended the oath as a necessary adaptation of well-tested Civil War methods to peacetime conditions. During the war, soldiers had attained cohesion and solidarity because they regularly faced armed enemy forces. Now the oath served as a partial surrogate for the enemy and was meant to instill in soldiers common values of loyalty to the state.[105]

That the manual touched on fundamental matters of the state's self-image was made clear by its subsequent fate. Little more than a month had passed after its introduction when the Agitation and Propaganda Section of the party's Central Committee, headed by Andrei Bubnov (later director of PUR), objected to several segments and concluded that "the manual needs reworking." The critics charged that the biographies of Marx, Lenin, and Kalinin contained untidy formulations and that several paragraphs of the Red oath were left without commentary. The Army Commissariat itself, in its report for 1922–1923, criticized the manual for its failure to address "more advanced" soldiers and units with large working-class contingents. PUR had adapted its program for an exclusively or largely peasant audience. The journal *Politrabotnik* complained that the manual paid inadequate attention to the moral and political obligations of soldiers in time of war and to the discipline appropriate in peacetime. PUR received instructions to rework the program during the

105. "Tsirkuliar PURa s raz''iasneniem tselei vvedeniia Krasnoi prisiagi," 17 July 1922, in PPR III, pp. 74–75.

spring and summer of 1923, but, judging by the resolutions of the national assembly of political workers convened in October 1923, PUR was far behind schedule.[106]

When it released the political manual in October 1922, PUR projected that the course of lectures could be completed by February 1923, in time for Red Army Day and the solemn swearing of the Red oath. February came and went, but few units came close to completion, so the deadline was extended to the next important holiday in the socialist calendar, May Day. That deadline, too, passed without significant achievements. Then summer maneuvers interrupted teaching activities, so PUR approved a further extension to September. In September, however, PUR issued a new winter course that used the old manual. "Whether we wanted to or not," wrote Aleksandr Shifres, "we came to resemble a squirrel running in circles." But worse than that, "some people wanted nothing more than to go on being squirrels until the end of time."[107] Shifres repeated Trotsky's complaints that the manual was still too far removed from current events. During late 1922 and early 1923, such events as the French occupation of the Ruhr, the Curzon ultimatum, and the murder of Soviet Ambassador Vatslav Vorovskii in Switzerland could have served as pretexts for a new intervention. But, Shifres complained, "all of these intruded into our systematic political work from the outside, disrupted the plans laid out, and contradicted the fundamental line." The manual was too abstract and formulaic, he charged. Its material lacked relevance; political workers needed to derive political lessons from current events.[108]

Many political workers shared Shifres's dissatisfaction with the political manual; furthermore, until the summer of 1923 political workers had no textbooks to accompany the political manual. Just as they had done during the Civil War, they turned to newspaper material for their lectures.[109] But these good intentions were stillborn because newspapers too had fallen on hard times, especially after the army press was put under a system of cost accounting that nearly bankrupted the entire operation. The Supreme Military Edi-

106. Suvenirov, *Kommunisticheskaia partiia*, pp. 213–14; *Otchet Narkomvoenmora za 1922/23 g.* (Moscow, 1925), pp. 164–65; *Politrabotnik* 6–7 (1923): 49; 1 (1924): 135. According to Gusev, the political manual was never finally approved by the Central Committee. See S. I. Gusev, "Nashi raznoglasiia v voennom dele," in *Grazhdanskaia voina i Krasnaia Armiia: Sbornik statei* (Moscow, 1958), p. 55.

107. A. Shifres, "Dvukhgodichnaia programma voenno-politicheskogo obucheniia krasnoarmeitsa," *SP* 1 (1924): 54.

108. A. Shifres, "Perspektivy zimnei raboty," *Politrabotnik* 6–7 (1923): 49–50.

109. *Voennyi vestnik* 22 (1923): 18; *Politrabotnik* 1 (1924): 136; Ivan D. Shevchenko, "Ideino-politicheskoe vospitanie lichnogo sostava Leningradskogo voennogo okruga v gody voennoi reformy (1924–1925 gg.)" (candidate's diss., Leningrad Higher Party School, 1979), p. 144.

torial Council appealed directly to the Central Committee to bail it out of its difficulties, but even after some subsidies were authorized to "rescue the army press," the council closed down most local press operations and cut back the circulation of the major papers that continued publishing.[110] The shortage of newspapers and the "low level of political knowledge" among the soldiers prompted political workers to experiment with techniques that did not rely so heavily on written materials. In one military district, following a lecture on the procedures for elections to local soviets, the staff organized "tactical elections," during which each type of weaponry represented a village, each platoon represented a *volost'*, each battery a district, and each administration a province.[111] At least through such exercises, soldiers were beginning to learn the rudiments of the new state's political structure.

Unfortunately, the introduction of the political manual could not alter the deplorable condition of the army and its political staff, so it did little to improve soldiers' attendance and their mastery of the program. Soldiers were attending only five to seven hours a month instead of the required twenty-four to twenty-five hours. The political staff still blamed excessive duty details for the absenteeism. But PUR had no real authority to regulate duty details, and because of the chronic understaffing of units that made the excessive duty details necessary, political workers attacked the problem in their characteristically ineffective fashion by instituting "attendance journals" for the soldiers. These journals quickly became nothing more than a formality: they did nothing to increase attendance, but only added to the responsibilities of political workers.[112] Qualified political workers remained in short supply, and class sizes still exceeded one hundred in many companies, despite the intention to conduct the classes as conversations. Instead of the lively discussions that were envisioned, political workers fell back on lectures.

PUR ordered further surveys to determine how well soldiers were mastering the new manual. Not surprisingly, the results were disheartening. Units regularly failed to make it through half the required course in the allotted time. Overall, only 15 percent of the soldiers were found to have performed well, 50 percent satisfactorily, and 35 percent poorly. It was disturbing enough that in some

110. For vivid accounts of the crisis of the army press, see M. Krylov, "O material'nom budushchem krasnoarmeiskoi pechati," *Politrabotnik* 8 (1923): 142, 159; also 4–5 (1924): 215; *Otchet o deiatel'nosti Otdela voennoi literatury pri RVSR i Vysshego voennogo redaktsionnogo soveta: S 1 ianv. 1921 g. po 31 dek. 1922 g.* (Moscow, 1923), pp. 14–17; B.N., "Beg s prepiatstviiami," *Zhurnalist* 8 (1923): 59–60.

111. Suvenirov, *Kommunisticheskaia partiia*, pp. 214–15.

112. *Politrabotnik* 6–7 (1923): 60; *Voennyi vestnik* 14 (1922): 54; S. E. Rabinovich, "Itogi okruzhnogo soveshchaniia politrabotnikov L.V.O.," *Politrabotnik* 4–5 (1924): 98–99.

districts 89 percent of Communist Red Army men failed the test, but more distressing that 32 percent of the political enlightenment workers themselves failed.[113] The senior political staff concluded that, despite considerably diminished expectations, the program was still overly ambitious. Either army conditions had to improve or the political manual had to be scaled down even further.

The Crisis in Discipline

The incessant tinkering with the programs of political education and the unrelenting demoralization of PUR's staff were symptomatic of a greater crisis that gradually alarmed more and more senior army and party leaders. By the end of 1922 the fighting was over. All the foreign interventionists' forces had left Soviet territory and the most threatening domestic insurrections had been defeated. Now army personnel felt justified in demanding improvements in their situation, but their appeals went unanswered, in part because the nation's economy continued to totter precariously on the brink of collapse and all available resources flowed to civilian industry, but also because the army's leadership was still groping about for a new organizational mission and structure. The RVSR slowly and hesitatingly proceeded with demobilization and with the transition from the mobile Civil War fronts to a peacetime system of permanent military districts. In February 1923 the Politburo again agreed to reduce the size of the army, this time to 600,000 men, "the minimum necessary for the security of the RSFSR." Within a few months, the nation's unremitting economic difficulties impelled the Central Committee to lower even this "minimal" figure to a final 562,000.[114] As the number of men dropped, the RVSR began organizational reforms that compounded the army's troubles.[115]

The frequent reorganizations eroded the morale not only of the commanders and troops but also of the political staffs, who sensed that all their efforts were in vain because sooner or later the units would be disbanded and reformed. Reports complained of "liquidationist" (*likvidatorskie*) and "despondent" (*upadochnye*) moods

113. Suvenirov, *Kommunisticheskaia partiia*, p. 215; Khripunov, "Kul'turnaia rabota," pp. 115–17; *Politrabotnik* 10–11 (1922): 41–46.

114. Suvenirov, *Kommunisticheskaia partiia*, pp. 48–49.

115. The changes in the Ukraine resembled the situation in most parts of the country until 1924. The Ukrainian Workers'-Peasants' Government formed the Kharkov Military District in January 1919. In February 1920 the Ukrainian Reserve Army merged with the district, but less than a year later the Reserve Army was disbanded. In April 1922 the RVSR dissolved the Kharkov District as well as the two-year-old Kiev Military District and placed the two districts' resources under the command of the Ukrainian and Crimean Armed Forces, which in turn was reorganized two months later into the Ukrainian Military District.

among soldiers, officers, and political workers alike. The troops often understood the disbanding of their units as punishment for some
fault of theirs. They became disheartened and indignant that, only
months after they had entered the Red Army, they were considered
criminals. The commissars bore the brunt of the troops' resentment
because they typically executed the "punitive" disbandments. Commissars called meetings to explain the purpose of each reorganization, but, to prevent the demoralized soldiers from deserting, they
also assigned convoys to accompany the reassigned troops to their
next destination.[116] Army commentators warned that discipline was
suffering a perilous decline across the country. Degtiarev, speaking
for PUR, insisted at the end of 1922 that the army "now looks more
like the Red Army of 1918–1919 than it looks like that of 1920, the
year of victory." He attributed the slackening of military discipline
to "general demobilization moods and the concessions made to the
petite bourgeoisie in the area of our economic construction."[117]
Degtiarev's criticisms echoed those of many in the army, particularly
in their negative attitude toward the conciliatory policies of the NEP.
In his address to the Tenth Congress of Soviets, Trotsky also pointed
to the threat of petit bourgeois influences and identified the army's
problems as "a weakening of comradely cohesion, a fall in revolutionary discipline, and a resurgence of certain features of the caste-
estate military regime."[118]

Trotsky's diagnosis was confirmed by numerous reports from political workers. Material conditions were so deplorable that there
was very little that a commissar or commander could do to compel a
disobedient soldier to desist from undesirable behavior. In fact, as
soldiers often preferred guardhouse punishment to the dreary routine of duty and drills, they systematically disregarded warnings.[119]
More important, the solidarity between troops and their commanding officers and commissars had all but disappeared. Suitable housing was scarce as civilians returned to their homes and military
personnel were forced to leave; consequently, officers increasingly
were quartered in private apartments and homes. Troops lived apart
from their superiors and began to grow apart in lifestyles as well.
Sensing no common mission and fate binding them together, soldiers saw little reason to obey commands. The commissars complained that the "petit bourgeois city apartments" subjected the

116. N. Tsyganov, "Vred chastykh rasformirovanii i pereformirovanii," *Krasnyi
strelok* 5 (1922): 43–44.

117. Lev Degtiarev, "Boevaia rol' komiacheek," *Put' politrabotnika* 6 (1922): 38.

118. Trotskii, "Pered perelomom," December 1922, in KVR, vol. 2, pt. 1, p. 403.

119. M. Titov, "Chem ia byl i chem stal," *Voennoe znanie* 7 (1922): 43; L. D.
Trotskii, *Put' politrabotnika* 7 (1922): 6–7.

officers to "gradual but persistent alien ideological influences."[120] Among those influences was the resurgence of a much-reviled practice of the Imperial Army, the assignment of orderlies (*denshchiki*) to perform menial household chores for officers and their wives. PUR warned that the degrading practices were "creating a gulf between the Red Army men and commanders and political workers" and recommended turning over guilty command personnel to a tribunal for "conspiracy and abetting the squandering of military resources."[121]

Even the Red commanders, those officers who earned their ranks as Communists during the Civil War, seemed only too eager to assume the old privileges that went with an officer's rank. The director of military schools, David Petrovskii, explained that the Red commanders' style of swaggering or self-conceit (*kraskomchvanstvo*) was a vestige of their "former oppressed status as workers and peasants before October 1917." Especially in their relations with civilians and subordinates, Petrovskii continued, the Red commanders demanded the rights and privileges of officers as understood by "peasants brought up under the old regime."[122] Red commanders chose to associate with the military specialists rather than with the troops, though they complained that they were overlooked when promotions were considered and that the military specialists continued to enjoy an unfair advantage. All officers were neglecting political work and sinking deeper into "political illiteracy," according to the frustrated political staff.[123] The "weakening of comradely cohesion" that Trotsky mentioned was pronounced in party circles as well. Nearly a third of the command staff were now party members; and commanders, together with the political staff, now accounted for six-sevenths of all party members in the army.[124] The rise in party

120. R. Shaposhnikov, *Osnovy politicheskoi raboty v RKKA* (Leningrad, 1927), p. 172. A novel by Semen Mikhailov, *Brigadnaia roshcha*, 2d ed. (Leningrad, 1930), depicts the mores in the postwar army. The hero complains that relations between officers and subordinates had lost the familiarity of the war period, when they addressed one other as "dear brother" and slapped one another on the shoulder. Now everything had become more cold and formal (p. 172).

121. Suvenirov, *Kommunisticheskaia partiia*, p. 234.

122. D. A. Petrovskii, *Voennaia shkola v gody revoliutsii* (Moscow, 1924), p. 113.

123. *Krasnyi boets* 13 (1922): 19, 15 (1922): 42; F. I. Golikov, "Obiazatel'noe politicheskoe obuchenie komsostava," *Politrabotnik* 8 (1923): 116; A. Shteingart, "Komandiry Krasnoi Armii po 1266 anketam," *Politrabotnik* 2–3 (1924): 77.

124. The percentage of party members among commanders tripled, from 10 percent in 1920 to 30 percent in 1923. This trend continued during the 1920s: by 1929 over half of all officers were in the Communist Party. See A. S. Bubnov, "VKP(b)," in *Bol'shaia sovetskaia entsiklopediia* (Moscow, 1930), 11:542. See also Rigby, *Communist Party*, p. 109.

membership among officers raised new fears that "class-alien elements" were entering the party out of impure motives. The military
delegates to the Tenth Congress of Soviets warned that "not only
elements of proletarian and semiproletarian origins" but also those
"of noble [origin]" were seeking admission.[125] Since an overwhelming majority of the party members in the army were now identified
with the "bosses," and since the bosses were growing ever more isolated from the daily lives of the soldiers, the party's influence
among the rank-and-file troops waned accordingly.[126]

As the authority of the political and command staffs declined,
lack of discipline among the troops increased. Officers and commissars responded with a variety of ineffective measures. Many tried to
win their troops to their side by cajoling them and treating them as
equals. Especially the Red commanders had the attitude that any
knowledge of precise regulations ought to be the exclusive preserve
of the military specialists. For men of such unassailable credentials
as themselves, a proper revolutionary consciousness quite sufficed
to keep army relations in order.[127] These commanders and commissars looked for "easy popularity among their subordinates and permitted all sorts of infractions in spite of orders from the higher
commanding officers and contrary to their own good sense."[128] They
defended their conduct, however, as instilling a new type of discipline, one befitting a socialist society and its army. After all, they
reminded their critics, early army manuals had stressed "conscious
revolutionary discipline." Even the author of the 1922 manual defined military honor as "the consciousness of one's own dignity"
and drew a sharp distinction between the "revolutionary discipline" of the Red Army and the "discipline of the cane" (paloch-
naia distsiplina) that had prevailed before the Revolution.[129] The
proponents of "conscious discipline" criticized other colleagues
who, in their opinion, erred too far in the direction of traditional,
unquestioning obedience. They accused these "holdovers of the tsa-

125. "Tsirkuliar PURa ob izuchenii prichin stremleniia v riady partii sredi ra-
zlichnykh sotsial'nykh sloev krasnoarmeitsev," 1 March 1923, in PPR III, pp. 133.
126. PUR issued a steady stream of circulars demanding "the involvement of nonparty Red Army men in the work of Communist cells," "the strengthening of the
party apparatus," and "the raising of party activism." See "Tsirkuliar PURa o priv-
lechenii bespartiinykh krasnoarmeitsev k rabote komiacheek," 17 July 1922, pp. 75–
76; "Tsirkuliar PURa ob ukreplenii partiinogo apparata Krasnoi armii," 14 October
1922, pp. 99–101; and "Tsirkuliar PURa o merakh po povysheniiu partiinoi aktivnosti," 24 November 1922, pp. 116–19; all in PPR III.
127. A. Vasil'ev, "Prestupnost' na zapadnom fronte," Krasnaia prisiaga 12 (1923):
171.
128. M. Efremov, "Eshche o distsipline," Voennoe znanie 16–17 (1921): 16–17.
129. Distsiplinarnyi ustav Raboche-Krest'ianskoi Krasnoi Armii (Petrograd, 1922),
pp. 1–22.

rist regime" not only of imposing the "discipline of the cane" but also of parade-field discipline (*mushtra*) and outright physical abuse of subordinates (*derzhimordstvo*).[130]

The issue of military discipline bore upon the often troubled relationship between the army and the Commissariat of Justice. The major area of contention remained the fate of the revolutionary tribunals that had survived from the martial-law regime.[131] The debate over military justice posed the same questions about the limits of the army's authority that the debate over Glavpolitprosvet had posed. Following the end of hostilities in many parts of the country, civilian judicial organs had taken over many of the functions that revolutionary military tribunals had previously fulfilled under martial law. The Commissariat of Justice again was proposing a total takeover of the judicial administration and a consolidation of all courts and tribunals under its jurisdiction. At the Tenth Party Congress the military delegates had decided not to present their theses on the army's punitive policy because of their controversial nature. But the next year the military delegates to the Eleventh Congress proposed that the Red Army command reorganize revolutionary military tribunals in all military districts and divisions and "transfer to them complete authority to serve Red Army units." A separate military penal system was necessary, they said, because three-quarters of the troops were peasants and because the army had far greater need for compulsion than civilian society did. They produced statistics that showed an alarming rise in the numbers of desertions and other military crimes throughout 1921. Characteristically, the military delegates held their civilian counterparts responsible for the deterioration in conditions. The army's revolutionary military tribunals had evolved the "necessary approach to the struggle with military crimes" during their four-year baptism by fire, but the same "could not be said either for the people's courts or for the military departments of provincial revolutionary tribunals," because the civilian organs "had no contact with the specific conditions of Red Army life" and their entire structure was ill suited to serve the needs of the Red Army.[132]

---

130. G. Kapralov, "Partiinoe stroitel'stvo v Krasnoi armii," *Krasnoarmeets* 2–3 (1921): 14.

131. Revolutionary military tribunals were sanctioned by a decree of VTsIK, "Polozhenie o revoliutsionnykh voennykh tribunalakh," 20 November 1919 (SU RSFSR 1919, no. 58). For a discussion of military law during the Civil War, see V. M. Chkhikvadze, *Sovetskoe voenno-ugolovnoe pravo* (Moscow, 1948), pp. 80–97. For a suggestive parallel from imperial Russian civil–military relations, see Fuller's chapter on civilians in military courts in *Civil–Military Conflict*, pp. 111–28.

132. "Postanovleniia, priniatye na soveshchanii voennykh delegatov XI parts"ezda," in *Odinnadtsatyi s"ezd*, pp. 700–701.

In this struggle with the civilian institutions, the army lost temporarily. At the end of the year, revolutionary military tribunals were
abolished under a new judicial code.[133] Military tribunals replaced
the revolutionary military tribunals and had their functions defined
by the criminal code for the RSFSR adopted in May 1922, which defined military crimes very narrowly in order to keep as much control as possible over the conduct of soldiers in the hands of civilian
organs.

The correct politics of discipline became a focus for discussions
in the army about the future of "socialist relations." But the discussions also produced temporary uncertainty, and all references to the
ill-defined concept of "conscious" or "revolutionary" discipline left
both political workers and officers, not to mention the soldiers themselves, unclear about their responsibilities and rights. The authors of
the 1922 manual asserted that the inconsistency in approaches dictated the need for "a general regulation of punishments for infractions for all military personnel, equal for all and excluding the
possibility of personal discretion by the commander."[134] Instead of
the arbitrary regime they now faced, soldiers needed to know that
each infraction carried with it a predictable countermeasure. When
punishments were left to the commander's discretion, the door was
open for soldiers to feel themselves to be the victims of injustice;
consequently, the punishments lost their force and, in fact, often
produced contrary results. Despite the strict regulations prescribed
in the new manual, however, an inspection tour in 1923 by the
Ukrainian Political Administration revealed the same unsystematic
and disorderly disciplining.[135]

133. "Polozhenie o sudoustroistve RSFSR," 22 November 1922. The debate was resumed a year later. See chap. 4 of this book.
134. *Distsiplinarnyi ustav*, pp. 5–6.
135. S. N. Orlovskii, "Revoliutsionnaia zakonnost'," *Krasnaia zvezda*, 20 June 1925,
p. 3.

PART TWO

The Frunze Reforms

CHAPTER 4

The Context of Reform,
January 1923–February 1924

If God doesn't help us ... and we get entangled in a war, we'll be thoroughly routed.

—Joseph Stalin, 1924

During the last months of 1922 and 1923 military commentators complained increasingly about the failure of the center to take decisive measures to reverse the decline in the army's morale and the rising incidence of indiscipline. For the moment the political leadership, including Trotsky, seemed to feel that the military situation was not so urgent as economic recovery; moreover, Soviet diplomats had gained a string of recognitions for the republic, and so had encouraged a sense of provisional security. As a consequence, little or nothing was done to respond to the crisis in the army. That situation changed dramatically at the beginning of 1923.[1] First, Foreign Commissar Georgii Chicherin's disarmament proposals failed to reduce the threatening arsenals of Soviet Russia's hostile neighbors: the Baltic states, Poland, Finland, and Rumania. Relations with these powers, each of which only recently had fought against the Red Army, remained tense. But far more alarming was the dramatic French occupation of the German Ruhr valley in January, which threatened the still fragile European peace and raised fears of another continental upheaval. Germany was Soviet Russia's closest ally; as the pariah nations in the Versailles settlement, the two states recently had signed secret agreements on military cooperation and public treaties on trade and commerce. The unstable situation in Germany provoked confused Soviet responses. The Comintern and the Commissariat of Foreign Affairs seemed to be operating at cross-purposes, one testing the waters for a renewal of revolution and the other try-

1. For a more thorough discussion of the diplomatic history of 1922–1923, see E. H. Carr, *The Interregnum, 1923–1924* (New York: Macmillan, 1954), pt. 2.

ing desperately to prevent the outbreak of hostilities. Tensions rose
higher in May, when Anglo-Soviet relations came close to being broken off. After a vigorous anti-Soviet propaganda campaign in the
British press, the Foreign Office delivered the "Curzon ultimatum"
to the Soviet government. If the Soviet government did not meet
stipulated conditions within ten days, the trade agreement signed in
March 1921 would be denounced and the British chargé d'affaires
would leave Moscow. The Soviet leadership feared that Britain was
preparing to resume its anti-Bolshevik crusade. The Comintern postponed its scheduled session until 10 June because of "the danger of
war." The visits of French Marshal Foch and the British chief of the
General Staff to Poland, followed by the assassination of a Soviet
delegate to the Lausanne conference, fueled the war scare.

Political workers in the army kept soldiers abreast of the threats to
international peace and organized campaigns of mass protest against
the British affronts to Soviet national dignity. Army newspapers carried the fiery answers of party and military leaders and their appeals to the troops to keep their powder dry.[2] Many officers and
political workers seemed to rejoice at the prospect of renewed fighting. "Is it worth it to take up routine work," one army reporter
asked, "when we could be pulled into a war to defend our Soviet
frontiers?"[3] The excitement of officers and political workers, however, met with apathy in the majority of soldiers. The political staff
failed to persuade the troops that they had any interest in the international struggles that were heating up. Once again they had to
learn the lesson of the Polish campaign, that a peasant army would
not fight an offensive war, especially when no foreign armies were
invading Soviet territory. More important, several high-ranking military officials concluded that the soldiers had had very little military training, and with their lack of discipline they could not be
counted on to obey their commanders. Even if the soldiers were
willing to fight, the Red Army was certain to face defeat in its first
confrontation with a modern European armed force. From bitter recent experience, the army command knew very well the considerable strengths of the German and Polish armies.

In late March Trotsky's enemies in the Central Committee seized
upon the military emergency and the ailing Lenin's temporary withdrawal from active politics to attempt to wrest control over the army
away from the people's commissar. Powerful politicians united by
their long-standing hatred for Trotsky appointed a special commission, whose members included Frunze, Dzerzhinsky, Voroshilov,

2. See Trotsky's speech on 1 May 1923 in KVR, vol. 3, pt. 2, pp. 82–84; and the
speeches reported in the national press on 13 May 1923.
3. Na strazhe 1 (1923): 5; for other reports on the extreme tension in early 1923
see Na strazhe 2 (1923): 3.

and the former director of defense industry, Petr Bogdanov, to review the nation's defense preparedness and to report to the Central
Committee on urgent remedial measures. Not surprisingly, the commission determined that the army command had no adequate mobilization plan for war and had failed even to make an inventory of
the nation's resources in preparation for such a plan. The Central
Committee ordered the army command immediately to formulate
operational, organizational, and mobilizational plans.[4] In June the
presidium of the party's Central Control Commission stepped up its
assault on Trotsky's commissariat by forming a special military commission to investigate the condition of the Red Army. The first
chairman, Valerian Kuibyshev,[5] had earned a reputation as a tough
party specialist on personnel purges and currently headed the su-
per–state inspection agency that had been formed from a merger of
the People's Commissariat of Workers'-Peasants' Inspection and the
party's Central Control Commission. Kuibyshev received instructions to study four military districts: the Western, Ukrainian, Moscow, and North Caucasus. After he got the investigation under way,
Kuibyshev was replaced by one of Trotsky's most determined foes,
Sergei Gusev. The investigation, which went on for the rest of 1923,
employed members of the Central Control Commission, the army
and naval inspectorates, and large numbers of military specialists.
When the results were compiled, Trotsky's ouster seemed inevitable.
A new era was beginning in the Red Army.

Communist Ethics and Generational Conflict

The descent of the investigative teams on the four military districts and assorted central agencies unleashed a flurry of activity.
Curiously, Trotsky seemed to prefer to stay out of his rivals' way. In
his memoirs, Trotsky claimed that ever since 1921 his "personal interests had shifted to another field"; from the moment the Civil War
ended, economic problems "had absorbed my time and attention to
a far greater extent than military matters."[6] Trotsky shared the opinion of many civilian political leaders that the army already had benefited from the considerable attention and resources of the state

4. See Suvenirov, *Kommunisticheskaia partiia*, pp. 62–63; and Il'ia Berkhin,
Voennaia reforma v SSSR (1924–1925) (Moscow, 1958), pp. 54–55.
5. In 1920 Kuibyshev had served with Frunze on the Revolutionary Military
Council of the Turkestan Front as the head of the front's political administration.
Most recently, Kuibyshev had completed an investigation of the trusts to determine
the political reliability and economic competence of management personnel. As
Kuibyshev's deputy, the Central Committee appointed another member of the Central
Control Commission and Civil War veteran, Nikolai Shvernik.
6. Leon Trotsky, *My Life* (New York: Scribner's, 1930), p. 518.

during the Civil War. He did not press for a large or regular budget for the peacetime army, nor was he interested in comprehensive restructuring of the army organization. His seeming indifference to the army's fate earned him still more enemies within the military elite. Although he retained his position as army commissar, by early 1921 his assistant, Sklianskii, had assumed most of the responsibilities for the army's day-to-day functioning.

Trotsky's major effort to alter the deplorable conditions in the army was his "emphasis on lifestyle" (kurs na byt). In a series of articles and speeches, which were based on discussions with delegates at a meeting of the party's propaganda workers in Moscow, Trotsky attacked current techniques of propaganda as inappropriate to existing conditions.[7] He asserted that attention to economic reconstruction and above all to culture should supplant the previous emphasis on politics, which he defined as "the conquest of power and its consolidation as a result of the Civil War," the building of the Red Army, the nationalization of the chief means of production, and the establishment of a state monopoly on foreign trade. Now that the Bolsheviks had consolidated their hold on state power, they had to overcome Russia's heritage of backwardness by teaching citizens to work "accurately, punctually, and economically" and soldiers to read and write, to use manuals and maps, and to cultivate "habits of tidiness, punctuality, and thrift." He warned that this transformation could not be achieved by some miraculous means, such as "a specially invented 'proletarian military doctrine' " that was "quite lacking in any real understanding of our actual problems." Trotsky fired a bold salvo against the advocates of both "proletarian military doctrine" and "proletarian culture";[8] it was high time, he declared, to give up such "miracles and childish quackeries." The nation must settle down to a long and patient struggle with the tyranny of habit and custom, must fight against religion, vodka, and the patriarchal family structure, and must introduce civility and politeness in daily relations. Because no government could transform life "without the broadest initiative of the masses," Trotsky called for citizens to join voluntary mass associations to implement the changes.

Trotsky was not alone in advocating the transformation of Russian culture. He invoked the authority of Lenin, who also proposed a retreat from the earlier techniques of political struggle in favor of a slower pace of daily change in culture and habits. Elsewhere, the

7. The articles were published as a volume in 1923, Voprosy byta (Moscow, 1923), and in English as Problems of Life (London, 1924). The citations here are from the first article in the series, "Not by Politics Alone," in Problems of Everyday Life, and Other Writings on Culture and Science (New York: Monad, 1973).

8. Trotsky dealt with the topic of "proletarian culture" in a special critical pamphlet entitled Literatura i revoliutsiia (Moscow, 1923). An American edition appeared in New York in 1957 as Literature and Revolution.

Soviet state was lending its support to a burgeoning network of "Time Leagues" that aimed to rationalize workplaces and habits along the lines advocated by Frederick W. Taylor in the United States. The army too had its Time League cells and other cells devoted to the "scientific organization of labor."[9] During the summer of 1923, under the leadership of Trotsky's ally and the new director of PUR, Vladimir Antonov-Ovseenko, senior political workers devised programs that incorporated the themes of retreat from "grand" or "pure" politics and improvement in the "lifestyle and culture" of the Red Army.[10]

But Trotsky erred politically in his characteristically tactless dismissal of the "proletarian" theories of his rivals, especially in the army and PUR. Lower-ranking political workers probably accurately perceived Trotsky's campaign as an accusation that they were politically unsophisticated and that their approach to political education had failed. They seized upon Trotsky's characterization of his program as an epoch of kul'turnichestvo to charge him with ideological heresy. Whereas Trotsky thought that he was redefining the tasks of the Revolution for a new era, they accused him of abandoning the Revolution altogether. Furthermore, many of his observations and suggestions reminded older party members of the arguments made by a group of intellectuals after the 1905 revolution. In their collected essays, titled Landmarks, the authors had advised fellow members of the intelligentsia to abandon their faith in popular revolt and instead to work to spread civic culture among the masses in a program of gradual reformism. For many Communists, the NEP was perceived as a return to capitalism, and to bolster their arguments, they pointed out that Mensheviks abroad and the conservative "Changing Landmarks" (smenovekhovstvo) group welcomed the NEP as a signal that the Bolsheviks finally had returned to their national senses.[11] After all, Trotsky had once been a Menshevik; per-

9. D. Er—ov, "Bor'ba za vremia," Krasnaia rota 28 (1923): 34–36; "Polozhenie ob organizatsii ligi 'Vremia' v chastiakh Krasnoi Armii Zapadnogo Fronta," Krasnaia prisiaga 3/24 (1924): 88–93. For more on the scientific organization of labor and Soviet Taylorism, see Kendall Bailes, "Alexei Gastev and the Controversy over Taylorism, 1918–1924," Soviet Studies 29 (July 1977): 373–94.

10. "Tsirkuliar Politupravleniia Zapfronta No. 112," Krasnaia prisiaga 12 (1923); N. Nekrasov, "Byt, 'chistaia' politika i kul'turnichestvo v Krasnoi Armii," Krasnaia prisiaga 12 (1923): 96–97; "2-e frontsoveshchanie 25–26 iiulia 1923," Krasnaia prisiaga 13 (1923): 21; V. Kasatkin, "Pochemu i dlia chego?" Krasnaia prisiaga 15 (1923): 14–16; B. Baratov, "O chem pora prizadumat'sia," Voennoe znanie 12 (1923): 74.

11. See especially Nikolai Ustrialov's essays in Smena vekh [Changing landmarks] (Prague, 1921) and Pod znakom revoliutsii (Harbin, 1927). The fears of many party members were also confirmed by a survey of Soviet officials published in Pravda on 1 September 1922. Nearly half the officials expressed support for the "Changing Landmarks" philosophy. Almost as many anticipated the collapse of state capitalism and a return to a more genuine form of capitalism.

haps it was not coincidental, in the words of Soviet polemicists, that Trotsky's views now echoed the Mensheviks' warnings that Russia was not ready for a socialist revolution, but first had to undergo a period of slow capitalist development.

More important, Trotsky's campaigns unwittingly contributed to the snowballing crisis in discipline by calling for a larger measure of popular participation to reform the habits of commanders, commissars, and rank-and-file party members. Coinciding with the Kuibyshev-Gusev investigations, the party commissions in the army, those bodies charged with monitoring the behavior of all Communists, began a review of the membership against the background of an often acrimonious discussion in the press and at divisional conferences of soldiers about "Communist ethics and lifestyle." The prescient Trotsky had warned that his call to reform habits and custom carried the risk of abuse by clumsy busybodies and might deteriorate into cant.[12] Something of the sort soon appeared in the army: soldiers, especially noncommunist soldiers, and lower-ranking political officers exploited the new campaign to vent their pent-up hostilities and sense of injustice against their superiors and to express their discontent with the changes in party policies at the center. The divisional party commissions that heard the complaints were carefully selected to include as many party members as possible who had experience in the pre-1917 Bolshevik underground and to exclude any army personnel who might have had a conflict of interest by virtue of their positions in the unit.[13] Summaries of the commissions' activities which appeared in the military press painted a revealing picture of the atmosphere prevailing in many units.

The most frequently cited "violations of party ethics" were drunkenness, card playing and other forms of gambling, observance of religious rites, unhealthy family relations, bourgeois prejudices, abuse of office, and appropriation of "NEP morals and practices." In 1923 charges were brought against 13 percent of the army's Communists and ended in the expulsion of 40 percent of those brought before the party commissions. The greatest number was expelled for religious practices (70 percent of all rank-and-file members who were so accused were purged), followed by violations of party discipline (52 percent) and drunkenness (30 percent). The broadly defined cate-

12. Trotsky, "How to Begin," in *Problems of Everyday Life*, p. 67.
13. According to official reports, 97 percent of the commission members in the four major military districts were Old Bolsheviks and a remarkable 75 percent claimed working-class origins: D. Milov, "Partiinaia rabota v Krasnoi Armii za pervuiu polovinu 1923 g.," in *Sbornik statei po partiinoi i politprosvetrabote v Krasnoi Armii i Flote v mirnoe vremia* (Moscow, 1923), p. 6.

gory of "violations of party discipline" included such relatively minor offenses as failure to pay dues or to attend meetings regularly, but such charges could also be brought against political groupings who spoke out against the policies of the ruling triumvirate. Political opponents in a unit were charged with petty squabbling, abuse of authority, careerism, or a "noncommunist lifestyle." Most of the people expelled were rank-and-file members, but one-third of all those charged with violations were commissars and political workers. Commentators in the army press explained that party members most likely to violate party ethics were Communists of peasant and white-collar origin who had joined the party in the most recent period; but nearly half of the charged political workers claimed working-class origins. The commissions found that these men from proletarian backgrounds tended to fraternize with the military specialists and through them made contacts with "petit bourgeois influences."[14]

More than anything else, the statistics reveal that two generations were waging a fierce struggle for control over the political staff. The party commissions exacerbated already existing tensions between the generations by frequently siding with lower-ranking party members against senior political workers and officers. The split was most pronounced between the directors of army political administrations and lower-level political instructors, and reflected significant differences in age, social background, and marital status. By late 1923, more than half of the directors declared their social origin to be neither peasant nor worker but "other," which meant intelligentsia or white-collar worker. Nearly two-thirds had joined the party either before or soon after the Revolution. For the lower ranks the picture was virtually the opposite. Peasants (45.7 percent) and workers (40.5 percent) predominated, as did those who had entered the party since 1918 (87 percent). By both criteria, the political instructors and lower-level personnel were much closer to rank-and-file soldiers. The overwhelming majority of *politruki* were peasant youths who had entered the party as soldiers during the Civil War. According to Vladimir Dunaevskii, the author of the most comprehensive survey of the political staff, these men were not the "most authoritative" group; that group consisted of workers with Red Guard experience or peasants who had served in the old army under the tsar and the Provisional Government. A third and rapidly growing group was

14. A. Krylov, "Obshchii obzor raboty partkomissii Krasnoi Armii i Flota," *Politrabotnik* 7 (1924): 46–50; Krylov, "Sostoianie partorganizatsii Krasnoi Armii na 1-oe maia 1924 g.," *Politrabotnik* 8–9 (1924): 85–86; P. Mirovitskii, "God prakticheskoi raboty," *Politrabotnik* 6–7 (1923): 103.

made up of largely peasant youths who had entered the party since 1921.[15]

Fortunately, Dunaevskii also devoted considerable attention to the attitudes of the political staff and identified some very revealing features of their political culture. Most of the lower-level personnel identified their lives and purpose with their careers in the army. Even the *politruki* of working-class origins, the "old men" among the instructors, considered themselves to have become déclassé during the World War and the Civil War. They had had little experience in industry before their military service in any case; 60 to 70 percent looked on political work in the army as their permanent career. Among the peasant component of the "old men," 40 percent called themselves *razryvniki*, or uprooted ones. They explained that they had broken their ties to their former villages, largely because they had come from the poorest sectors of the peasantry and because their households had been devastated during the war and the famine. These men, too, looked on the army as their only career. According to Dunaevskii, the "old men" were the "most serious" among army political workers. They were the "heroic type of revolutionary professional Communist," men who had not left the party after the Kronstadt mutiny and the introduction of NEP. They were similar in background and experience to the Red commanders, who also looked on the army as their permanent career.

The soldiers and lower-ranking political workers turned the investigation and purge of the party's membership into a "campaign against overindulgence" (*izlishestva*). Above all, the campaign against overindulgence was directed against the perceived entrenchment of an increasingly privileged officer and senior political staff. The disgruntled men who brought the complaints skillfully adopted the rhetoric of the party's "official" criticisms of the army and of the charges that were exchanged during the increasingly heated intraparty struggle among the elite factions competing for Lenin's mantle. Party commissions heard charges that inequality had become the norm of army life and that "NEP ethics" was corroding the army's "comradely cohesion." The commissions affirmed soldiers' indictments of their superiors and defended their fines and punishments as measures to restore the party's authority in the army and to reestablish "comradely cohesion." Without such cohesion, they argued, soldiers could not be expected to respect the authority of their superiors and discipline would continue to decline. And soldiers could not obey superiors who would not share with them the hardships of daily life in the army, but instead chose to set themselves apart in lifestyles that the soldiers deemed undeserved.

The party commissions and the complainants almost unanimously attributed the slackening of standards among the army elite to the conditions of NEP Russia. Indeed, for many military men, especially for those who had joined the party since October 1917, NEP meant a return to normal life. These men married, began raising families, establishing households, and pursuing education and leisure activities. Accordingly, they had less time and were less willing to make the sacrifices that the party had demanded of them for so many years. Many Communists now felt they had delayed decisions about their personal lives long enough. After all, were not influential party leaders—Trotsky and Lenin and many others—advocating a retreat from the "grand" politics of the Civil War and its tremendous personal sacrifices and urging that society focus on improving the details of daily life?

At least since the Civil War, however, other large and vocal groups in the party identified communism precisely with the sacrifices of the Civil War and found it exceedingly difficult to make the transition to peacetime life.[16] One political worker declared that "there was nothing all that terrible about suffering. I came from a poor peasant background and was accustomed to living in much worse conditions." As a party member, he promised, "I can endure anything." Another party member suggested that the solution to the problem of inequality that pervaded army relations was social leveling—"raise the lower categories up to the higher ones, and lower the higher ones."[17] Dunaevskii scornfully explained that most of the younger men operated at an "unbelievably low level in political the-

16. Stephen Cohen refers to two "cultures" within the Communist Party after the Civil War—a "war communist culture" and a "NEP culture." What united the men and women who shared each culture were sets of attitudes toward the Civil War experience. The "war communists" favored the style of command and asceticism, while the pro-NEP members favored persuasion and took a more positive view of material comforts. See Cohen's chapter "Rethinking Bolshevism" in *Bukharin*, pp. 123–59. An especially pessimistic view of party members who could not adjust to the vagaries of life in the NEP years is seen in a short story by Aleksei Tolstoy about the fate of a woman army commander who is driven to murder by the unbearable conditions of her postarmy life and employment: "Gadiuka," in *Sobranie sochinenii*, vol. 4 (Moscow, 1958), pp. 180–221. *Gadiuka* literally means adder or viper, and here stresses the atmosphere of poisoned lives and relationships that Tolstoy sees as the tragic fate of these Civil War misfits. For years after its publication in 1928, Tolstoy's story excited emotions at readers' conferences and demonstrative trials of the heroine (ibid., pp. 818–20).

17. N. Dernov, "Byt i rabota v armii v otsenke samikh partiitsev," *SP* 1 (1924): 13–14.

ory." Especially the peasants who had joined the party in the early post-1917 period threatened to deteriorate into "dead political capital" if they failed to gain some "serious political knowledge." The senior political officers who were bearing the brunt of the assault on "petit bourgeois lifestyles" concurred that their critics' leveling program was a typical "infantile left-wing" delusion of unsophisticated holdovers from the Civil War period. The director of the Western Front's political administration, Vasilii Kasatkin, accused the younger men of pursuing the campaign against overindulgence with excessive self-indulgence of their own.[18] And a colleague of Kasatkin's, V. Chernevskii, turned the tables on the lower ranks and accused them of "petit bourgeois" leveling for their absurdly excessive intervention in the personal lives of party members. Chernevskii reported that the "levelers" were banning party members from owning gold and silver objects, playing billiards, drinking beer, and "even possessing small collections of private books."[19] The last item reveals the clearly anti-intellectual coloration of the campaign.

Unintimidated, the levelers pressed for the right to interfere in the private lives of party members who had deviated "from a proper Communist view on various aspects of life."[20] They transformed the "emphasis on lifestyle" into a campaign for what they called Communist ethics. The lower-ranking moralists were especially troubled by the family lives of party members and directed their vitriol against the wives of commanders and senior political staff officials. Here too the generational factor provides background for the acrimonious investigations. Most of the resentful young soldiers and *politruki* were unmarried, and, conversely, their elder superiors lived in separate quarters with their families.[21] When critics accused them of excessive "attraction to a petit bourgeois life through family ties," they were pointing to a widespread postrevolutionary marriage pattern that had attracted attention in civilian party organizations as well: Communists were marrying women who could not claim peasant or working-class origins.[22] During the treacherous years following the Revolution, the daughters of Russia's former elites

18. Vasilii Kasatkin, "Partrabota posle prizyva 1902 g.," *Politrabotnik* 6 (1924): 11.

19. V. Chernevskii, "Bor'ba s izlishestvami v Krasnoi Armii," *Politrabotnik* 4–5 (1924): 72.

20. N. P. Komarov, "Opyt izucheniia byta kommunistov," *SP* 6 (1924): 21–22.

21. These statements are based on considerable impressionistic evidence, but no statistics on marriage patterns among military personnel are available until the 1926 census. At the time of the census, two-thirds of the lower-ranking command and political staff—as well as the rank-and-file soldiers—were bachelors. See E. Ioselaniani, "Partiinost' i obrazovatel'nyi tsenz voennosluzhashchikh sukhoputnykh voisk (dannye perepisi RKKA v dekabre 1926 goda)," *Statisticheskoe obozrenie* 11 (1928): 103.

22. See, e.g., E. Kviring, "Zheny i byt," in *O morali*, pp. 87–88, cited in S. Ivanovich, *Krasnaia armiia* (Paris, 1931), pp. 228–29.

desperately sought matches with men of proper revolutionary credentials to protect themselves and their families. Red Army families were exempted from forced labor and various taxes and entitled to subsidies for food and housing. Now that a restored private economy was encouraging the revival of a "new petite bourgeoisie," these women had begun "to show their true colors," according to the party commissions, "in their demands for more material goods and better living conditions."[23] Indeed, married political workers expressed far greater dissatisfaction with their material conditions than did their bachelor counterparts. They complained of overwork, poor housing, and inadequate salaries. Demanding wives distracted their Communist husbands from performing their party obligations. Under the influence of their wives, these political workers and commanders withdrew from party work and lost touch with the nonparty masses because they placed "their personal interests above the interests of the party and the working class."[24] Wives from unsuitable social backgrounds brought religion into their homes, even though nearly all party members in the army claimed to have been nonbelievers since their late teens. Unsatisfying family situations contributed to a disturbingly high rate of alcoholism among party members. The surveys indicated that this phenomenon remained confined largely to the senior staff members and officers.[25]

Under the assault of the moralizing commissions, married Communists whose wives were neither party members nor from "toiling" backgrounds were forced to defend their personal lives. Some claimed, with apparent sincerity, that they were in fact doing the party a service by drawing women from the nontoiling classes into the party's sphere and reeducating them in the proper spirit. Others insisted that they would have liked to marry a politically more suitable woman, but women Communists were in short supply. More, however, admitted frankly that female communists and Komsomol members made fine comrades but bad wives. "If only they could be a bit more feminine," one married official argued, "Communist bachelors would associate exclusively with them." Of course, every Communist was looking not only for a woman but for a friend and comrade as well. But, he added, men preferred "someone neat, dressed as well as possible, tidy, and with a more or less pleasant appearance." Such girls, he claimed, were most likely to come from a petit bourgeois environment. Besides, after working all day, "you

23. Apse, "Itogi anonimnoi ankety po obsledovaniiu byta kommunistov UVO (po 1463 anketam)," *Politrabotnik* 6 (1924): 38–39; A. Krylov, "Boleznennye iavleniia v partorganizatsii Krasnoi Armii i Flota," *Politrabotnik* 4–5 (1924): 47.

24. F. Anulov, "Byt komsostava," *Voennyi vestnik* 40 (1923): 35; K. Rol', "Byt Krasnoi Armii i 'Krasnaia zvezda,'" *Krasnaia zvezda*, 1 January 1925, p. 5.

25. Apse, "Itogi," pp. 36, 37, 42; V. Zibert, "Ob odnoi bolezni v nashikh riadakh," *SP* 2 (1924): 12–13.

want to come home to a nice domestic setting where you can relax."
A Communist wife could not provide such a setting because she
would be working no less than you. The militant moralists would
have none of these feeble rationalizations. They demanded that
"weak" Communists either change their lifestyles or leave the party.
Many chose the latter alternative and left voluntarily; many others
were expelled by the party commissions, whose investigations frequently had tragic outcomes. Accused party members broke with
their families and many later faced heavy financial burdens when
they were required to help support their children. An alarming
number of party members, apparently unable to cope with the conflicting claims of home and party, committed suicide.[26]

The private lives of unmarried officers and senior political staff
members were not altogether immune to the wrath of their subordinates and the party's moralists, who pointed to a revival of heinous
practices from the Imperial Army as symptoms of degeneration.
Among army elites both suicides and duels tied to love intrigues
and scandals gained in popularity.[27] Duels were especially frequent
among the cadets in the new military academies, whose instructors came overwhelmingly from careers in the Imperial Army. The
party journalist Mikhail Kol'tsov demanded an end to the army's
"Onegins" and "Childe Harolds" and decried the resurgence of the
"Philistine" ethos of Aleksandr Kuprin's novel The Duel. Characteristically, he attributed "Philistinism" to the "NEP petite bourgeoisie."[28] Party commissions and cell meetings condemned all
dueling activity and expelled guilty members. The reported rise in
suicides strikingly revealed the degree to which daily life and personal relations had been poisoned in the atmosphere of the postwar
army. Marital problems and romantic intrigues were only part of the
reason for the desperate acts of military men. Injured pride was a
common motivation mentioned in the notes that suicides left behind
them. Another frequent reason was the intolerable material deprivation and unsatisfying intellectual and spiritual life in garrison
towns.[29] Expulsion from the party drove many to take their own
lives, even as others declared that they would not take their expul-

26. Apse, "Itogi," pp. 32, 34–36; Krylov, "Boleznennye," pp. 50–51; Dernov, "Byt i
rabota," pp. 12–13.
27. Krylov, "Boleznennye," p. 52; I. Filatov, "Po povodu odnogo samoubiistva,"
Voennyi vestnik 9 (1924): 24–25. Filatov identified himself as a Red commander.
28. M. Kol'tsov, "Doloi armeiskikh Oneginykh i Chail'd-Garol'dov!" Pravda, 4 July
1923; "Dikovinnoe delo," Voennyi vestnik 20 (1923): 36; Griboedov, "Neudachnoe na-
padenie (po povodu dueli v Krasnoi Armii)," Voennyi vestnik 21 (1923): 46–47; R.
Muklevich, "O dueli," Voennyi vestnik 23 (1923): 43–44.
29. S. Fil'chenko, "Opyt issledovaniia partiinogo byta," Krasnyi boets 9 (1924): 37.

sion lying down. "Either I appeal to a higher organ, or I enter [the party] again on general qualifications, or I'll shoot everyone who is responsible for my leaving the party," one embittered Communist threatened.[30]

All these party ills—suicides, troubled domestic lives, drunkenness, careerism, unbridled self-interest—eroded any sense of solidarity among the army's elites and their authority in the eyes of the soldiers. On the wane was the revolutionary enthusiasm that had postponed or muted the surfacing of fierce personal rivalries during the Civil War, when Communists were united in the face of a common and mortal enemy. Many demoralized political workers felt the state had abandoned them to uncertain fates and the NEP policies had compromised their revolution. They perceived their self-indulgent bosses to be an inextricable part of the greater problem of morale facing the peacetime army. Not surprisingly, the generational split that sundered the army on so many other issues also divided it with regard to the NEP political settlement. When PUR conducted a survey of its staff in early 1924, 91 percent of the senior political staff declared themselves to be in favor of NEP. In contrast, a quarter of the lower-ranking political workers and Red commanders considered NEP to be "a harmful turn in the development of the Revolution." Between one-fifth and one-half felt that their material situation had improved little since the end of the Civil War, and, when asked whom they considered to be the winners under NEP, they answered, "The bourgeoisie."[31] The generational split shaped many of the sharp political differences that were now tearing apart the army's elites. The senior political staff was older, less "democratic" by social origins, married, and better educated. They now associated themselves with the political and economic arrangement called NEP, while their younger subordinates considered their superiors to be part of a new privileged "bourgeoisie" of bureaucrats who cared little and did even less for the simple people.

Trotsky's Struggle for Power

While the sundry campaigns for Communist lifestyle and against overindulgence were under way, two other struggles among the political elite forced themselves into army affairs: the potentially revolutionary situation in Germany and Trotsky's fight to hold onto his prominent place in the party and state. Because Trotsky was still at least nominally head of the Red Army and because the army ex-

30. Dernov, "Byt i rabota," p. 15. See an earlier article about the alarming rise in suicides among military personnel by D. Rogin in *Vestnik statistiki* 9–12 (1922): 111.
31. Apse, "Itogi," p. 36.

pected to be called to defend the republic in the event of a new
European war resulting from a German revolution, the larger national and international struggles impinged on and complicated politics in the army, already poisoned by the investigations and
campaigns.

In the fall of 1923, against a background of mounting economic
and social crisis, the German Communists formed coalitions with
left-wing socialists, made preparations for a general strike, and actually attempted an armed coup in Hamburg. A takeover of the German state was called off. In Moscow the Politburo, although
generally in favor of a German revolution, was divided over how
much support was appropriate at this stage. Trotsky was most enthusiastic in encouraging the German Communist Party to seize
power, Zinoviev was less enthusiastic, and Stalin was cautious because he foresaw no revolution in Germany until spring at the earliest. Despite the hesitations of several leaders, the Soviet government
sent military advisers and a delegation headed by Karl Radek to
monitor events in Germany and offer assistance.

The Red Army was put on unofficial alert, but no full-scale mobilization was ever ordered. The slogan of the year was "One does not
get ready during a war; one must be ready for war." Articles on political work in wartime appeared for the first time since the Civil
War. The October assembly of political workers declared that their
immediate task was to "explain to soldiers the meaning and essence
of the civil war that has begun in Germany." They also demanded
that party organizations conduct "military propaganda" among the
civilian populace to instill "revolutionary combat moods and interest in military affairs."[32] And, in anticipation of a possible Red
Army move into Central Europe, officers were encouraged to enroll
in Polish and German language courses. By late fall reports of extreme "nervous tensions" among the army's Communists provoked
alarm that war fever was getting out of hand.[33] The political workers, especially the lower-ranking *politruki*, and Red commanders

32. "21–26 oktiabria 1923 g. Vsesoiuznoe soveshchanie politrabotnikov Krasnoi
Armii i Flota," in *Vsearmeiskie soveshchaniia*, pp. 303–6. See also "Iz rezoliutsii 3
Vsesoiuznogo soveshchaniia politrabotnikov Krasnoi Armii i Flota," in ibid., pp. 64–
119. The assembly was addressed by Trotsky ("Sovremennoe polozhenie i zadachi
voennogo stroitel'stva," in KVR, vol. 3, pt. 2, pp. 146–72), Antonov-Ovseenko, and
PUR's assistant director, Mikhail Landa.
33. *Politrabotnik* 11 (1923): 5–6, 94. For more details on these events, see E. H.
Carr, *Interregnum*, chap. 9. A delegate of the Central Committee of the German Communist Party reported that when he visited Tukhachevsky's headquarters at Smolensk in April, he found the Red Army men eager "to march with arms in their hands
to the aid of the German and Polish proletariat," and that the command staff was
equally ready for combat against Poland. Carr claims that Frunze and Voroshilov favored a military offensive against Poland, but the Curzon ultimatum had taken the
wind out of these plans (p. 215).

welcomed the possibility of new fighting and hoped that a new war might infuse some revolutionary enthusiasm into the moribund political climate of NEP Russia. By contrast, the reaction of the overwhelming majority of peasant soldiers to the German crisis of 1923 was indifference. Ironically, the soldiers' apathy seemed only to fuel the ardor of the political workers, who concocted a peculiar explanation that attributed the soldiers' apathy to their "revolutionary impatience." According to this interpretation, the troops felt that events were moving too slowly and that "the old woman, History, needed to be whipped on." Typically, the senior political staff had a more commonsensical explanation that reflected their greater resignation to circumstances. For the, army agitation failed because the peasant soldiers saw little or no connection between the German events and their own lives and households. Peasants simply did not support offensive revolutionary wars.[34] The senior staff, though it praised the revolutionary enthusiasm of their junior army comrades, lamented the failure of their "revolutionary reason." The frenzy of late spring and late fall "had been a banal thing, and one that we must reject," concluded one writer.[35] From the point of view of the junior political officer, his superiors had turned their backs on the Revolution and surrendered to the "petit bourgeois" self-indulgence that NEP had bred among the bosses.

A related struggle was taking place at the apex of political power. By mid-November the German revolution had ended and order was restored throughout the country. In the aftermath of the defeat, the Soviet leadership disagreed over how to understand the implications of what had just occurred. Two factions confronted each other with radically different interpretations. Stalin argued that the German proletariat had not been ripe for revolution and that any comparison between the recent situation and the one faced by the Bolsheviks in October 1917 was inappropriate. Trotsky remained insistent that the conditions had been ripe for a revolution and, by stressing the parallel between October 1917 and October 1923, accused the German leaders of spoiling the chances for success. For a large part of the party, the West had betrayed Russian hopes for world revolution. Although Stalin did not enunciate his doctrine of "socialism in one country" until the following year, the failure of the German revolution dealt a serious blow to those party leaders who continued to look to the West for the genuine proletarian revolution. Trotsky in particular continued to hope that the European proletariat might yet save the Russian Revolution from degenerating into Bonapartism. In future debates, however, he would have to explain why the most de-

34. Vasilii Kasatkin, "Germanskaia revoliutsiia i russkii krest'ianin," *Krasnaia prisiaga* 19 (1923): 3–4.
35. *Na strazhe* 2 (1923): 3.

veloped proletariat in Europe had failed to follow "backward" Russia's example.[36] Despite subsequent war scares during the 1920s, never again did the nation's mood reach the fever pitch of 1923. In the army the failure of the German revolution dramatically transformed the once jubilantly expectant mood to one of defeatism. "Revolution is subsiding. We overestimated its potential," an army reporter conceded. "Capital is stronger than labor in Germany." Just a short time earlier it had seemed that the revived enthusiasm of the Civil War might triumph over the prosaic doldrums of NEP Russia. Now the double failure of the revolution and the attempts to create enthusiasm among the troops for the hoped-for war reinforced the general mood of dissatisfaction with the course of events since the end of the Civil War.

As Trotsky tied his fate ever more firmly to the future of revolution both abroad and at home, the struggles among the party's leaders took a new turn. The debate over the German revolution overlapped with a debate over domestic policy. In the summer, labor unrest had alarmed the party and compelled it to consider how to address workers' grievances. On 8 October Trotsky addressed a letter to the members of the party's Central Committee in which he criticized their policies in several areas. A week later forty-six prominent party members signed a statement demanding that the Central Committee convene an emergency conference to review the political and economic condition of the country. The Forty-six were not a unified group; their numbers included former Workers' Oppositionists and Democratic Centralists, such as Vladimir Smirnov and Andrei Bubnov, men who had little sympathy for Trotsky. Also among the, however, were close political friends of Trotsky who held important posts in the army, including Ivan Smirnov, PUR director Antonov-Ovseenko, and Nikolai Muralov, commander of the Moscow Military District.[37] Trotsky and the Forty-six demanded that the Politburo devise a comprehensive economic policy that would allow the state to take a more direct role through economic planning. Their criticisms of economic policy led them to demand political reform as well. They protested against the increasingly widespread practice of appointing party secretaries and against the constraints on discussion at party gatherings. The Forty-six also demanded that the ban on party factions be lifted or relaxed because it had opened the door for one faction to form a dictatorship over the party.

36. Isaac Deutscher, *Stalin: A Political Biography* (New York: Oxford University Press, 1966), pp. 289–90, offers a persuasive hypothesis about the impact of the German events on Trotsky's defeat by Stalin.

37. Isaac Deutscher, *The Prophet Unarmed: Trotsky, 1921–1929* (New York: Oxford University Press, 1959), pp. 106–26.

Faced with this challenge to their policies, the Central Committee majority threatened disciplinary sanctions if the oppositionists circulated their incendiary document among the general party membership. They also sent trusted and effective agitators to party organizations to squash any grass-roots support for the opposition and to whip up support for the majority's policies. In the last week of October, at an enlarged session of the Central Committee, they censured Trotsky and reprimanded the Forty-six. At the same time, the plenum acknowledged the criticisms of the oppositionists and approved a program of "inner-party democracy"; furthermore, they endorsed an "intensification of the struggle against overindulgence and the deteriorating influence of NEP on certain elements of the party."[38] On 7 November Zinoviev pledged to restore democracy within the party. *Pravda* and other newspapers invited Communists to discuss all matters of party life. Among the prominent Communists who accepted the invitation was Trotsky. In a series of articles published in *Pravda*, he repeated most of his criticisms of the existing state of affairs in the party and state apparatus.[39] Among his targets was the army's political staff, in particular the military correspondents, whom he charged with "killing all independent thought" by writing in clichés about everything important. Even their accounts of the feats of Civil War heroes, he claimed, sacrificed the truth for an inspirational lie.[40] The point of this excursus was to identify resistance to initiative and tradition in the army with the same unbending attitudes among contemporary party members. By attacking the old guard in the party and the political staff in the army, Trotsky was alienating two very influential constituencies whose hostility toward his proposals would soon help end his career.

PUR's director, Antonov-Ovseenko, also threw himself into the fray. When army newspapers called for open discussions, several party organizations passed resolutions siding with the oppositionists' positions. Party members who had suffered from punitive measures during the recent investigations were particularly active in the opposition. At the end of December Antonov-Ovseenko took the bold step of sanctioning the complete restoration of party democracy in the army. Without the knowledge of the Central Committee, he distributed a circular authorizing the election of party cell secretaries and bureaus without the previously required confirmation of a

38. "Ob"edinennyi plenum TsK i TsKK sovmestno s predstaviteliami 10 partorganizatsii," 25–27 October 1923, in *KPSS v rezoliutsiiakh*, 2:495–96.

39. Trotsky's articles appeared later as the pamphlet *Novyi kurs* (Moscow, 1924), published in English as *The New Course* (New York, 1943).

40. Trotsky repeated all these charges against army correspondents in a speech to journalists, "Rech' na Vsesoiuznom soveshchanii zhurnalistov," *Politrabotnik* 7 (1924): 39.

political department and requiring commissars to account for all their actions in regular reports to party cells. Three days earlier, also without informing the Central Committee, he had set 1 February 1924 as the date for a conference of party cells of the military academies, higher educational institutions, and the Air Force staff, institutions where he hoped to garner more support for Trotsky's platform.

Antonov-Ovseenko wrote his own very harshly worded letter to the Central Committee on 27 December 1923. He reminded the party bosses that the army was not a group of "courtiers to the throne of party hierarchies," and that the party feuds had been harmful to morale in the army. "This cannot go on for long," he warned. "Only one thing remains—to appeal to the peasant masses who wear the uniforms of Red Army soldiers and call to order the leaders who have gone too far."[41] Within weeks, meetings of party members in the army were proposing permanent military assemblies to decide all questions of army life. It was as if the soldiers' committees of 1917 and 1918 had won a new lease on life. Party members demanded the right to discuss all commands before their release. Antonov-Ovseenko and his sympathizers appealed to the disgruntled party masses to dismantle the entire commissar system and to take out their hostilities against the political departments that placed constraints on their own political activity. In an address to the Moscow garrison, Antonov-Ovseenko declared that the military cells "were solidly behind Trotsky."[42] Probably he was exaggerating the sympathy for the opposition, but certainly in Moscow and Petrograd Trotsky's position received a sympathetic hearing. Elsewhere the discussions started only after considerable delay. Outside the capitals, party members had only a vague idea of the issues under contention.

However strong the opposition may have been, it brought a swift and decisive response from the Central Committee majority. In a plenary meeting convened on 12 January 1924, the Central Control Commission reprimanded the defiant army cells and the Orgburo demanded the removal of Antonov-Ovseenko from the directorship of PUR. Clearly the leadership could not ignore a virtual threat of

41. Anton Antonov-Ovseenko, The Time of Stalin: Portrait of a Tyranny, trans. George Saunders (New York: Harper & Row, 1981), pp. 35–36. The author is the son of the hero of the Revolution. As the source for his father's threatening letter, he cites the unpublished memoirs of Mikhail Poliak, then head of PUR's press department.

42. Deutscher, Prophet Unarmed, p. 117. For details on the political struggles in the army, see Otchet Politicheskogo upravleniia Leningradskogo voennogo okruga: Mai 1923 g.–mai 1924 g. (Leningrad, 1924), pp. 51–52; Shaposhnikov, Osnovy, pp. 76–77; M. Kachelin, "Itogi partiinoi diskussii v K.K.A.," Krasnyi boets 6 (1924): 22; KPSS v rezoliutsiiakh, 2:508–9; Suvenirov, Kommunisticheskaia partiia, p. 138; Politrabotnik 1 (1924): 223; Otchet Narkomvoenmora za 1922/23 g., p. 226.

mutiny from the army's chief political officer. Antonov-Ovseenko was replaced on 17 January by Andrei Bubnov, who must have promised to purge the army thoroughly and eliminate the possibility of any Praetorian Guard revolt. Bubnov's first act as director of PUR

Andrei Bubnov, director, Political Administration of the Revolutionary Military Council of the USSR, 1924–1929. From A. S. Bubnov, *O Krasnoi Armii* (Moscow, 1958).

was to revoke Antonov-Ovseenko's circular sanctioning party democracy in the army. He reinstated the practice of appointing political workers and, in a second circular, explained how the recent decisions on party democracy voted by the Thirteenth Party Conference were to be implemented by army cells. The elective principle applied exclusively to the lowest level of party organization (company and regimental cells) and to party commissions. All the rest of the political apparatus, because it served functions of administrative and political control, was to be appointed from above. The special imperatives of the military mission did not permit the army's Communists the luxury of the type of political life that civilians enjoyed; rather, "side by side with party discipline there exists an especially strict and consistently applied military discipline." Bubnov stressed that "together with comradely relations, there must be a superior–subordinate relationship."[43] Although Bubnov needed nearly another year to enforce his stricter policies, he made it clear that PUR would no longer tolerate the civilizing deviations that had so threatened the combat mission of the army in recent months.

On 21 January 1924, a few days after Bubnov began his political house-cleaning operations, Vladimir Lenin died. As party leaders paid tribute to his career, they sought to outdo one another in calling for party unity in this time of grave tragedy and political crisis. Bubnov instructed political workers to assure the young peasant soldiers that Lenin's death did not portend any changes in the Soviet government's rural policies. The political staff should try to direct the sympathy that the troops felt for the passing of their great leader toward forging stronger ties of loyalty to the Soviet state and the Communist Party.[44] Despite Bubnov's reassurances, Lenin's death did signal a sharp turn in the fate of the army. With Lenin's hesitating but constant support now gone, Trotsky no longer made any effort to halt the army's takeover by his opponents. The party plenum that convened just one week after Lenin died appointed an authoritative commission to discuss the condition of the Red Army. The commission, headed by Gusev, included Frunze, Voroshilov, Mikhail Lashevich, Aleksandr Orekhov, Aleksandr Egorov, Grigorii Ordzhonikidze, Iosif Unshlikht, Nikolai Shvernik, I. M. Voronin, Andrei Andreev, and the new director of PUR, Andrei Bubnov.[45] No close political ally of Trotsky had a voice on the commission, which rep-

43. "Tsirkuliar PURa s raz"iasneniem reshenii XIII konferentsii RKP(b) o vnutri-partiinoi demokratii v sviazi s osobennostiami organizatsii Krasnoi Armii i Flota," 13 February 1924, in PPR III, pp. 185–92.

44. "Tsirkuliar PURa o zadachakh raboty po izucheniiu deiatel'nosti V. I. Lenina i leninizma," 16 February 1924, in PPR III, pp. 193–98.

45. Soviet historians give various dates for the commission's creation. Berkhin, in Voennaia reforma, pp. 59–60, claims that the plenum that met at the end of January 1924 formed the commission. This assertion is confirmed in an introduction to a report by Frunze published in Voenno-istoricheskii zhurnal 6 (1966): 66n. Nikolai Kuz'min, in Na strazhe mirnogo truda (1921–1940 gg.) (Moscow, 1959), pp. 21–22, argues that the commission was selected even before Lenin's death, at the plenum convened on 14–15 January. Berkhin cites army archives, while Kuz'min cites the Central Party Archives.

resented a substantial majority of the men who would rule the country for the next decade and beyond.

The commission's first act was to present the findings of the military commission appointed back in June 1923, whose report had been held up until Trotsky's enemies were confident that he could no longer place obstacles in the way of their reform plans. Not surprisingly, the commission's conclusions were alarming: "The Red Army is not a reliable fighting force."[46] They identified the most serious shortcomings in several volumes of findings. One set of criticisms focused on the absence of any serious strategic thinking at the top of the military chain of command. The war scare of 1923 had revealed that army headquarters had no realistic plan for mobilization in the event of war; moreover, the current organizational structure and personnel at army headquarters rendered it unsuitable for the tasks of preparing the country's defense and directing the army. Frunze already had made similar charges against army headquarters and Deputy Army Commissar Sklianskii in March and again in October 1923. This time Gusev scathingly referred to Trotsky and the high command as "specialists and generals who were well advanced in age." Trotsky himself, Gusev claimed, did nothing in the RVSR. He left the entire leadership of the army in the hands of his deputy, Sklianskii, and the chief of staff, Pavel Lebedev, an aristocratic holdover from the Imperial General Staff Academy. In support of his charges, Gusev cited a letter from Commander Ieronim Uborevich, in which he complained that the RVSR operated in an atmosphere heavy with "the spirit of the Sukhomlinov period."[47] Tsarist self-seekers were stabbing in the dark and had no perceptible system to their workings. Army headquarters still had no single view about the purpose and structure of the army and had not approved a single standardized manual for any of the service branches.[48]

A second focus of the critical findings was the area of administration and logistics. The RVSR had yet to introduce a regular system of units and formations in the army, though the Civil War had ended three years earlier. The rear organizations were still cumbersome

46. Gusev's report and the discussion that followed in the Central Committee are described in Berkhin, *Voennaia reforma*, and a candidate's dissertation by Dmitrii Pikha, "Bor'ba Kommunisticheskoi partii za ukreplenie Sovetskikh Vooruzhennykh Sil v 1924–1928 godakh" (Kiev State University, 1964). Both works quote extensively from the unpublished protocols of the meeting, which are held in the Central Party Archives.

47. Vladimir Sukhomlinov (1848–1926) was director of the General Staff Academy from 1908 to 1909 and war minister from 1909 to 1915. He was dismissed from his post in 1915 and charged with malfeasance, corruption, and treason for failing to prepare the army adequately for war. He was arrested in 1916, freed, rearrested in 1917, and sentenced to life imprisonment at hard labor. In 1918 he either escaped or was released on grounds of advanced age, and he emigrated to Germany.

48. Berkhin, *Voennaia reforma*, pp. 60–62.

and swollen, the weapons supply system was inadequate for any future war, and food and clothing supply also continued to present a deplorable picture. Finally, the commission drew attention to problems of staff morale and low professional standards. The organizational chaos at the top made itself felt in the extreme instability of

Mikhail Frunze, people's commissar of the army and navy, chairman of the Revolutionary Military Council of the USSR, 1925. From M. V. Frunze, *Sobranie sochinenii*, 3 vols. (Moscow, 1926–1929), courtesy of Division of Art, Prints, and Photographs, The New York Public Library, Astor, Lenox, and Tilden Foundations.

command personnel at the bottom. The commission bemoaned the shortage of officers, in some units reaching 50 percent, and their low qualifications. The report found that not more than 25,000 officers educated in Soviet military schools remained on duty. Of the 87,000 officers who had graduated from these schools during the Civil War,

30,000 had died and an equal number had been demobilized. Furthermore, as many as 45 percent of the officers came from unsuitable social backgrounds and over 5 percent were former White officers. These complaints were familiar from the reports of political workers and the resolutions voted by party members and nonparty soldiers at their frequent assemblies. Of course, after the recent near-mutinies under Antonov-Ovseenko, the commission also found the state of political work in the army to be "unsatisfactory."

After hearing the commission's report, the plenum discussed the findings and recommended further investigation, but also ordered the Politburo to begin action on the most urgent recommendations. On 3 March Frunze replaced Sklianskii as deputy commissar, but in fact assumed de facto control over the army. A few days later he formed a new RVSR, which included most of Trotsky's prominent opponents in the army: Frunze, Voroshilov, Bubnov, Ordzhonikidze, Semen Budennyi, Sergei Kamenev, Shalva Eliava, and Aleksandr Miasnikov. Although Trotsky's enemies certainly used the commission as a forum for political struggle against him, they did not fabricate the alarming findings. The army had been in a serious state of decline since the end of the Civil War, and Trotsky, again by his own admission, had lost interest in military matters. Still, the deplorable condition of the nation's economy and the postwar demobilization played a large role in the army's crisis; perhaps even a more attentive Trotsky would have been unable to remedy all the army's ills in these difficult conditions. Wherever the truth may lie, Trotsky's authority in the army now was irrevocably shaken, and the mandated army reform would be executed without his participation. By the time the Central Committee formally relieved Trotsky of his duties, in January 1925, Frunze already had been administering the army for nearly a year.

CHAPTER 5

Militarization:
Officers and Soldiers

Enough of sentimentalizing and sugar-and-honey democratic methods for
educating a soldier. Revolutionary armies, and that includes ours, come to
consciousness only via mountains of corpses.
                                                —Aleksandr Sediakin, 1925

Militia Compromise and Conscription

Frunze, Gusev, Bubnov, and the entire Revolutionary Military
Council[1] directed the first stage of the reforms in close communication with the Central Committee. The major organizational reform
was the transition to a mixed system of regular cadre army and territorial militia. Frunze announced that he would expand and overhaul the territorial militia system, but that it would be preserved
alongside the regular army. The proponents of the standing army
had had to compromise with the advocates of the militia, in large
measure because the Soviet state simply could not afford a large
armed force while it was still trying to restore its struggling economy. Under the terms of the compromise, the regular army's size
was fixed at 562,000 men. This number equaled only one-third of
the eligible recruit pool, made up of all twenty-two-year-old males
not disqualified for physical, legal, political, or economic reasons.
The term of duty for regular troops was fixed at two full years. All
remaining eligible males were to enlist in territorial divisions for
shorter, staggered terms. Militia troops reported for duty two months
each year, usually during the summer, for a total of four years.[2]

1. On 28 August 1923 the Revolutionary Military Council of the Republic (Russian initials RVSR) was renamed the Revolutionary Military Council of the USSR
(RVS SSSR, hereafter RVS for convenience's sake).
2. By 1 October 1925 the RVS had formed twenty-six regular cadre divisions and
thirty-six territorial militia divisions. In addition, there was one territorial militia
cavalry division and one regiment of armored trains. See Kuz'min, Na strazhe, p. 31.

During the initial year of the transition to the mixed system, regular army personnel fiercely resisted attempts to transfer them to the militia formations. An assistant to Frunze recalled that senior political workers "considered it shameful to be transferred from a regular to a territorial one because they assumed that a territorial unit was 'second rate.' " Many military men predicted that the experiment would not last long.[3] Frunze shared the anxieties of many prominent military men. From the military point of view, he explained, "if we had had before us a choice between a regular army of 1.5 to 2 million men and the current system of the militia, . . . all the arguments would have been in favor of the former." But, he complained, "we were not given that choice."[4]

In exchange for its acceptance of the mixed system, the army leadership won several concessions, the first of which was a victory over Vsevobuch. Until 1923 territorial units had been assigned loosely to Vsevobuch's jurisdiction. Now all territorial units were placed firmly under the command of the Army Commissariat and in a position decidedly subordinate to the regular army's administrative and supply systems. Vsevobuch no longer competed for real authority over any part of the military's operations. Podvoiskii's organization was completely dismantled in 1923 and its staff and resources were absorbed by the RVS. Podvoiskii subsequently devoted most of his energies to organizing mass sports programs. Second, all surviving special assignment detachments, *chony*, merged with regular army units. Most recently the detachments had passed from Vsevobuch to the Cheka, then to the GPU. Third, in the territorial formations a core of regular soldiers and officers, optimally between 10 and 15 percent, would be assigned to train and coordinate the militia troops. Despite these measures to bolster the preparedness of the militia forces, the army's leaders considered the militia training program inadequate to guarantee the nation's defense; consequently, the territorial formations were located exclusively in those districts that did not share a border with a foreign country.[5] Furthermore, the party made a solemn promise to expand its role in pre-induction training, another responsibility that the now extinct Vsevobuch recently had claimed. Finally, as the RVS began to expand the territorial system, it also completed the reorganization of the existing fronts and autonomous armies into a uniform system of military districts.

3. "Vospominaniia o Frunze," *SP* 27–28 (1925): 37.
4. M. V. Frunze, "Kadrovaia armiia i militsiia," in *Sobranie sochinenii*, 3 vols. (Moscow/Leningrad, 1926 and 1929), 3:289.
5. The Volga Military District, for example, consisted wholly of territorial divisions.

All in all, the terms of the compromise represented an important, albeit qualified, victory for the proponents of the regular army. By 1924 only a few outspoken antimilitarists, such as Podvoiskii and some of his Vsevobuch colleagues, questioned the need for a standing army for the foreseeable future. Their hoped-for opportunity to exploit the demobilization to transform the Red Army into a "truly socialist militia" had passed. To complicate matters further, Trotsky's competing version of the militia army had shared little with the ideal envisioned by the staff of Vsevobuch. Most likely, Trotsky's championing of the militia system had only damaged its chances of gaining greater favor among his growing camp of enemies. Now, six years after the Revolution, the party formally reversed its earlier stand. Instead of declaring the regular army a temporary stage in the transition to a genuine people's militia, as the party congresses of the Civil War had insisted, the party now defended the mixed system as a necessary compromise until the nation could afford to maintain a large standing army. Even more telling about the regular army's victory was the character and structure of the territorial militia formations. The militia that emerged was a mockery of the original militia ideals defended by Podvoiskii and his allies, the Military Opposition, and most especially the Red Guards. Nothing remained of that ideal but the principles of short terms of duty and territorial recruitment. By all other criteria, the militia closely resembled the regular army.

The administrative reorganization enabled the army command to make their first serious attempt to introduce system into recruitment, length of service, and promotion policies. In 1922 Sovnarkom had passed a new law on conscription, but because of the instability of the army's apparatus, the call-up procedures failed to alleviate the confusion in the local military commissariats. According to the 1922 law, all eligible twenty-year-old male citizens were to be called up during February and March each year, to begin service on April 1, and to be released the following fall. For the first time, terms of duty were fixed for each of the service branches. At first the army command determined that, given their budget constraints, the 800,000-man conscript pool ideally could pass through the army in one year; but soldiers needed two years for adequate military training. As a result, the military and political leadership settled on a compromise term of one and one-half years for conscripts in the infantry and artillery.[6] The first year's experience revealed a whole

6. Temporary deferments were granted for sickness, immaturity, and completion of one's education. Certain "backward nationality" groups were exempted from service, as were persons who had been deprived of the franchise by a court sentence or who by virtue of their class hostility to the Soviet state could not be entrusted with arms. Certain difficult family and property situations entitled soldiers to terms of

series of problems, mostly stemming from the persistently high turn-over, the ongoing demobilization and reorganization, desertion, and extremely poor health among twenty-year-olds.[7] The 1923 military commission devoted special attention to the problems of manpower turnover. Frunze presented a new standardized recruitment and pro-cessing schedule for 1924, with basic terms of duty set at two years for all Soviet citizens eligible to serve. The RVS followed Frunze's temporary measure with a series of orders fixing the length of ser-vice at two years and regulating leaves, assignments, and transfers. All disfranchised persons were obliged to register in service units *(komandy obsluzhivaniia)* to perform nonmilitary duty for the army. Any such man unable to serve for any reason was to pay a special military tax.[8]

The first "normal" call-up in 1924 did not run smoothly. First of all, budget shortfalls due to a poor harvest forced the RVS to call up 100,000 fewer men than the army command had determined were necessary to bring units up to desired strength.[9] Then the special call-up originally scheduled for March was delayed until May. When recruitment finally got under way, peasant protest meetings met the recruitment drive in every military district. The fall call-up coincided with the first major overhaul of both the military districts and the central apparatus. Again the chaos at the top triggered protests at local recruitment centers. Recruiters warned that drill in-structors would have to pay dearly for the confusion because re-cruits whose first contact with the army was the poorly run call-up would have little respect for order and discipline. Director of Army Recruitment L. Malinovskii lamented that nothing had changed dur-ing the first year of the reorganization. "The old Russian style of

only six months. For more details, see Berkhin, *Voennaia reforma*, pp. 239–42; Berkhin cites "Ob obiazatel'noi voinskoi povinnosti grazhdan RSFSR," *Sobranie za-konov i rasporiazhenii Raboche-Krest'ianskogo pravitel'stva RSFSR* 61 (1922): 786.

7. The spring call-up was inconvenient for peasants, while the fall release left the army short until the next spring call-up. A second call-up in the fall was decreed for those who had shortened terms of six months. The twice-yearly call-up proved to be too much work for the local commissariats and a six-month term too little time to learn any important military skills.

8. The conscription age was raised from twenty to twenty-one to raise the level of physical fitness of the cohort. Recruitment drives would occur once yearly in the fall: "O srokakh sluzhby v RKKA, RKKF, i voiskakh OGPU," *Vestnik TsIK, SNK i STO SSSR* 4 (1924): 116. On the service units see "O poriadke zachisleniia grazhdan v komandy obsluzhivaniia v 1924 godu," *Vestnik* 3 (1924): 76, cited in Berkhin, *Voen-naia reforma*, pp. 246–47.

9. The original army plan had called for 610,000 men to begin military service; the revised plan lowered that number to 554,000. Frunze had calculated expenses at 427 million rubles, but received only 395 million. See his frank report to a plenum of the RVS convened between 24 November and 1 December 1924, "Ob itogakh reorga-nizatsii Krasnoi Armii," *Voenno-istoricheskii zhurnal* 6 (1966): 66–75 and 8 (1966): 64–72.

working by groping about and relying on chance" continued to set the tone for recruiters, who exhibited "an entirely impermissible attitude toward living human beings." The predictable result, Malinovskii observed, was "the lowering of the morale of the young recruit."[10] On top of all these travails, the RVS had released a large number of low- and middle-ranking officers, leaving many units with no drill instructors or other teaching personnel. "I can say with absolute certainty," Frunze confessed, "that during the course of this year we did not have a Red Army, if we mean by this an organized and trained force."[11]

After the miserable performance of the army in 1924, Sovnarkom devised yet another law on conscription, which remained in force until 1939.[12] The Law on Obligatory Military Service detailed a system of exemptions and deferments and new regulations for minority nationality groups. The conscription system not only accorded with the army command's projections for manpower needs but, like earlier service laws, defined categories of citizenship in the Soviet state. Disfranchised persons were no longer obliged to enlist in special service units, which had been abandoned during peacetime, but they were still required to pay a special military tax, which would go to social security offices for support of invalids of the Civil War. Women were eligible to serve on a voluntary basis during peacetime; in the event of war, the Army Commissariat might ask the state to decree obligatory service for them as well. The new law, together with the major organizational and personnel changes that Frunze was able to complete by the fall of 1925 and the general economic recovery across the nation, finally yielded the desired results. According to the army's annual report, over 90 percent of all eligible males appeared for induction. Cases of self-mutilation and simulation were pleasantly rare. Even many men eligible for deferments and other special benefits were not claiming them.[13]

The Remaking of the Officer Corps

Organizational stability was the crucial prerequisite for the reformers' plans to restructure relations of authority in the army, the

10. L. Malinovskii, Foreword, in A. Dobrovol'skii, N. Sokolov, and A. Speranskii, *Organizatsiia i tekhnika protsessa priema novobrantsev v otdel'noi voiskovoi chasti* (Moscow, 1925), pp. 4–6; see also D. Zuev, "V ozhidanii 1902 goda," *Na strazhe* 9 (1924): 24; "Gotov'tes' k prizyvu," *Krasnaia zvezda*, 24 July 1925, p. 1.

11. Frunze, "Ob itogakh reorganizatsii," p. 70.

12. "Zakon ob obiazatel'noi voennoi sluzhbe," *Sobranie zakonov* 62 (1925): 463, cited in Berkhin, *Voennaia reforma*, p. 250.

13. *Otchet Narkomvoenmora za 1925/26 g.*, p. 74, cited in Berkhin, *Voennaia reforma*, p. 255.

most far-reaching component of the reform programs. Under the catchword of "militarization" the team of Frunze, Gusev, and Bubnov introduced a series of measures designed to create a favorable environment in which the officers could expect their authority to be respected and the soldiers could expect a firm policy on discipline. By "militarization" the reformers actually meant the remilitarization of an institution that was perceived to have lost its distinctive military spirit because civilian organizations and practices had so penetrated the army's way of conducting its affairs. Though Frunze became the most eloquent and tireless spokesman for militarization, Voroshilov eventually took up the campaign, as did Bubnov, Gusev, and Mikhail Tukhachevsky. Just as the compromise that was reached on a mixed system of territorial militia and regular cadre army signaled a reevaluation and rejection of a series of political ideas integral to an earlier stage of the Revolution, so the program of militarization marked a change in the leadership's attitude about the internal workings of an army that looked to be ever more permanent. Above all, militarization signaled a decisive defeat for the commune model of army life which the Military Opposition had defended not so long ago. In proposing the interrelated set of reforms known as militarization, the army's leadership acknowledged that lack of discipline was a complex political, social, cultural, and even economic problem that could not be resolved without a coherent plan.

The reform team chose as the centerpiece of their militarization program the gradual phasing out of the practice of dual command, by which the watchdog commissars had been required to countersign all officers' orders before soldiers were obliged to obey them. As the state came to trust its officers more, especially those who had passed the test of loyalty during the Civil War, the commissars' responsibility for control over them lost its urgency. All authority that previously had been shared by officer and commissar now was to be unified in the hands of a trusted officer. The institution of the commissar and the practice of dual command had been justified as temporary policies dictated by the large and threatening presence of the military specialists. From the beginning, however, dual command had introduced ambiguity, tension, and often hostility into officers' relations with commissars, thereby diminishing the authority of both groups in soldiers' eyes. In practice the lines of command had been fluid during most of the Civil War, and areas of jurisdiction confused and disputed, most often because commissars could not resist the temptation to involve themselves in operational matters that were supposed to be the exclusive preserve of the military specialists. One-man command was seen as an effective antidote to what both officers and commissars called "bureaucratization" in the army, by which they meant excessive parallelism and the burdensome paperwork that went with it. Harried political workers complained that paper shuffling had come to replace all meaningful activities.[14] At least these admissions vindicated Smirnov, who had predicted, as spokesman for the Military Opposition, that dual command would strip commissars and political workers of real military authority and they would degenerate into mere chancellery employees.

The army command had contemplated the transition to one-man command even before the reform commissions had set to work. During Gusev's tenure at PUR, as we have seen, a 1922 regulation stipulated that if a commander or agency head had been a member of the party for no fewer than two years "and if he were sufficiently prepared for political leadership," then the relevant political department had the right to appoint an assistant for political matters instead of a full-fledged commissar. The responsibilities of the assistant were defined as "administrative-political" and "political enlightenment work."[15] Little progress was made then in implementing the reform because shortly after Gusev issued the regulation, Trotsky reassigned him to the Turkestan front. Again in March 1923 Sklianskii signed an order introducing limited one-man command in the central military administration.[16] Sklianskii indicated that the transition to one-man command in these agencies would accord with the stipulations set forth in the 1922 regulation, so it was clear that little progress had been made even a year later.

The reform team opened the door for the introduction of unified or one-man command (edinonachalie) by dismissing many senior and middle-ranking military specialists. In April Frunze reported that he had begun trimming and improving the political profile of the army's central administration. Red commanders and Communists with administrative experience were moving into positions vacated by the purge of "unreliable military specialists."[17] The larger

---

14. I. N., "Na novye rel'sy," Na strazhe 10–11 (1924); see also Politrabotnik 6–7 (1923): 4; V. Kasatkin, "Perspektivy raboty," Politrabotnik 4–5 (1924): 164–65. In a 1923 survey of political workers, the respondents admitted that 50 percent of all reports they wrote were fabricated, that hoodwinking was commonplace, and that they and their colleagues took a "formal bureaucratic approach"; "Udovletvoriaet li politruka rabota," SP 1 (1924): 51.

15. "Polozhenie o komissarakh Krasnoi Armii i Flota," 3 January 1922, in PPR III, pp. 56–65.

16. "Prikaz Revvoensoveta Respubliki o vvedenii edinonachaliia v upravleniiakh, uchrezhdeniiakh i zavedeniiakh voennogo vedomstva," 15 March 1923, in PPR III, pp. 134–35.

17. By the end of the year, Frunze claimed, the central administration had been reduced by 40 to 50 percent. Not only did large numbers of former Imperial Army officers continue in service after the Civil War, but an investigative commission located 2,598 former officers and military bureaucrats who had served in the White

presence of party members, predominantly of working-class origins and with Civil War experience, was said to be bolstering troop morale.[18] Still the reform proceeded slowly. The army leadership hesitated to move any faster than it did in large measure because there were too few officers and commissars who satisfied both the political and military requirements necessary to place unified command in their hands. Very few Red commanders had any formal military education; they had gained their skills in combat. But, surprisingly, they also were poor in political understanding, or, as their commissar counterparts expressed it, they were politically illiterate. The commissars, on the other hand, shone in the political sphere but at best had roughly the same level of military expertise as the Red commanders. As the military schools and academies underwent their own reorganization and reforms, they began to raise the level of military expertise of the Red commanders and commissars, but the process was frustratingly slow. The military specialists, for their part, had formal military training, but were even less politically literate than the Red commanders. Until the army command had adequate numbers of trusted Red commanders to replace the military specialists, dual command could not be abandoned altogether.

To speed up the personnel changes and to raise the overall professional level of the officer corps, Soviet military schools and academies began turning out more graduates. During the first year, however, dismissals outpaced promotions and graduations. Only in 1925 did the numbers of officers and administrative personnel begin to climb again. The percentage of Communists among the military elite rose from nearly 23 percent of the officers and 18.8 percent of the administrative personnel in 1923 to over 40.9 percent of the combined staffs in 1925.[19] To address the problem of inadequate officer political preparation, the RVS commanded that the entire officer corps successfully complete a "minimum program of political knowledge" by the end of the summer of 1924. Whenever possible, officers were to involve themselves in political enlightenment work.

---

armies. By 1 January 1925 that number had dropped to 377. See *Otchet Narkomvoenmora za 1923/24 g.*, pp. 66, 73; *Otchet Narkomvoenmora za 1924/25 g.*, pp. 127, 316, cited in Berkhin, *Voennaia reforma*, p. 261.

18. In the Leningrad Military District the administration was reduced by 33.5 percent. See Shevchenko's dissertation, "Ideino-politicheskoe vospitanie," pp. 84–85. Party members in the central apparatus rose from 12 to 25 percent. The percentage who claimed proletarian origins climbed to 50. See Pikha, "Bor'ba," pp. 83–84, 86.

19. In 1923 the Army Commissariat listed 74,910 officers and administrative personnel. That number dropped to 53,003 in 1924, but rose in 1925 to 76,273 men, 15 percent of the entire army. That number included officers (58.1%), political staff (19.4%), administrative personnel (18.6%), medical staff (3%), and veterinary staff (0.9%): Berkhin, *Voennaia reforma*, p. 262.

To add teeth to these measures, Frunze indicated that an officer's performance in political enlightenment work would enter his personnel record for review when he came up for promotion.[20]

In June 1924 the Central Committee's Orgburo decided that enough progress had been made in reducing the differences between the political and military staffs and decreed the transition to one-man command for the entire army. It appointed Bubnov to head a commission to set the pace and determine the process for implementing the transition. At a Central Committee meeting on 28 July, which heard the commission's report, Frunze spoke enthusiastically in favor of the transition. Stalin underlined the need to make the transition as quickly as possible and criticized those who were urging excessive caution.[21] A month later, in symbolic recognition of the army leadership's commitment to the reform, Frunze abolished the titles of Red commander and military specialist and decreed one title for all officers, commander of the Workers'-Peasants' Red Army.[22]

Despite a general consensus among Red commanders, commissars, and military specialists that the army was in deplorable condition, the reforms from above sparked considerable fears among all three groups. From the outset, the reforms met great resistance; consequently, they were implemented in stages beginning in the summer of 1924 and continuing through 1925. In large measure military personnel simply feared the unknown future that awaited them. The concept of one-man command had entered the political and military debates before any real consensus had been reached on a clear definition of the new arrangement. Most important, the leadership faced a decision about the future of the commissars. Clearly commissars still had a role to play in monitoring the political and moral condition of the troops subordinate to them, but where would they stand in relation to an officer entrusted with one-man command? The rumors and later the official announcement that the RVS intended to implement one-man command throughout the army provoked panic in the political administration. The political staff feared that the army's new leaders were about to abandon them for the embraces of the officer corps and pointed to a series of articles in the officers' journal, Voennyi vestnik, which proposed the very mergers of the political organs with the operational staff that the commissars were protesting. The articles only confirmed the widely held perception

20. "Prikaz RVS SSSR o vovlechenii komandnogo sostava v politiko-prosvetitel'nuiu rabotu v chastiakh Krasnoi Armii," 8 April 1924, in PPR III, pp. 205–6.

21. Petrov, Stroitel'stvo, pp. 159–60.

22. Berkhin, Voennaia reforma, pp. 263, 293.

that officers were eager to rid themselves of the political commissar and his bothersome educational programs. Political workers demanded that only commanders who were also party members be considered for promotion. They also lobbied for more rigorous examinations in political literacy for commanders. In September 1924 the directors of political departments in the Western Military District expressed their grave reservations about the wholesale move to the new command principle. They recommended that one-man command be implemented very gradually, and only for commanders with "respectable" party careers.[23]

The September resolution served as the model for one adopted by an army-wide meeting of political directors convened in November. Frunze and Iosif Unshlikht appeared before the meeting to defend the reform program, but failed to assuage all the delegates' fears. The directors expressed approval for the reorganizations in the central and local military agencies, but they demanded a temporary halt to further reforms until the success of the initial changes could be determined. They even gave their grudging approval to the territorial militia system, "despite a series of problems," but insisted that civilian soviet and party organizations fulfill their share of the responsibilities and contribute to the costs of organizing the militia formations. On the most troubling question of one-man command, however, the directors urged caution and demanded an affirmation from the center that the transition to one-man command would not "in any way diminish the role of political work, or the significance of political organs in the Red Army." The most important task of the one-man commander, the directors insisted, should be to raise the authority of the political apparatus and its work. They called on PUR to combat the attitude that political work was now to be deemphasized, held by "part of the officer corps," and to ban the practice of transforming political departments into sections of officers' staffs.[24] Bubnov drafted a resolution incorporating the convention's reservations and recommendations. The RVS conceded that the current reoganization "will meet with considerable difficulties and can be implemented only in part." It forbade commanders to merge political departments with their staff organizations, and ordered commanders to preserve the autonomy of all political organs and to respect the important role of political work in the Red Army. At the

23. Ibid., p. 294.

24. "Rezoliutsii Vsesoiuznogo soveshchaniia nachal'nikov politupravlenii okrugov, flotov, voenkomov korpusov, divizii, nachal'nikov politotdelov divizii," 17–27 November 1924, in *Vsearmeiskie soveshchaniia*, pp. 157–83; see esp. documents 87–88.

same time, the RVS also recommended a measure that clearly went against the wishes of the political workers: that even nonparty officers be eligible for promotion to one-man command.[25]

Noncommunist officers, particularly military specialists, feared that their days were numbered. Indeed, beginning in 1924 certification commissions vigorously began promoting Communist commanders, graduates of Soviet military academies, and hundreds of commissars who were considered to have the requisite administrative or combat experience. The purges of military specialists in the administrative apparatus also fueled their fears. Noncommunist officers charged that the Red Army leadership unwisely had committed itself to 100 percent "communization." Frunze, himself a Red commander, attempted to allay the noncommunists' suspicions by assuring them that there was "no possible way" that the army command could achieve 100 percent "communization" of its officer corps, even if it wanted to do so. "One-man command," he promised, "is in no way tied to a wholesale communization of the Red Army." The noncommunist officer will have "a secure place in the ranks of the Red Army."[26]

Eventually Frunze had to make more than mere rhetorical concessions to the influential critics of one-man command: he slowed the entire process. The reformers postponed the transition indefinitely in the navy and in all nationalities units, institutions that remained politically very sensitive. In the regular army Frunze limited the reform to the lowest command levels for the time being; furthermore, he ordered a more thorough scrutiny of the social origins and party service records of all men brought up for promotion. The considerable resistance effectively slowed the changeover to one-man command. By 1 October 1925, more than a year after the Orgburo publicly announced the reform, only 14 percent of the highest-ranking officers exercised full command. Voroshilov tried to force the tempo of the transition after he succeeded Frunze in late 1925, but resistance persisted.[27] The changeover proceeded more rapidly in the lower ranks, but the reform was pronounced completed only in 1931.[28] Despite the delays, both the RVS and the party's Central

25. "Rezoliutsiia plenuma RVS SSSR o prakticheskikh shagakh po provedeniiu edinonachaliia," 24 November–1 December 1924, in PPR III, pp. 233–34; Petrov, Stroitel'stvo, p. 160.

26. M. V. Frunze, "Itogi plenuma RVS SSSR," 20 December 1924, in Sobranie sochinenii, 2:182.

27. Berkhin, Voennaia reforma, pp. 306, 311.

28. By April 1925, one-man command had been implemented among 14 percent of divisional commanders and 26 percent of regimental commanders. Six months later those figures rose to 44 and 33 percent, respectively. See Iu. P. Petrov, "Deiatel'nost' Kommunisticheskoi partii po provedeniiu edinonachaliia v Vooruzhennykh Silakh (1925–1931 gody)," Voenno-istoricheskii zhurnal 5 (1963): 18–19. By 1 October 1925,

Committee refused to retreat from their commitment to raise the authority of the officer corps. "There is to be no turning back," Frunze insisted.[29]

Frunze defended the policy as one dictated by the course of events and by the evolution of the commissar's role from that of control to that of administration and organization. Although he contended that there was no reason to view this evolution as a decline in the commissars' influence, he sent out very mixed signals to military personnel. In a speech to students at the Red Army's military academy, he seemed ready to part company with the commissars altogether. "If we have to fight in two or three years," he speculated, "we'll need commissars." But, he added, if before the next war the army should be able to improve its political situation and inner cohesion, "then perhaps we'll be able to get by without commissars."[30] No one doubted any longer that the army's leaders were elevating the officer corps in status and authority at the expense of the political staff. In a letter to all political workers, the Central Committee secretary, Andrei Andreev, lent official sanction to the elevated status of the officer corps. "There is no doubt," he declared, " that the transition to one-man command will increase the social and political weight of the command staff."[31] And despite Frunze's and Bubnov's reassurances that political work still occupied a prominent place in the structure of the Red Army, officers won permission not to attend the political classes that were obligatory for the troops, in a reversal of the most recent concessions to the political staff. After investigating an outpouring of officer complaints, the Commission on the Overload of the Command and Political Staffs concluded that officers could not meet all the expectations that were stipulated in the regulations on one-man command if they also retained their obligations in political enlightenment.[32] Officers were still required to participate in one mass social organization on a regular basis. In 1925 a new regulation on army commissars affixed the commissars' demotion in status. The most recent regulation, that from 1922, still authorized the commissars to exercise political control over the activities of Red Army men, commanders, and the administrative and

---

73 percent of all corps commanders, 80 percent of all brigade commanders, and 54 percent of all directors of military educational institutions held one-man commands. See Berkhin, *Voennaia reforma*, p. 306.

29. Frunze, "Itogi plenuma," p. 180.

30. Petrov, *Stroitel'stvo*, p. 164n.

31. A. Andreev, "Ob edinonachalii v Krasnoi armii," 6 March 1925, in *KPSS o vooruzhennykh silakh Sovetskogo Soiuza* (1981), p. 228.

32. Chief of Staff Sergei Kamenev chaired the commission, which met in March 1925 and included representatives of the General Staff, PUR, and the editorial board of *Krasnaia zvezda*. The RVS issued a decree based on the commission's recommendations in May. See *Na strazhe* 12–13 (1924): 14–15 and 7 (1925): 8; *Krasnaia zvezda*, 24 March 1925, p. 1.

economic staffs. Now "commissars were appointed first of all to direct and conduct day-to-day party and political work" and "to ensure the education and training of the personnel of the Red Army
and Navy in a spirit of class cohesion and Communist enlightenment." Conspicuously absent was any reference to monitoring officers' conduct.[33]

Political workers justifiably felt themselves to be demoted to mere
coordinators of political enlightenment work. Many were complaining that they saw no alternative but to retire before they were dismissed. To forestall the loss of so many talented men to civilian life
and to preclude their total embitterment with the army command,
Frunze offered the commissars an avenue for promotion if they were
willing to improve their military skills. The RVS and PUR launched
a campaign for the "militarization of the political staff," offering incentives for political workers to return to school for military
training.[34] In fact, hundreds of political workers took advantage of
the educational opportunities and enrolled in military academies.
Almost without exception, they were promoted to one-man commands after they completed their training. In early 1925 the certification commissions reviewed the service records of the entire
political and officer staffs and promoted large numbers of political
workers to military commands.[35]

The RVS conceived the transition to one-man command as only
the first step in its program to elevate the authority of the officer
corps. Because the powers and responsibilities of officers were to
grow under the provisions of *edinonachalie* and also because officers had been complaining for years about their unreasonable work
loads, the army's leaders decided to expand the number and responsibilities of junior officers (*mladshii komsostav*). In large measure
the junior officers were meant to serve as a buffer between the senior officers and the regular troops. In this sense, they corresponded
to the noncommissioned officers of the most Western armies. They
were to take responsibility for activities that required the most close-
range and constant daily contact with the troops, such as routine
drilling and training. The Red Army, much like its imperial predecessor, had so far been unable to attract enough men to fill the middle ranks. Now the junior officer was designated a key component of
the new structure of authority, "the foundation upon which rests the

33. Berkin cites "Vremennoe polozhenie o voennykh komissarakh RKKA i RKKF,"
30 June 1925, in *Sputnik molodogo komandira* (Moscow, 1927), p. 506. See his *Voennaia reforma*, pp. 395–96.
34. Frunze, "Krasnaia Armiia na rubezhe 8-go goda ee sushchestvovaniia," 25 February 1925, in *Sobranie*, 3:124–25; L. S., "Itogi dvukh soveshchanii," *Krasnaia rota* 22
(1925): 4; Andreev, "Ob edinonachalii," p. 227.
35. Petrov, "Deiatel'nost'," p. 17.

entire matter of discipline," according to Frunze, who placed himself squarely behind the new policy. The junior command staff, he
said, would be a "unique transmitter of all educational influences
from above."[36]

A new disciplinary code assigned more punitive powers to the
junior officers. Bubnov called on all commissars, procurators, military tribunals, and party cells to devote special attention to raising
the authority of the command staff and of the junior officers in particular. To combat the poverty that discouraged men from remaining
in the service, the RVS marked out a long-range plan to raise substantially the level of benefits available to the junior officers.[37] Finally, in yet another blow to the political staff, the junior officers too
were freed from the requirement to attend all political classes with
the troops, although they still were obliged to attend some. PUR justified the move as an effort to free the junior officers for more
strictly military functions, especially the coordination of training
and drill with their superior officers.[38]

With the approval of the first military budget for 1924, the RVS
earmarked large sums to improve the material conditions of all military men, but most especially of the officer corps. Frunze appealed
for pay raises and larger expenditures for housing so that officers
would no longer have to live in civilian quarters or in dilapidated
barracks. He compared the low wages of Soviet officers with those in
bourgeois armies and complained that officers could not even look
forward to an adequate pension after retirement.[39] In June 1924 the
RVS raised officers' pay by an average of 21 percent. Another raise in
November increased officers' pay by one-third and that of regular
troops three and one-half times. Allowances for living quarters were
raised, and the pension program was put on a solid footing.[40] In
early 1925 Stalin lent his authoritative support to Frunze's petition
for an increase in the military budget. Stalin pointed to growing tensions in the international arena as justification for the greater expenditures at a time of fiscal tightening.[41]

36. Frunze, "Kadrovaia armiia i militsiia," in *Sobranie*, 3:287. See also the statement on the importance of the junior officer in *Materialy soveshchaniia po
vneshkol'noi rabote v RKKA* (Moscow, 1927), 57.

37. N. Polev, *Komandnyi sostav RKKA i inostrannykh armii* (Leningrad, 1927), p.
215; A. Shteingart, "Komandiry Krasnoi Armii po 1266 anketam," *Politrabotnik* 2–3
(1924): 80.

38. N. Tatarintsev, "Itogi soveshchaniia voenno-sudebnykh rabotnikov," *Krasnyi
boets* 6 (1925): 6–7; SP 2 (1926): 54.

39. M. V. Frunze, "Oborona strany (Doklad na III s''ezde sovetov)," in *Krasnaia
armiia i oborona Sovetskogo soiuza* (Moscow, 1925), pp. 36–39.

40. Berkhin, *Voennaia reforma*, pp. 326–27; *Krasnaia zvezda*, 6 June 1925, p. 1; 13
January 1925, p. 4; December 1925; *Sobranie zakonov* 62 (1925): 463.

41. Stalin, "Rech' na plenume TsK RKP(b)," 19 January 1925, in *Sochineniia*, 7:
11–14.

Plenary session of the Revolutionary Military Council of the USSR, November 1924. From M. V. Frunze, *Sobranie sochinenii*, 3 vols. (Moscow, 1926–1929), courtesy of Division of Art, Prints, and Photographs, The New York Public Library, Astor, Lenox, and Tilden Foundations.

The package of measures designed to raise the authority and living standards of the officer corps gradually accomplished one of the RVS's goals, a reduction in personnel turnover. Not only did an officer's career become more attractive, but the officer corps was revitalized by the promotion of younger men and by the reentry into army service of the graduates of Soviet military schools. The new officers inherited the places freed by the retirement and dismissal of many exhausted veterans of the recent wars and by the purges of politically "alien" or "unreliable" military specialists and Trotsky-ists. The Red Army now had a loyal and increasingly well-trained group of officers who would remain in place until the military purges of the mid-1930s.

Trade Union Methods and Iron Discipline

In 1925 the RVS issued new uniforms designed clearly to distinguish commanders, political workers, and regular soldiers. The new

Members of the Revolutionary Military Council of the USSR, 1925: (*left to right*) Sergei Kamenev, Kliment Voroshilov, Mikhail Frunze, Iosif Unshlikht, Andrei Bubnov. From M. V. Frunze, *Sobranie sochinenii*, 3 vols. (Moscow, 1926–1929), courtesy of Division of Art, Prints, and Photographs, The New York Public Library, Astor, Lenox, and Tilden Foundations.

uniforms symbolized how much attitudes toward authority and rank had changed since the Revolution, when soldiers tore off officers' epaulettes and demanded to be treated with dignity as citizens. Gone was the familiarity between officers and troops which veterans recalled from the Civil War. Now that the state had an officer corps that claimed proper social origins in the workers and peasants, it relentlessly sought to reinstate strict, traditional military discipline for regular soldiers. This reform, too, met with considerable resistance; consequently, it was implemented piecemeal and gradually over several years.

The Military Commission declared that indiscipline had reached a state of crisis. Frunze, in his extraordinarily candid address to a plenum of the RVS in late November 1924, admitted that the initial reforms actually had compounded the officers' problems. The chaotic recruitment drive brought disgruntled soldiers into units that were short of instructors and whose commanders also had fallen prey to "demobilization moods." By late fall 1924 Frunze warned that the situation had become threatening.[42] The crisis extended from careless attitudes toward uniforms and physical appearance to systematic refusal to obey superiors' commands. A senior political worker complained, "We had instances when Red Army men, knowing that discipline in the Red Army rested on a fully conscious sense of duty," fell to discussing with their commander the orders they had just been given, all this "while standing in formation." Soldiers seemed to understand conscious discipline to mean that in every case they were to be persuaded that a given order was reasonable before obeying it.[43] The defenders of "conscious discipline" continued to argue that the Red Army was distinguished from its tsarist predecessor precisely by the comradely relations between officers and troops, based on appeals to reason and consciousness. This imperative to safeguard the special type of discipline in the new army had been one of the arguments of the Military Opposition at the Eighth Party Congress and an integral component of the commune model.

Once the reform team was satisfied that the first stages of their scheme were being slowly implemented, they embarked on a campaign to win support for changing attitudes toward discipline in the army, once again under the slogan of militarization. Especially in the area of military training, civilian methods of persuasion and debate—"trade union methods," as Stalin and Trotsky, among others, disparagingly called them[44]—had eroded discipline and combat readiness in the Red Army. The opponents of "trade union methods" often raised the issue of the Red Army's overwhelmingly peasant character. Perhaps, the advocates of traditional discipline argued, if the Red Army were still composed primarily of proletarians, as it was during the very first months of the Soviet Republic's existence, then "conscious discipline" might suffice to guarantee obedience to orders. But, unfortunately, the class composition was no longer so conducive to risky experiments with the nation's defense. A peasant

---

42. Frunze, "Ob itogakh," *Voenno-istoricheskii zhurnal* 8 (1966): 68.

43. N. P. Komarov, "Distsiplina i nachal'niki," *Krasnaia zvezda*, 11 December 1925, p. 3.

44. See Stalin's remarks at the Tenth Party Congress in 1921, when he compared "trade union methods" to the far preferable "military methods," in which persuasion was secondary to coercion: "Nashi raznoglasiia," reprinted from *Pravda*, 19 January 1921, in Stalin, *Sochineniia*, 5:4–14. The negative attitude toward trade unions had a prehistory of its own. Bolsheviks had recent and painful memories of their failure to penetrate the trade union leadership before and during 1917. The strongest Bolshevik support among workers during 1917 came from factory committees that challenged the authority of the Menshevik- and SR-dominated trade union hierarchies. See also the positions of Bukharin and Lenin during the trade union debates in 1920 and 1921, in Daniels, *Conscience of the Revolution*, pp. 129–36, 156–59.

soldier lacked the "consciousness" that allowed for the luxury of a more lenient form of authority in the military. In fact, most military leaders no longer believed that even an army composed predominantly of proletarians could operate according to the comradely rules of the Civil War. And, of course, the military specialists had never favored "conscious discipline."

In January 1925 Frunze officially opened the door for a reevaluation of Red Army policy with an address titled "Lenin and the Red Army," in which he couched the issue of military discipline in the context of Lenin's views on party discipline.[45] By invoking Lenin's authority and choosing party discipline as his analogy, Frunze at one stroke linked the current intraparty struggle to the politics of the military; and he also posed the army as a model of relations in society. Lenin, in a typically polemic article titled "Infantile Disorders of Left Communism," had tried to bring around the Left Communists, whose membership overlapped with that of the Military Opposition, from their quasi-anarchist rejection of state authority to a more "orthodox" appreciation of the realities of political power.[46] Lenin offered a paradigm for the relationship between the nonproletarian masses and the vanguard Bolshevik party; the masses lacked revolutionary consciousness, and only the party could foster it in them. These views revealed how thoroughly Lenin repudiated the commune model of 1917, even though many of his ideas about the vanguard and masses had appeared in prerevolutionary works, most notably *What Is to Be Done?* In a similar fashion, Frunze distanced himself and the army command from the commune model of armed force. In his address, the army command stood in for the party and the Red Army masses filled the place of the nonproletarians who lacked the essential consciousness necessary to build genuine socialism. After establishing his analogy of the party and army command, Frunze proceeded to the real issue of contention, the proper Marxist attitude toward discipline—an attitude, he claimed, that "certain of our military workers do not entirely understand." He established three conditions for army discipline to be effective: first, the officer corps and political staffs must be as selfless and steadfast as the party itself; second, the army command must maintain "living and organic contact" with the Red Army masses; third, the sol-

45. M. V. Frunze, "Lenin i Krasnaia Armiia," *SP* 18 (1925): 1–5. Frunze addressed a solemn meeting at the Military Academy of the Red Army on the occasion of the first anniversary of Lenin's death.

46. Lenin wrote the work in April 1920; see "Detskaia bolezn' 'levizny' v kommunizme," in *PSS*, 41:1–104.

dier masses must be convinced of the correctness of "our leadership" on the basis of the actions and behavior of the army's elite. Next he turned to his most controversial thesis. It was impossible, he maintained, to have "inner conscious discipline" without attention to external details of order. "To achieve this order we must, and here it is absolutely inevitable, employ the familiar elements of *mushtra.*" The word *mushtra* and its variant *mushtrovka* came from the rhetoric of the Imperial Army and carried connotations of extremely harsh drill-sergeant discipline. It was a style of command that had been associated with the military specialists, and they had been the only ones to employ the term favorably. If a Red commander or commissar had uttered the word during the Civil War, invariably he would have done so with opprobrium. By 1925, however, a significant part of the Civil War generation of commanders and commissars had also developed a revulsion for the "trade union methods" of persuasion which civilian organizations tried to introduce in the army. Once Frunze pronounced the previously unmentionable word, he opened wide the gates for those who had remained silent for fear they would be accused of reviving reactionary ideology.

Two days after Frunze's address in Moscow, the political workers of the Ukrainian Military District convened to discuss two items, one-man command and discipline. PUR director Bubnov arrived to win support for the reform team's policies. Vladimir Zatonskii, now director of the Ukrainian District's Political Administration, delivered the official report on disciplinary policy, in which he complained about inconsistency in commanders' practices and demanded "planned, systematic inculcation of discipline."[47] Notably, Zatonskii did not use the term "conscious discipline." Bubnov appeared in other military districts to proselytize the new discipline and issued a special circular in which he outlined measures to combat the widespread "weakening of discipline."[48] In April 1925 Bubnov chaired a commission to draft a new disciplinary code to replace the 1922 version. The military press aired the commission's discussions and elicited an impassioned debate on the role and type of discipline suitable for a socialist army. Frunze declared that the time for looking the other way at infractions of discipline was over. Officers could no longer complain that difficult material conditions prevented them from pursuing a determined course in this area. "Now," he proclaimed, "we are waging a decisive struggle against

47. *Krasnaia zvezda,* 27 January 1925, p. 4.
48. "Tsirkuliar PU RKKA o merakh po ukrepleniiu voinskoi distsipliny v chastiakh Krasnoi Armii i Flota," 10 February 1925, in *PPR* III, pp. 252–54.

all slovenliness, loose discipline, negligence, and unconscious attitudes toward service."[49]

An articulate and vocal Red Army officer, Aleksandr Sediakin, the current commander of the Volga Military District and a frequent writer on military training,[50] assailed "the ignoramuses who persist in their campaign for conscious and revolutionary discipline." For an army to be distinguished from civilian society—otherwise what sort of army could it be?—a certain kind of discipline was required. To expect discipline to rest on "consciousness," Sediakin argued, "is not realistic at all; moreover, it is the most naive romanticism." Even the army's Communists and Komsomol members were not spared Sediakin's jibes, for "these most loyal cadres did not demonstrate by their example any good intentions of conscious subordination to the demands of military discipline." If party and Komsomol members could not be counted on to demonstrate the necessary consciousness, Sediakin queried, how could the "revolutionary romantics" hope for any better behavior from illiterate peasant recruits?[51] Sediakin insisted that, from the first minute of his army service, a soldier had to be made aware that he was not just serving time, nor was army life designed for his entertainment. The army was "a severe, often very severe, school of life and combat." Never in history had anyone attained military success "with sentimentalizing and sugar-and-honey democratic methods of educating a soldier." Revolutionary armies "come to consciousness only via mountains of corpses." The only way to ensure victory in war is to instill the strictest discipline and to make the most severe demands on soldiers. After all, he concluded, military discipline "has given to the ruling classes thus far the capacity to wage war with masses to whom the genuine aims of battle remain unknown." Did it make sense for the Red Army to enter into battle with "the cohesion of class discipline alone, when military discipline could better guarantee success?" Se-

49. Frunze, "Krasnaia armiia i oborona Sovetskogo Soiuza," 19 May 1925, in *Sobranie*, 3:233.

50. A brief biography of Sediakin in the Soviet journal of military history notes that Sediakin was "precise and painstaking to the point of pedantry" in matters of military service. Sediakin, of peasant background, graduated from an agricultural technical school before the Revolution and worked as a land surveyor. He served in the World War, attaining the rank of staff captain *(shtabs-kapitan)* by February 1917. He joined the party in May 1917 and rose quickly through a series of commands during the Civil War. Sediakin's views on military training became even more influential after 1927, when he was appointed director of the Training and Drill Administration of the Red Army. He was one of the organizers of the journal for officers, *Voennyi vestnik*. See *Voenno-istoricheskii zhurnal* 11 (1963): 123–26.

51. A. Sediakin, "Puti stroitel'stva boesposobnoi armii," *Voennyi vestnik* 8 (1925): 214–15. For more complaints about the inability of party and Komsomol members to learn habits of subordination, see A. Rudoi, "Iacheika, distsiplina i voennyi uklon v rabote (V poriadke ucheta 9-i kavdivizii)," *SP* 17 (1925): 19.

diakin did not advocate sending troops into battle unaware of "the genuine aims of battle," but his harsh attacks on the "romantic" advocates of "soft discipline" showed how far the debate on disciplinary policy had moved in the few short months since Frunze's opening salvoes. Especially now that the army had an officer corps of suitably "democratic" social background, it was argued, forms of discipline that superficially resembled those of tsarist times were fundamentally different because the social and political setting of Soviet Russia drastically altered the character of all relations of authority. In other words, *mushtra* administered by an officer of proletarian social origins was a perfectly Marxist and revolutionary policy, even more so because the army was overwhelmingly made up of peasant conscripts. State and party leaders had been making very similar arguments about the need to curtail industrial democracy because of the deproletarianization of the Russian working class and the danger of petit bourgeois influences in NEP society. The political elite concluded from its often peculiar forms of class analysis that because power now was formally in the hands of the proletariat, higher state and party organs were able to preserve the proper form of consciousness necessary to construct a socialist order. Just as strikes and other forms of collective worker protest were virtually banned, so soldiers would have to obey unquestioningly and leave their civilian ideas about politics at home.

The proponents of "conscious" or "soft" discipline were losing ground fast. Only a year earlier they still had been able to keep references to *mushtra* out of sanctioned political discourse. But now Sediakin's views appeared in a lead editorial of the official mouthpiece of the Red Army officer corps, *Voennyi vestnik*. When his opponents dared to criticize Sediakin or others who shared his views, they received harsh rebukes and insulting epithets. "Once and for all," another military spokesman on training matters demanded, "we must expunge from our conduct everything that is 'from democracy' "; furthermore, all "the little chats" with commanders must end, together with "the straggling and slovenliness."[52] What became clear during the debates over discipline was that a growing and influential group of military men resented the intrusion of civilians and what they scorned as civilian techniques into the army's way of operating. This was certainly not the first time that military men had expressed their dissatisfaction with the state of civil-military relations. But at least since the Civil War, they had suffered what they perceived as substantial defeats at the hands of their civilian antagonists; now they sensed that the tables might be turning in their favor. Indeed, they had altered the parameters of acceptable discourse

52. Khadaev, "Zadachi shestogo goda," *Krasnyi kursant* 7 (1925): 2.

in the spheres of discipline and civil-military relations. They insisted on a special army structure of authority which allowed them unimpeded control over their own organization and personnel.

In the case of discipline, the real issue was how to define a suitable and effective system of punishments. Discussion revolved around who should be punished for which crimes, a scale of punishments, and who had the right to punish in which settings. The proponents of "conscious" discipline located allies within the civilian judicial establishment. To a large degree the struggles were an extension of conventional bureaucratic politics because the civilians were advancing their own institutional interests: they wanted greater authority for their own organization. But the struggles also had a genuinely ideological component as well. Even during the Civil War civilian authorities had contested the creation of a separate military organism within the socialist state, but then the major institutional contender for control over soldiers' and officers' lives was Vsevobuch. Later the Commissariat of Enlightenment's Glavpolitprosvet temporarily and ineffectively challenged PUR for control of political enlightenment. Now that both of those organizations had lost their political clout, leadership in the struggle for civilian control over military affairs fell to the judicial apparatus.

The judicial workers had a long history of opposition to military practices, but under martial law during the Civil War, civilians had had to remain silent while military tribunals administered justice throughout most of the country. Military tribunals were not the only challenge to civilian efforts to attain control over "revolutionary socialist legality." From the beginning, the Commissariat of Justice had had a second formidable opponent in the Cheka and its successor, the GPU.[53] In this particular battle, the Cheka unwittingly aided the army in undermining all claims that the civilians advanced. As late as 1923 military tribunals were still trying citizens, mostly civilians, charged with counterrevolutionary activity during the Civil War.[54] Justice Commissar Nikolai Krylenko objected to the survival of the military tribunals as an "illegal separate judicial system." Civilian judicial personnel throughout the country viewed the tribunals as organs of summary justice. What civilian authorities objected to most strenuously, however, was the military's definition of crime, which in their opinion was far too comprehensive.

53. See Leggett, *Cheka;* and Lennard Gerson, *The Secret Police in Lenin's Russia* (Philadelphia: Temple University Press, 1976). Once again, for an interesting parallel from late imperial Russia, see Fuller's account of the struggles over justice after the 1905 Revolution in *Civil-Military Conflict*, chap. 5.

54. See, e.g., the report on the activities of the Military Tribunal at the Western Front, A. Vasil'ev, "Prestupnost' na zapadnom fronte," *Krasnaia prisiaga* 12 (1923): 169–70, 173–74.

In October 1924 an attempt to settle these contentious issues was made in the "Regulation on Military Crimes," the first national military criminal code. In fact, the regulation was a version of the Justice Commissariat's 1922 criminal code; the major innovation was a definition of the legal subject. Only those citizens currently serving in the military or those eligible for but evading service illegally could be tried for military crimes. This definition represented a victory for the civilian judicial administration because it excluded military authorities from all but the most narrowly defined army environment. In addition, the Commissariat of Justice succeeded in adding a further category of military crime that protected civilian society from the depredations of military personnel. The regulation declared as illegal any "violence perpetrated on the civilian population by a serviceman during wartime or in battle conditions."[55]

The regulation met resistance from military judicial authorities, who convened in February 1925 to devise a strategy for persuading the nation's leadership that the army's effectiveness rested on a peculiar punitive policy.[56] The delegates passed a resolution that answered their civilian critics point by point. In army conditions, they declared, the overriding concern is effective discipline; therefore, not only acts punishable under civilian criminal codes but infractions of discipline that fall outside those narrow categories must be punished. "The spread of such infractions can only undermine the combat readiness of a unit."[57] It was precisely these infractions that made up the largest category of military crimes. Above all, military tribunals heard cases involving soldiers who were absent without leave (still called deserters), who refused to obey commands, who violated regulations outlined in service manuals, and who damaged equipment. The next largest category, malfeasance and economic crimes—bribe taking, theft of state property, embezzlement, and squandering—troubled civilian officials considerably less, though they still felt it was their obligation, not their military counterparts', to try such cases.

Military tribunals regularly jailed violators for what civilians considered to be minor infractions. The civilian spokesmen protested that a jail term amounted to disfranchisement for the convicted man

55. Chkhikvadze, *Sovetskoe voenno-ugolovnoe pravo*, pp. 98–99.
56. The convention was chaired by Valentin Trifonov, president of the Military Collegium of the Supreme Court. The report on crime in the army was delivered by Nikolai Kuz'min, procurator of the Military Collegium. Kuz'min had risen to his post through the army's Political Administration. He had served as director of the political administrations on the Turkestan front and later in the Siberian Military District. He headed the Military Training Administration just before his appointment to the procuracy. He was succeeded at the Training Administration by Sediakin.
57. Tatarintsev, "Itogi soveshchaniia voenno-sudebnykh rabotnikov," *Krasnyi boets* 6 (1925): 5–6.

and could turn otherwise loyal soldiers into "disseminators of harmful influence in the army." At least on this point the civilians won a concession. The convention resolved not to disfranchise soldiers who received sentences of less than a year, but to assign these soldiers to punitive detachments that would correspond to the correctional institutions for civilian lawbreakers. Furthermore, the military delegates promised to "exchange information" with other judicial bodies outside the army. The civilians had to content themselves with the minimal control opportunities afforded by such exchanges of information.

On the fundamental issue of a distinctive punitive policy for the army, however, the delegates stood their ground. "Everything that has been said," concluded the delegate V. Malkis, "compels us, the tribunal personnel, to insist that our unified class punitive policy" demands methods distinctive from those by which "our civilian judicial organs" operate. The special methods of the army reflected the "interests, conditions, and everyday life of the Red Army."[58] The strident tone of the army delegates' arguments made its way into the provisional disciplinary code that the RVS promulgated in September 1925. The new code incorporated the two-pronged approach of increasing the authority of the officer corps and sanctioning harsher punishments for infractions of discipline by regular troops. The code obliged all military personnel "to observe with precision the order established in the Red Army by the laws and service manuals and all supporting commands and directives of superiors." Superiors had the responsibility to encourage and reward subordinates who distinguished themselves by their obedient conduct and to punish the negligent and the insubordinate. In a combat situation superiors had the right and obligation to employ "armed force" against those who failed to obey orders.

The major difference between the new code and its 1919 and 1922 predecessors was the introduction of a hierarchy of punitive measures that were to be applied to different categories of personnel. The 1919 code had recognized only one category of punishment for all servicemen. Now the punishments for regular troops would differ from those prescribed for officers. A regular soldier could be publicly reprimanded, for example, but an officer no longer faced such humiliation. Finally, the code expanded the types of recommended "prophylactic measures" so that superiors had a broader range of techniques to apply for the now highly differentiated categories of infractions that soldiers and lower-ranking officers might commit.[59] Separate punitive policies for officers and regular troops had also

58. V. Malkis, "Karatel'naia politika v Krasnoi Armii (k soveshchaniiu voennykh tribunalov i voennoi prokuratury)," *Krasnaia zvezda*, 21 February 1925, p. 1.
59. Berkhin, *Voennaia reforma*, pp. 369–71.

been a target of the Military Opposition at the Eighth Party Congress. The 1925 code signaled yet another defeat for the opposition's commune model of army relations. The revisions were justified by the need to increase the authority of the officer corps.

As soon as the discussion of discipline began, the army's critics warned that the new punitive policies threatened a wave of mass desertions. At the Third Congress of Soviets, in May 1925, Frunze, in his first major public appearance as army commissar since he replaced Trotsky, dispelled such alarmist predictions with a barrage of statistics. Instead of chasing away soldiers, he argued, the tougher disciplinary measures had produced a sharp drop in desertion, from 8 percent in 1923 to 0.1 percent in 1925.[60] After the promulgation of the new disciplinary code, military districts registered significant decreases in the incidence of military crimes. The number of violators dropped, as did the number of arrests, which were replaced by less severe punishments. All reports by judicial authorities attributed the improved situation to the reform program.[61] The reforms were intended to eliminate the excessive arbitrariness of army disciplinary policies, which had been a major source of discontent and sense of injustice among soldiers. Soldiers and officers now had clearer ideas about what they could expect from one another. Indeed, if harsh measures no longer needed to be applied to guarantee soldiers' obedience, then the reformers had achieved a remarkable degree of success.

60. Frunze, "Doklad na III-em s''ezde sovetov," *Krasnaia zvezda*, 22 May 1925, p. 3. The May congress was the third since the proclamation of the Soviet Union in 1922. The congresses cited in earlier chapters were meetings of the soviets of the RS-FSR (the Russian Soviet Federated Socialist Republic).

61. See, e.g., the reports from the Ukrainian Military District for 1926–1928, cited from archival materials in Pikha, "Bor'ba," p. 186–87.

CHAPTER 6

Peasants, Civilians, and Army Politics

As it is only by means of a well-regulated standing army that a civilized country can be defended; so it is only by means of it that a barbarous country can be suddenly and tolerably civilized.

—Adam Smith, *Wealth of Nations*

Rural Politics and the Peacetime Army

The reforms in discipline and especially the compromise of a mixed system of territorial and regular armies posed new problems and presented new opportunities for the national political and military leadership in the area of rural policy. At the beginning of 1925 Frunze addressed an assembly of party cell secretaries about the contribution that secretaries in territorial units were especially well situated to make: they had an almost unparalleled opportunity to learn about peasant life and to strengthen the link between town and country. Indeed, these opportunities made the demands on territorial personnel far greater than those placed on political activists in regular units, in part because ties to civilian organizations would of necessity be closer in territorial formations. Because political work in the territorial formations was more complicated, party activists needed to exercise special caution and maintain a steady balance between military tasks and tasks oriented toward a primarily agricultural audience. Frunze disclosed that reports indicated "deviations" in the direction of excessive attention to rural propaganda at the expense of military training. It was imperative, he reminded the delegates, that they keep in mind that an army is above all "an instrument of war."[1]

1. M. V. Frunze, "Territorial'noe stroitel'stvo i rabota v derevne," 27 February 1925, in *Izbrannye proizvedeniia* (1957), 2:220–37. Boris Zorin, the deputy director of PUR's Agitation and Propaganda Department, also noted the excessive attention that

In drawing the secretaries' attention to "peasant deviations," Frunze identified a dilemma that went to the heart of the evolving civil–military relations in peacetime Russia. The army's leadership was dedicated to the greater political goal of building new bases of state authority in the countryside; after all, the army had a direct interest in the rural population, for it was from the countryside that the overwhelming majority of soldiers and many officers would come for the foreseeable future. PUR committed large resources to civic education and especially to encouraging peasant soldiers to help in "building socialism." Building socialism gradually was coming to mean a noncapitalist path to heavy industrialization with a pronounced defense orientation and the creation of a political class at the local level which shared a commitment to the leadership's agenda. At the same time, however, the overriding priority of the army's elite was to maintain a well-disciplined and well-outfitted armed force to defend the nation as it proceeded to "build socialism peacefully." Because the army and party leaders saw the Red Army as an army of a new type, one that embodied new missions and a new form of civil–military relations, the delicate balance between the often contradictory dual orientation permeated all questions of organization and instruction.

The "peasant question" also heightened the tensions that the political struggles injected into party life during 1923 and 1924. The "scissors crisis"[2] in late autumn 1923 raised concerns among the party's leadership that the peasantry might abandon the "worker-peasant link" that underlay the state's economic and political stability. As the party leaders responded to the perceived crisis, they began to divide over economic policies, and especially over rural policies. An influential part of the party's leaders, whose spokesman was Grigorii Zinoviev, the Petrograd party chief, advocated more conciliatory policies toward the peasantry. At the Twelfth Party Congress, in April 1923, Zinoviev defended himself against Iurii Larin's charges that he was guilty of "peasant deviation."[3] Lev Kamenev, speaking in support of Zinoviev's proposal to reduce the

political workers were devoting to "peasant moods," to the detriment of purely military and political education: B. P. Zorin, "Osnovnye uspekhi," *Krasnaia Armiia v 1924 g. i "Krasnaia zvezda"* (Moscow, 1925), pp. 260–61.

2. The "scissors crisis" was the result of a sharp disparity between high prices for industrial goods and low prices for agricultural products. In an address before a party assembly, Trotsky used a diagram to show rising and falling price curves, hence "scissors." Bolshevik leaders feared that peasants, faced with unfavorable terms of trade, would withdraw from the market. For more details on agrarian policy, see E. H. Carr, *Socialism in One Country, 1924–26,* 3 vols. (New York: Macmillan, 1958–1964), 1:191–99.

3. *Dvenadtsatyi s''ezd RKP(b), 17–25 aprelia 1923 goda: Stenograficheskii otchet* (Moscow, 1968); for Zinoviev's remarks, see pp. 28–30, 38–45; for Larin's response, see pp. 111–15.

tax burden on peasants, cited a letter from Frunze, who recently had returned from a visit to Ivanovo-Voznesensk. Frunze was distressed by the serious discontent of the peasantry with Soviet policies and warned, "We have evidently gone beyond those economic limits that are politically permissible."[4] When Frunze moved higher in the army command and replaced Trotsky's deputy army commissar, Sklianskii, Zinoviev gained an influential ally for his conciliatory policies.

Both Frunze and Bubnov advocated moderation and patience with peasant recruits, especially after the alarming behavior of peasants during the spring 1924 recruitment drive. Despite substantial efforts to ensure that the simultaneous demobilization and call-up would run smoothly,[5] the combination of administrative disorganization and peasant discontent produced a near disaster. In several military districts, and especially at the assemblies of men called up for service in the territorial militia units, peasants turned the induction campaigns into political demonstrations against the unjust agricultural tax. "They take taxes, but give nothing in return," the peasants complained, according to one political worker. The protestors demanded that peasants be permitted to form their own trade union to defend their interests. In one brigade, the inductees actually formed a Union of Grain Growers. Political workers reported back to Moscow that peasants complained of discrimination by the proletarian dictatorship. After all, they worked far more hours a day than the average worker, yet the same workers "lived in clover," while peasants toiled away in penury.[6] The demonstrators called into question the very linchpin of the New Economic Policy, the so-called worker-peasant alliance (smychka), according to which the cities promised low prices on industrial goods for the peasants who provided them with foodstuffs. The demonstrations at induction centers were part of a broader upsurge in political discontent among the peasants, referred to in party documents as "peasant moods." The press also reported a rise in "kulak terrorism," including the harrassment and even murder of rural newspaper correspondents who uncovered

4. Ibid., p. 435.
5. The Central Committee ordered local party organizations to arrange, wherever possible, festive sendoffs and lectures about recent measures taken to improve the workings of the soviet administration. Likewise, the newcomers should find a warm welcome and well-provisioned induction operation: *Izvestiia TsK RKP(b)* 5 (1924): 28, cited in Suvenirov, *Kommunisticheskaia partiia*, p. 108.
6. Berkhin cites reports from the Tula provincial party committee, among others, in military archives: *Voennaia reforma*, pp. 103–4. See also Frunze's comments on the bungled spring call-up in "Ob itogakh reorganizatsii Krasnoi Armii," *Voenno-istoricheskii zhurnal* 6 (1966): 64. According to Frunze's extremely critical remarks, the army fell short of its induction plans by 100,000 men.

abuses of authority, moonshine operations, and intimidation by kulaks.[7]

At the Thirteenth Party Congress, in May 1924, Zinoviev, together with Mikhail Kalinin, once again appealed for more concessions to the peasantry. He decried the common tendency to brand every prosperous peasant a kulak and suggested, "We should not be only the party of the city." Zinoviev was opposed by no less than Nadezhda Krupskaia, Lenin's widow, and Aleksei Rykov, who spoke against adopting too conciliatory a policy and advocated turning the peasant committees of mutual aid into agencies for waging class warfare in the countryside, evoking the spirit of the Civil War. Krupskaia, among others, also proposed sending tens of thousands of party activists into the villages to raise the deplorably low cultural level of the peasant masses. She paid a surprising compliment in passing to the Red Army as "a tremendous school of culture, and an organization contributing to the firm alliance between working class and peasantry." In the congress's final resolution on cultural work in the countryside, the Red Army was assigned an important role in "communication with the village" by means of veterans, the permanent staff of the territorial units, youths undergoing pre-induction processing, and soldiers' letters.[8]

During the summer of 1924, army maneuvers continued to be plagued by organizational problems. At the end of August peasants rose up in arms in Georgia. Army units were called in to crush the rebellions. Stalin explicitly linked the Georgian disturbances to the peasant revolts in Tambov and the sailors' mutiny at Kronstadt in 1921.[9] Both he and Zinoviev called attention to the wave of murders of village correspondents as signs of greater troubles in rural society. Petitions continued to pour into Moscow from around the country as peasants demanded more conciliatory rural policies from the state. Finally, over considerable opposition, Zinoviev won support for a policy of turning "a face to the countryside." The agricultural tax was lowered, and restrictions were eased for peasants who wished to hire labor and lease land.

The apparent shift in party tactics toward the peasantry baffled political workers in the army. In November 1924 directors of politi-

7. See Carr, *Interregnum*, pp. 213–15, 261–63.

8. *Trinadtsatyi s''ezd RKP(b), Mai 1924 goda: Stenograficheskii otchet* (Moscow, 1963); for Zinoviev's report to the congress, see pp. 36–109; Kalinin's speech, pp. 434–52; Krupskaia's remarks, pp. 452–65; Rykov, pp. 472–78. For a summary of the discussion about party policy in the countryside, see Carr, *Interregnum*, pp. 144–49. The peasant committees of mutual aid were formed by the People's Commissariat of Social Welfare to distribute relief during the great famine of 1921–1922. Since then the committees had vitually ceased to function because they had no clear mandate.

9. Stalin, "O 'Dymovke,' " 26 November 1925, in *Sochineniia*, 7:19–24; also "K voprosu o proletariate i krest'ianstve," 27 January 1925, in ibid., p. 31.

cal administrations heard from party leaders that in their attempts to transform peasants into loyal proletarians, they had been guilty of "depeasantization," which seemed to mean that peasants' needs and interests had not been considered with sufficient sympathy. Political departments had taken too harsh a line in screening peasant applicants for party membership. The Ukrainian Military District was chastized after it issued an order suspending any further admissions of peasant soldiers.[10] At the February 1925 meeting of party cell secretaries, Bubnov spoke about the controversial issue of admitting peasants to party organizations and the party's national policies toward the rural population. Earlier, in the spirit of Zinoviev's conciliatory line, Bubnov had exhorted party cells to encourage more peasants to join both the party and Komsomol, but he advised them to be very careful about the social origins of prospective candidates, making sure in every case that poor peasants had first priority and that only "the best part of the middle peasantry be considered." More important, he chastized those party and Komsomol members who continued to oppose the admission of peasants, especially into Komsomol, because they were in essence abdicating any role in guiding the political development of masses of rural youth. Besides, any growth of Komsomol's numbers in the army would have to come from expanding peasant membership.[11] Bubnov insisted on maintaining the party as an elite core, while relegating Komsomol to the function of appealing to the broader populace. In his address to the assembly, Bubnov repeated many of the themes that Zinoviev had been promoting in his tours across the country to explain the party's "face to the countryside" program. He advised moderation and patience because "general conditions in the countryside now are very complicated." Political workers should expect that "the moods and vacillations in the countryside will find the most keen and immediate reflection in the army." If the secretaries persisted in expecting peasant youths to be reeducated in one fell swoop, Bubnov warned, the army would find itself facing a whole series of "difficulties that we will not be able to solve easily." As a beginning, he exhorted the party activists to "banish decisively" from their speech any phrases associated with the notion of "depeasantization." Rather than try to make the peasant into a conscious proletarian, as Gusev had advocated in the first postwar years, all political workers and mass organizations, including the party and Komsomol, should fo-

---

10. *Politrabotnik* 7 (1924): 24; SP 2 (1924): 57; *Krasnaia zvezda*, 6 March 1925, p.3.
    11. "Tsirkuliar PU RKKA i TsK RLKSM o povyshenii rosta riadov RLKSM v armii," 24 January 1925, in PPR III, p. 247–49.

cus on the more modest goal of "transforming the peasant in the army into a Red soldier."[12]

The party secretaries rebuffed Bubnov's entreaties and vocally disagreed with many of the concessions in the party's "face to the countryside." The delegates accused Bubnov of backsliding on the peasant question, of adapting army slogans to "the limitations of the peasantry, and of making them softer." The secretaries attributed Bubnov's errors to a weakening of the party's will in its relations with the countryside, which in itself was a consequence of the lax principles of membership recruitment that some political leaders were advocating. The party secretaries directly linked their vision of the party as a vanguard organization and their unwillingness to resign themselves to the conciliationist policies of the center toward the peasantry. The adherents of the vanguard model warned that PUR would not be able to maintain the party's revolutionary élan and its explicit commitment to societal transformation if it lost its elitist character. If it did not guard itself against the petit bourgeois influences that prevailed in the broader civilian society and in the overwhelmingly peasant majority of conscript soldiers, the party would be defeated by Russia's historic backwardness and the cause of socialism would be lost forever.

The secretaries' defiant opinion evidently was shared by many of the men they represented. Boris Zorin, deputy director of PUR's Agitation and Propaganda Department, reported with alarm in late spring 1925 that a very significant layer in the army's lower-ranking party apparatus were convinced that "our policy in the village serves the interests of the kulaks at the expense of both the poor and middle peasantry."[13] These were the very "depeasantizers" whom Bubnov had rebuked in his recent speeches. According to Zorin, excessively antipeasant activists were giving soldiers the mistaken impression that the party and Soviet state were biased against diligent and thrifty peasants. "The result," Zorin complained, "is that in our army you can find several thousand soldiers who absolutely sincerely think that the poorer a peasant is, the better he is for the Soviet state," and, even worse, "that to be a permanently poor peasant means to render the Soviet state a great service."[14] The depeasantizers especially abused the term "kulak," according to Zorin, Bubnov, and Zinoviev himself. To be labeled a kulak, an exploiter of others'

12. *Krasnaia zvezda*, 6 March 1925, p. 18; *Soveshchanie sekretarei iacheek pri PURe: Stenograficheskii otchet* (Moscow, 1925), p. 134; Evdokimov, *Politicheskie zaniatiia*, p. 17.

13. B. P. Zorin, "Eshche o derevenskom voprose v agitatsii i propagande v Krasnoi Armii," *SP* 20 (1925): 1.

14. B. P. Zorin, " 'Derevenskii vopros' v agitatsii i propagande v Krasnoi Armii," *SP* 19 (1925): 4.

labor, was to suffer a grave charge. The Soviet constitution denied kulaks many benefits of citizenship, including the right to vote in soviet elections and to participate in national political life. Despite official assurances that conscripts were carefully screened to keep kulaks out of the army (according to PUR, at the most only 2 to 3 percent may have outwitted the military commissariats), political workers alleged that 10 percent of the troops in some units were kulaks. Party cells kept lists of kulaks—or "antirevolutionary elements," as they were called—which included those who asked "malicious" questions at meetings and during political classes, those who disputed elections in party cells, and in general "those who showed themselves to be more or less active." Any peasant whose family owned "an extra pair of bulls" was charged with harboring sympathies for kulaks. Because of the hostility directed against these soldiers, "even middle peasants were declaring themselves to be poor peasants, apparently assuming that a middle peasant did not have sufficient trust."[15]

Zorin and other senior political workers characteristically attributed these attitudes to the "low level of political development" among party and Komsomol activists. But the rift between PUR's top leadership and its agents in military units reflected the fundamental gaps in social origins and political outlook that persisted into the mid-1920s. A senior official who was critical of the depeasantizers explained that Komsomol members, "mostly landless peasants and workers," were not able to deal tactfully with peasant soldiers, "who are primarily middle peasants." Instead of the patience that Zinoviev and Bubnov were counseling, the activists frequently "shot from the hip in typical rash Komsomol fashion, throwing about on any pretense the words 'kulak' and 'counterrevolution.'" The Komsomol members thereby created "a certain stratification among the soldiers."[16] The younger activists grew increasingly impatient with their older, less "proletarian" superiors. In a sense, the depeasantizers were indicating to the party leadership that fundamental ambiguities had entered the official policy toward the countryside. Turning a face to the countryside, whatever else it might have meant, certainly signaled a reevaluation of the appropriate bases of support for a state that still called itself revolutionary and socialist. And the depeasantizers not surprisingly believed that they were adhering faithfully to what they had learned in the army. In the context of incessant criticism of NEP moods and petit bourgeois influences, soldiers learned that anyone who lived by the profit mo-

15. N. D., "Izuchenie krasnoarmeitsev," *Krasnaia rota* 5 (1925): 20; *Krasnyi boets* 5 (1925): 4–5; M. Romanovskii, "O seredniake v Krasnoi Armii," *Krasnaia rota* 5 (1925): 7.
16. I. Tashlitskii, "Komsomol v Krasnoi Armii," *SP* 5 (1924): 20–21.

tive and who gained wealth by exploiting others' labor was morally and politically dangerous. After all, the gist of political enlightenment in the army had been that most peasants were unreliable political allies. Poor peasants and hired rural laborers came closest in their political experiences to developing the requisite proletarian consciousness; the overwhelming majority, the middle peasants, had split political personalities because they could be both exploiter and exploited. Now Zinoviev was admonishing political workers for abusing the label "kulak" to silence their critics among nonparty soldiers. He resorted to extremely contorted arguments to justify the policies he was promoting in conjunction with the turn to the countryside. "It is precisely so that we can wage a successful struggle with the kulak," he explained to the inhospitable political staff, "that we need to fight with all our strength against the current tendency to declare any industrious peasant a kulak."[17] "Face to the countryside" was interpreted by the lower-ranking party and Komsomol activists as a retreat from the party's fundamental principles. One very alarmed political worker reported that some party cells were taking the slogan to mean that the Communist Party had abandoned its self-identification as the vanguard of the proletariat and now was a "workers' and peasants' party." In accordance with the party's new image, one cell had concluded that it should admit all peasants who submitted membership applications, regardless of their property holdings or their "political physiognomy." When the troubled political worker charged the party leadership with placing its wager "no longer on the proletariat, but on the peasantry," he came dangerously close to the charges that Trotsky and other oppositionists were making.[18]

By early summer 1925, the party's leadership had split over the wisdom of extending further concessions to the peasants. In May 1925 Stalin, who apparently sensed that a substantial number of party members resented the conciliatory policies, rejected Bukharin's entreaty to the peasants to enrich themselves.[19] Later Stalin, Molotov, and Andreev, in an unpublished letter to the editors of Komsomol'skaia pravda, declared that the concessions to the peasantry had introduced considerable confusion and errors into party work. Bukharin's slogan was "not ours and is wrong . . . Our slogan is socialist accumulation." Certainly, they admitted, the peasantry is the only available ally who can provide the proletariat with direct assistance, but they reminded their audience that the peasantry

17. "Chto oznachaet lozung 'litsom k derevne'? (Iz stat'i tov. G. Zinov'eva)," Krasnaia zvezda, 14 January 1925, p. 3.

18. A. Bakov, "Ob odnom opasnom uklone," Krasnyi boets 1 (1925): 40–41.

19. Stalin, "K itogam rabot XIV konferentsii RKP(b)," 9 May 1925, in Sochineniia, 7:111. Stalin reported to the party aktiv of the Moscow organization.

was "not a very strong ally." Stalin, Molotov, and Andreev also rejected as utterly unacceptable another proposal that party and Komsomol activists compete for influence among nonparty peasants, in fact suggesting a sanctioning of pluralist politics.[20] Zinoviev made the first public allusion to the ongoing debate in a speech to a Leningrad conference of party workers in the Red Army. He once again criticized those party members and peasants who had incorrectly interpreted his "face to the countryside" campaign as a "wager on the kulak."[21] Then in late autumn 1925 Zinoviev and Kamenev reversed themselves and attacked Bukharin, at first in veiled references and then directly. Not surprisingly, Krupskaia joined them in attacking Bukharin. By November even Bukharin recanted publicly and disavowed his former slogan, "Enrich yourselves."[22]

The depeasantizers in the army welcomed the attacks and disavowals as a return to more or less normal policies. But only after the Fourteenth Party Congress, in December 1925—the "industrialization congress"—did their superiors in PUR come around to a tougher line. In a manual on political work, Leonid Degtiarev urged that political workers not change their attitude toward "the current kulak class and toward all other exploiting groups." A full two years before the party center would take coercive measures to requisition "surplus" grain and four years before it embarked on mass collectivization, Degtiarev advised, "Forbid them [the kulaks] to take part in any agencies of the Soviet government, isolate them, confiscate all that part of their wealth which should go to satisfy the interests of the toiling masses, levy heavier taxes on them, and, in the case of the slightest resistance, wage merciless struggle and wholesale confiscation of their property."[23] The political program of Degtiarev's manual was a triumph for the depeasantizers, who thwarted the center's conciliatory plans and advanced their own rural political program in the party and Komsomol organizations they controlled.

20. The letter, "Vsem chlenam redaktsii 'Komsomol'skoi pravdy,' " 2 June 1925, is reproduced in Stalin, *Sochineniia*, 7:153–55. The authors criticize Bukharin's slogan indirectly, choosing a series of articles by Aleksei Stetskii, "Novyi etap novoi ekonomicheskoi politiki," and A. Slepkov, "O leninskom nasledstve." (Stetskii served in the Political Administration of the Eastern Front during the Civil War.)

21. *Pravda*, 30 June 1925; *Leningradskaia Pravda*, 1 July 1925, cited in Carr, *Socialism in One Country*, 1:308n.

22. See Carr, *Socialism in One Country*, 1:303–12, 319–31, on the debate over peasant policy during the summer and autumn of 1925. In 1927 Bukharin praised the Red Army as a school of socialist training. "We have the broadest masses drawn into state work, and the remolding by these masses of the state apparatus. This process unmakes our basic classes, depeasantizes the peasantry and deproletarianizes the proletariat": *Pravda*, 24 November 1927, cited in E. H. Carr and R. W. Davies, *Foundations of a Planned Economy, 1926–1929*, 2 vols. in 3 (New York: Macmillan, 1969–1971), 2:333.

23. L. S. Degtiarev, *Politrabota v Krasnoi Armii* (Leningrad, 1925), p. 142.

Militarization of the Civilian Populace

Political workers' views on rural politics formed part of the larger struggle over the army's relations with the civilian society that fed and supplied it. Ultimately, the army's leaders were not content to confine their militarization campaign to the military alone. In 1924 Frunze, Bubnov, Voroshilov, and Tukhachevsky went on the road to persuade the civilian populace that it had an essential role in helping the army defend the nation: civilians should learn basic military skills and develop an organizational network capable of rapidly mobilizing large numbers of men and women in the event of war. Frunze justified what he called "the militarization of the civilian populace" by the constraints imposed on the army. The small size and budget of the standing army and the unreliable territorial militia system failed to ensure the level of combat readiness demanded by modern warfare. "We cannot prepare the country for defense," he warned, "if we rely solely on our military resources."[24] In one speech after another, the reform team at the top of the army argued that only a society permeated by military values could successfully defend the country in future wars, which would be fought not just between armies but between entire mobilized populations. Many of these ideas originated in the theses that Frunze and Gusev had defended at the Tenth and Eleventh Party Congresses. The World War had offered a foretaste of life in a fully mobilized society. But now the militarizers demanded a restructured peacetime civil-military relationship that approximated wartime conditions. As a first step, Frunze proposed that the Army Commissariat designate representatives to sit in the collegia of the relevant civilian people's commissariats and in such institutions as VSNKh (the Supreme Council of the National Economy). As a model of profitable collaboration between civilian and military agencies he pointed to the Main Medical Administration (Glavsanupr), which brought together civilian medical personnel with the military commissariats to monitor draft-age males' health and to conduct regular hygiene programs, including inoculation campaigns. Frunze insisted that "this work proceed *not* in the direction of the civilianization of our [military] apparatus," a threat he claimed to be a very real one; rather, "we must set as our goal the greater militarization of civilian institutions in anticipation of defending the country during an armed confrontation."[25] Civilian party newspapers promised to feature regular military sections to keep the public better informed about life in the Red Army. In order to improve coordination of pre-induction training, a task that was still left to civilians because the military budget could not meet all

24. Frunze, "Ob itogakh," pp. 73–74.
25. Ibid., p. 74.

the army's needs, army commissars won voting rights in civilian party committees in garrison cities. Many of these gains came as a result of Bubnov's struggles with the civilian party organization over issues of accountability for and intervention in army affairs.[26]

The militarizers' first target was the national school system. "All the efforts of the Commissariat of Enlightenment should be planned with an eye to serving the needs of defense," Frunze wrote in an essay devoted to the role of the rear in future wars. He pointed to the example of the United States, where universities trained officers in a "reserve officers' training corps." He acknowledged educators' fears that closer ties between the Enlightenment Commissariat and the army would plant the seeds of a new militarism, but he dismissed their anxieties as evidence that "petit bourgeois sentimental moods" persisted among them and that they failed entirely to comprehend "the essence and character of the tasks facing the Workers' and Peasants' Republic." Indeed, if educators would only cooperate in this venture, the nation would benefit from having "cultured, literate, and politically educated soldier-citizens." Frunze hinted to the civilian educators that the status of their commissariat might rise if they devoted themselves wholeheartedly to the serious task of military preparation.[27] In late 1924 PUR and the RVS won a pledge from civilian culture and enlightenment organizations to aid in preparing the populace for war and "in disseminating military knowledge in the country."

Leonid Degtiarev, the author of the army's standard manual on political education, also defended the militarization proposals, this time before the national Teachers' Congress in 1925. He too had heard the educators predict that military instruction would destroy the pedagogical principles of the labor schools by "diminishing the initiative and creative activity of pupils, introducing the stupefying aspects of military drill," and lowering morals. But these educators were wrong, he retorted. They forgot that the Red Army differed radically from its tsarist predecessor. And Degtiarev sounded a more menacing note when he reminded those who "giggled about militarization of the school" how Lenin had once answered his political

26. "O sozdanii komissii po vovlecheniiu grazhdanskikh kul'tprosvetorganizatsii v rabote po voennoi podgotovke naseleniia i po rasprostraneniiu v strane voennykh znanii," 19 November 1924, in *Sbornik prikazov RVS SSSR* (Moscow, 1924); L. Rozov, "Voennye otdely v grazhdanskoi pechati," *Krasnaia rota* 22 (1925): 76; see also "Polozhenie o vzaimootnosheniiakh politorganov i partorganizatsii," 11 August 1924, in *PPR* III, p. 217, and "O doprizyvnoi podgotovke," 26 September 1924, in *KPSS o vooruzhennykh silakh* (1981), pp. 216–17.

27. M. V. Frunze, "Front i tyl v voine budushchego," in *Izbrannye proizvedeniia* (1957), 2:133–43. The essay appeared in Frunze's anthology *Na novykh putiakh* (Moscow, 1925), and earlier as the introduction to P. Karatygin's *Obshchie osnovy mobilizatsii promyshlennosti dlia nuzhd voiny* (Moscow, 1925). Walter Jacobs translated the article as "Front and Rear in War of the Future" in his *Frunze*, pp. 167–78.

opponents, particularly the Mensheviks, who scoffed at what they sarcastically called Red militarism: "There are stupid people who scream about Red militarism. They are political rogues."[28] Military spokesmen had a long history of hostile relations with the Commissariat of Enlightenment, but now they felt no qualms about enlisting Lunacharsky in their campaign to raise the general level of popular awareness of the army's mission and to spread military skills with the aid of teachers. Lunacharsky lent at least his rhetorical authority to the militarization campaign. He explained to the teachers that although "no one had stated flatly that defense comes first, then the economy, and in third place is education," nevertheless "life itself has forced us to establish these priorities."[29] In his unflagging efforts to raise his commissariat's prestige and win it a commensurately greater share of the nation's resources, Lunacharsky now acquiesced in the army's demands. Not long before he had conceded a major defeat during the struggles over Glavpolitprosvet. The delegates to the Teachers' Congress took an oath to do their utmost to prepare their pupils for service in the Red Army. The Enlightenment Commissariat agreed to appoint a "military director" and four to twelve teachers to aid him in organizing military courses in institutions of higher learning.[30]

Predictably, the military spokesmen found constant shortcomings in the work of their civilian counterparts. A year after the Central Committee had ordered civilian newspapers to publicize military affairs, a political worker in the Ukrainian Military District complained that most newspapers still lacked military sections. Those that had introduced such a section were concerned exclusively with campaigns for call-ups or demobilization. "As soon as the campaign is over," the observer commented, "the section goes into hiding again for a long time."[31] Military propaganda was to be a full-time concern for editorial boards. And apparently local civilian committees diverted too few resources to the pre-induction programs for which they were responsible, most likely because their budgets too were stretched to meet more pressing organizational needs. The national budget that was approved for fiscal year 1925–1926 allocated

28. L. S. Degtiarev, "Oborona strany i narodnoe prosveshchenie," in *Oborona strany i grazhdanskaia shkola,* ed. Degtiarev and N. F. Artemenko (Moscow/Leningrad, 1927), pp. 102, 106. The anthology in which Degtiarev's address appears consists of speeches delivered to the Teachers' Congress.

29. A. Lunacharskii, "Iz doklada na I-om vsesoiuznom uchitel'skom s"ezde," in *Oborona strany,* p. 73.

30. Another army spokesman at the congress, N. F. Artemenko, chastized civil engineers. "There can be no two opinions," he warned, "about the need to extirpate the current unfortunate and serious detachment of civilian engineering from the military department": Artemenko, "Prakticheskoe razreshenie voprosa," in *Oborona strany,* p. 136.

31. Rozov, "Voennye otdely," p. 76.

central funds to subsidize the vital programs, thereby freeing local treasuries from responsibility for financing them; furthermore, political departments took a more aggressive role in appointing and getting military personnel elected to civilian party bodies.[32]

The army's elite did not consider, however, that the mere inculcation of military values in the populace would suffice to guarantee that the nation could withstand an assault by a modern army equipped with the latest technological weaponry. Rather, they pressed for a nationwide commitment to industrialization, the creation of a large proletariat, and a high priority to defense industry. The army command argued from a virtually unique vantage point on the problems of the new state because they had to look both outside to the international arena and inside to domestic political and economic developments. During the 1920s the major European powers and Japan were rearming at an alarming pace, and Soviet diplomatic efforts to slow or halt the arms race were enjoying little success. The Soviet Union's relations with the outside world continued to be characterized by war scares and unstable diplomatic agreements. The military leadership concluded that as long as the Soviet Republic remained an overwhelmingly agricultural nation, it risked defeat at the hands of a more sophisticated industrial power. Peasant Russia, according to Frunze, could not sustain an "army suitable for fighting a war" because a peasant did not have "the feeling of strength, faith in himself, or capacity to make independent decisions, precisely that capacity which life itself instills in a worker."[33] At a graduation breakfast meeting at the Military Academy, Frunze challenged civilian party and state institutions to fulfill the promise of the October Revolution by launching an industrialization program. Frunze was responding to Soviet president Kalinin, who had just addressed the graduates and exhorted them to create "a proletarian October in the field of military science." Frunze retorted that the "objective conditions" did not exist for such a revolution in the field of military science. "At that moment when we can count on not a million-man working class, but rather a ten- or fifteen-million proletariat," he promised, "both our strategy and tactics will begin to take on an altogether different character." The industrialization of Soviet society depended above all on "the work of our civilian institutions"; therefore, Frunze challenged Comrade Kalinin to achieve an "October" in the Soviet economy before he asked for any

---

32. *Sovetskie vooruzhennye sily: Istoriia stroitel'stva* (Moscow, 1978), pp. 152–53. During 1925 more than 100 political workers in the Leningrad Military District were elected to executive party bodies in provincial, regional, and district organizations. See Shevchenko, "Ideino-politicheskoe," p. 93.

33. Frunze, *Sobranie sochinenii*, 2:197.

decisive changes in the army's situation.[34] Frunze, and even more sharply Tukhachevsky, as deputy chief of staff, focused on several

Kliment Voroshilov, people's commissar of the army and navy, chairman of the Revolutionary Military Council of the USSR, 1925–1934; commissar of defense, 1934–1940. From *Raboche-krest'ianskaia Krasnaia Armiia* (Moscow, 1938), courtesy of Division of Art, Prints, and Photographs, The New York Public Library, Astor, Lenox, and Tilden Foundations.

34. "Rech' M. V. Frunze na torzhestvennom zavtrake, posviashchennom 5-mu vypusku slushatelei Akademii," 5 August 1925, published for the first time in M. V. Frunze, *Izbrannye proizvedeniia* (Moscow, 1977), pp. 432–33.

key economic sectors in their campaign for national mobilization. They singled out the budding tractor industry to play a prominent role on future battlefields because track-laying tractors could supplement the numbers of tanks and replace horses to draw heavy artillery. The communication and transportation sectors were similarly seen as liable to military service.[35]

Just as personnel in the Commissariat of Enlightenment resisted the appeals to militarize education, key civilian economic administrators disputed army claims to first priority in the peacetime budget. Reportedly Dzerzhinsky, now chairman of VSNKh, complained that the countryside deserved first stake on industrial goods because otherwise the worker-peasant link that served as the cornerstone of the regime's economic and social policies might be jeopardized. He ranked the military in last place, behind the demands of the peasant market, the urban populations, the commune system, and the rail industry. Dzerzhinsky defended his list of priorities in 1924 and again at the Fourteenth Party Conference in April 1925.[36] The military proved unable to win a substantially larger share of the national budget.

To overcome the often considerable resistance of the civilian institutions, Frunze, Tukhachevsky, and, later, Voroshilov worked to reshape and expand a burgeoning network of volunteer organizations that popularized aviation and chemical warfare among civilians.[37] These mass organizations had grown out of the local initiative of factories and even an occasional village to mobilize public support and economic resources to help the state with its defense needs. By 1925 the Society of Friends of the Air Fleet (ODVF) listed 2 million members. The society capitalized on the enthusiasm for airplanes in the early decades of the twentieth century to encourage citizens to

35. In adition to Frunze's article "Front i tyl," see accounts of his other addresses in the 1925 issues of *Krasnaia zvezda*. His address before the Third Congress of Soviets was printed in the issue of 22 May, p. 2; his speech on the tasks of the army is in the issue of 19 February, p. 2; other important works are P. Karatygin's *Obshchie osnovy;* M. N. Tukhachevskii, *Voprosy sovremennoi strategii* (Moscow, 1926). For a brief introduction to some of the major military thinkers on economic mobilization, see Michael Checinski, "The Economics of Defense in the USSR," *Survey* 29 (Spring 1985): 59–78, esp. 70n.

36. N. Valentinov (Vol'skii), *Novaia ekonomicheskaia politika i krizis partii posle smerti Lenina: Vospominaniia* (Stanford, Calif.: Hoover Institution Press, 1971). Valentinov, a former Menshevik, worked in the highest circles of VSNKh in the 1920s and met regularly with former Mensheviks occupying comparable positions elsewhere in the economic administration. His memoirs, although not everywhere reliable, report a great deal of high-level political gossip.

37. One could also argue that the secret collaboration between the Reichswehr and the Red Army was born out of the need to circumvent recalcitrant civilian economic bureaucrats. For more on the history of the collaboration, see Erickson, *Soviet High Command,* pp. 144–63, 247–82.

train as pilots or engineers.[38] Typically trade unions organized subscription campaigns to build individual airplanes. A second mass
organization, the Chemistry Society, Dobrokhim, disseminated popular information extolling the virtues of modern chemistry and instructed citizens about the dangers of chemical warfare, thereby
serving as a prototype for civil defense organizations. The Military
Scientific Society already had very close ties to the army. In 1920
the party organization attached to the General Staff Academy organized the society's first circles to study the World War and the Civil
War for the purposes of developing a modern program of officer education. The society, which aimed to raise professional standards
among Red Army officers, laid the foundations for the first Soviet
military archives and military historiography, and published a
monthly journal and several volumes devoted to military strategy
and tactics. By autumn 1924 the Military Scientific Society counted
50,000 members.[39]

In May 1925 Frunze appealed to the delegates of the first national
convention of the Military Scientific Society to broaden their organization's mission beyond the confines of the army and take an active part in the campaign to militarize civilian society. At first the
delegates ignored his appeals; they saw themselves as purveyors of
military professionalism among the officer corps, not as populariz-
ers of military knowledge for civilians. For the same reasons of professional integrity, the delegates rebuffed Frunze's proposal that they
merge with the Friends of the Air Fleet and the Chemistry Society to
create one mass organization not only to inculcate military values
and habits but also to build support for larger military budgets.[40]
The Friends of the Air Fleet and the Chemistry Society did merge in
1925 to become Aviakhim. Finally in 1926, one year after Frunze's

38. On the popularity of airplanes and aviation, see Jeffrey Brooks, "Popular and
Public Values in the Soviet Press, 1921–1928," paper presented at Conference on Popular Culture—East and West, Bloomington, Ind., 1 May 1986, p. 11.

39. The most informative work on the history of the volunteer societies is William
E. Odom, The Soviet Volunteers: Modernization and Bureaucracy in a Public Mass
Organization (Princeton: Princeton University Press, 1973); on the early history of the
Military Scientific Society, see N. Lomov and T. Kin, "Dobrovol'nye voenno-nauchnye
obshchestva (Iz istorii sozdaniia)," Voenno-istoricheskii zhurnal 5 (1975): 122–26.
The official organs of the society were Krasnaia armiia (1921–1922), Voina i tekhnika
(1923–1924), and Voina i revoliutsiia (from 1925).

40. Frunze, "Nashe voennoe stroitel'stvo i zadachi voenno-nauchnogo obshchestva: Doklad na pervom Vsesoiuznom soveshchanii VNO SSSR," 22 May 1925, in
Izbrannye proizvedeniia (1957), 2:340–55; translated by Walter Jacobs as "Our Military Construction and the Tasks of the Military Scientific Societies," in Frunze, pp.
179–94. Trotsky earlier warned that the army had ulterior motives and that its leaders
were intent on gaining greater access to the civilian economy through the volunteer
societies. See "Vozdushnyi flot—v poriadke dnia," 4 March 1923, in KVR, vol. 3, pt.
2, p. 182. This was also Valentinov's conclusion about the militarization campaign:
Novaia ekonomicheskaia, p. 119.

death, the Military Scientific Society agreed to alter the organization's mission and became the Society for Aid to Defense (OSO). A year later, the renamed society finally merged with Aviakhim to become Osoaviakhim. At the second congress of the new mass organization, Osoaviakhim claimed almost 5 million members.

After nearly two years of intensive lobbying by the military leadership, now augmented by the nationwide campaigns of the mass organizations, the Fourteenth Party Congress in December 1925 resolved to take "*all necessary measures* to bolster the strength of the Red Army and Navy." The Fourteenth Party Congress became known as the "congress of industrialization" because the prominent topic for discussion was when and how the nation should launch its industrialization program; moreover, the industrialization issue had become tied inextricably with the escalating battle for party leadership among the various factions, with Zinoviev and Kamenev now allied against Stalin. When Kamenev was forced out of his post as deputy of Sovnarkom, and also as president of the Council of Labor and Defense, he was replaced by two deputies, Valerian Kuibyshev and Ian Rudzutak. Kuibyshev had prior experience in high-level political posts in the army, having briefly served as chairman for the nation's electrification administration, and most recently as chairman of the Central Control Commission, in which capacity he had supervised a purge of the state administration. Rudzutak also had experience in both military and industrial politics.[41] Both Kuibyshev and Rudzutak became strong proponents of the defense industry. As soon as Kuibyshev took over as chairman of VSNKh upon Dzerzhinsky's death in 1926, he carried out a drastic reform to centralize the defense industry in a unified committee, Voenprom.[42]

Frunze's militarization drive sowed the seeds for a reorientation of economic policies toward defense needs, but it also legitimized a strengthening of military and patriotic elements in the Soviet political culture of the late 1920s and early 1930s. The measures implemented under the catchword of "militarization" emerged from the confluence of several trends in Russian and European society since the beginning of the twentieth century. Even before the Great War, Russian officers, impressed by the patriotism, enthusiasm, and self-sacrifice of Japanese soldiers during the 1904–1905 war, proposed programs to improve Russian troop motivation by milita-

41. For Kuibyshev's career in the Civil War and at VSNKh, see the biography *Valerian Vladimirovich Kuibyshev* by G. V. Kuibysheva, O. A. Lezhava, N. V. Nelidov, and A. F. Khavin (Moscow, 1966). For a discussion of the political struggles at the Fourteenth Party Congress, see Carr, *Socialism in One Country*, 2:131–52.

42. For more on the reorganization of the defense industry, see Carr and Davies, *Foundations of a Planned Economy*, 1:426–31.

rizing the entire population, including schoolchildren.[43] Following 1918, nearly everywhere in Europe governments emerged from the years of prolonged "total" warfare with boards of national economic planning, propaganda techniques, and experience with general mobilizations of the populace. In Russia the War Industries Committee system brought together representatives of the imperial bureaucracy, business elites, and even labor to coordinate supply for the military, while successive ministers of agriculture experimented with schemes of price controls, grain monopolies, and goods exchange to feed the civilian populace. During the short life of the Provisional Government the Menshevik economist Vladimir Groman advocated nothing less than "the militarization of the national economy" as a starting point from which to introduce principles of socialist planning.[44]

During the Civil War, the Bolshevik government implemented a set of often contradictory policies that came to be known collectively as "war communism," or "military communism." The new leaders embraced extensive governmental intervention in most sectors of the economy and acted to exclude the workings of the free "spontaneous" market. The Civil War often forced a retreat from a more comprehensive vision of planning because of a shortage of qualified personnel and halfhearted societal cooperation. The state concentrated its efforts on the twin aims of defense and industrial mobilization in the Council on Labor and Defense, which functioned until 1937. Ironically, even Podvoiskii's militia ideals, as embodied in Vsevobuch, promoted the virtual dissolution of the boundaries that traditionally had separated the civilian sphere from the military. Podvoiskii frequently harked back to a vision of Spartan society, thoroughly militarized and united behind common ideals. Of

43. See Fuller, Civil-Military Conflict, pp. 195–96, 207. Fuller suggests that "at least some tsarist soldiers, such as Bonch-Bruevich, Brusilov, and Barsukov, could hope that Bolshevism might be exactly that mass political movement which could instill the patriotism which was the chief element in victory," and that the Bolsheviks' readiness to resort to mass mobilization attracted many military specialists to service in the Red Army (p. 263).

44. On the wartime mobilization of economies in Europe see Karl Kautsky, The Social Revolution, trans. A. M. Simons and May Wood Simons (Chicago: C. H. Kerr, 1916). On the War Industries Committees, see Lewis Siegelbaum, The Politics of Industrial Mobilization in Russia (New York: St. Martin's Press, 1983). On the militarization of Russian industry during World War I, see B. Grave, "Militarizatsiia promyshlennosti i rossiiskii proletariat v gody pervoi mirovoi voiny," in Iz istorii rabochego klassa i revoliutsionnogo dvizheniia (Moscow, 1958); on Groman's ideas, see Naum Jasny, Soviet Economists of the Twenties (Cambridge: Cambridge University Press, 1972), pp. 97–102.

course, this ideal presupposed a citizen-soldier who was literate, cultured, and socialist.[45]

Within the army itself, a vocal company of militarizers coalesced in the officer corps, many of whom had a low opinion of the civilian bureaucracy and a lively sense of their own professional virtues. In often arrogant tones, military spokesmen contended that they had developed far better techniques for managing the nation's scarce resources than had their civilian counterparts. For example, the army sponsored hundreds of circles affiliated with the national Time League. Army Time Leaguers pointed with pride to the respect that military methods of organization enjoyed among the civilian organizations, for whom the phrase "in a military way" (*po voennomu*) meant quickly and precisely.[46] When the Council on Labor and Defense formed a committee on standardization of the Soviet economy, which was to introduce the metric system, the editor of the Red Army's daily *Krasnaia zvezda* boasted that the army, as the nation's number one mass consumer, had a considerable headstart in standardizing weaponry and military equipment. He urged the further "militarization" of several categories of consumer items that had potential military uses, including horseshoes, peasant carts, and harness gear. "Standardization, or the introduction of uniform types," concluded the editor, "is one of the most burning questions of the modern age."[47]

The militarizers, although they often couched their self-promoting arguments in the rhetoric of national mobilization for future wars, frequently went further in their enthusiasm to offer the army as a model of order and efficiency for society at large to emulate. Military spokesmen argued that because Russia lacked the industrial base and cultural practices of capitalist societies, the military could become "an organizing factor of tremendous importance."[48] This asser-

---

45. The best recent book on "war communism" is Malle, *Economic Organization of War Communism*; on Nikolai Podvoiskii and Sparta, see "Osnovy revoliutsionnoi voiny i taktiki v internatsional'noi mezhduklassovoi bor'be," in *Revoliutsionnaia voina*; and in *Vooruzhennyi narod*, the official journal of Vsevobuch; finally, ideas about national mobilization can be found in Nikolai Bukharin and Evgenii Preobrazhenskii, *ABC of Communism* (London: Communist Party of Great Britain, 1927), and Trotsky's pamphlet *Terrorism and Communism* (London: New Park, 1975). At the Twelfth Party Congress, Trotsky defended the realism of his proposals for introducing planning into the economy by pointing to the Red Army as a planned economy that could not be brought under the laws of the market. See *Dvenadtsatyi s''ezd RKP(b)*, p. 336.

46. D. Er—ov, "Bor'ba za vremia," *Krasnaia rota* 28 (1923): 34–36; see also the charter for one of the army's time leagues, "Polozhenie ob organizatsii ligi 'Vremia' v chastiakh Krasnoi Armii Zapadnogo Fronta," *Krasnaia prisiaga* 3/24 (1924): 88–93.

47. "Polozhenie o komitete po standartizatsii pri Sovete Truda i Oborony," *Krasnaia zvezda*, 17 October 1925, p. 1.

48. V. Shch—ii, "NOT i Armiia," *Krasnyi boets* 6 (1924): 67.

tion too had some roots in the army's claims since at least 1918 that it was more than a purely military school, but also a cultural and political institution. But only rarely before had military personnel had the audacity to suggest that the army offered an alternate model, or a supplementary force, to the industrial factory in the tasks of disciplining the Russian populace for the construction of socialism.

That audacity hinted at a fundamental reorientation of the nation's leaders and their understanding of the Revolution which had been under way since at least the end of the Civil War. Initially the industrial factory was held up as the model for socialist society because it was the locus for the development of a politically conscious proletariat. The Imperial Army, on the contrary, symbolized everything that was reactionary about the autocracy. The factory was so embedded in the state's notions of its own legitimacy that in 1922 the army's disciplinary manual still justified a strict but "conscious" disciplinary regime for soldiers by appealing to the model of factory discipline. Just as in the factory, where mistakes or careless habits could put expensive and sensitive machines out of commission, so in the army slipshod conduct opened the door to disaster and even loss of lives. The discipline of the factory, "conscious discipline," had the added advantage of ensuring equality and fairness in relations between managers and workers.[49] The rather sanguine perspective on factory discipline gradually underwent a substantial transformation, which was tied to the leaders' reevaluation of the Russian proletariat. After all, the Russian proletariat had never numbered more than 3 million before the Revolution. And since the Civil War party commentators had frequently decried the "deproletarianization" of the country and the related deterioration of factory discipline. Party and Komsomol organizers in the army complained that working-class conscripts brought with them habits and attitudes that were inappropriate to military conditions.[50]

The military writers who championed unquestioning discipline, after the reforms provided them a more hospitable environment in which to express their views, found factory discipline inadequate to the needs of the army. Especially since the term *mushtra* had reentered the politically acceptable vocabulary of military writers, factory discipline was increasingly seen as inferior to the discipline that the reform team was introducing into the Red Army's ranks. Above all else, the militarization drive had as its goal the shaping of a strictly regulated environment in which soldiers obeyed their superiors without question. In a popular pamphlet intended to explain

49. *Distsiplinarnyi ustav*, pp. 8–9.
50. The complaints of party and Komsomol organizers began as early as the Civil War, but the ambiguities embodied in the formulation "conscious revolutionary discipline" kept military writers from deriding factory discipline itself.

army life to civilian "military clubs," the authors conceded that "a specifically factory order and discipline," including measures against truancy and shirking, "guaranteed the necessary work of the factory." But, they insisted, in the army "this order must be even more precisely established and the discipline more firm," because together they "make of the army one iron fist." All military personnel must have "one interest, one concern. Personal life must be subordinated to the interests of the Soviet state." A factory worker, after all, submitted to discipline only within the factory walls. His personal life remained subject to undesirable influences at home or in the street. Every aspect of a soldier's waking hours, however, was organized by a set of manuals. "In the army," declared the authors of the popular pamphlet, "everything is strictly adjusted and fitted as in a timepiece."[51] Time and space served to reinforce the army's order. "Without supervision and order," soldiers were instructed, they would "turn the barracks into a breeding ground for crime and disease." That was why "we must build barracks life in a rational and orderly fashion."[52]

The army's political workers argued that their job in processing young recruits yielded far better results and was perhaps easier than the job of a political activist in a factory or elsewhere. Because every aspect of a soldier's life was precisely regulated, at least ideally, and because the soldier existed in a grid of authority relations that embodied the exacting demands of military discipline, the political worker felt himself able to wield greater leverage over his wards' political "reprocessing" than his civilian counterpart. But also because the typical recruit was a peasant lad fresh from the village, at once backward and exceedingly curious about the world outside his village, political workers felt that these young men "yielded easily to political work."[53] A peasant lad would be especially susceptible because he was removed from his familiar surroundings and all the pernicious influences that reinforced his undesirable attitudes and practices: his wife and family, the village priest and religion, petty traders and moonshiners.

51. S. Belitskii, V. Popov, and N. Beliaev, eds., *Besedy o voennom dele i Krasnoi armii: Sbornik dlia kruzhkov voennykh znanii na fabrikakh, zavodakh, pri klubakh i shkolakh*, 2d ed. (Moscow, 1928), p. 49.

52. The 1924 manual designated precise procedures for arranging beds, labeling all items, and setting up Lenin corners in every barracks. Regulations also covered care of uniforms, card playing, smoking, conduct in lavatories, lighting, heating, and food storage. See *Vremennyi ustav vnutrennei sluzhby RKKA (1924)* (Moscow, 1935), pp. 38–45.

53. Ia. B., "Udovletvoriaet li politruka rabota?" *SP* 1 (1924): 47–48. The author of this fascinating article on job satisfaction among the political staff based his conclusions on the responses to questionnaires he distributed to hundreds of his co-workers in the army.

In every speech that Frunze, Voroshilov, and all other high-ranking military figures made before civilian forums to whom they appealed for larger budgets and for support of the militarization drive, the military men underscored the army's record in transforming raw peasant recruits into Red Army men and Soviet citizens. In a nation that was desperately short of qualified schoolteachers, the army offered itself as a second Commissariat of Enlightenment. Formerly illiterate peasants returned home from the army with the rudiments of a general education and a taste of urban culture. Their gratitude toward the army bolstered their loyalty to the state that the army defended. Furthermore, the army's leaders promised that their particular school of military service trained administrative cadres for the great task of "building socialism" in a country that was also desperately wanting in loyal agents who knew the ropes of local administration, especially in the rural areas to which the soldiers would return after they completed their service. Indeed, the army was a respectable, if not the best, school of socialism in the Soviet Republic. Gradually the militarizers won broad support for assigning first priority to defense needs in the national economy and in education and culture. Still, acquiescence did not signal a victory of the army over civilian political leaders. Not all militarizers were military men; they included prominent civilians as diverse as Podvoiskii with his vision of a proletarian Sparta and the Menshevik economist Vladimir Groman, who foresaw the introduction of socialism via the Civil War economy, and also men with prior military experience who now occupied civilian administrative posts, such as Kuibyshev at VSNKh and Gusev in the Central Control Commission. A loosely defined consensus on civil–military relations brought these men together, often in spite of disputes over other aspects of their political beliefs, and even blurred the distinctions that separated the oppositionists from the emerging Stalin leadership.

The Party and Komsomol

The crisis in discipline that so alarmed the Central Committee spilled over into the political challenge of Trotsky's allies to the triumvirate of Stalin, Zinoviev, and Kamenev. Because Trotsky still had influential supporters in the army, especially the recent director of the Political Administration, Antonov-Ovseenko, the lines distinguishing the military from the political crises were increasingly blurred. In early 1924 Frunze chaired a plenary session of the RVS to resolve the political crisis in the army. The plenum recommended many of the now standard responses by the military's leadership to party troubles. First, the RVS directed PUR's new director, Andrei

Bubnov, to eradicate all "liquidationist tendencies," by which it meant expelling or dissuading from their political views all party members who wanted to dismantle the army's system of political departments and subordinate party cells. Antonov-Ovseenko's recent campaign for "democracy" in party organizations had been precisely such a "liquidationist tendency." Next the RVS recommended that PUR eradicate the "elements of caste ethos [*elementy kastovosti*]" in the army's party organizations, where Communists were little involved in the work of the party and consequently failed to exert any healthy influence on army political life. PUR, however, was unwilling to concede any genuine autonomy to members' organizations at the lower levels. Curiously, the party's senior representatives in the army saw no contradiction between the goal of increased participation and the means of reducing autonomy.

Second, the RVS ordered PUR to increase its political effectiveness by improving its structure, reducing its staff, and improving its personnel. This recommendation required the Political Administration to establish a clear hierarchy in its structure, to define responsibilities and powers at each level, and to conduct the purge that Bubnov already was planning. Third, the RVS recommended that PUR improve political instruction in the army, "rid it of the spirit of apoliticism and pure *kul'turnichestvo*," and instill in it "a class political character." These euphemisms bespoke the leadership's concern that the political staff was failing to secure loyalty to their basic policies, and as a result, party members in some parts of the army had fallen easy prey to the appeals of the oppositionists. Finally, the RVS recommended drawing as many Communist officers as possible into party and political activities, political instruction, and "soviet work."[54]

Even before the Frunze team launched its ambitious reform program, the Central Committee instructed Bubnov to crush the mutiny among the party and Komsomol members who recently had backed the oppositionists' claims against the ruling faction. Bubnov initiated his directorship of PUR by revoking Antonov-Ovseenko's circular calling for party democracy in the army. He then supervised a purge of the oppositionists at the top of his organization. Senior political workers who had proven their loyalty to the triumvirate replaced men who had supported Trotsky.[55]

54. Berkhin, *Voennaia reforma*, p. 386. Berkhin's account indicates that the plenary session of the RVS convened in January or February 1924.

55. Anton Bulin became the director of the political administration of the notorious Moscow District, where at least one-third of the party members had voted no confidence in the current national leadership. A special investigation of party organizations at headquarters and in military schools was conducted and "many chance elements," including former members of "petit bourgeois parties" (Mensheviks and

As Bubnov was consolidating his position at PUR, he instructed the directors of political administrations to review the records of all party members in order to prevent any further demonstrations of disloyalty such as the army recently had witnessed. In the aftermath of Antonov-Ovseenko's partially successful campaign to garner support for the oppositionists' platforms, the Central Committee dispatched men with solid Bolshevik credentials who were loyal to the ruling triumvirate to discover why certain party organizations had succumbed to the oppositionists' appeals. The investigators attributed most of the blame to the youth, inexperience, and rural origins of the largest part of the party's mass membership in the army and, in particular, to the influx of student youth during the fall 1923 mobilization. Indeed, since the Civil War the party regularly mobilized for military service party members who were the same age as the recruits. Because the older, more experienced party members had returned to civilian life, the lowest rungs of the party organizations were occupied by twenty-one-year-olds. The party's investigators reported that the young Communists did not enjoy the authority among their peers that their older predecessors had had during the Civil War.[56]

The investigators' diagnosis of the party's ills substantially shaped the remedy that was concocted by the army's political leadership. PUR responded to the findings with a variety of measures that coincided with the first nationwide call-up conducted according to the plan devised by the reform commission in spring 1924. Party members who were eligible for call-up were ordered to appear at induction centers one month early to receive instructions on how to prepare for the arrival of their nonparty peers.[57] While the rest of the party was in the throes of the campaign to recruit new members from the factory bench following Lenin's death, the army's recruitment drives ground to a nearly complete halt. After alarming experiences with military students in the fall of 1923 and with the peasants during the spring call-up in 1924, army organizations hesitated to enroll members among the rank-and-file recruits.[58] By July

SRs), were discovered in the ranks of the Trotskyist opposition: Petrov, Stroitel'stvo politorganov, p. 150. Antonov-Ovseenko also claimed that Trotsky's appeal was strongest among the cadets and the army's highest administrators.

56. See, e.g., the report from the Leningrad Military District, Otchet Politicheskogo upravleniia Leningradskogo voennogo okruga, pp. 53–54; also Otchet Narkomvoenmora za 1923/24 g., p. 226, cited in Berkhin, Voennaia reforma, p. 261; V. Kasatkin, "Partrabota posle prizyva 1902 g.," Politrabotnik 6 (1924): 14.

57. Izvestiia TsK RKP(b) 5 (1924): 28, cited in Suvenirov, Kommunisticheskaia partiia, p. 108.

58. For a discussion of the Lenin enrollment, its origins, and its results, see Rigby, Communist Party Membership, pp. 110–31.

party membership had dropped to 24,500, the lowest level since the beginning of the Civil War, even though the number of candidate members rose to 12,417. Most of the secretaries of company-level party cells were demobilized, leaving the lowest levels without experienced organizers. The regularly scheduled demobilization of the twenty-three-year-old soldiers in the spring of 1924 explains part of the drop in numbers. But the moratorium on new admissions from the rank and file also contributed to the lower numbers. Because there were fewer party members among the new recruits, the army's organization came to be more notably a preserve of the officers and political staff.[59] As had happened so often before, the measure designed to improve the political situation initially worsened conditions in the army.

The political crisis in the army had become a concern for the national party membership and was discussed at party conferences and congresses. When the delegates to the Thirteenth Party Congress, in May 1924, delivered the official diagnosis of the party's ills in the army, they resorted to rhetoric that dated back at least as far as the end of the Civil War. Then, civilians hostile to the military's methods, together with many of the army's own political workers, criticized the leadership of PUR for allowing party work in the army to diverge from the life of the party as a whole, for not exercising proper guidance over its subordinate affiliates, and for not maintaining healthy ties with local civilian party organizations as a result. At that time the critics charged Trotsky and his immediate subordinates with relying excessively on the military specialists and relegating the commissars and party members to decidedly secondary functions. Now a new generation of party members leveled the same charges, but the nearly identical rhetoric concealed a very new type of political struggle. In fact, Trotsky and Antonov-Ovseenko advocated greater democracy for party cells in the army in the hope that military Communists would support the oppositionists' challenge to the Central Committee triumvirate. When delegates to the Thirteenth Congress charged the army's leadership with separating party life in the army from the life of the party as a whole, they now meant that

59. In January 1924 the army counted 31,595 full and 8,055 candidate members. In July those numbers were 24,468 and 12,417, respectively. A third of the members of party organizations were candidates. Of the full members, regular soldiers had accounted for 34 percent of the total in January; after the demobilization, that percentage was down to 24.6. See Berkhin, *Voennaia reforma*, pp. 401–2. Berkhin's figures differ from those presented in *Desiat' let Krasnoi armii*, which lists 51,816 members and candidates in January 1924 and 49,491 in October 1924 (p. 42), but these figures too are the lowest since the army was organized in 1918.

Trotsky and his supporters were threatening to split the party into factions and to use their institutional bases in the army to challenge the Central Committee's authority.[60]

Bubnov, armed with the authority of the Central Committee majority and the approval of the May party congress, proceeded to implement the directives. He translated the reform team's slogan of militarization to mean that party and Komsomol members should be enlisted in the campaign to reinforce strict discipline and to bolster the authority of the officer corps; first, therefore, he would have to enforce even stricter discipline among party members. On the basis of his analysis of PUR's shortcomings under his predecessor, Antonov-Ovseenko, he proposed thoroughgoing changes in organization, personnel, and political instruction. Bubnov had the good fortune to retain his directorship of PUR for nearly six years, a period unprecedented in the army's history. Although he, too, experienced difficulties in implementing some of his reforms, he clearly left a strong imprint on the army's political administration before he replaced Lunacharsky as commissar of enlightenment in 1929.

After he had installed loyal allies in key positions at PUR, Bubnov moved to consolidate all party and Komsomol work exclusively in PUR's hands. The envisioned changes involved two sets of relationships, those among army bureaucracies and civil–military relations, the latter considerably more tortured than the former. First, Bubnov subordinated all agencies of political control in army-related institutions to his administration. The major autonomous organization here remained the special political secretariat of the Main Administration of Military Educational Institutions (GUVUZ). Especially in light of the support that students in military schools had shown for the oppositionists, the purging of the GUVUZ secretariat and its transfer to PUR's control was designated an urgent priority. Indeed, during 1924 and 1925 the RVS temporarily reduced the number of military schools. Although Frunze claimed that the schools were too expensive and were turning out too many commanders, the schools' performance during the recent political struggles must have entered into the deliberations on how best to respond to the budget shortfalls.[61]

The more sensitive and contentious set of relationships that Bub-

---

60. "Ob ocherednykh zadachakh partiinogo stroitel'stva," in *Trinadtsatyi s"ezd*, p. 614.

61. The new organizational framework was ratified in "Polozhenie o Politicheskom upravlenii Raboche-Krest'ianskoi Krasnoi Armii (mirnogo vremeni)," 7 September 1925, in *PPR* III, pp. 324–30. For the shutdown of military schools, see Frunze's report "Ob itogakh reorganizatsii Krasnoi Armii," *Voenno-istoricheskii zhurnal* (1966): 72. Frunze had calculated the army's operating budget at 427 million rubles, but he received only 395 million from Sovnarkom.

nov's organizational reforms touched were the army's ties to civilian organizations. Here Bubnov was caught in a dilemma. On the one hand, because the army's small budget was unable to cover all recruitment, training, and outfitting costs, the military leadership had no alternative but to turn to civilian organizations for additional funds and personnel. Especially in the first years after the Civil War, many units came to depend on civilian patrons for essential supplies.[62] On the other hand, the army's personnel, and PUR in particular, resented civilian institutions' intrusion in military affairs and they repudiated the techniques and attitudes that civilians brought with them. Army personnel invariably criticized those areas for which civilian institutions had responsibility, especially in preparing draft-age males for induction and in informing the civilian population about upcoming maneuvers.[63] At the least, the civilian intrusions confused the lines of authority in the army.[64] Since the beginning of the army's existence, civilian party committees had resisted the army's claim to extraterritoriality and demanded that they have control over party members in military units stationed in their localities. Bubnov's first victory was to centralize in the army's political departments all personnel records and authority over party members serving in regular and special units, and those studying in

62. During the Civil War, civilian government agencies and organizations "adopted" military units in a practice that became known as *shefstvo* (patronage). Initially the patrons were expected to exert a healthy political influence on military life, in the manner of Vsevobuch and Glavpolitprosvet. After the Civil War, when the military's finances entered their bleakest period, army units came to look upon their patrons as "milk cows" and complained bitterly when the civilians could not deliver material aid or when they interfered in army life. See "Materialy k soveshchaniiu voennykh delegatov XIII s"ezda RKP(b): Sostoianie shefstva v Krasnoi Armii," *Politrabotnik* 6 (1924): 95–96; "Prakticheskie predlozheniia PURa o shefstve v Krasnoi Armii i Flote," *Politrabotnik* 6 (1924): 98; T. G., "Pora vnesti izmeneniia," *Krasnyi boets* 9 (1924): 52; *Otchet Politicheskogo upravleniia Leningradskogo voennogo okruga*, pp. 13–14.

63. See the irate comments of a political worker following the 1923 summer maneuvers, N. Vasil'ev, "Itogi frontovykh manevrov," *Krasnaia prisiaga* 17 (1923): 15; and the thorough instructions about helping with certain army tasks sent by the Central Committee to all provincial and regional party committees, "Ob usilenii raboty v Krasnoi Armii," 29 October 1923, in *KPSS o vooruzhennykh silakh*, pp. 210–11.

64. As late as 1923 some civilian party district committees *(raikomy)* still were supervising political organs for special assignment detachments. They also collaborated with the political secretariat of GUVUZ in directing the activities of party members in military schools. Even the political departments of infantry units were not indisputably under the jurisdiction of PUR. In both Leningrad and Moscow the provincial party committees regularly called meetings of party members in the army and created "military bureaus" to coordinate all party activities with the local army political administration. See Shevchenko, "Ideino-politicheskoe," pp. 89–90. For the activities of the Moscow provincial committee, see Berkhin, *Voennaia reforma*, pp. 387–88. Because the political situation in Moscow continued to be especially volatile, Voroshilov, the new commander of the Moscow Military District, was appointed to head a commission to draft a new regulation on civilian-military relations.

military schools. The Central Committee thereby recognized the army's practice of organizing party institutions along extraterritorial lines.

Next, not only did PUR's staff win the party's sanction to keep out civilian intruders from those areas it jealously guarded for itself, but the official rhetoric about strengthening the ties between military and civilian organizations was employed to reverse the previous order of intrusion. Now the army's political staff was encouraged to take a more active part in the activities of their civilian counterparts. Commissars and directors of political departments were directed to enter local party committees in areas where their units were stationed. Ostensibly this measure was designed to improve the performance of the civilian organs in pre-induction training and induction, and to give the army a greater say in the affairs of garrison towns and frontier areas in particular. Political departments were obliged to coordinate their "most significant directives and instructions" with civilian organizations, but the latter had no formal right to revoke any instructions that related to matters of party or political work in the army. For local civilian party committees, an August 1924 "Regulation on Relations" clearly represented a defeat. They were required to put their resources and personnel at the military's disposal through the agency of the political departments, but they were left little say as to how those resources and personnel were to be used. All civilian "military bureaus" were henceforth abolished. The one loophole left open for civilian organizations to exert some control over party life in the army was Article 12 of the regulation, which obliged party commissions in the army to send their decisions on admission and expulsion of members to the relevant civilian party counterparts. A November meeting of senior political workers requested that the Central Committee reconsider Article 12 because it "considerably undercut" the army's authority to regulate the affairs of its own staff. The military delegates to the Fourteenth Party Conference, in May 1925, repeated their complaints about excessive civilian interference in personnel matters. Finally, in June 1925, the Central Committee closed the loophole when it conceded that the requirement to present decisions to civilian organizations for confirmation produced excessive parallelism and was ignored by the army's political departments, a condition it resolved by transferring all authority over party members in the army to military organizations exclusively.[65]

65. "Polozhenie o vzaimootnosheniiakh politorganov i partorganizatsii Krasnoi Armii i Flota s partkomami i organizatsiiami RKP(b)," 11 August 1924, in *PPR* III, pp. 217–20; on the June 1925 amendment see *PPR* III, p. 533, n. 56. The regulation, though adopted in August, was not distributed till 27 October 1924, suggesting that civilian organizations did not concede all their rights immediately. For evidence that

Even after Bubnov managed to consolidate his authority within the army's political administration and to introduce some order in the realm of civil–military relations, his troubles were far from over. Because of the changing policies in regard to admission of soldiers to party membership and because of the ever-louder complaints made by young Communists that their views were being ignored, the Komsomol organizations in the army confronted Bubnov with new problems. The twenty-one-year-old cohort that arrived in spring 1924 gave the army its first large numbers of Komsomol members. Many of the recruits had only recently joined Komsomol.[66] Komsomol quickly was becoming the Red Army man's organization, while the party itself was more and more evolving into the institution of the officers and political staff. Among the rank and file, Komsomol members outnumbered party members by 4 or 5 to 1. These trends forced the party to reevaluate the relationships between Komsomol and party in the army, an issue that was under scrutiny and being contested outside the army as well.

As long as party members had substantially outnumbered Komsomol members, the problems of Komsomol organization remained eclipsed by more pressing demands. But now Komsomol's leaders tried to seize what they perceived to be an opportunity to bolster their organization's flagging fortunes. They recommended that the party upgrade Komsomol's status by sanctioning the creation of "collectives-cells in the army."[67] But the party could not relinquish all its authority over soldiers' conduct, so in February 1923 the Central Committee reaffirmed its ban on Komsomol cells and ordered party cells to appoint an "organizer" to direct the daily activities of Komsomol members. Komsomol members were required to attend all open meetings of party cells, where they could speak but could not vote. They were excluded from closed party meetings; nonetheless, they were expected to carry out all party assignments. The Central Committee avoided any reference to questions of admission

political departments were ignoring art. 12, see P. Tsel'min, "K novomu polozheniiu o voennykh partiinykh komissiakh," *SP* 29 (1925): 29–30. For the November convention's resolution on art. 12, see "Soveshchanie politrabotnikov Krasnoi Armii i Flota," *Na strazhe* 25 (1924): 53.

66. By 1 October one-half of the army's 30,000 members had entered Komsomol in the past year.

67. Since 1919 the Central Committee had prohibited, as a threat to military cohesion, the formation of Komsomol organizations that operated independently of party organizations. The ban had never been entirely successful. Some Komsomol members continued to organize their own cells occasionally on the grounds that party members paid them no attention and they felt worse off than the homeless orphans who had been wandering throughout the country since the Civil War. For more on the Komsomol during the Civil War and immediate postwar years, see Tirado, *Young Guard!*; *Bol'shaia Sovetskaia Entsiklopediia* (Moscow 1930), 11:640–41; the protocols of the congresses and conferences; and N. Sumskoi, *Komsomol'skaia rabota v Krasnoi Armii* (Moscow/Leningrad, 1929).

and expulsion of members; presumably these matters remained in the hands of the appropriate civilian organizations.[68] Until 1924 PUR successfully resisted all of Komsomol's attempts to carve out greater power for itself in the army. Like members of other civilian organizations that sacrificed personnel and resources to the army, Komsomol members felt justified in demanding some say in the conduct of their own affairs and even in the greater political life of military units. The proposal of "collectives-cells" met with opposition at the assembly of military delegates to the Thirteenth Party Congress, in May 1924, and at the Sixth Komsomol Congress, Bubnov warned that Komsomol work in the Red Army required stricter subordination to party control.

Komsomol members who entered army service in the spring of 1924 were full of enthusiasm and eager to conduct political work, but during their first hoped-for opportunity, the summer field maneuver, party members resisted or ignored their efforts. The young activists complained that the Party members wanted to "de-Komsomolize" them and refused to give them any authority. Their demands for autonomous cells and their complaints to political departments replicated the appeals of their national leadership. In July, in response to the pressures at the top and from below, the Central Committee met the Komsomol leaders less than halfway and sanctioned the formation of "assistance groups" (gruppy sodeistviia) in army units. The new organizations could not elect their own executive boards and remained subordinate to the "organizer" appointed by the unit's party cell. Furthermore, the Central Committee listed no new rights or responsibilities for the groups short of a vague duty "to assist the party."[69] Clearly, in the face of party members' hostility to their junior partners' ambitions, the Central Committee's concessions made little headway in resolving the conflicts between the two groups. Still, the "assistance groups" caught hold with soldiers, and their numbers rose rapidly, from 230 in October 1924 to 3,740 in July 1925.[70]

Not only did Bubnov have to work out a compromise within the army over areas in which it was permissible for party members to guide their junior partners in Komsomol, but he also extracted a few concessions from the civilian youth leadership. First, the national Komsomol leaders very reluctantly conceded that the special condi-

68. "Polozhenie o rabote RKSM v Krasnoi Armii i Flote," 9 February 1923, in PPR III, pp. 129–30.

69. Sumskoi, Komsomol'skaia rabota, pp. 14–15; VLKSM v rezoliutsiiakh ego s''ezdov i konferentsii, 1918–1928 gg. (Moscow, 1929), pp. 183–86; Shestoi s''ezd Leninskogo kommunisticheskogo soiuza molodezhi: Stenograficheskii otchet, 12–18 iiulia 1924 g. (Moscow/Leningrad, 1924), pp. 55, 317–18, 324; P. Tashlitskii, "Partorganizatsiia i rabota KSM," SP 14 (1925): 16.

70. Petrov, Stroitel'stvo, pp. 203, 204.

tions of Komsomol work in the army dictated an exceptional set of relationships with the party and the political departments. In fact, civilian youth organizations, like their civilian party counterparts, lost any meaningful role in directing the affairs of their members serving in military units. The civilian party organizations even intervened—not unselfishly, for they too wanted more say in Komsomol politics—on behalf of Komsomol and offered to conduct investigations of Komsomol work in army units. Army spokesmen at Komsomol assemblies consistently defeated all such proposals.[71] In effect, the army succeeded in fending off another threatened incursion by civilian political activists in military life.

The second important concession that Bubnov wrung from the national Komsomol leadership pertained to the age limit for Komsomol membership. In the civilian Komsomol, membership was open to young citizens aged fourteen to twenty-three. Under the new service requirements, soldiers entered the army during the year they turned twenty-two, so many completed their term of duty only after turning twenty-four. Under the national Komsomol rules, twenty-four-year-olds automatically lost their active membership. In the army this age limit operated to exclude tens of thousands of soldiers from any direct involvement in a formal political structure. One solution would have been for the party organizations to grant candidate-member status to Komsomol members who turned twenty-four, but throwing open the doors to party membership in 1924 and 1925, especially to peasants, was out of the question because party organizers were "regulating" their membership's growth to keep out "careerists and politically unreliable elements." At the end of 1924 assemblies of Komsomol organizers in the army proposed that the rules be amended to permit Red Army personnel to remain active members through the age of twenty-four. At first the civilian organizations rejected the military delegates' suggestions. The rules, the civilians explained, already provided for twenty-four-year-olds to remain in the organization, but without the right to vote. The military delegates responded that the rules "in essence condemned Red Army soldiers who are Komsomol members to passive membership."[72] In May 1925 persistent pressure from the army's Komsomol and party activists finally induced PUR's leadership to reach a compromise solution with Komsomol's central committee. Twenty-four-

71. The provincial party committees did win approval to investigate Komsomol activities, but only after the investigations had been cleared and coordinated through the appropriate army political department. They could make recommendations to political departments, which would decide whether and where to implement them. See the account of a Ukrainian assembly of Komsomol organizers meeting in late 1924 in Gr. Kul', "Voprosy Krasnoi Armii na Vseukrainskom soveshchanii orginstrov LKSMU," *Krasnaia rota* 57 (1924): 30–32.

72. Ibid., pp. 32–33.

year-olds remained active members in the army's organizations, but the age limit of twenty-three held for acceptance of new members.[73] Once again the army won official acknowledgment, as well as the commensurate political authority, that the special conditions of military life warranted unique privileges that set its political organizations apart from their national civilian membership.

Bubnov's half-year tenure in office had just begun to show positive results in reducing organizational confusion and political discontent when Trotsky, still formally head of the Red Army, launched his next and most desperate challenge to the triumvirate. Again Bubnov counterattacked, and his army-wide agitation campaign produced ringing denunciations of Trotsky's harmful behavior. The denunciations testified to the success of PUR's recent purge. By the fall of 1924, when once again Trotsky appealed to party members to support him against the triumvirate, even the military schools passed resolutions denouncing Trotsky's attempt "to replace Leninism with Trotskyism."[74] In November 1924 Bubnov called a nationwide assembly of senior political workers, who passed a resolution demanding Trotsky's dismissal from the Army Commissariat. Trotsky, ill with malaria, did not appear before the delegates to defend himself. Shortly thereafter, the authoritative party cell of the RVS also demanded his dismissal. On 15 January 1925 Trotsky asked the Central Committee to relieve him of his post as chairman of RVS. The Central Committee plenum appointed Frunze to succeed him.

To assess the damage wrought by the upsetting events of 1924, the Central Committee ordered a thorough investigation of the condition of party cells in the army.[75] Not surprisingly, the investigators un-

73. Sumskoi, *Komsomol'skaia rabota*, pp. 8–9; "Tsirkuliar o prodlenii sroka prebyvaniia v riadakh RLKSM komsomol'tsam, prokhodiashchim sluzhbu v Krasnoi Armii i Flote," 30 May 1925, noted in *PPR* III, p. 551.

74. According to Iona Iakir, the new director of military schools, "100 percent of all party organizations in military schools declared themselves in favor of the Central Committee's line": *Krasnaia zvezda*, 9 April 1925, cited in Petrov, *Stroitel'stvo*, p. 151. The pretext for the party struggles in the fall was the appearance of Trotsky's preface to a volume of his speeches and writings of 1917, titled "The Lessons of October." Trotsky vindicated his role in the October Revolution and impugned the conduct of his current opponents in the Central Committee, mainly Zinoviev and Kamenev, but also Rykov, Kalinin, and other Old Bolsheviks who had failed Lenin during the crucial days of planning for insurrection. For Trotsky's essay and the responses of his major assailants, see *Ob "Urokakh Oktiabria"* (Leningrad, 1924) and a later volume, *Za leninizm* (Leningrad, 1925). For Deutscher's account of the political struggles in late 1924, see *Prophet Unarmed*, pp. 151–63.

75. Initially the Central Committee had ordered the investigation in August 1924, but it did not form the investigative commission till the end of the year. In January and February 1925, after Trotsky's dismissal, teams were dispatched to four military districts, the Special Caucasian Army, and the vessels of the Black Sea Fleet. See Petrov, *Stroitel'stvo*, p. 187.

covered several serious problems, which they summarized as the lack of participation by soldiers in party activities and a formal approach to political work. Both of these shortcomings eroded the effectiveness of party organizations in reaching their intended mass constituencies. (Trotsky had made similar charges of bureaucratization earlier in the year.) The reporters complained that party cells showed little life or initiative, but instead were accustomed solely to accepting orders from above. They also criticized the widespread replacement of elections to party bodies with appointments from above: the one area of party activity where the elective principle was still officially sanctioned, the election of cell secretaries and bureaus, was consistently violated. Komsomol members too complained that they continued to be obstructed in their efforts to take a greater part in political life. Party members forbade their junior colleagues from exercising any control over admission and expulsion of their own members. Having no say over key aspects of their organizational life, Komsomol members also became "passive" and uncooperative. The inactivity of lower-level party organizations took a particularly heavy toll on the campaign to instill stricter discipline in troops, but cells also did little or nothing to counteract the "peasant moods" that had so alarmed the party's leadership during the spring and autumn.

The investigative commission blamed most of the problems on demographic changes in the party and the recruiting policies of the preceding year. The major explanation was the exceedingly small number of party members among rank-and-file troops. Most soldiers remained outside of both party and Komsomol organizations. Officers and political workers were so burdened by the new demands placed on them by the reforms that they could devote little attention to strictly political affairs.[76] The report of the investigative commission was the main topic of discussion at an assembly of party cell secretaries that Bubnov convened at the end of February 1925, the same assembly that Frunze addressed on the challenges of rural party work.[77] The party's Orgburo had come to the conclusion that the only remedy for the army's unhealthy condition was to involve more soldiers in the reform measures. The investigative team recommended that party recruitment be stepped up and that political departments revive the company-level cells that had disappeared as a result of the demobilization and consequent depletion of party numbers at the lowest rungs of the army organization. These recommendations fell on eager ears. The secretaries enthusiastically endorsed measures giving themselves more authority in working with party

76. Berkhin, *Voennaia reforma*, pp. 408–9.
77. For a summary of the assembly, see Petrov, *Stroitel'stvo*, pp. 186–91; for the official proceedings, see *Soveshchanie sekretarei iacheek pri PURe*.

and Komsomol members, with nonparty soldiers, and, for those serving in territorial units, with peasants generally. Bubnov delivered an address on the secretaries' important role in instilling discipline and on party membership policies. Several other speakers proposed that the delegates play a greater role in the nation's political life. Of course, these speeches too pleased the secretaries.

Frunze addressed the party secretaries on the contentious issue of the party's future in Soviet society, a matter that had pitted party leaders against the rank and file at every recent conference and congress. His speech also went to the heart of the secretaries' future political roles. Military and political leaders took different positions on the party's appropriate size and social composition. These positions were inextricably tied to competing visions of the party's role in society. Some wanted a mass party that was representative of broad segments across society. Such a mass, representative party would ensure the leaders healthy ties to the nation. Others argued that only a vanguard elitist party could uphold the strict discipline that was essential in the coming struggle for socialism in Russia. The prerevolutionary political debates between Mensheviks and Bolsheviks over the appropriate model for a revolutionary party were playing themselves out in new forums and new social and political contexts. Too large a party could not guarantee an effective political vanguard, but too small a party would limit access to the greater populace. The party, Frunze held, "must remain as a relatively not very large core, but a core [nonetheless], consisting of tested individuals, tempered by the Revolution." Such a core must stand firmly by a "class proletarian point of view," the only effective "guarantee against all deviations." Too large a party ran the risk of degenerating into "something diffuse and soft-bodied," incapable of carrying out its political mission.[78] In the army, the party's vanguard role was linked to strict discipline and thereby became an integral part of the militarization campaign.[79]

The vision of the party as vanguard also appealed to the depeasantizers because they firmly believed that admitting many peasants to party membership would only dilute "resolute proletarian consciousness" with petit bourgeois conciliatory influences. The determined resistance of lower-ranking party and Komsomol activists, who were most influential in deciding on admission to their organizations, frustrated the plans of PUR's leaders both to expand numbers and to ease the admission requirements for nonproletarian

78. Frunze, "Territorial'noe stroitel'stvo i rabota v derevne," in *Izbrannye proizvedeniia* (1957), 2:234–35.
79. Party commissions were ordered to devote special attention to violations of the new disciplinary codes. Their investigations in late spring and early summer helped to reduce infractions substantially. See Petrov, *Stroitel'stvo*, pp. 190n, 191.

applicants. Party membership did expand. Indeed, starting in 1926 the army's party organizations grew more rapidly than the entire national party organization. From the all-time low of less than 50,000 in 1924, the army's organizations added nearly 10,000 new members every year until 1930. But the party's statistics reveal significant changes in the composition of membership and hint at the antagonism that endured at the organization's lower levels.

First, the proportion of candidates rose steadily, suggesting that party commissions and political departments were requiring applicants to undergo longer probation periods before they were admitted to full membership.[80] Second, the percentage of peasants also dropped steadily, while the social category known as "others," consisting mainly of white-collar workers, remained relatively steady. Military men of proletarian origins accounted for the largest growth between 1924 and 1930, when they made up nearly 60 percent of the total membership, the percentage that peasants had represented in 1923.[81] The figures for the army closely follow trends in the party at large, but whereas the party had committed itself to a policy of "proletarianization" of its membership, PUR's leaders initially had pushed for easing admission for peasants and white-collar workers. Most likely the depeasantizers can claim credit for bringing army membership closer to the national norms.[82]

Finally, party membership in the army underwent changes in breakdown by army occupation and status. In the early 1920s the most pronounced trend was to concentrate party membership among the officer corps and political staff. As one-man command was introduced after 1925, the number of political workers dropped yearly. Between 1925 and 1929 their share of the total membership was halved. As officers and regular soldiers assumed more responsibilities for political education in the army, they also filled the places formerly held by the political staff in the party.[83] By the autumn of

80. The most complete statistics on party membership are found in Suvenirov, *Kommunisticheskaia partiia*, pp. 112–13. Suvenirov compiled his tables from PUR and party handbooks. The percentage of full members in party organizations reached a high of 84.2 percent in 1923 (15.8 percent were candidates). The percentage of candidates rose to 40 in 1926.

81. Except for 1928, when the number of "others" rose dramatically to 27 percent of the total membership, white-collar representation fluctuated between 13 and 16 percent. The percentage of peasants dropped from 56.3 in 1923 to 29.0 in 1930. Workers rose from 31.4 precent in 1923 to 58.3 in 1930. See ibid., p. 112.

82. For statistics on national membership trends, see Rigby, *Communist Party Membership*, p. 116.

83. In 1925 officers accounted for 31 percent (18,106 total), military cadets 20.6 (11,909), political workers 24.5 (14,155), and regular troops 16.3 (9,412). In 1929 officers accounted for nearly half of the total membership, 48.8 percent (45, 419 total), cadets dropped to 11.6 (10,774), the political staff dropped to 12.1 percent (11,266), and regular troops rose to 23.6 percent (21,936). See Suvenirov, *Kommunisticheskaia partiia*, p. 113.

1927 the "party saturation" of the army (ratio of party members to total military personnel) attained a remarkable high of 16.1 percent, a figure twenty times greater than that for the population at large and even several times greater than the party saturation of the proletariat itself.[84]

Many of the processes that were changing party membership were replicated in Komsomol. Beginning in 1924, Komsomol's numbers in the army not only grew more rapidly than the national Komsomol organization itself but far outpaced even the rate of the party's expansion in the army. From the 30,000 Komsomol members registered in 1924, their numbers climbed to 177,000 by the middle of 1930 and 250,000 by the end of 1931.[85] Like the party's organizations, Komsomol subjected larger numbers of applicants to longer probation periods as candidate members, but unlike the party's organizations, Komsomol embraced soldiers, some junior officers, and a few military cadets. Peasants dominated the new Komsomol in the army, although workers continued to make up nearly one-third. The category of "others" remained below 10 percent.[86] Komsomol's phenomenal growth suggests that the depeasantizers were at least willing to conform to PUR's behest on Komsomol membership policy, once Bubnov and his co-workers assured the lower-ranking party members that they would have a vital role in directing Komsomol activities.

Military and many civilian leaders, most notably Stalin and his close political allies, used the vanguard model to argue that it was unlikely that the party could achieve its ambitious goals if it tolerated the type of democratic political culture that the oppositionists were advocating.[87] Military leaders defended the vanguard role of the party in the army by pointing to the backwardness of Russia, with its overwhelmingly rural economy and peasant population, and to the current international situation, which demanded unflagging vigilance and unquestioning obedience from soldiers. Virtually the same arguments surfaced during the course of every struggle between military and civilian spokesmen. The civilians argued that the wartime emergency was over, and therefore the army had no further claim to the privileged position. Their organizations' more dem-

84. *Piatnadtsatyi s''ezd VKP(b): Stenograficheskii otchet* (Moscow/Leningrad, 1928), p. 100, cited in Suvenirov, *Kommunisticheskaia partiia*, p. 111.

85. *Desiat' let Krasnoi armii*, p. 54; Petrov, *Stroitel'stvo*, pp. 252, 254.

86. *Desiat' let Krasnoi armii*, p. 56.

87. Stalin's views on the issue of party democracy came remarkably close to the arguments made by military men. At the Thirteenth Party Conference, in January 1924, he asserted that internal party democracy was possible only if Soviet industry and the industrial proletariat grew dramatically, and if the Soviet Republic were free from threat of foreign attack. See Stalin, "Doklad ob ocherednykh zadachakh partiinogo stroitel'stva," 17 January 1924, in *Sochineniia*, 6:7–8.

ocratic political styles served as the only effective guarantee against the emergence of a new officer caste and the politically unacceptable relations that had characterized the tsarist army. Furthermore, now that the army had become an important recruiting agency for both the party and Komsomol, a strong civilian influence on the new members in the army assumed far greater urgency.

With equal conviction military men argued that civilians failed to appreciate the nature of an army, and particularly of the Red Army. Above all, the type of discipline required to compel a soldier to fight differed markedly from the discipline observable in civilian society, even in the best-run factory setting. Unfortunately, they went on to argue, the typical Red Army conscript lacked even the discipline of a factory worker because the Red Army was and would remain an overwhelmingly peasant organization. In the current period of international tensions and constant threat to the security of the Soviet state, civilian experiments were entirely out of the question. Moreover, the army setting provided a unique opportunity to remake the undisciplined peasant conscripts into conscious Soviet citizens, but only if they were effectively isolated from everything in their environment that reinforced their familiar and undesirable lifestyles. Therefore, the military spokesmen concluded, they required total control over the special educational environment they had developed since the formation of the Red Army in the Civil War. By the mid-1920s the army's arguments appeared to be triumphing. The goal of militarization forced a gamut of civilian organizations, including the party, Komsomol, and the educational and judicial establishments, to forgo large measures of institutional authority over daily affairs in the army.

PART THREE

A School of Socialism

CHAPTER 7

Militarization and Sovietization: Political Culture in the Postreform Army

We must take a new attitude toward the army—as a cultural force through which we can reeducate the nation.

—*Krasnyi boets*, 1924

Toward the Two-Year Program

The 1923 investigative commission that set the army reforms in motion ordered a thorough overhaul of the system of political education for soldiers and junior officers. Gusev, as chairman of the commission, now had his opportunity to undo the work of his successors as directors of PUR, Serebriakov and Antonov-Ovseenko, both of whom had joined the Trotskyist opposition. Bubnov, currently director of PUR, convened regular assemblies of political workers and surveyed attendance records, literacy examinations, and the opinions of instructors on ways to improve PUR's techniques. Actually, by the end of 1923 an assembly of political workers had adopted a "unified system of political education" based on the political manual (*politustav*); however, as long as the army remained a "revolving door" for personnel, as it was portrayed by the investigative commission and by several army commentators, and short on funds in every sector, PUR was unable to implement any of the new schemes.[1] A year later, at the end of 1924, Bubnov set in motion a major reevaluation of political education in line with the reforms in army life that Frunze was overseeing.

The overhaul came in response to alarming reports in the spring of 1924 that party conscripts, called up one month earlier than their

1. In spring 1924 Gusev complained that no decisions on political education had been implemented since at least early 1922: *Politrabotnik* 4–5 (1924): 16.

nonparty peers, revealed extremely weak knowledge of "the Bolshevik party line, the party's struggle with Menshevism, with other alien political groups, and of [the party's] tactics."[2] Next PUR divulged the disturbing findings of another survey, this time of *politruki*, that the army's primary teaching staff were "just barely educated." Nearly nine-tenths of the instructors had no more than two years of primary education and were not competent in Russian history, geography, natural science, fractions, percentages (which figured prominently in the visual aids PUR distributed), or analysis of literary texts. They could not even "*read aloud in a distinct, competent, or expressive manner.*" Given the lack of preparation, the authors of the report concluded, *politruki* had become "superficial know-it-alls."[3]

In the meantime, the political staff was subjecting the soldiers to a battery of surveys in the hope of gaining a more refined sense of the targets of their educational work. Political workers exploited every opportunity to gather information about each soldier: private conversations with him, his letters home, observations during political instruction, and reports from party and Komsomol members in the unit. The staff's curiosity seemed to know no bounds. What effect did political events, holidays, or participation in festive demonstrations and mass campaigns have on the soldier? Was he religious? Did he frequent theaters and libraries? Which books did he prefer? How wealthy was his family? Did they own a horse or other livestock? How large were their landholdings?[4] The survey quickly gained a prominent place in the array of indispensable techniques for transforming peasant recruits into soldiers and citizens. The political staff shared the modern faith of large sectors of the new Soviet bureaucracy that their statistics represented a form of control over the populations surveyed; furthermore, they could use the statistics to buttress their arguments for one or another type of educational approach.

Since the level of political literacy among the instructors and party members had been found to be so low, it was hardly surprising that soldiers also performed abysmally when they were examined on what the political staff felt to be the rudiments of a civic education.[5] The senior political staff in Chita and Leningrad admin-

2. V. Zibert, "O bol'shevistskom vospitanii," *Na strazhe* 25 (1924): 9–10.
3. Ravdel', "Ob obshchem obrazovanii politrukov," *Na strazhe* 6–7 (1924): 61; *Politrabotnik* 8–9 (1924): 72.
4. A. Solov'ev, "Postanovka raboty po izucheniiu krasnoarmeitsev," *SP* 23 (1925): 26; A. Shifres, "Kak izuchat' krasnoarmeitsa?" *SP* 5 (1924): 60, and "Pervye itogi izucheniia molodogo krasnoarmeitsa," *Politrabotnik* 7 (1924): 20; Kuznetsov, *Metodika politzaniatii*, p. 138.
5. S. E. Rabinovich, "Chto pokazala proverka politzaniatii krasnoarmeitsev LVO," *SP* 26 (1925): 39; V. Kasatkin, "Ob uchete opyta," *Politrabotnik* 6 (1924): 78.

istered the army's first standardized vocabulary tests to Red Army soldiers to check the efficacy of their staffs' labors in conveying the political agenda and rhetoric of the nation's leaders. The vocabulary that appeared in the tests came from the most frequently used terms in army and party newspapers and the teaching guides for political lectures. The multiple-choice word identifications tested soldiers' knowledge of political figures, cities, abbreviations, and foreign phrases.[6] On the basis of the vocabulary tests, the army's language specialists concluded that peasant soldiers had considerably smaller vocabularies—some estimates put them as low as 800 to 2,000 words in active use—than other social groups and that they were unfamiliar with many words that had entered the Russian language since the Revolution. "Let's be frank," a political worker admonished, "when we speak about banks, stock exchanges, parliaments, trusts, finance kings, and democracies, we are not being understood and we won't be understood."[7]

Perhaps more troubling was the discovery that even when soldiers used such words, they understood them in a sense that was entirely different from the understanding of their urban, more educated counterparts. One such disparity was seen in the soldiers' readings of the word *soglashatel'*, which literally means conciliator or compromiser, but in the pre-1917 discourse of socialists and revolutionaries had come to mean a traitor to the workers' cause. Lenin and the Bolsheviks had used the term to malign the Socialist Revolutionary and Menshevik parties for their participation in the "bourgeois" coalitions of the Provisional Government in 1917. Indeed, the only "proper" choice among the four offered was "Menshevik." Several soldiers, reading *soglasie* as the order and harmony that the regime declared to exist between workers and peasants, wrote in the name of Lenin, ostensibly because he "had implemented harmony in Russia."[8] The commentators concluded that the soldiers simply did not know any better, but some hinted that the soldiers might be resorting to a well-known peasant strategy in dealings with outside authorities and were playing dumb, knowing full well the meaning of *soglashatel'*. If the soldiers' responses were read this way, they

6. For more on the early history of the army's vocabulary surveys, see I. N. Shpil'rein, D. I. Reitynbarg, and G. O. Netskii, *Iazyk krasnoarmeitsa* (Moscow/Leningrad, 1928). The authors worked in the Psychotechnic Section of the State Institute of Experimental Psychology. The Psychotechnic Section conducted the most ambitious study of soldiers' language in 1924–1925. Its findings are the main topic of *Iazyk krasnoarmeitsa*.

7. N. Iarov, "Podkhod k auditorii i teme," *Krasnyi boets* 6 (1924): 20.

8. A. Shifres, "Kak izuchat' krasnoarmeitsa?" *SP* 5 (1924): 60; E. Kosmin, *Politicheskaia rabota v territorial'nykh chastiakh* (Moscow/Leningrad, 1928), pp. 62–63.

might have been accusing Lenin of betraying the Revolution.[9] Other
evidence revealed that peasants derived rather original etymologies
for contemporary Soviet political terms which were clearly colored
by their distrust of the national leadership. For example, peasants
used several variants in reference to *VTsIK* (the All-Russian Central
Executive Committee, the body that constitutionally held supreme
power in the country) which revealed sarcastic anti-Semitic sentiments: "Shmol'nyi" (a Yiddish *sh* replacing the *s* in "Smol'nyi,"
Lenin's headquarters during the October Revolution and the first
seat of Sovnarkom), "Tsentrozhid" (Central Administration of Yids,
a parody of the centralized trusts and economic agencies set up during the Civil War), and *prezhidium* (again a Yiddish *zh* replacing the
z in *prezidium* to create *zhid*.[10] At least these ingenious renderings
refute political workers' rose-colored explanation that soldiers dis-
torted political terms at random and reveal an attitude widespread
among peasants—that the new Soviet elite was the latest in a series
of arbitrary rulers imposed on them from outside. The visible role of
Jews in the party and state hierarchy shaped peasant understanding
of the changes in political power since the Revolution.

PUR officially adhered to the explanation that soldiers, because
they were from working-class or poor peasant backgrounds(!), initially held antistate views out of ignorance and resentment of the
kulaks' hegemony over village political life. In their nearly Socratic
equation of virtue with knowledge, PUR spokesmen asserted that as
soon as the soldiers were instructed in the scientifically grounded
Marxist truths found in the political manual, and thereby were redi-
rected from the pernicious influences of their petit bourgeois rural
environment, they would recognize that their real interests were being served by the workers'-peasants' government. The political literacy examinations would enable the political staff to chart the
soldiers' ascent from the realm of political unconsciousness to genuine proletarian consciousness.

The political literacy examination was one of many tests and techniques that the army's staff used to gain knowledge about the soldiers they were assigned to reeducate. In early 1924 N. Rabichev,
assistant director of the Ukrainian Military District's political administration, painted a highly revealing portrait of the twenty-one-
year-old conscripts who were arriving from the local induction
centers. His description of the typical soldier's political physiognomy matched the observations of most political workers. "The new
inductees arrive to a man very religious," Rabichev began. The first

9. John Bushnell writes of this strategy of self-defense in the Imperial Army, "The
wisdom of stupidity was peasant wisdom": *Mutiny amid Repression*, pp. 22–23.
10. S. I. Kartsevskii, *Iazyk, voina i revoliutsiia* (Berlin: Russkoe universal'noe
izdatel'stvo, 1923), p. 36.

thing they did on arrival in the barracks was cross themselves. They prayed every evening, kept their crosses and icons from home, and wrote to their parents that "God is not honored in the barracks." Not surprisingly, there was hardly a Komsomol member among them. The soldier, Rabichev went on, evinced a guarded, if not initially hostile, attitude toward his commander, toward Communists, and toward the city in general. His attitudes had been formed by conversations about rural hardships back home during the Civil War. The new recruit probably did not remember prerevolutionary life, nor was it likely that he had served in a military unit before, but he might have been involved in banditry. Certainly he had heard grumbling about food commissars, forced grain requisitioning, the Cheka terror, and the antiprofiteering detachments that blocked entry to the cities for many years. No doubt his relatives and neighbors bemoaned their unfair share of the nation's tax burden.

Rabichev's picture of the new recruit was not entirely bleak, however. Surely the peasant was full of suspicions and fears about the regime that had compelled him to leave his family and familiar surroundings, but he also had an all-consuming curiosity about both army life and especially "the awesome Soviet city." During his first days he longed to walk about town, go to libraries and clubs, and especially to shops and stands. His release from quarantine was a momentous and joyous event. Whether he knew it or not, Rabichev observed, the soldier was testing all that he knew and all that he was learning against what he found outside the barracks. A soldier's initial curiosity acted as a powerful lever for the political staff to begin his reeducation; but, warned Rabichev, the soldier's first acquaintances outside the barracks gate would be influential in shaping his new attitudes. Too often those first acquaintances were representatives of the urban petite bourgeoisie, "the woman who sells seeds, the nearby shopkeeper, the church on the corner, and, a little farther away, the market and the town prostitute."[11]

PUR's job was to replace one set of loyalties and attachments with another. As a Red commander put it, "Our mission is to destroy the old regime in the hearts and minds of the Red Army men."[12] Political workers had to guard soldiers from unwholesome environmental influences and convey to them "correct" political information; moreover, a soldier had to know why and against which enemies he was fighting, and he had to want to fight and to be prepared to give up his life.[13] To accomplish this vital mission, PUR unveiled a new

11. N. Rabichev, "Nyneshnii krasnoarmeets i politchas," *Politrabotnik* 2–3 (1924): 57–58, 60.
12. Vasil'ev, "'Zhiv kurilka'!" *Voennyi vestnik* 1 (1923): 22.
13. Kosmin, *Politicheskaia rabota*, pp. 43–44.

two-year scheme of political education in July 1925.[14] The most comprehensive statement to date of the aims and methods of political education, it revealed the values that the nation's political elite saw fit to convey to its soldiers. PUR presented the new program as the product of discussions and practical trials conducted over several years. And, despite the adaptations necessitated by prevailing social, political, and cultural conditions, the authors insisted that their scheme was grounded in the best traditions of scientific Marxism and revolutionary praxis.

The three fundamental pillars of the two-year program were "militarization, sovietization, and internationalization." As dictated by the unifying concept of the Frunze reforms, militarization occupied the most prominent place in the two-year program. The primary task of all education, in both content and form, was to guarantee combat readiness and soldier morale. The entire first year of a soldier's education was designed to transform "the peasant who was called to serve in the Red Army into a Soviet soldier who had a clear idea of the Red Army, its aims, organization, and history." Political education in military themes accompanied the purely military instruction that all recruits underwent in the Red Army's version of boot camp. The two-year program was augmented by the militarization of all extracurricular activities.[15] PUR instructed political workers to conduct their cultural and educational work so as to reinforce the measures for improving discipline. The political staff arranged their lessons with the aid of guidebooks and articles in the military press. The authors of the aids continually reminded the instructors that although the Red Army differed fundamentally from the tsarist army, it still was an instrument of warfare. M. Korol', a senior political worker, cautioned against putting "too much hope in the consciousness, the ideological level, and other no doubt wonderful traits of the Red Army man." Discipline was discipline. If much of Red Army military instruction resembled tsarist techniques, there were, after all, only so many ways to issue such commands as "at ease," "fire," and "double time." The guard watch and sentry "perform the same function in our army that they performed in the tsarist army." The execution of commands, the system of military subordination, orders and reports, the psychological and physical traits of a fighter, the capacity to operate as a member of a unit— "these characteristics," wrote Korol', "lie at the base of military organizations in general, independent of the class base on which the

14. *Sbornik prikazov i tsirkuliarov PU RKKA SSSR No. 21: Dvukhletniaia programma politzaniatii s krasnoarmeitsami s ob"iasnitel'noi zapiskoi* (Moscow, 1925).
15. "Iz tsirkuliara PU RKKA o merakh po uluchsheniiu vneshkol'noi raboty v armii," 3 August 1925, in PPR III, pp. 315–24, esp. pp. 319–20.

The Red Army is the school of citizenship. Courtesy of Poster Collection, Hoover Institution Archives, Stanford University.

armed forces are constructed."[16] Korol' claimed that he too believed "in the enthusiasm of our worker-peasant masses," but he defined the class consciousness that he deemed essential for a soldier as the will to fight and win with "class hatred for the enemy and love for the socialist fatherland."[17] Proletarian consciousness for Korol' was little more than militant Soviet patriotism. Indeed, following the army reforms, little distinguished the statements of authoritative spokesmen such as Korol' from what Trotsky had advocated during his own tenure as army commissar and from what contemporaries then called "vulgar militarist" or "militarist-culturist tendencies" (voenizatorski-kul'turnicheskie tendentsii),[18] but of course no one repeated such charges any more.

16. M. Korol', *Voprosy voenno-politicheskogo vospitaniia v Krasnoi Armii* (Moscow/Leningrad, 1927), pp. 23–24. See also Kosmin, *Politicheskaia rabota*, p. 45.
17. Korol', *Voprosy*, pp. 4, 6, 11–12.
18. Such epithets are also routinely used by contemporary Soviet historians to defame Trotsky's reputation. See Suvenirov, *Kommunisticheskaia partiia*, p. 81.

During a soldier's second year in service, he was to begin the portion of his political training designed to transform him into a loyal, informed Soviet citizen and potentially a cadre who might enter the Soviet bureaucracy upon release from the military. The dominant theme of sovietization was to instill in the peasant soldier the conviction that the proper political settlement for Soviet Russia was "the bond of workers and peasants under the leadership of the working class and its party." Finally, in third place was "internationalization," which was described as education about the foreign policy of the Soviet state. This was by far the least satisfactorily conceived portion of the program. It was assigned neither a fixed number of hours nor a recommended set of themes and left for discussion "during the course of the entire program."[19] In 1924 several senior political workers had recommended that internationalization be dropped altogether, on the grounds that it was unfeasible and that political instructors would have a large enough task merely to convince the average soldier of "the indisputable need for the defense of the Soviet state," let alone for any internationalist mission.[20] Just as proletarian consciousness was equated with Soviet patriotism, internationalism underwent a shift in meaning that accorded the interests of the Soviet state the indisputably highest priority for the international revolutionary movement.

The two-year program remained in force with minor revisions until the mid-1930s.[21] On the model of the tiered system of education

19. PUR instructions allotted 280 hours of political education during a soldier's first year and 190 during the second. See *Dvukhletniaia programma politzaniatii s krasnoarmeitsami: Sbornik prikazov i tsirkuliarov Politicheskogo Upravleniia RKKA SSSR* (Moscow, 1928), p. 5; Suvenirov, *Kommunisticheskaia partiia*, pp. 216–17, 219.

20. *Vsesoiuznoe soveshchanie nachpuokrov, nachpuflotov, voenkomkorov, voenkomdivov i nachpodivov, 17–22 noiabria 1924 g.: Stenograficheskii otchet* (Moscow, 1924), p. 99.

21. At the end of 1937, following the first two five-year plans of industrialization and the mechanization of the army, PUR amended the general educational requirements for all military personnel to upgrade their technical skills. Soldiers and officers were expected to have greater mastery of mathematics and the sciences. See "Direktiva PU RKKA o dal'neishem sovershenstvovanii obshchebrazovatel'noi podgotovki komandno-nachal'stvuiushchego i riadovogo sostava armii," 31 December 1937, in *Partiino-politicheskaia rabota v Krasnoi Armii: Dokumenty, iiul' 1929 g.– mai 1941 g.* (Moscow, 1985) (hereafter PPR IV), pp. 339–40. The Soviet government adopted a new law on "treason against the Motherland" in June 1934; consequently, at the beginning of 1939 the text of the military oath was revised and given new stress in all political education. See "Direktiva PU RKKA o poriadke priniatiia, izucheniia i raz''iasneniia novogo teksta voennoi prisiagi," 3 January 1939, in PPR IV, pp. 362–64. Finally, after the publication of the *History of the Communist Party of the Soviet Union (Bolsheviks): Short Course* in 1938, party education also underwent a fundamental restructuring. See "Direktiva PU RKKA ob izuchenii postanovleniia TsK VKP(b) 'O postanovke partiinoi propagandy v sviazi s vypuskom "Kratkogo kursa istorii VKP(b)," ' " 15 November 1938, in PPR IV, p. 357.

for party and Komsomol members, the political staff tried more effi-
ciently to reach its diverse publics with three variants of the two-
year program, one for literate soldiers, another for the semiliterate,
and a third for the illiterate. In 1927 PUR increased the number of
exercises in militarization after the spring war scare.[22]

The Army as Family and School

Above all, soldiers had to learn to identify their individual fates
with the well-being of their fellow soldiers and their superiors and
with the army as a whole. To cultivate a sense of solidarity, political
workers created a collective memory, "combat traditions," for their
units by constructing a history of heroes and heroic battles which
was intended to inculcate the military virtues of honor, self-
sacrifice, and obedience. "Every Red Army man should know the
history of his unit," proclaimed V. A. Kamskii, a senior political
worker who wrote extensively on the creation of military
traditions.[23] The few veterans of the Revolution and Civil War who
remained on active duty recounted the deeds of the young soldiers'
predecessors. Soldiers were encouraged to contact other veterans
and to collect documents for the unit's archives. Calendars that
highlighted important Civil War battles, biographies of fallen heroes,
and all banners and decorations awarded to the unit hung in honored corners of the soldiers' clubs. In addition to 10 February, which
had been fixed since 1919 as Red Army Day, units celebrated significant dates in their own history. While the political staff worked to
strengthen the soldiers' attachment to the military unit, they linked
that loyalty to larger bodies, regiments and armies, and to the Red
Army as a whole.[24]

The history of sports in the army illustrates how creative the political staff could be in building loyalty and implementing the reforms, and also how comprehensively they understood the bases of
authority and the techniques needed to inculcate desired traits in

22. *Sbornik prikazov i tsirkuliarov PU RKKA SSSR No. 15: Dvukhletniaia programma politzaniatii s krasnoarmeitsami* (Moscow, 1927); Suvenirov, *Kommunisticheskaia partiia*, pp. 219, 220.
23. V. A. Kamskii, "O vospitanii boevykh traditsii," *Voennyi vestnik* 37 (1925): 57.
On earlier efforts to create new traditions, see Vlavin, "Vechera vospominanii v
Oktiabr'skuiu godovshchinu," *Voennoe znanie* 10 (1922): 34; N. Krasnopol'skii, "Za-
kreplenie traditsii v chastiakh," *Krasnaia prisiaga* 15 (1923): 98–105. For further recommended techniques to instill loyalty to the unit, see *Materialy soveshchaniia po
vneshkol'noi rabote*, pp. 16–17; "Prikaz RVS SSSR No. 816," *Krasnoarmeiskii spravochnik*, 12 August 1925, p. 2.
24. Kamskii recommended adjusting the lyrics of a unit's "traditional" fighting
song so that it linked the soldier's unit with the greater mission of the Red Army: "O
vospitanii," p. 57.

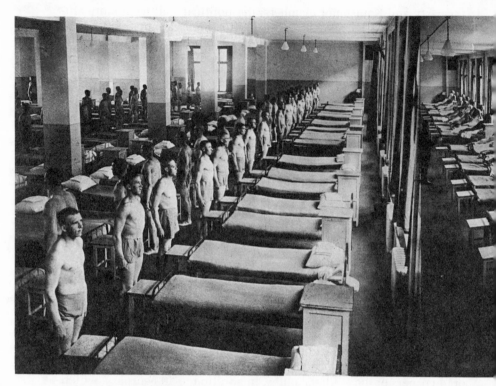

Morning exercises in a Red Army barracks. From *Raboche-krest'ianskaia Krasnaia Armiia* (Moscow, 1938), courtesy of Division of Art, Prints, and Photographs, The New York Public Library, Astor, Lenox, and Tilden Foundations.

soldiers. Beginning in 1924, the nation's sports enthusiasts seized on Frunze's campaign for militarizing the populace to win army approval for enhancing the role of sports activities in military education. Before 1924 the army had devoted few resources to sports, or physical culture, as it was then called.[25] In part sports fell victim to the same budgetary and personnel shortages that afflicted all army activities. But the initially slow introduction of sports into military training was also attributed to the hostility of commanders and peasant soldiers. According to those political workers who favored a greater role for sports, many officers, both former imperial officers and red commanders, considered sports to be pure amusement that diverted soldiers' energies from traditional military

25. For the early history of Soviet sports, see the excellent study by James Riordan, *Sport in Soviet Society* (Cambridge: Cambridge University Press, 1977), esp. chaps. 3 and 4. Riordan argues (pp. 85, 95–96) that sports was a battleground for pro- and antimilitary political leaders.

drills and exercises.[26] For their part, peasants viewed the strange twistings and games as excessive physical exertion, typical upper-class foolishness.[27]

Once the army's leaders launched the militarization program, the sports enthusiasts sensed they might have found new allies for their cause. They argued that collective physical activities promoted unit solidarity and bolstered discipline because sports accustomed soldiers to following strictly established rules and required them to work together as a team to win. In this way, the budding Soviet sports movement played a vital role in the campaign for building loyalty. Armies and divisions fielded their own soccer teams and track-and-field squads. Soldiers followed the wins and losses of their teams in the daily sports columns of central and district newspapers. Military educators debated the relative virtues of several types of sports, and concluded that team activities clearly were preferable to competitions that pitted individual soldiers against each other. The varieties of sports activities that stressed individual competition ran the risk of encouraging "petit bourgeois" attitudes, whereas collective sports activities fostered appropriately "proletarian" virtues. Sports certainly had other benefits to recommend them to the army leadership, most obviously in improving the physical condition of the soldiers. But it was the arguments for discipline and solidarity that dominated the public debates. By 1927, an assembly of army sports activists proposed that soldiers receive demerits for violating game rules or exhibiting "uncomradely relations" during training or competition.[28]

As the political workers tried to build a new set of primary loyalties for the soldiers, they frequently referred to the army as a large family. They contrasted a caricatured version of the tsarist army, where officers and soldiers came from two distinct classes and cultures, with the workers'-peasants' Red Army, where officers and soldiers came from "one great family of toilers." Both stood guard over the peaceful labor of "their brothers, the workers and peasants."[29] Political workers merged the rhetoric of class solidarity with a

26. N. Rakitin, "Fizkul'tura v Krasnoi Armii za god," *Krasnaia zvezda*, 1 January 1925, p. 8; Boguslavskii, "Fakty i mysli o sporte," *SP* 6 (1924): 29; V. V., "Sport na komandnykh kursakh," *Voennoe znanie* 4 (1921): 10–11.

27. P. Neimark, "Kurs na zdorovogo boitsa," *Krasnaia zvezda*, 31 May 1925, p. 3; B. P. Zorin, *Krasnaia Armiia i oborona SSSR* (Moscow/Leningrad, 1926), p. 50.

28. *Materialy soveshchaniia po vneshkol'noi rabote v RKKA*, p. 112. For a glimpse of the fascinating debates about sports in the army, see V. Kal'pus, "Voenizatsiia fizkul'tury," *Krasnaia zvezda*, 2 December 1925, p. 3; and "Fizicheskaia kul'tura i voennaia podgotovka molodezhi," in *Voennaia rabota komsomola: Sbornik statei* (Moscow/Leningrad, 1927), pp. 104–7, 110–11; Be—v, "O rabote sportchetverok," *Krasnaia rota* 47 (1924): 129–30.

29. V. Tal', *Istoriia Krasnoi armii* (Moscow/Leningrad, 1929), p. 184.

model of family relations. During the Civil War, revolutionary soldiers and political workers had invoked another model of relations based on the ideal comradeship of socialist party members. Then, Bolshevik propagandists and the army's commanders frequently began their orders with the revolutionary greeting "Comrades Red Army men!"[30] But as the military reformers introduced more strictly regulated hierarchies in the relations between officers and soldiers, the model began to change imperceptibly. Memoirs and military fiction show relations in the Red Army even in the 1920s as considerably less formal than they had been in the Imperial Army; however, the same literature also makes clear that relations were no longer what they once had been, especially during the early years of the Civil War.[31] Soldiers continued to address their commanders as "comrade commander" even after the reforms, but now kinship symbolism accommodated the greater degree of inequality that was widely accepted as appropriate and even essential for the smooth functioning of the military organization.[32] Army spokesmen used the rhetoric of class solidarity and the family with increasing frequency and that of comradeship with ever more qualifications. During the 1920s, the army's symbolic parent was the Revolution. The Red Army was the "child" (detishche) of the Revolution. Later Lenin assumed the role of parent, especially after he died in 1924. Still later, Stalin supplanted Lenin as father of all Soviet soldiers.

Political workers highlighted two practical aspects of the family imagery for soldiers. First, just as families looked out for the well-being of their members, the army looked out for the welfare of its personnel and their families. Second, families brought up their young to have useful skills and knowledge, so that they could build their own lives after they left the family hearth. Now the army pro-

30. See the pamphlets and brochures reproduced in *Plamennoe slovo: Listovki grazhdanskoi voiny (1918–1922 gg.)* (Moscow, 1967), documents no. 20, 33, 57, 81, 82, 108, 110, 146.

31. See, e.g., the following passage from Semen Mikhailov's novel *Brigadnaia roshcha*: "At one time, 1919 or 1920, you could go up to a soldier, address him simply as 'dear brother,' slap him on the shoulder. . . . This was considered the only way [of communicating], and not only your immediate superior but even an army commander could resort to such familiarity and no one would be amazed. But with the new generation in the Red Army, which hasn't even heard about the way things were in the Civil War days, one has to talk in a different fashion" (p. 172).

32. For example, Korol' explained that some measure of comradely relations was necessary to guard against overly formal discipline, but that the army faced a far greater danger than formal discipline if "excessively broad comradely relations went beyond the bounds of military discipline": *Voprosy*, pp. 11–12. For some suggestive insights into the political uses of kinship symbolism in the Stalin years, see Katerina Clark, "Utopian Anthropology as a Context for Stalinist Literature," in *Stalinism: Essays in Historical Interpretation*, ed. Robert C. Tucker (New York: Norton, 1977), pp. 180–98.

Red Army men reading letters from home. From the journal *Krasnoarmeets*, courtesy of
The Hoover Institution, Stanford University.

vided its "sons" with education in a wide range of fields, from techniques for improved crop yields to political campaigning skills
for soviet elections, as well as opportunities for advancement
through higher military education. The welfare and educational aspects of the Red Army's "family" self-image were at the center of
soldiers' concerns in the thousands of letters they wrote to the con-
sultative bureaus that PUR set up in 1923.[33] The specialists at these
bureaus referred soldiers to relevant laws and organizational structures to which they could appeal if they wanted to enroll in a school

33. The volume of soldiers' mail grew so rapidly that a year later the RVS formed
the Central Bureau of Red Army Letters, which, as a regular supplement to the popular journal *Krasnoarmeets*, published hundreds of letters followed by answers from
competent specialists. The supplement was titled *Krasnoarmeiskii spravochnik*.
Monthly summary reports from the Bureau of Red Army Letters also appeared in
Krasnaia zvezda.

or if they felt that their family's needs were being ignored by local administrators. Most of the letters addressed to the Central Bureau of Red Army Letters centered on tax exemptions and benefits for servicemen and their families, and postservice educational opportunities.

By 1925 the administration for dispensing the panoply of benefits promised to soldiers and veterans was so large and unwieldy that Sovnarkom ordered an extensive reorganization. A new All-Russian Committee for Aid to Invalid, Sick, and Wounded Red Army Men and to the Families of Soldiers Killed in Action swallowed up the myriad interdepartmental commissions that had grown up to handle specific aid programs.[34] The committee assigned responsibility for dispensing benefits at the local level to rural soviets and peasant mutual aid committees (krest'ianskie komitety vzaimopomoshchi, or krestkomy). Unfortunately for the soldiers, the local agencies were notoriously delinquent in fulfilling all the urgent tasks assigned to them. When soldiers' and veterans' complaints flooded the Central Bureau, the civilian Commissariat of Justice stepped in to spur local officials to action. Justice Commissar Dmitrii Kurskii warned all provincial and regional procurators' offices and court chairmen that irregularities in dispensing benefits to impoverished Red Army families would have dire consequences for the morale of the armed forces. A month later, VTsIK instructed all soviet organizations to assign first priority to the rights and interests of military personnel and their families. Negligent officials would be subject to criminal prosecution.[35]

Soldiers placed their hopes in their political officers when local agencies failed them. Political departments enthusiastically backed up the soldiers' complaints with letters to local prosecutors because, they had concluded, "our local soviet organs satisfy the needs of the Red Army men only under pressure from the procurator's office." These complaints against local authorities rarely were successfully contested.[36] In extreme cases of persistent neglect or obstinacy, po-

34. Among the new committee's disbursement tasks were credits for Red Army households, forest allotments, free acquisition of horses rejected by the army, housing privileges, special employment opportunities and social insurance, health benefits, education quotas, and a series of deductions or exemptions from taxes on agriculture, rent, income, government seals, and hunting licenses. See Krasnoarmeiskii spravochnik, 1924–1927, passim.

35. See reports in Krasnaia zvezda, 13 January 1925, p. 3; 10 July 1925, p. 4; 17 September 1925, p. 4; M. A. Kokorin, Voennaia rabota partiinoi iacheiki (Moscow/Leningrad, 1929), pp. 103–4; Krasnoarmeiskii spravochnik, 17 August 1927, p. 2.

36. P. I. Sokolov, "Bol'she vnimaniia!" Krasnaia zvezda, February 1925; for earlier examples of this practice, see I. Ruderman, "Politrabota vo vremia sbora 2-oi Belorusskoi Terdivizii," Krasnaia prisiaga 17 (1923): 95.

litical departments sent plenipotentiaries to the villages to put direct pressure on delinquent officials. "As a rule," one political worker noted, "the soldiers and even the average peasants consider military [officials] better than their own."[37] This was hardly surprising, because the military agents, after all, had a far more enviable role than their civilian counterparts in the villages. The rural soviets primarily extracted wealth and obligations from the local populace, whereas the military's representatives interceded on behalf of indignant soldiers, veterans, and their families to award what amounted to an extensive system of privileges. The practice of appealing to army officials for aid attained a considerable degree of institutionalization during the 1920s. Appeals went as high as the army commissar himself. During the first six months of Voroshilov's tenure in 1926, he reportedly received 3,000 letters of appeal.[38] Political workers used such appeals to build soldiers' loyalty to the army's leaders. Soldiers learned about Voroshilov's revolutionary past in a special lesson devoted to his biography.[39]

By its various interventions the state not only won the soldiers' loyalty but—perhaps unwittingly—created a new semiprivileged stratum in villages across the country. Veterans and their families came to expect the workers'-peasants' state to guarantee them a better material existence than that enjoyed by other families. Moreover, because many peasant households had suffered devastating economic losses during the absence of their primary breadwinners, soldiers' and veterans' appeals were often desperate calls to save them from total ruin. After the needy families met with resistance from old village elites and new officials, no doubt they bore long-standing and bitter grudges for many years. Indeed, military families very likely contributed to a polarization in many villages which resembled what Soviet historians have called "class stratification" in the countryside. Their struggles for the entitlements promised them added to the tensions of rural politics.

37. A. Maevich, "Po 19-i territorial'noi," *Krasnaia zvezda*, 24 January 1925, p. 3.

38. One-third of the letters came from active-duty servicemen, the remainder from veterans who still "considered the Red Army to be their own organization." The letters were divided roughly evenly among appeals for help in settling disputes over pensions and subsidies, advice on how to gain admission to military schools, and recommendations on how to conduct political and educational work among the peasantry. See Vladislav Kardashov, *Voroshilov* (Moscow, 1976), p. 231.

39. See the 1928 edition of *Dvukhletniaia programma politzaniatii s krasnoarmeitsami*, Conversation no. 10, "Biografiia Klimentiia Efremovicha Voroshilova," pp. 32–33. Voroshilov frequently reminded audiences that he had honest working-class roots. His biography included such details as the paltry wages he had earned as a miner, his sufferings in tsarist prisons, and his Civil War heroism. He was known in the army as Grandfather or Uncle Klim (Ded Klim). Other Civil War heroes figured prominently in political lessons, including Budennyi, Bliukher, Uborevich, Iakir, and Kotovskii.

Political workers not only administered welfare programs but promoted the army as a school, "a second Commissariat of Enlightenment," in the words of Deputy Army Commissar Iosif Unshlikht. Indeed, Unshlikht's claims were not hyperbole, for as late as the 1927–1928 fiscal year, the army spent several times as much on mass and adult education as did the civilian Commissariat of Enlightenment.[40] Frunze, addressing men about to be demobilized in 1925, felt confident that they "would never bear any grudges against the Red Army. It has given you everything it could," including literacy, an education in politics "because workers and peasants are now building their own government and need to know how to administer their society," and ways to understand nature, "how to combat it, how to use its powers to the benefit of your farming."[41] In addition to the education available to all soldiers, the army offered special educational opportunities for soldiers who wanted to advance up the ladder of the military or state hierarchy. In 1926 applicants to army schools in the Moscow Military District were running at between four and eight per available place.[42] The great career expectations of prospective servicemen had occasional unwanted consequences. Inductees who viewed the army as little more than a school to prepare them for a good position tended to resist the regimentation that greeted them in the barracks. In the fall of 1928 Komsomol's Central Committee exhorted its local organizations, which played a large role in preparing draft-age youth for military service, to stop "embellishing the conditions of army service" and to keep firmly in mind that the army was above all a *military* school.[43]

Despite the problems occasioned by overly enthusiastic Komsomol instructors, the efforts to promote the military as both school and welfare agency positively affected the attitudes of substantial numbers of young Soviet citizens toward military service. In 1924 a political worker surveyed 200 noncommunist soldiers about how their preservice impressions had stacked up against their actual experience of army life. Even then the results were very encouraging. Over half the soldiers claimed that they had had positive impressions of army life before entering. Even the one-third who had heard about the severe shortages of food and clothing or that the Red

40. Ivanovich, *Krasnaia armiia*, p. 92. For 1927–1928 the army spent 5 rubles 80 kopecks per capita on political enlightenment, while the equivalent per capita expenditure of the Enlightenment Commissariat was 1 ruble 7 kopecks. During that year the army earmarked 3,260,000 rubles for political enlightenment. See *Desiat' let Krasnoi Armii*, p. 76.
41. See the foreword by M. V. Frunze in *Demobilizovannye na derevenskoi rabote: Krasnoarmeiskie pis'ma*, ed. M. Mikula (Moscow, 1926), p. 6.
42. B. Bogdanov, "Itogi komplektovaniia voennykh shkol M.V.O. v 1926 g.," *SP* 51–52 (1926): 39.
43. *Izvestiia*, 25 August 1928.

Army was "a band of robbers" asserted that they had not believed those tales. Most encouraging of all for the political staff, more than three-quarters of the surveyed soldiers found army life "entirely satisfactory."[44] In 1926, on the eve of their return home after two years of service, another group of soldiers was asked about their attitudes when they were called up. Nearly two-thirds claimed to have joined the army willingly, one-fifth simply had resigned themselves to an inescapable obligation, and 4 percent had gone unwillingly. Most professed that they had had no distinct impressions of army life, but a significant 12.7 percent answered that they had viewed the army as a school for workers and peasants.[45]

Although army spokesmen typically found nothing at all suspect in the rather sanguine impressions of military life, especially when their own reports were full of complaints about hardships and disorganization, more tangible data corroborated their sense that popular attitudes were indeed changing in the direction of greater willingness to serve and even to consider the military as an attractive career option. The number of draft-age citizens who failed to show up for induction dropped steadily throughout the 1920s,[46] as did self-mutilation and simulation of illness to avoid service. In fact, one doctor reported that especially poor peasants actually were concealing physical deformities and illnesses to avoid rejection for military service. Several peasants asked to have their cases reconsidered after they had been rejected on grounds of poor health so that, according to the doctor, "they wouldn't lose their chance to see the world and its people."[47] For many peasant youths, military service was a ticket out of the patriarchal regime of village life. Numerous studies of rural life in the 1920s attest to young peasants'

---

44. P. Kuz'min, "Itogi izucheniia politiko-moral'nogo sostoianiia krasnoarmeitsev," *SP* 3 (1924): 56–57.

45. I. Krupnik, "Nekotorye itogi raboty s 1902 godom," *SP* 52 (1926): 18–19; see also Kosmin, *Politicheskaia rabota*, p. 54; *Krasnaia zvezda*, 15 June 1927; *Voennyi vestnik* 35 (1928).

46. On the drop in evasion of service, see Frunze's speech to the Third Congress of Soviets, *Krasnaia zvezda*, 22 May 1925, p. 3; see also the account of a call-up for a territorial unit, "O iavke na obshchii territorial'nyi sbor peremennogo sostava, mladshego nachsostava i krasnoarmeiskikh chastei 64 strelkovoi divizii," 26 August 1929, Smolensk Archives, WKP 215. Of the 9,605 men eligible for call-up, 8,324 appeared on schedule and 628 showed up late, for a total of 93.2 percent of the projected number.

47. On the decline in self-multilation, see Degtiarev, *Politrabota v Krasnoi Armii*, p. 80; on soldiers denying their health problems to avoid being rejected, see G. Kvasnitskii, "Zdorov'e prizyvnikov," *Krasnaia rota* 55–56 (1924): 143. Dr. Kvasnitskii conducted the first systematic health inventory of the draft-age male population in the Ukraine and Crimea in May 1924.

dreams of leaving the village or, in any case, peasant work.[48] Once they had a taste of city life and a glimpse of the new opportunities for careers in the army or bureaucracy, many soldiers tried hard not to return home. Correspondents for army newspapers kept in contact with as many veterans from their units as possible. They too reported that demobilized soldiers looked back on their service with fondness, especially when they returned to their "dark and uncultured villages."[49]

Soviet Patriotism and Leninism

Political workers built on soldiers' loyalty to the army to forge a firm attachment to the new political order. The lessons devoted to "sovietization" included elementary information about government institutions and laws, geography, and a version of Russian and world history that was intended to reinforce the party leaders' claim to be the rightful rulers over Soviet society. The political staff followed the pattern they used to build loyalty to the army by starting with the smallest unit, the most familiar places and names in a peasant soldier's home environment. Each soldier learned how to locate his native village on a map and prepared a short talk for his peers about the economic and cultural significance of his region. A particularly talented instructor had the soldiers link their individual regions with the larger national economy, thereby expanding their loyalty from family and village to the Soviet state. For a peasant the term rodina connoted the area immediately surrounding his native village. For the new Soviet political class, however, just as for their liberal predecessors in the short-lived Provisional Government, rodina represented a far larger area, the territory that made up the modern nation-state they were attempting to build, as well as a group of ideas about Russian national interests and power.

In a variation on the technique of constructing military histories for the soldiers, political workers taught episodes from the nation's

48. See, e.g., A. M. Bol'shakov, Derevnia, 1917–1927 (Moscow, 1927), esp. Academician Ol'denburg's introduction, pp. iv, vii; also Ia. I. Burov, Derevnia na perelome (Moscow/Leningrad, 1926), pp. 94–95. Many peasant youths were sold on the attractive Red Army uniforms because, after all, looking good "was far from the last thing on a peasant boy's mind": N. Rabichev, "Nyneshnii krasnoarmeets i politchas," Politrabotnik 2–3 (1924): 57.

49. Voenkor D. Ivanov, "Uroki demobilizatsii," Na strazhe 15 (1924): 11; see also letters in Demobilizovannye na derevenskoi rabote, passim. For an early account of an elder peasant's pride in his officer sons, see "Peasant Officers," in Geoffrey Gorer and John Rickman, The People of Great Russia: A Psychological Study (New York: Chanticleer, 1950), pp. 75–82.

past to instill sentiments of patriotism for the Soviet order. They clearly saw soldiers' memories of past events as a technique for recasting their loyalties and behavior. The Revolution and Civil War periods were crucial to persuade soldiers of the historical legitimacy that the Soviet state claimed for itself, and, as PUR directives reminded the political staff, the number of soldiers who had any familiarity with the Civil War and Revolution, let alone life in prerevolutionary Russia, was dwindling every year. "The mass of Red Army men have not thought through the history of the Civil War," declared one Feidulov, a political worker: he suggested that political education should have as its primary goal "the overcoming of false impressions of the Civil War." Today's soldier, Feidulov warned, probably remembered the Civil War not so much as the heroic combat of workers and peasants as the forced grain requisitioning campaigns, when his father hid the "surpluses" and the food detachments took them away. Nor did today's soldier, Feidulov continued, understand why the Civil War was fought or "the hatred that compelled his fathers and brothers to fight against the landowners." He probably had no recollections whatsoever of the landowners and did not associate them with "oppression, with the zemstvo land captain or the village policeman." In other words, today's soldiers had no historical memory that political workers could use to build loyalty to the Soviet state and instill hatred for all oppressors. Feidulov charged political instructors with creating "fierce hatred, wrath, and contempt for the bourgeoisie" by means of illustrations from current events and the Russian past.[50]

While the soldiers were being exposed to the correct version of the Russian past and assimilating the expanded sense of a native land, they also learned to identify the nations that bordered the Soviet state and to distinguish enemies from friends. Because, as the instructors taught, the Soviet state was encircled by largely hostile capitalist powers that covetously eyed the riches of the former Russian empire, the state was obliged to maintain an army for defense of its frontiers. Soldiers were taught that foreign powers conspired to overturn the Soviet experiment in proletarian rule because the example of the Russian Revolution offered great hopes to oppressed workers everywhere and threatened the domestic security of all bourgeois states. Thus every war scare during the 1920s became a political lesson about the international situation of the embattled Soviet state, and maps became essential tools to create the

---

50. Feidulov, "Materialy k III-mu razdelu dvukhletnei programmy," *SP* (1926): 38; see similar complaints about soldiers' lack of correct historical perspective and similar recommendations in Korol', *Voprosy*, p. 60.

citizen-soldier's new national identity.[51] The friends of the Soviet state, the soldiers were taught, were the workers of foreign countries and oppressed peoples everywhere. To forge symbolic ties of moral support with foreign workers, thousands of soldiers enrolled in the International Organization for Aid to Imprisoned Fighters for the Revolution (MOPR). At meetings of MOPR cells, soldiers "adopted" notorious foreign prisons and carried on correspondence with men and women who were imprisoned for their revolutionary activities. Soldiers contributed meager donations for the maintenance of foreign political prisoners and for the victims of "White terror." The "personal" relationships that soldiers nurtured encouraged them to follow the fates of their adopted foreign comrades in the daily press and on the map.[52] For similar ends, the leaders of foreign governments that were sympathetic to the Soviet Union or of foreign revolutionary or progressive political parties frequently paid ceremonial visits to Red Army units, who "adopted" them as well.[53] Political workers took advantage of these visits and MOPR activities to educate the soldiers in the values of "internationalism," the third and most ill-defined pillar of the two-year program of political education.

Just as soldiers learned the important events in the life of their commander in chief, Voroshilov, and other military leaders, they also learned about the nation's civilian leadership. President Mikhail Kalinin was an ideal figure for explaining to peasant soldiers how, in the new political order, a peasant not unlike themselves could rise to become the head of a revolutionary state. Kalinin came from a middle peasant family, had taught himself to read, and had worked as a lathe operator in a cartridge factory. Kalinin made frequent visits to army units, where he heard soldiers' petitions and answered their questions. He was proclaimed to be a living embodiment of the worker-peasant bond that underlay the Soviet political arrangement.[54] The biographies of important party and state leaders appeared on the pages of soldiers' mass-circulation newspapers and journals. Many of these leaders, like Kalinin, paid

51. V. M. Kamskii, "O geograficheskoi karte," Voennyi vestnik 9 (1925): 41. For some intriguing comments on geography and the national discourse, see Michel Foucault, "Questions on Geography," in his Power/Knowledge: Selected Interviews and Other Writings, 1972–1977, ed. Conlin Gordon (New York: Panthèon, 1980), pp. 63–67.

52. "Beseda s chlenom ispolkoma MOPR P. N. Lepeshinskim," Krasnaia zvezda, 16 May 1925, p. 4; M. Movetskii, Krasnaia armiia i MOPR (Moscow, 1926), pp. 7–8. By 1926 MOPR officials claimed 250,000 members in the Red Army.

53. See, e.g., Krasnaia zvezda's reports on Chiang Kai-shek's visit in 1925.

54. Kalinin's and Aleksei Rykov's biographies are the subjects of Conversation no. 23 in Dvukhletniaia programma, pp. 61–63.

regular visits to Red Army units to explain national policies and assure the soldiers of the government's constant attention.

Lenin's biography became a central theme of the sovietization cycle, and what some historians have called the "Lenin cult"[55] owed a great deal of its popularity to the army's program of political education. After Lenin's death, Boris Zorin, PUR's head of agitation and propaganda, proposed that the entire political enlightenment program be called "Leninist Bolshevik study and training." Although Lenin actively discouraged any idealization of his person, he endured first public expressions of sympathy when he suffered a bullet wound from a would-be assassin in the summer of 1918 and then public commemorations of his fiftieth birthday in 1920.[56] His death in January 1924 ended months of a national obsession during which newspaper readers followed the doctors' reports on his failing health. The aura of reverence that quickly surrounded Lenin's name and life was the product of a genuine outpouring of public sympathy, as well as of a calculated scheme to wrap the leadership in the mantle of the fallen leader. Trotsky, Stalin, and Zinoviev each defended his own political platform by designating himself as the true interpreter of "Leninism." In the army, as elsewhere in society, the reverential attitude toward Lenin served to discourage officers from criticizing state policy, much as once the cult of the emperor had discouraged imperial officers from political thinking.[57] Army units joined the mourning nation and renamed the Red corners in soldiers' clubs in Lenin's honor. Within three weeks after his death, the volume of resolutions to rename units and schools after Lenin mounted so high that PUR drafted a fixed procedure for processing the petitions.[58]

Actually, Lenin's death left the army's leadership in a state of panic. From the countryside came reports that some disgruntled peasants expected the Soviet regime to fall and that the imperialist powers would take advantage of the confusion at the top to launch a new anti-Bolshevik crusade. In the early 1920s the frequent war scares regularly provoked panicked waves of buying and hoarding

---

55. Nina Tumarkin, *Lenin Lives! The Lenin Cult in Soviet Russia* (Cambridge: Harvard University Press, 1983).

56. In 1919 the journal *Krasnoarmeets* refused to print a poem about Lenin on the grounds that the heroes of the new revolutionary order were not individuals, but the proletariat; a year later, however, it printed a poem in honor of Lenin's fiftieth birthday. See *Krasnoarmeets* 3 (1919) and 21–22 (1920).

57. Fuller, *Civil-Military Conflict*, p. 30. Fuller argues that "a full-blown cult of the Emperor . . . encouraged officers to confuse the dynastic and military interest."

58. "Tsirkuliar o poriadke predstavlenii khodataistv o prisvoenii chastiam, uchrezhdeniiam i zavedeniiam RKKA imeni V. I. Lenina," 16 February 1924, in PPR III, p. 556.

and predictions of the Bolsheviks' fall from power. Soldiers' moods
reflected these anxieties. At conferences, political workers reported,
the troops worried that the capitalists might attempt an invasion in
the weeks between April, when one age cohort would be released,
and the end of May, when the next cohort was scheduled to be
called up. "That means," one soldier commented, "that for a whole
month the country will be weakened."[59] PUR responded quickly to
the uneasiness. Bubnov warned political workers to exercise special
discretion during these tragic moments. Many soldiers, he observed,
were displaying the same cautious attitude that was evident in the
villages, where "the peasantry was awaiting some confirmation that
Soviet power, even after the death of its leader, would continue the
same politics of support for the peasant economy" and for the
worker-peasant bond that Lenin had been promoting during the NEP.
At the same time, Bubnov continued, undoubtedly the soldiers were
profoundly upset by Lenin's death. He instructed political workers
"to take all this into account and make these sentiments the point of
departure for our work among the nonparty masses."[60] Bubnov
urged the political staff to divert the reverential sentiments for the
deceased Lenin into channels to promote broader state and army
goals. Soldiers should be encouraged to imitate Lenin in everything
and should replace the great loss the nation suffered by intensifying
their own work. A PUR circular formulated Lenin's testament as a
pledge to maintain and strengthen the worker-peasant bond, to
strengthen the Soviet state and the Red Army, and to unify the "Leninist" party of Communists. In Lenin's teachings soldiers had another weapon with which to arm themselves for the coming battles
with world capital.[61] And, beginning in April 1924, all military district newspapers carried a daily section headed "What Comrade Lenin Taught." In 1925, on the first anniversary of Lenin's death, PUR

59. *Krasnaia rota* 43–44 (1924): 100; on earlier rumors of war and invasions in the
countryside see Ia. Shafir, *Gazeta i derevnia* (Moscow, 1923), pp. 30, 110–12, 116–17,
137. Jeffrey Brooks writes ("Popular and Public Values," unpublished paper, p. 14):
"Rumors of war sold newspapers, and Soviet journalists played on readers' fears to
portray Bolshevik leaders as defenders of Russia against her enemies. This appeal to
patriotism was most apparent during the war scares of 1923 and 1927, but it was also
characteristic of the Soviet press throughout the 1920s."
60. "Tsirkuliar PURa o zadachakh raboty po izucheniiu deiatel'nosti V. I. Lenina i
leninizma," 16 February 1924, in *PPR* III, pp. 193–98. See also A. Bubnov and M.
Rafes, "Izuchenie leninizma v Krasnoi armii (Instruktsiia Politicheskogo Upravleniia
RVS SSSR)," *Kommunisticheskoe prosveshchenie* 1 (1924): 72; "Lenin i leninizm v
Krasnoi armii," *Politrabotnik* 2–3 (1924): 19.
61. "Tsirkuliar PURa o zadachakh," pp. 193–94; see also an official army obituary
of Lenin, "Prikaz Glavnachvuz SSSR no. 39," *Voennoe znanie* (1924): 126.

issued a list of recommended literature headed by Stalin's pamphlet *On Lenin and Leninism.*[62]

Army political departments helped soldiers and peasants in nearby villages organize Lenin memorial ceremonies. At least a few political workers expressed some discomfort at the disturbing resemblance of the new ceremonies to religious services. From Voronezh, A. Maevich complained that the Lenin evenings "turned into the biography of some sort of new saint." He objected that accounts of Lenin's debates had become "a purely Gospel narrative about how the young Lenin beat down the obstinacy of the impious old populists."[63] Obviously PUR was determined to capitalize on all the rhetoric and symbolism available in Russian political and religious culture to create an air of solemnity around Lenin's figure. Extensive instruction on how to organize a Lenin evening on the anniversary of the founding of the Red Army conveys the tone of these highly theatrical festivities. The lights go out, the curtain opens. Center stage and up front is a representation of a large book, volume 15 of Lenin's collected works. Upstage is a bust of Lenin against a red background. To the left stand a group of male and female workers, to the right a group of Red Army men. Light falls on the bust of Lenin and the book: the people are in semidarkness. The male workers declaim in unison, "The Red Army was created by Red October." The female workers answer, "The Red Army was created by Comrade Lenin." The entire chorus declares, "The Red Army is the armed alliance of workers and peasants forged with the steel binding of communism."

A voice from deep in the stage recites in "melodeclamation":

> In the turbulent days, like a tempest,
> In the nightmarish days, like unto night,
> When the people, knitting their brows,
> Decided to have done with their slavery,
> —You were created from a handful of daring ones,
> From a handful of fearless eagles,
> Not in days but in fleeting hours,
> In battles you grew and became strong
> And carried forward to victories
> The banner bravely raised.

---

62. "Literatura po leninizmu," *SP* 8–9 (1925): 24–40; see also Andrei Bubnov, "Velikii stroitel'," and Ia. Bronin, "K voprosu pred"istorii Krasnoi Armii (Opyt izucheniia voprosa po sochineniiam Lenina)," both in *SP* 8–9 (1925); "Pomoshch' samoobrazovaniiu: Kratkaia programma po izucheniiu leninizma po skheme Stalina," *Krasnyi boets* 13 (1924): 58.

63. A. Maevich, "Po 19-i territorial'noi," *Krasnaia zvezda,* 26 January 1925, p. 3.

A Red Army man declares, "The Red Army has completed the school of Comrade Lenin. Under his leadership, it has carried high the red banner of communism from victory to victory. True to the testament of Il'ich, it will carry his banner onward to new victories."

A choir sings from behind the stage:

Need will not break us
Poverty will not bend us over
Capricious fate is not master over us
Nevermore, nevermore. . . .
Comrades, we celebrate the seventh anniversary of the Red Army.

A voice from the audience: "Without Lenin." All repeat, "Without Lenin." A male voice declaims, "He who created the Red Army— the first army of the proletarian revolution in the world—is no more."[64] The script continues to fill a program lasting several hours.

Several aspects of the celebration are noteworthy for the army's formulation of Lenin's "testament." First, within two months after Trotsky had resigned as army commissar and as chairman of the Revolutionary Military Council, his name was dropped from the anniversary celebration. All of his accomplishments in building the Red Army were transferred to Lenin, who, as the embodiment of Red October, was also the progenitor of the Red Army. No mention of any other military or political leader distracts from the solemn focus on Lenin. Second, the Red Army is firmly embedded in the mythology of the Revolution. Indeed, it is a creation of the Revolution, which is ongoing and looks forward to new battles and new victories, even without Lenin's wise leadership, for Lenin left behind his testament, symbolized by the larger-than-life volume of his writings and the bust. Finally, although the ceremony celebrates the worker-peasant alliance, the two groups on stage represent workers and Red Army men. Peasants in uniform, rather than peasants as such, are the truly reliable allies of the revolutionary proletariat.

64. Setlin, "Godovshchina Krasnoi Armii v biblioteke (iz opyta klubnoi bib-lioteki)," *Krasnoarmeiskii bibliotekar'* 3 (1925): 90.

CHAPTER 8

The Red Army and the Worker-Peasant Alliance, 1925–1930

The Red Army is the village resettled in the city and the barracks.

—V. Lugovskoi, 1925

Cadres for the Countryside

The political arrangement under which peasants and workers co-existed in the Soviet republic, known as the worker-peasant alliance or link (smychka), was the central theme of all educational and cultural activities devoted to sovietization. The preface to nearly every PUR directive to political workers began with the equivalent of "Because the overwhelming majority of Red Army men are peasants . . ." And, indeed, because of the large numbers of peasant recruits, the state's relations with the peasantry and the history of the party in the countryside became a focus for discussions about the appropriate content of political education. The director of PUR's Department for School Programs, Andrei Dushak, forthrightly stated that any narration of the past must serve to reaffirm "the historical correctness of the Bolsheviks," especially their "faith in the strength of the working class as the hegemonic force of the Revolution and in the revolutionary potential of the peasantry as an ally for the working class."[1] Political workers must shun any form of "objectivism," which Dushak defined as striving to stand above the issues, above events, and above the competing sides. Political workers had to persuade peasant soldiers that the state foresaw a meaningful role for them in the emerging political order, but soldiers would have to accept the fact that the leading role went to the proletariat. If a peasant

1. A. I. Dushak, Metodika i organizatsiia partiinogo prosveshcheniia (Moscow, 1927), pp. 29, 32.

soldier should ask why workers, and not peasants, held power in the
Soviet state, the political worker should answer categorically that
"no other authority is possible." Until the Revolution, capitalists
had provided the political classes of modern nations, but the Revolution had raised to power a second world-historical class, the proletariat; and peasants, as history has demonstrated, are incapable of
organizing a large modern state. For the peasantry, destined to remain subservient to the better-organized classes of the world, the
choice between capitalism and socialism should be clear. Unfortunately, according to a guidebook for political workers, peasants are
given to vacillation, in contrast to the workers, who are "the most
determined and unwavering advocates of socialism." And because
the new Soviet state remains surrounded on all sides by enemies,
"the slightest vacillations, the slightest doubt or wrong step, can
threaten ruin."[2]

The stance assumed by Dushak and Kuznetsov conformed to the
victory of the army's depeasantizers. In discussions about the Civil
War, for example, instructors underscored the vacillations of the
peasantry by identifying the kulaks as active participants in the
anti-Soviet counterrevolution. They "could not reconcile themselves
to the nationalization of the land, the confiscation of surpluses, and
their loss of the possibility of becoming new landowners and exploiting the poor and middle peasant masses in the countryside."
Unfortunately, owing to the cultural backwardness that prevailed in
large parts of the country, certain parts of the middle and poor peasantry failed to understand the real motives of the kulaks in opposing
the new political order and joined with the counterrevolutionaries.
In succeeding lessons, instructors told soldiers that kulaks and the
"kulak-wealthy segment" of the Cossacks provided fertile soil for recruiting soldiers to the White armies. But once peasants had a taste
of the new dictatorship that the Whites offered them, they abandoned their households and ran off to join Red partisan bands. Only
when the peasants came over to the side of the beleaguered workers
could the job of crushing the counterrevolution be finished, but the
peasantry's initial vacillations had cost both them and the workers
irredeemable losses in lives and livelihoods.

The instructors portrayed the revolutions of 1905 and 1917 in similar ways to explain that, although peasants clearly suffered exploitation under the old regime and therefore demonstrated considerable
revolutionary potential, only the organizing power of a disciplined
proletariat and its vanguard party, the Bolsheviks, transformed the
historically isolated and elemental outbursts of tormented peasants

2. Kuznetsov, *Metodika*, pp. 6–7; for similar statements, see Ia. G. Bronin, *Politgramota komsomol'tsa: Uchebnik dlia komsomol'skikh politshkol pervoi stupeni*
(Moscow/Leningrad, 1927), pp. 135–36.

into a movement of effective political resistance. Workers provided fighters for the Revolution in far greater proportions than did the peasants. The peasants should see for themselves the indisputable importance of discipline for maintaining a combat-ready army. The same discipline was essential for success in the political struggle.[3]

Political workers were not quite so naive as to believe that lectures and readings alone would fundamentally alter peasants' impressions of workers and the unjust burdens that the countryside had to bear for the national welfare. To dissuade the soldiers from their notions that workers had a far easier life than peasants—an attitude referred to as "peasant envy"—political departments organized frequent excursions of Red Army men to factories, mines, and other proletarian work sites. Typically the workers designated a welcoming party, delivered a few stirring speeches about the benefits of the worker-peasant alliance, demonstrated how various pieces of their machinery worked, and concluded with a joint meal. Political workers reported that after soldiers spent a couple of hours in a deep mine, they came away with the impression that the miners worked in much less favorable conditions than even the poorest peasants back home.[4] Finally, and most important perhaps, the state backed up the political staff in assuring the soldiers of the important place they occupied in the political and social order by means of the schooling and welfare benefits and the frequent visits by party and state leaders to the barracks and summer camps.

The true test of the army's ambitious programs to remake the peasant recruit into "an active fighter for socialism" was his performance after he completed his two-year service obligation. A soldier could stay in the army, seek urban employment, or return home to the countryside. After the Frunze reforms, the prestige of a military career rose steadily; more and more soldiers entered military schools and elected careers with the military. For most of the 1920s, however, the army command kept the numbers of schools and of military men enrolled in them at a low level. They explained that the network of schools was turning out more commanders than the army needed after the reform; however, the long-term reorganization, the purges of unreliable military specialists, shortages of teachers, and primarily the army's chronic budgetary constraints also kept the number of places low.[5] Finally, beginning in 1925, and es-

3. See secs. 3 and 4 in Dvukhletniaia programma, pp. 67–100.

4. Kokorin, Voennaia rabota partiinoi iacheiki, p. 89; see also G. Grigorov, Otpuskniki v derevne (Leningrad, 1926), pp. 4–5.

5. On the reorganization of the military school system, see Berkhin, Voennaia reforma, pp. 270–89; Erickson, Soviet High Command, pp. 194–95. On the inadequate budget, see Voroshilov's complaints in "Otchet Narkomvoenmora IV Vsesoiuznomu s"ezdu Sovetov," in Oborona SSSR: Izbrannye stat'i, rechi i pis'ma (Moscow, 1937), pp. 134–36.

pecially after 1928, the army command made a concerted effort to raise the percentage of proletarians among the students in military schools. A conscious discriminatory policy favored applicants from working-class backgrounds over those of peasant or white-collar origins.[6] For the overwhelming majority of soldiers, consequently, a military career was ruled out.

Soldiers who came from towns and cities returned home. They were joined by many peasant soldiers who resolved to make their future in the city rather than face uncertain or bleak prospects in the countryside. As more and more soldiers remained in the towns, however, their prospects too became increasingly uncertain. Unemployment rose steadily through the 1920s and remained well over one million from 1923 on. Officials of the Commissariat of Labor attributed most of the high urban unemployment to the influx of unskilled peasants.[7] From accounts in army newspapers and constant appeals by army officials to civilian organizations and private factory owners to grant veterans special priority in hiring, it is clear that soldiers and junior officers joined the ranks of the unemployed in growing numbers. As early as 1923 the army had warned soldiers not to expect to find employment in the most desirable cities and urged that they consider organizing agricultural communes or artels instead.[8] The following year the army pressured labor exchanges to find work for demobilized soldiers before anyone else was placed. City governments set up cafeterias and dormitories with some funding from the Central Commission for Aid to Demobilized Red Army Men.[9] By September 1925, however, central army newspapers warned that Moscow, Leningrad, Vladivostok, the Crimea, and Turkestan were "infected with unemployment" and enterprises were refusing to hire former soldiers to fill existing vacancies.[10]

6. The Central Committee, in a circular letter issued in June 1925, demanded that more attention be paid to improving the class composition of applicants for military schools: *Izvestiia TsK RKP(b)*, no 21 (96) (June 1925), cited in Berkhin, *Voennaia reforma*, p. 273. For the statistical results of the campaign, see Berkhin, p. 286.

7. On 1 January 1924, officially registered unemployed stood at 1,240,000; on 1 September 1925, at 1,300,000: Carr, *Socialism in One Country*, 1:388–98. The figures for 1925–1926 were 1,017,200; for 1926–1927, 1,241,500; for 1927–1928, 1,289,800: Carr and Davies, *Foundations of a Planned Economy*, 1:456.

8. *Krasnaia rota* 27 (1923): 109–10. In Fedor Panferov's novel *Bruski*, the first two volumes of which appeared in 1930, an army veteran, Kirill Zhdarkin, returns to his native village and, after a fitful start, sets up a commune.

9. For labor legislation requiring industrial employers to assign high priority to hiring army veterans, see Margaret Dewar, *Labour Policy in the USSR, 1917–1928* (London and New York: Royal Institute of International Affairs, 1956), pp. 111, 114, 213, 219, 246, 283, 387. Generally the legislation treated veterans as equal to proletarians in their rights to industrial jobs.

10. *Krasnaia rota* 17 (1925): 79; *Krasnaia zvezda*, 1925 issues, 8, 16, and 25 January; 17 February; 16 and 23 October; 9 December. The Moscow labor exchange listed 100 enterprises that refused to hire former soldiers.

A representative of a Red Army cultural patronage organization (kul'tshef) reads a report to a peasant meeting. From the journal *Krasnoarmeets*, courtesy of The Hoover Institution, Stanford University.

Former soldiers queuing up at labor exchanges became a familiar part of the NEP landscape. As the army began reviewing plans to find employment for soldiers, PUR organized prerelease short courses in several skills.

The overwhelming majority of soldiers returned to their villages and looked to resume some sort of rural livelihood. Their political instructors sent them home with a mission to combat ignorance and "construct a new rural life according to the legacy of Il'ich." The soldiers were urged to "take a quick look around, determine the major needs in their village," and call together the Communists, Komsomol members, and other demobilized soldiers to "create a nucleus for the struggle with the sores of rural life."[11] Until 1925, how-

11. *Krasnoarmeets* 59/60 (1924).

ever, these men were given no more systematic preparation in reconstructing life in the village than a package of literature and a subscription to one or more newspapers. Despite former soldiers' lack of preparation, they had clear ideas of the countryside's ills. They returned home expecting only the worst from local authorities. During political lessons, instructors warned about inefficient and corrupt soviet officials, who were highlighted in press exposés. Not surprisingly, such instructors, including many of the depeasantizers whom Zinoviev and Bubnov had rebuked at various times, bred contempt for local officials in a large number of soldiers, who concluded that it was their mission to "turn everything upside down" and restore decent government. In one of its many surveys of soldiers on the eve of demobilization, the Ukrainian District Political Administration polled the Kharkov garrison about the political attitudes they were taking home with them. The respondents were intent on "remaking," "dispersing," and otherwise upsetting the existing rural order. The alarmed author of the report charged that the average Red Army man "no longer knows the village." He had an idea of how the village was supposed to be, according to Soviet laws and decrees; unfortunately, however, he had little guidance in his well-intentioned but ill-informed crusade.[12]

Soldiers' disgust with local government was only reinforced by the contrast between the festive sendoffs organized for them at demobilization time and the indifference or hostility they met on arriving home. Soldiers typically returned to a village with other men who had been inducted at the same time. At least in the first months after they returned, many wrote regular letters back to their units. The military newspapers reprinted hundreds of these letters during 1924 and 1925. Former soldiers reported increasing tensions in the villages as they tried to put into practice the ideas they had absorbed during military service. Four soldiers who returned home from one division immediately began to fight against "the abuses of rural authorities, the deceitful behavior of the village priest, and against moonshine." The soldiers reported that the kulaks quickly got angry with them, but expected the soldiers' efforts to be wasted. "The comrades paid no heed to these mutterings," they reported, "and carried on with their work."[13] Elsewhere "kulak" resistance took more violent forms. A returnee mobilized several older former servicemen, who summoned a "congress of dischargees" in the village and discussed ways to organize a struggle against "darkness,

12. Iung, "O nastroeniiakh uvolennykh v zapas krasnoarmeitsev i o nekotorykh itogakh nashei raboty," *Krasnaia rota* 43–44 (1924): 98–100; see also a PUR study summarized in Suvenirov, *Kommunisticheskaia partiia*, pp. 249–50.
13. Vyrvich, *Krasnaia armiia v bor'be s negramotnost'iu*, p. 75; see also Ia. Iakovlev, *Derevnia, kak ona est'* (Moscow, 1923), pp. 70–71.

religion, moonshine, and other evils." A "local agent who was looking out for the interests of the [soviet] chairman" arrested the whole "congress." After they finally won their release, the former soldiers appealed to their old unit for advice on what to do next.[14] Soldiers who wanted to return to farming or to set up their own households for the first time also faced formidable obstacles. Typically many had occupied the lowest rungs of village society before their military service, either as the youngest sons of independent heads of households or as hired labor for wealthier peasants. When these returnees attempted to gain readmission to their former households, the village communal administration often rejected their applications, especially if they muttered anything about remaking the rural economy. Some particularly tenacious veterans banded together to form communes or artels on the outskirts of the village, where the writ of the communal assembly did not run. Although precise numbers for these experimental Red Army communes and artels are not available, the military press regularly publicized their creation and accomplishments. Typically, the press coverage highlighted the heroic efforts of the former Red Army men in combating the resistance of local villagers.[15] In all these reports of heightened rural tensions, a part of the political leadership that was allied with Stalin found evidence for their assertion that the countryside was undergoing increasingly sharp stratification, even if the term was not used in the same sense in which Soviet historians have used it to date.[16]

Organizing veterans in the village and forming experimental agricultural artels were only two of the returning soldiers' responses to the resistance they met from local authorities. A third and far more

14. P. Tashlitskii, "O sviazi s demobilizovannymi," *Politrabotnik* 7 (1924): 110–11.

15. See Panferov's novel *Bruski* for an account of early experiments; see also A. F. Chmyga, *Ocherki po istorii kolkhoznogo dvizheniia na Ukraine (1921–1925)* (Moscow, 1959), pp. 82–89; *Za chto borolis': Rasskazy krasnoarmeitsev-otpusknikov i ikh druzei o nashei bor'be za sotsializm i ob uchastii krasnoarmeitsev-otpusknikov v bor'be za sotsialisticheskoe pereustroistvo derevni* (Moscow/Leningrad, 1928), p. 68; R. M. Bedzhanian, "Kommunisticheskaia partiia—organizator aktivnogo uchastiia Krasnoi Armii v sotsialisticheskom stroitel'stve (1918–1932)" (doctoral diss., Lenin Military Political Academy, Moscow, 1969), p. 528; Pikha, "Bor'ba Kommunisticheskoi partii" (diss.), pp. 274–75; *Krasnaia zvezda*, 10 June 1925. The army also collaborated with the Commissariat of Agriculture in dispatching former soldiers to strategically important border areas in the Far East and Transbaikal to set up agricultural colonies. When soldiers heard about the success or survival of a Red Army colony, they frequently requested to be demobilized to the same area, and the numbers of pioneers and their families grew each year. See *Krasnoarmeiskii spravochnik*, 29 July 1924, p. 5, and 31 May 1925, p. 4; M. Ritman, *Pylaiushchie budni: Krasnoarmeiskie agitkolonny v sotsialisticheskom pereustroistve derevni* (Moscow, 1930), p. 24; P. Kh. Chausov, "Rol' Krasnoi armii v kolkhoznom stroitel'stve na Dal'nem Vostoke v 1927–1932 gg." (candidate's diss., Irkutsk State University, 1966), pp. 7–8.

16. For a discussion of the debates during the 1920s about the economic and social changes in the countryside, see Lewin, *Russian Peasants and Soviet Power*, pp. 41–80, 132–71.

widespread response, resignation and withdrawal, greatly alarmed political workers and party leaders. Most soldiers, when they confronted defiant local officials, eventually threw up their hands in despair and tried to settle back into a quieter but probably frustrated existence. This was a particularly likely response for a soldier who returned home alone or whose village had no Komsomol or party cell. Iakov Iakovlev, a frequent and authoritative writer on rural life, wrote that soldiers were "eaten up by the countryside. Its inertia sucks them dry."[17] Soldiers who had been Communists in the army often failed to register with their local organizations and allowed their memberships to expire. Iakovlev reported that only after an entire hour of conversation with one peasant did he discover that the man had been the chairman of his party cell in his army unit. "I came home to the village," the former soldier explained, "and here was the age-old inertia. It was a long way to the *volost'* cell, and none of my acquaintances were members, so I didn't bother to register." Iakovlev's diagnosis, however, was not altogether grim. The very fact that former soldiers felt resigned to the dismal prospects of life in the countryside still set them apart from fellow villagers who had not served in the army or had spent little time in a city. He contrasted the typical villagers, who saw themselves as "a frightened folk," with the former Red Army men, who, wherever he observed them, behaved in anything but a servile and submissive manner. Rather, the former soldier, because "he was accustomed to ordering men about his cell," took every expression of disagreement he heard as hostility to the Soviet state; in fact, he was a new Soviet "Sergeant Prishibeev."[18]

PUR and party officials viewed these developments with mixed emotions. On the one hand, the soldiers' military experience and their exposure to previously unfamiliar cultural and social settings gave them a sense that their lives could be different. Of course, many expressed disappointment after they left the army. A poor peasant wrote that he was bored to death because "there are no cultures [sic] of any kind," whereas in the army he had grown accustomed to attending the theater and reading newspapers. "But here," he lamented, "besides my work, there is only loathsome boredom, not a single amusement."[19] On the other hand, inexperienced and

---

17. Iakovlev, *Derevnia*, pp. 66–67.
18. Ibid., pp. 71–72.
19. A. Osipov, "Krasnoarmeiskii molodniak," *Politrabotnik* 7 (1924): 26–27; see also D. Ivanov, "I v oblasti religioznoi est' interesnaia cherta," *Na strazhe* 15 (1924): 12–13; "Trudovoi den'," *Krasnaia zvezda*, 9 September 1925, p. 4; N. Brykin, *V novoi derevne: Ocherki derevenskogo byta* (Leningrad, 1925), p. 21.

ambitious soldiers often attacked local elites and thereby polarized the villages. If the soldiers managed to win a majority of the peasants to their side, then the center had reason to be satisfied with their nascent rural political class. If, however, the former soldiers alienated a majority of the villagers, then the heightened tensions they introduced were likely to have undesired consequences. Not only were former soldiers forming their own communes, but they reported back to their units that, in the face of village opposition to their attempts to "strengthen soviet power," they set up their own rural soviets and party and Komsomol cells, published their own newspapers, and even submitted separate slates of candidates for the elections to the soviets. One alarmed observer noted that these separate slates made it look as if the soldiers had formed their own political parties, a clearly impermissible development.[20]

All these trends—increasing urban unemployment, the slow pace of change and resistance to it in the villages, the state's growing commitment to a transformation of the national economy, and the army's already considerable experience in turning out cadres who were conversant with and often loyal to the greater goals of the Soviet state—led to a reevaluation of existing programs for soldiers about to return home. The outcome was an expanded commitment to training former military men in specific tasks to aid them in "building socialism" in the countryside. In July 1925 the party's Central Committee ordered all political departments to organize courses for soldiers who were scheduled for demobilization in September. Soldiers enrolled in the twelve- to fifteen-day courses were to be housed in one dormitory and freed from all other tasks and drill assignments for the duration of their service.[21] PUR allocated funds for the new programs, which trained soldiers to become cooperative workers, policemen,[22] tractor operators, lower-level soviet employees, directors of reading rooms, and even film projectionists. Army newspaper correspondents were hastily retrained as village

20. S. Sorkin, "Ob aktivnosti terameitsev na sele," *Krasnaia rota* 1–2 (1924): 72–73; see also A. Kruglov-Landa, "Nashe popolnenie i nashi 'stariki,' " *SP* 6 (1924): 46; N. Kurdin, *Sovetskoe stroitel'stvo na sele i zadachi krasnoarmeitsa-otpusknika* (Moscow, 1925), p. 73.

21. "Kursy dlia demobilizovannykh krasnoarmeitsev," *Krasnaia zvezda*, 4 July 1925, p. 4.

22. As early as May 1923 the Commissariat of Internal Affairs had recommended filling the ranks of the rural police force with demobilized Red Army men because, despite a purge of the police force, "elements hostile to the Soviet regime still remain in its ranks, and therefore in the future it will be imperative to examine seriously the social composition of the staff and systematically weed out all unnecessary elements." Former soldiers were considered to be "healthy elements." See Kizilov, *NKVD*, p. 114.

correspondents. At first the courses trained modest numbers of soldiers. Following the Fifteenth Party Congress, in December 1927, when the party pledged itself to collectivization, PUR expanded the programs.[23]

In the spirit of Frunze's campaign to militarize the civilian population, former soldiers supplemented and often supplanted an absent or very weak network of loyal technical and administrative personnel in the countryside; moreover, the state's leaders increasingly looked to the veterans as a nascent rural political class capable of helping them to extend their authority over a still remote peasantry. When the center called for reelections to the soviets in the spring of 1926 because they had fallen into the hands of "bourgeois elements"—that is, peasants who refused to obey the center's dictates—army political departments prepared soldiers to take an active part in the election campaigns by arranging mock elections to fictional congresses from the *volost'* to the national level.[24] Soldiers took an active part in the election campaign. The Central Committee plenum that summarized the election results expressed disappointment in the overall turnout of rural proletarians and poor peasants, but extreme pleasure in the victories of former Red Army men, who won over half the seats in the *volost'*-level executive committees and one-third in rural soviets.[25]

Certainly by 1928 the army was devoting considerable resources to training soldiers as part of a new political class prepared to aid the center in its efforts to remake the countryside. Deputy Army Commissar Unshlikht told a meeting of party members that their job was to reeducate the young men "so that they return to the countryside as propagators of the ideas of socialism." He warned them that theirs was "a task of exceeding difficulty," for it meant releasing annually into the countryside hundreds of thousands of "new builders of socialism, who after they return home from the ranks of the Red Army, understand, reason, and behave differently than they behaved two years earlier."[26] Many of the army's leaders were certain, however, that their own future and the defense of the nation depended on the successful outcome of this exceedingly difficult task. Frunze

23. Between 1925 and 1927 the Red Army schooled 65,501 men in rural work. During 1928 alone the army sent 68,000 cadres to the countryside, including 3,687 directors of collective farms. See V. F. Klochkov, "Rol' Krasnoi Armii v likvidatsii negramotnosti i podgotovke kadrov dlia sela v gody sotsialisticheskogo stroitel'stva," *Istoriia SSSR* 3 (1980): 77.

24. "Pokazatel'nye s"ezdy sovetov," *Krasnaia zvezda*, 14 August 1925, p. 4.

25. Former soldiers also won positions as chairmen in 53 percent of the rural soviets and 70 percent of the executive committees. See *Perevybory v sovety RSFSR v 1925–1926 gg.* (Moscow, 1926), p. 35; K. E. Voroshilov, *Stat'i i rechi* (Moscow, 1937), p. 171.

26. *Krasnaia zvezda*, 15 November 1928.

had warned in 1925 that the Red Army could not be counted on to win wars against increasingly better-equipped armies so long as the Soviet Union remained a backward, agrarian nation. The army's expanded commitment to training specialists in the broad array of administrative and technical fields that were crucial to any scheme for rural transformation occupied a key role in the emerging redefinition of the worker-peasant alliance that served as the rhetorical framework of economic and social policies during the 1920s. In the changing political environment of the late 1920s, the countryside offered its sons to the army, which in turn invested more and more resources in the training of new organizers of the rural economy.

The generally positive results of the political staff's programs reaffirmed the staff in its educational mission and methods. But in the conditions of the compromised political settlement of the NEP, the attitudes and practices that soldiers learned during their military service often had tragic outcomes. The suicide of a soldier in late summer 1929 reveals the tensions that surfaced as the soldiers tried to make sense of the political order of Russia in the 1920s by using what they had learned in the army. Comrade Parsh, a twenty-three-year-old peasant soldier, before shooting himself fatally, left a poignant note, in which he poured out his despair about his hopeless future after he had failed to gain admission to a higher military school. Parsh's letter was included in a confidential report by the political officer of an unnamed division headquartered in Smolensk. Because he so movingly captured the moods of many soldiers and because his letter is a rare uncensored document from party archives, it is worth describing at some length. Parsh begs his comrades not to condemn him for his suicide. He explains, "I perish because I am a *batrak*," a hired rural laborer. He was scheduled to be released in a few weeks, but had been unable to find other employment. "There was no point in wandering around the earth, it was better to end my life, that way I won't bother others and won't suffer myself." Parsh thanks the Red Army for teaching him to read and write, but has a few harsh words about his superior, the battery commander, who conducted himself "like a kulak and not in a proletarian manner." If he had spent more time in the unit, "he would have had a bullet in his head" by now. In his extremely disjointed note, Parsh appeals to his comrades to distribute his effects to poor Red Army men. "And then, comrades, don't think that because he [sic] violated the church, God punished him." No, "it was my own nervous condition that drove me to this incident." Parsh beseeches his comrades to write to his brother; "otherwise, he will do the same thing. Better that I am the only fool." Once again he explains that it is his nervous condition, "his life situation itself at the end of his service," and the fact that no one will help him that have driven him to end his suffering. Apparently not seeing the contradiction in his previous appeal to urge his brother to avoid sharing his fate, Parsh proffers some confused counsel to other *batraki* who have no qualifications. "Better to resolve [on the same act as he] and not to suffer, because Soviet power has nothing but grief from us and we cause ourselves grief as well." After a final complaint about the party secretary's lack of interest in helping him out of his predicament, Parsh concludes, "This is all that I wanted to say before my own death and so, Long live the leader of the proletariat and Soviet power under the guidance of the Communist Party."[27]

The political officer who filed the intelligence report noted that Parsh had joined the party only the year before. Parsh had applied for an extended tour of active duty, but his application had been rejected because he was "badly prepared, learned poorly, and was insufficiently disciplined." Before his fatal shooting, there were no reports of earlier attempts or any discussions of suicide. The political officer concluded that Parsh killed himself because he was disappointed with "his life as a *batrak* after demobilization."[28]

Parsh expresses a curious amalgam of loyalty to the army, even to the state, and a pained sense of injustice and hopelessness. He reviles his own social background as a hired rural laborer and disparages an arrogant commander as a kulak. The bleak picture he paints of village life places him in the camp of the militant depeasantizers. During his military service he achieved literacy and was notorious for desecrating a church in an outburst of atheist outrage. He had linked his future plans to a military career in order to escape his dreary former life. When his hopes were disappointed, he could not imagine any other life, so he shot himself. Parsh's suicide note reveals a great deal about life in the Red Army during the 1920s. First of all, this despairing soldier was not alone in taking his life.[29] At several times after the Revolution, alarmingly high rates of suicide among party members and military men had been discussed in party meetings and in the periodical press. Suicide was explicitly linked to political discontent or moral and spiritual exhaustion.[30]

27. Smolensk Archives, WKP 215, "Politdonesenie," 25 September 1929.
28. Ibid.
29. On suicides, see *Krasnyi boets* 9 (1924): 37; P. Tsel'min, "O samoubiistvakh," *SP* 13 (1926): 20–22; and Voroshilov's remarks in a speech to military delegates in April 1927, in his *Oborona SSSR*, pp. 75–76.
30. In early 1921 large numbers of suicides followed the bloody suppression of a sailors' mutiny against Soviet power at the former revolutionary fortress of Kronstadt and the subsequent introduction of the New Economic Policy. Tens of thousands resolved on less drastic solutions by resigning from the party. These men and women, many of them young, were thought to have killed themselves or resigned out of a sense that Lenin's regime had betrayed them and everything they had fought for by turning arms against the sailors who protested in the name of the Revolution against the injustices of the Bolsheviks' rural policies in particular, and by permitting the

Parsh too ties his suicide to his nervous condition, which he explains as stemming from the anxieties he faced as he neared the end of his term of duty in the army. He ruled out a return to the countryside, where he had no prospects but to resume his life as a hired agricultural laborer for a wealthier peasant, perhaps even for a kulak. He also ruled out an urban profession because in the cities unemployment was well over a million in early 1929.

Ironically, both the unattractive future that awaited him in the countryside and the urban unemployment were in large measure the unwitting consequences of official economic policies. The most attractive option he saw for himself was to pursue a career in the army by gaining admission to a military academy. Parsh mentions no family ties but for a poor brother, who apparently was living in the same dire straits that Parsh despaired of escaping. His loyalties were to the army and to his army comrades, to whom he bequeathed his remaining possessions. The army had provided him with basic literacy and the fundamentals of a new world view, including an antireligious education. And, very significantly, the army system of political education had equipped him with a new rhetoric and set of categories with which he made some sense of his predicament. The language of class stratification—"kulak" for a wealthy peasant, *batrak* for a hired laborer—were words that Bolshevik and Soviet authorities introduced into the political vocabulary of the countryside, largely through men like Parsh himself. When Parsh found his commanding officer overbearing and abusive, he accused him of kulak and "unproletarian" behavior. A peasant soldier learned to equate "proletarian" with "virtuous" or "just." Parsh expressed himself at least partially in Bolshevik social and political categories.

At the same time Parsh clearly reviled his own social status, as a reflection of his experience of the 1920s. Although the state officially proclaimed that its legitimacy was grounded on an alliance between the workers, poor peasants, and hired laborers, in fact the state's economic policies discriminated against the poorest peasants in favor of their more powerful neighbors, the so-called middle

---

return of private capital in the form of petty trading and the leasing of nationalized industries to foreign and domestic private citizens. Another explanation that was often offered was that these men and women suffered nervous exhaustion from the years of deprivation and stress during the Revolution, the Civil War, and, for many, the trials of prerevolutionary underground party work. And nervous exhaustion was frequently blamed for the petty bickering and foul atmospheres in party collectives around the country. In 1923 and 1924 members of the Trotskyist opposition were reported to be killing themselves or resigning after they sensed that their leader's political chances were slipping away and that the Revolution was veering toward reaction in the hands of Trotsky's political opponents: "14.1 percent of all [party] members who died in the first quarter of 1925 and 11.9 percent of all candidates who died were suicides;" according to *Izvestiia TsK*, 7 September 1925, cited in Leonard Schapiro, *The Communist Party of the Soviet Union*, 2d ed. (New York: Vintage, 1971), p. 314n.

peasants and kulaks.[31] Moreover, the political worker who handled Parsh's suicide also noted that he was poorly educated and had bad work habits. This condition, too, was often associated with farm labor's inferior place in the village hierarchy. Ironically, wealthier peasants were the most literate and skilled rural inhabitants. Their economic hegemony translated into political and cultural domination in the village. The state had made only paltry efforts to break that stranglehold by the end of the 1920s. When Parsh found his last hope of gaining admission to a military school dashed, he saw no way out but to end his miserable existence.

For all his complaints about his prospects outside the army and the abusive officer in his unit, however, Parsh felt strong loyalties to both the army and the Communist Party. These attitudes contrasted dramatically with the attitudes an analogous peasant soldier in the Imperial Army would have held toward his officers and the political order he served. Although peasants had been known to rise in the ranks of the Imperial Army, they were notable exceptions; moreover, even officers did not enjoy much prestige, and a military career was "popularly reviled by the educated classes."[32] That the Red Army became for peasants and workers an institution for upward social mobility and a welcome alternative to village life amounted to a remarkable change in perspective on military service from the prerevolutionary period. And if the political workers succeeded in transferring the loyalty soldiers felt for the army to the state's larger goal of social transformation, then a leadership committed to a plan of radical social revolution in the countryside might assume that soldiers and veterans could be counted on to help in the building of socialism.

Soldiers and Collectivization

In December 1927 the Fifteenth Party Congress resolved to reorganize the Soviet rural order according to the still rather vague principles of collectivization. The army figured prominently in the ambitious plans. The delegates congratulated former servicemen for their substantial role in propagating socialism in the village and urged them to take even greater roles in existing political and cultural organizations.[33] During the winter of 1927–1928 the center,

31. On the condition of hired rural laborers and poor peasants, see Lewin, *Russian Peasants*, pp. 49–60.
32. Fuller, *Civil-Military Conflict*, p. 262.
33. "O rabote v derevne," in *Piatnadtsatyi s"ezd VKP (b)*, pp. 1420–21, 1467. See also Krupskaia's remarks on the Red Army as an increasingly important national cultural center, in ibid., p. 1253.

fearing shortfalls in peasant deliveries to the market, resumed grain requisitioning to combat alleged "kulak hoarding." The political staff closely monitored the behavior of peasant soldiers for hostile reactions to the emergency coercive measures. In February 1928 PUR convened a special meeting of directors of political administrations to evaluate how the army had come through the tense winter months. The directors delivered generally favorable reports and promised "not to permit even a trace of indifference or casual attitudes toward soldiers' moods"; their anxieties, however, were revealed in a resolution urging the center to proceed with caution.[34] The grumblings of soldiers during the winter grain requisitioning troubled the more than eighty delegates who attended the second army-wide Assembly of Secretaries of Party Cells. The secretaries confessed that party members had not responded with the requisite haste to the protests of certain soldiers and had allowed "a distortion of the class line in our political and educational work." As a lamentable consequence of these failings, the party secretaries reported, many soldiers expressed "nationalist, anti-Semitic, and sectarian [religious]" sentiments, as well as objections to the new policies in the countryside. The delegates pledged to devote special attention to soldiers who received letters from hostile "kulak elements" or who had been home on furlough during recent months. Despite the undesirable conduct of the politically "illiterate" soldiers, however, the delegates joined their superiors, the directors of political administrations, in expressing overall satisfaction with the health of the army.[35]

Having passed its first test with reasonably good marks, the army received a more demanding assignment. PUR won a large budget increase for 1928–1929 to expand its collaboration with the Commissariat of Agriculture in training soldiers as rural technicians and administrative personnel.[36] In August PUR declared that it would turn out 68,000 collective farmers and an equal number of "organizers of military work in the village," that is, former soldiers who formed local branches of the Aviation and Chemistry Society (Aviakhim), conducted pre-induction courses for peasant youths, and pro-

---

34. "O politiko-moral'nom sostoianii RKKA v sviazi s provodimymi khlebozagotovkami," February 1928, cited in Pikha, "Bor'ba Kommunisticheskoi partii," p. 238.

35. For a discussion of soldiers' disapproval of the requisitioning campaign, see A. Grichmanov, "Ko vtoromu vsearmeiskomu soveshchaniiu sekretarei iacheek," *Voennyi vestnik* 11 (1928): 3; on manifestations of "nationalism, anti-Semitism, and [religious] sects," see N. Kudrin, "Krasnoarmeiskaia pechat' i voenkory letom," *Voennyi vestnik* 18 (1928): 40. The convention met 23–31 March 1928. See B. P. Zorin, "Itogi vtorogo soveshchaniia sekretarei partiinykh organizatsii RKKA," *Voennyi vestnik* 13 (1928): 3.

36. PUR's budget grew by 75 percent, whereas the Army Commissariat's increased by only 13 percent. See Z. Pertsovskii, "Voprosy material'nogo obespecheniia partpolitprosvetraboty," *Voennyi vestnik* 20 (1929): 36.

pagandized the army's virtues among the rural populace.[37] Because PUR had given its staff such short notice, however, the political departments fulfilled only 6 to 7 percent of their quotas in graduating collective farmers and "military organizers." Few former soldiers entered collective farms, a disappointment that PUR attributed to the inadequacy of political departments' efforts to coordinate their programs with local agricultural organs and collective farm centers. When, in March and April 1929, soldiers were sent to the fields to help peasants with sowing, the Central Committee complained that the Army performed poorly and called for "a drastic change" in planning for soldiers' participation in future campaigns.[38] Soldiers returned from the sowing with fresh impressions of the center's rural policies.

The troubles during the winter of 1927–1928 were the warning signals of a wave of dissent among peasant soldiers which rose as the collectivization campaign gathered force. In the summer of 1928 a lead editorial in *Krasnaia zvezda* warned all political workers and local military commissariats to be on guard against disfranchised persons and "class-alien and socially dangerous elements [who] had begun to penetrate the ranks of the Red Army."[39] If a kulak or other disfranchised person succeeded in convincing an induction board that he was a poor or middle peasant, then he could qualify for full citizenship privileges. Because record keeping in the provinces was still very poor, enterprising kulaks and other "former people" were able to alter their legal status with relative ease. The Omsk regional executive committee reported that "kulaks" from European Russia were traveling to Siberia to enlist in the army because in Siberia, where peasants were on average wealthier than those in European Russia, they could be counted as middle peasants and thereby remove their political disabilities.[40] In May and June 1929 political workers reported a "particularly sharp rise in all sorts of negative phenomena in the barracks." The wave of dissent coincided with the "intensification of measures of social pressure on the kulaks who

37. See "Direktiva No. 92132," 20/22 August 1928, in PPR III, p. 539n.

38. "Postanovlenie TsK VKP(b) o podgotovke otpusknikov v RKKA," 12 April 1929, in KPSS o vooruzhennykh silakh (1981), pp. 256–57. For a discussion of the shortcomings, see "O podgotovke otpusknikov," Voennyi vestnik 16 (1929): 2–5; "Kolkhoz i Krasnaia Armiia," Krasnaia zvezda, 12 May 1929; "Direktiva PU RKKA ob uluchshenii dela podgotovki iz otpusknikov kadrov dlia sotsialisticheskogo pereustroistva sel'-skogo khoziaistva," 3/8 May 1929, in PPR III, pp. 502–7.

39. Krasnaia zvezda, 10 August 1928; a similar warning appeared also on 11 October 1928. The Second Army-wide Convention of Secretaries of Party Cells also heard reports from delegates who claimed to have uncovered "nests" of kulak elements among the most belligerent soldiers: ibid., 29 March 1928.

40. V. I. Varenov, Pomoshch' Krasnoi Armii v razvitii kolkhoznogo stroitel'stva, 1929–1933 gg: Po materialam Sibirskogo voennogo okruga (Moscow, 1978), pp. 39–40; see also p. 42.

Soldiers help harvest the grain. From *Raboche-krest'ianskaia Krasnaia Armiia* (Moscow, 1938), courtesy of Division of Art, Prints, and Photographs, The New York Public Library, Astor, Lenox, and Tilden Foundations.

were hiding grain." During political classes many peasant soldiers disputed instructors' claims that kulaks' power was growing in the villages. According to reports political workers submitted to their superiors, peasant soldiers representing the "wealthy part" of the village spoke out for "the general interests of the peasantry" and denied the existence of class stratification in the countryside. "There are no kulaks in the village any longer," the belligerent soldiers declared. "Everyone works the same, only the poor peasant doesn't want to work." These "wealthy" peasants also tried to persuade other peasant soldiers to cut back on their sowing because "the more you sow, the more taxes they'll squeeze out of you." And, of course, the defiant soldiers incited peasant "envy for the working class" by declaring that workers lived better than peasants.[41] Sol-

41. See reports from Ukrainian party archives cited in Pikha, "Bor'ba Kommunisticheskoi partii," p. 237; and the protocol of a "typical" political class on the regime's attitude toward kulaks and middle and poor peasants, "Politzaniatie, kak ono est' (Stenogramma politzaniatiia v I vzvode 3 roty N polka)," *Voennyi vestnik* 10 (1929): 37–42. The editors noted that the lesson contained major methodological and political errors, but they included this particular lesson because it was illustrative of much of the army's political work. See also numerous references to "peasant moods" among soldiers in several issues of *Krasnaia zvezda* during 1929; and K. G. I., "Khleboza-

diers quickly caught on to the possible gains they could reap from
the initial confusion of the collectivization campaign. Many requested early demobilization in the spring of 1929, ostensibly to
enter a collective farm. PUR castigated all political departments
that had encouraged such attitudes and advised them to heed the
center's directives with the utmost prudence.[42] Soldiers who protested against collectivization were arrested and sentenced; military
authorities forbade peasants to visit soldiers on the grounds that
they were disseminating anti-Soviet propaganda. Finally, political
workers were ordered to monitor more carefully all letters addressed to soldiers because peasants, especially in anonymous letters, were denouncing Soviet policies and inciting soldiers to acts of
disobedience.[43]

In 1929 programs for training collective farmers also raised the
first alarms among officers, who feared that the new civilian agenda
threatened to disrupt normal military training procedures and to
subject the army once again to the ill-conceived designs of grasping
politicians. In May 1929 the All-Union Council of Collective Farms
created a special military section to provide instructors for army political departments, opening the doors to another band of outsiders
unlikely to understand the special needs of the military organization. "Preparation for the countryside" before demobilization, which
occupied soldiers for a few weeks in 1927, filled nearly the entire
second year of their political education beginning in 1929.[44] At least
initially, the army's political staff did not object to the role that military personnel were playing in the countryside. They participated
in the collectivization campaign on an equal footing with high-
ranking civilian central and regional party officials. During the first
half of 1929, for example, the director of the political administration
of the Siberian Military District, Avgust Mezis, arrived in Tomsk as a
plenipotentiary for collectivization on assignment from the Siberian
krai party committee. After he completed his work in Tomsk, Mezis
moved to Irkutsk, where he conducted assemblies of "peasant workers" who were charged with implementing the collectivization policies, thence to the district party conference in Achinsk as the

gotovki, vliianie kulachestva i zadachi partiino-politicheskoi raboty," Voennyi vestnik
34 (1929): 32; I. Dubov, "Polkovaia pechat' i bor'ba za general'nuiu liniiu partii,"
Voennyi vestnik 42 (1929): 34.

42. "Direktiva o nedopustimosti dosrochnogo uvol'neniia krasnoarmeitsev iz ria-
dov RKKA v sviazi s vstupleniem v kolkhozy," 13 May 1929, in PPR III, p. 561.

43. See reports for 1930 in Varenov, Pomoshch' Krasnoi Armii, pp. 41, 43–44.

44. G. S. Agafonov, "Kommunisticheskaia partiia—organizator aktivnogo uchastiia
Krasnoi Armii v sotsialisticheskom preobrazovanii derevni v 1926–1932 gg. (na materialakh Ukrainy)" (candidate's diss., Lenin Military Political Academy, Moscow,
1976), p. 11.

Villagers arrive at a Red Army garrison. From the journal *Krasnoarmeets*, courtesy of
The Hoover Institution, Stanford University.

official representative of the *krai* party bureau.[45] Political workers in
other districts fulfilled similar missions during 1929 and 1930, pri-

45. Varenov, *Pomoshch' Krasnoi Armii*, p. 146. Mezis, a former Latvian revolutionary, rose rapidly in the army's political administration after the Civil War. He graduated from the Tolmachev Military Political Academy in 1927. In August 1927 he was
appointed deputy director of the political administration of the Ukrainian Military
District, then in May 1928 deputy director in the Siberian Military District, where
almost immediately he was promoted to director. Following his successes with the
initial phase of collectivization in Siberia, he was transferred to the strategically sensitive Special Far Eastern Army, where he served as director of political administration and member of the Revolutionary Military Council. He remained in high
positions in the political administration until he was shot in 1937.

marily because civilian agencies were desperately short of personnel.[46]

As the tempo of the collectivization drive gained speed in 1929, the national political leaders increasingly involved the army in all aspects of the campaign. In June Voroshilov, together with Aleksandr Muralov (signing for the chairman of the All-Union Resettlement Committee attached to VTsIK) and Grigorii Kaminskii (chairman of the All-Union Council of Collective Farms), approved a directive to revolutionary military councils in all military districts which outlined the correct procedures for drawing demobilized Red Army men and junior officers into the collective farm movement. The directive complained that the collective farm movement already was experiencing "a critical shortage" of "well-prepared and politically literate cadres who came directly from the countryside itself and from its most active and vanguard elements." Especially now, the center's extremely ambitious goal to bring millions of peasants into the collective farm system during the immediate five-year period and the critical shortage of reliable local agents to implement its goal inclined the national leadership to view the Red Army as "a powerful reservoir" of personnel. Voroshilov, Muralov, and Kaminskii advised political departments to use informal organizations of soldiers from the same region, zemliachestva, to create "initiative groups" who would return to a village with a united front. They encouraged soldiers to consider moving to the outlying border regions and urged republic-level agricultural commissariats to recruit soldiers to already existing farms "without violating the basic principle of voluntary entry into collective farms." Finally, Sovnarkom promised to grant a series of substantial tax exemptions and other benefits to collective farms that were organized by Red Army men or that accepted former soldiers as members.[47] Despite reports of some resistance on the part of soldiers, referred to as "kulak moods" and anti-Semitism, the party declared itself satisfied with the condition of the army in July 1929 and resolved to step up soldiers' involvement in the transformation of the countryside.[48] Soldiers were

46. Klochkov, "Rol' Krasnoi Armii," p. 136.
47. "Direktiva Vsesoiuznogo pereselencheskogo komiteta pri VTsIK SSSR, RVS SSSR i Vsesoiuznogo soveta kolkhozov revvoensovetam okrugov i flotov, narkomzemam soiuznykh respublik, kolkhoztsentram o poriadke ispol'zovaniia krasnoarmeitsev i mladshikh komandirov-otpusknikov v kolkhoznom stroitel'stve," June 1929, in PPR III, pp. 514–18. Although the published source for this directive lists N. Muralov as signing for the chairman of the All-Union Resettlement Committee, probably the actual co-author was Aleksandr Muralov, first deputy commissar and then commissar of agriculture for the RSFSR in 1929. See R. W. Davies, Industrialization of Soviet Russia, vol. 1: The Socialist Offensive: The Collectivization of Soviet Agriculture, 1929–1930 (Cambridge: Harvard University Press, 1980), p. 169n.
48. "O sostoianii oborony SSSR: Iz postanovleniia TsK VKP(b)," 15 July 1929, in PPR IV, pp. 14–16.

sent to help with the grain procurement drives across the country in August and September and campaigned actively for seats in yet another round of reelections to the soviets. Former soldiers won more than 40 percent of the seats in village, raion, district, and republican soviets.[49]

The men who graduated from the army's personnel training courses left an uneven record of achievement. Predictably, soldiers who had undergone two years of service in a regular unit proved far more reliable at carrying out the center's wishes than their counterparts who had served in the territorial militia forces. Soldiers reported arriving home to find that not one territorial soldier had joined the collective farm. Usually after the arrival of the more reliable regular troops, the number of collective farmers rose dramatically. Political workers concluded that the militia soldiers had fallen under the influence of local kulaks, but they had long been warning their superiors and civilian political leaders who would listen that the territorial militia system simply did not afford adequate opportunities to remake a peasant's political and cultural profile.[50] The army-trained cadres also fell prey to many of the same "excesses" that characterized the entire national collectivization drive. Soldiers were charged with "striving for high percentages," or fixing arbitrary quotas attainable only by coercion; they violated "the principle of voluntary collectivization" also by exerting blatant and masked forms of pressure on other soldiers. They antagonized villagers by "tactless" methods. They were also guilty of "gigantomania," that is, organizing farms that were too large to be economically and organizationally viable.[51]

Not surprisingly, the former soldiers reported numerous cases of peasant, or "kulak," resistance. When one brigade called a meeting in a village to organize a collective farm, the twenty-five "kulak" families managed to break up the meeting and persuaded the villagers to table any such proposals indefinitely. The soldiers had convened the meeting without conducting any prior agitational work or even consulting with the representatives of the presumably sympathetic village poor. Army units were dispatched to put down the protests.[52] Although soldiers were quick to brand as kulaks any peasants who resisted their energetic aid in collectivizing, it is clear that resistance was widespread among many families that had been

49. "Direktivy ob aktivnom uchastii chastei Krasnoi Armii v khlebozagotovitel'-nykh rabotakh 1929 goda," 5, 19/22 July 1929, in *PPR* III, p. 559; "Demobilizovannye v sovetakh," *Voennyi vestnik* 1 (1930): 68.
50. I. I. Geller, *Krasnaia armiia na fronte kollektivizatsii* (Samara, 1930), pp. 7, 18. Iosif Geller was a PUR instructor who specialized in training soldiers to work for their local military newspapers.
51. See Bedzhanian, "Kommunisticheskaia partiia," pp. 46–47.
52. Geller, *Krasnaia armiia*, pp. 16–17.

registered as poor and middle peasants before the collectivization
drive began.[53] A military man who had been assigned to a civilian
organization for implementing the collectivization policies arrested
twenty "poor and middle peasants" for refusing to join a collective
farm.[54] More often, however, military units sent brigades of soldiers
to "assist" the poor peasants and demobilized soldiers in organizing
against kulaks. During election campaigns, servicemen packed meetings and shouted down "kulaks and kulak agents."[55] Ironically, the
soldiers who now were urging and sometimes threatening their fellow villagers to join the great collective farm movement resembled
the soldiers who returned home in 1917 to spread the message of the
Revolution and incite peasants to seize land and expel the land-
lords. Only now the soldiers' message often fell on deaf ears. The
new revolution that the soldiers were bringing appealed largely to
the outcasts from village society.

Despite all the difficulties that the political staff encountered in
fulfilling its new mission, by the end of 1929 the center proudly
claimed that "you will undoubtedly find a former Red Army man as
leader and organizer in every reading cottage, cooperative, land as-
sociation, and kolkhoz."[56] The official organ of the collectivization
drive, Kollektivist, announced that 25,000 veterans' families had
joined or formed 200 Red Army collective farms, most of them in
the Ukraine, along the Volga, and in the Far East.[57] Although 25,000
families represented less than 10 percent of the total number of soldiers released annually from military service, still the figures added
to the zeal of the political and administrative bodies charged with
the collectivization drive. In October the Agriculture Commissariat
reported to the Council on Labor and Defense that it needed 182,075
personnel for state and collective farms. The commissariat estimated
that only half of them could be provided from the existing network
of educational institutions. At most, another 2,000 men could be removed from unemployment lists at the labor exchanges and sent to

53. On the abuse of the term "kulak" during collectivization, see Merle Fainsod,
Smolensk under Soviet Rule (New York: Vintage, 1963), pp. 244–47.
54. Bedzhanian, "Kommunisticheskaia partiia," p. 590. For reports of armed conflict between military units and peasants, see Krasnaia zvezda, 9 July, 17 October,
and 20 November 1929.
55. Agafonov, "Kommunisticheskaia partiia," p. 16; Chausov, "Rol' Krasnoi armii,"
pp. 9–10; Varenov, Pomoshch' Krasnoi Armii, p. 136.
56. Sel'skokhoziaistvennaia gazeta, 23 November 1929, cited in Davies, Socialist
Offensive, p. 207.
57. Kollektivist 3 (1930): 2. PUR discouraged soldiers from seeking resettlement in
Siberia, the Far East, the Urals, and Kazakhstan, ostensibly because the state land
fund alloted for collective farms in those areas had been exhausted for 1929. First
priority went to soldiers who would join already existing collective farms. Dzyza
listed the largest Red Army collective farms in "Krasnaia Armiia i zadachi kolkhoznogo stroitel'stva," Voennyi vestnik 4 (1930): 36–37.

the countryside. Therefore, representatives of the Agriculture Commissariat had no choice but to turn to the army to fill the gap. They even flattered the army: "The experience of 1929 demonstrates that the Red Army can handle this assignment."[58]

A military writer who signed himself Dzyza and who was sympathetic to the Agriculture Commissariat's ambitious plans rebuked the army's political organs and party organizations for dragging their feet on training more soldiers for collective farm work. "Here and there this is explained by a wish to receive exhaustive directives from above. But," he exasperatedly objected, "we already have the resolution of the November plenum of the Central Committee and the January [1930] resolution on the tempo of collectivization." Dzyza dismissed commanders' fears that increased attention to the collectivization campaign would reduce the time devoted to combat preparedness. "These fears have absolutely no serious foundations," he declared. He reminded these timid souls that throughout the entire post-Civil War period, the army had successfully served double duty by combining military and political training with "political and cultural influences on the countryside by means of the whole mass of Red Army men and commanders."[59]

On 30 January 1930 Voroshilov, responding to pressures from the leaders of the collectivization campaign, announced that the Red Army would train 100,000 "workers for the countryside," including no fewer than 75,000 specifically for the collective farm system. They were to be cadres "capable of managing collective farms and specific types of work in them; of servicing tractors, combines, and complex farm machinery"; and, of course, of serving as "vanguard fighters for the transformation of simple collective farms into higher forms." Accordingly, they were to be selected from volunteers who were either poor peasants, hired farm laborers, or workers.[60] Five days earlier, the new director of PUR, Ian Gamarnik, had ordered all political workers to focus on the new slogan of the agricultural campaign, "Liquidation of the kulak as a class," but not to forget that not one minute of military training should be sacrificed for the collectivization programs.[61] By the end of 1930, 103,000 soldiers and jun-

58. "Kadry dlia kolkhozov i sovkhozov," Voennyi vestnik 37 (1929): 53.
59. Dzyza, "Krasnaia Armiia," p. 32.
60. "Postanovlenie RVS SSSR ob uchastii Krasnoi Armii v kolkhoznom stroitel'stve," 30 January 1930, in PPR IV, pp. 44–46. PUR followed Voroshilov's resolution with its own instructions, "Direktiva PU RKKA o podgotovke v armii kolkhoznykh kadrov," 8 February 1930, in ibid., pp. 47–49.
61. Ia. Gamarnik, "Novaia obstanovka—novaia politika, novye lozungi," Krasnaia zvezda, 25 January 1930; see also "Iz direktivy PU RKKA o rabote s krasnoarmeitsami po raz"iasneniiu politiki partii, napravlennoi na likvidatsiiu kulachestva kak klassa," 31 January 1930, in PPR IV, pp. 46–47. Gamarnik warned the political staff to expect the kulaks, now "fighting to the death," to do everything possible to win the middle peasants to their position.

Ian Gamarnik, director, Political Administration of the Revolutionary Military Council of the USSR, 1929–1937. From *Raboche-krest'-ianskaia Krasnaia Armiia* (Moscow, 1938), courtesy of Division of Art, Prints, and Photographs, The New York Public Library, Astor, Lenox, and Tilden Foundations.

ior officers had completed crash courses at the end of their service terms and left the army for their new assignments as builders of socialism in the countryside.

Although the Agriculture Commissariat's enthusiasm and willingness to tap what appeared to be a perpetual spring of rural cadres gave rise to ever more ambitious projections, part of the army leadership made a successful effort to slow the pace of collectivization at least temporarily. The Agriculture Commissariat now expected the army to graduate 100,000 rural cadres during each year of the five-year plan.[62] Within a month after Voroshilov's pledge to turn out 100,000 cadres and well before those promised cadres had completed their training, certain members of the army command and political administration balked at any further large-scale involvement of military personnel in the collectivization campaign and demanded that any Red Army families who had been dispossessed as kulaks in the heat of the recent campaign have their full rights restored and receive compensation for any damages they had suffered. The objections of the military leadership to the collectivization methods are reported in foreign diplomatic notes, but they also can be substantiated by a radical change in the army's commitment to preparing cadres during 1930.[63] According to British and French diplomatic sources, Voroshilov himself "warned Stalin early in 1930 that he would not be responsible for the army if the latter persisted in the process of ruthless and indiscriminate collectivization." "Certain members" of the government feared military action by Poland if morale fell too low in the Red Army.[64] Italian diplomats denied that Voroshilov intervened; rather, Gamarnik, at an expanded meeting of the Politburo in late February, demanded an end to the forced pace of collectivization and the policy of liquidating the kulaks, or "they would no longer be able to count on the Red Army." Significantly, Gamarnik received support from his predecessor as director of PUR, Andrei Bubnov, now commissar of enlightenment. According to the Italian version of the meeting, all those attending voted in favor of Gamarnik's proposed policy changes except Stalin and Molotov. Outvoted, Stalin retired to write the article "Dizzy from Success," published on 2 March, in which he called a halt to forced collectivization.[65]

62. For a discussion of the Narkomzem schemes, see "Kadry dlia kolkhozov," reprinted from *Sel'skaia gazeta* 168 (1929) in *Voennyi vestnik* 37 (1929): 53; and Dzyza, "Krasnaia Armiia," p. 35.

63. Stalin also chose the central army daily, *Krasnaia zvezda* (21 January 1930), to correct "two inaccuracies in the formulations" of the policy of "liquidating the kulaks as a class," hinting that certain military leaders had taken too soft a line in the matter: Stalin, *Sochineniia*, 12:178–83.

64. Report in the archives of the British Foreign Office, cited in Davies, *Socialist Offensive*, p. 280. Also in Jonathan Haslam, *Soviet Foreign Policy, 1930–1933: The Impact of the Depression* (London: Macmillan, 1983), pp. 121–22.

65. Haslam, *Soviet Foreign Policy*, p. 122. Stalin's speech, "Golovokruzhenie ot uspekhov: K voprosam kolkhoznogo dvizheniia," appeared in *Pravda*, 2 March 1930, and is also reproduced in Stalin, *Sochineniia*, 12:191–99. The Italian reports that

Whoever initiated the changes in rural policy, they were certain to find support among influential parts of the military command, who even earlier had protested openly that the cadre training programs were upsetting military education and that all sense of balance had been lost. The protests stemmed in large measure from the recent sense of pride that high-ranking officers felt in the army. At the end of 1929 the Special Far Eastern Army, under the command of the Civil War hero Vasilii Bliukher, handily defeated Chinese troops.[66] Also by the end of the 1920s the vast majority of the officer corps had undergone higher military education and had developed a professional ethos that was reflected in the military press.[67] Military professionals feared that "civilizing" influences once again threatened to deprive the nation of a combat-ready military instrument. Just as an influential component of both the military and political command had warned in 1922 and 1923 that the army was losing its distinctively military character in the face of excessive demands from civilian politicians, so now they sounded the alarm again. In February the editor of the army's central daily newspaper, *Krasnaia zvezda*, had warned readers that "if there were no threat of invasion, then we wouldn't need an army, but rather peasant universities, soviet and party schools, and courses for collective farm workers." But such a threat did exist, quite palpably in the form of

Gamarnik was instrumental in reversing the campaigns of the winter of 1929–1930 are supported circumstantially by the almost complete silence of Voroshilov on any matters relating to collectivization for several months after the crisis. See Samuel Harper, *Making Bolsheviks* (Chicago: University of Chicago Press, 1931), p. 137. If the Italian reports are accurate, then either Gamarnik had been enforcing a policy with which he vehemently disagreed or he changed his mind decisively once the adverse consequences of the collectivization drive on soldiers' morale emerged. John Erickson, *Soviet High Command*, p. 356, disputes the claims that the High Command opposed Stalin's policy of collectivization.

66. Janos Decsy, who studied at the Frunze Military Academy in 1956, recalls that lecturers on military history told students that Bliukher, Ieronim, Uborevich, and Iona Iakir (the first two men were of peasant origin and had served in the Great War) were particularly vocal in opposing collectivization; interview, 16 April 1988. Matitiahu Mayzel, in his introduction to the Hebrew translation of Marshal Zhukov's memoirs, also claims that Bliukher tried to dissuade Stalin from pursuing collectivization, and at least succeeded in blocking the drive in his jurisdiction, the Far East: *Zichrornot Hamarshal Zhukov* (Tel Aviv: Maarachot, 1982), p. 29. I thank Amir Wiener for pointing out this information to me. For details on the Special Far Eastern Army, see Erickson, *Soviet High Command*, pp. 240–46.

67. Voroshilov claimed that by 1928 only 3,968 officers of a total of 23,889 had not completed advanced courses in military institutes: Voroshilov, *Stat'i i rechi*, p. 230, cited in *KPSS i stroitel'stvo vooruzhennykh sil SSSR* (Moscow, 1959), p. 276. Since 1923 officers had their own professional journal, *Voennyi vestnik*; in 1927 it absorbed nearly all educational journals, including the organ of the political staff, *Sputnik politrabotnika*. For works of military theory, see B. M. Shaposhnikov, *Mozg armii*, 3 vols. (Moscow, 1927–1929); V. K. Triandafillov, *Kharakter operatsii sovremennykh armii* (Moscow, 1929); A. A. Svechin, *Strategiia*, 2d ed. (Moscow, 1927); Tukhachevskii, *Voprosy sovremennoi strategii*; and the 1929 army field manual.

the militarist pronouncements of the Polish government. In such conditions it was entirely impermissible that, as the infantry corps in one regiment reported, political workers were telling soldiers that at the present moment inattention to military preparedness was "a natural thing, because the entire country, and accordingly the army, is laboring on the main task of complete collectivization and the destruction of the kulak as a class."[68] "We often forget," wrote the editor, "that military matters are the primary profession of the regular staff of the armed forces. It is not a normal situation that in several units of the Moscow garrison, between 50 and 80 percent of the officers are busy during the evenings in civilian educational institutions."[69] PUR spokesmen warned that the long-term absence of officers from their units in connection with the collectivization drive had taken a considerable toll on combat readiness. Even some civilian party officials were ready to question the army's involvement in the collectivization campaign. In an address to a Siberian party conference, the first secretary of the Siberian committee, R. I. Eikhe, a Civil War veteran, agreed that it was necessary for the civilian party organizations to strengthen ties with the Red Army and to use "our military comrades in civilian work. But," he added, "to take a commander or political worker away from his unit for two to three months is not an accomplishment, but a blunder and a mistake."[70]

As soon as Stalin announced the temporary retreat from all-out collectivization, a new slogan, "Struggle to strengthen military studies," replaced all previous slogans devoted to the collectivization campaign. Beginning in the summer of 1930, the number of commanders and political officers departing for work in the countryside dropped sharply. To remedy the threatened deterioration in discipline, PUR ordered the upcoming conferences of division-level party representatives to return the attention of the entire staff of the Red Army to military training. "The active participation by the Red Army in the socialist construction of the Soviet Union," the editor of *Voennyi vestnik* advised, "should not be reflected in the execution of the primary training plans of military units." The editor angrily warned that "not one hour, not one minute of military training" should be sacrificed.[71] Other senior political workers now demanded the elimination of all "head-spinning"—an obvious refer-

68. *Krasnaia zvezda*, 22 February 1930; see also issues from 9 and 12 February and 13 March 1930.
69. *Krasnaia zvezda*, 20 February 1930.
70. Eikhe's address is reported in *Sovetskaia Sibir'*, 11 June 1930; see also PUR's directive of 15 March 1930; both documents cited in Varenov, *Pomoshch' Krasnoi Armii*, pp. 147–48.
71. "Povysit' boevuiu podgotovku i mobilizatsionnuiu gotovnost'," *Voennyi vestnik* 7 (1930): 2; also "K partiinym konferentsiiam," *Voennyi vestnik* 8 (1930): 3.

ence to Stalin's "dizzy" speech—moods in the army's party organizations. Intelligence pouring in from the countryside made it clear that these pernicious moods had "taken hold rather solidly here and there." The only way to "foster the political condition and morale of the Red Army masses" was for the army's party organizations to put an end to "all distortions" as quickly as possible. In other words, the excesses of Red Army collectivizers—among other agents of collectivization—were contributing to widespread peasant discontent. When letters and visits from relatives brought news of the substantial coercion that the center was unleashing in the countryside, that discontent very quickly found its way back to the army, producing grumblings and open opposition.

PUR especially denounced military men who permitted "distortions" in their conduct toward the families of soldiers and officers in the villages, many of whom fell into the lists of kulaks and lost their property and rights as citizens.[72] The Central Committee, in a special resolution on "the struggle with distortions of the party's line on the collectivization movement," singled out the protection of Red Army families and their property as a priority of the highest urgency. In a curious exemption from the otherwise "strict regulations," all party committees were to admit to membership kulaks and people otherwise deprived of their voting rights if their families included "Red partisans, Red Army and Navy men, and rural teachers who were loyal to the Soviet regime," provided the latter vouched for the reliability of their relatives.[73] Thus at every step of its tortured path toward rapid transformation of the countryside, the national leadership was forced to compromise its ambitious goals, in large measure out of concern for the country's physical survival in the international arena. As the overwhelming majority of soldiers were peasants and a growing part of the peasantry were demobilized soldiers, a major upheaval in the countryside could have a devastating effect on the military.

Although PUR shifted its attention back to more narrowly military tasks, the army nonetheless graduated 103,000 cadres for the countryside by the end of 1930. Just as civilian party officials in many regions ignored Stalin's call to reverse the recent policies, many army personnel persisted in attaining the rapid breakthrough for

72. A. Aleksandrov, "Sovremennyi etap kolkhoznogo stroitel'stva i zadachi part-politraboty v RKKA," Voennyi vestnik 19 (1930): 7–11. For evidence of violence committed against veterans and Red Army families, see the memoirs of Lev Kopelev, The Education of a True Believer, trans. Gary Kern (New York: Harper & Row, 1980), p. 270; also Fainsod, Smolensk under Soviet Rule, p. 244; for a fictional account, see Mikhail Sholokhov, Seeds of Tomorrow, trans. Stephen Garry (New York: Knopf, 1935).

73. "Postanovlenie TsK VKP(b) o bor'be s iskrivleniiami partlinii v kolkhoznom dvizhenii," 14 March 1930, in KPSS v rezoliutsiiakh, 5:104.

which they had been preparing. PUR had to exert considerable pressure to rein in the overly enthusiastic collectivizers. Army and party leaders satisfied themselves with reports that more than 70 percent of all troops who left the army in late spring 1930 joined collective farms.[74] In their letters home, many soldiers exhorted their families to join the new farms. A soldier in the Belorussian Military District wrote to his father, "I want you and advise you to join the collective farm." He warned that upon demobilization, he would join one himself, and "if you don't join, then you are no father to me, and I am no son to you." A second soldier wrote his family, "You are sitting in a dark corner and listening to kulaks. Don't listen to them. . . . Enough of living as hired hands, go to the commune or to a collective farm." The family of the second soldier wrote back that they had read his letter at a village assembly, and the entire village had decided to join a collective farm.[75]

In the collective farms that former soldiers established in the frontier regions, the new farmers brought with them the organizational principles and work attitudes acquired during their two years of service. Many continued to address one another by their military ranks. Former soldiers who abandoned the often precarious agricultural experiments were reviled as "deserters from the front of socialist construction" who harbored "opportunistic attitudes to hardship."[76] According to one chronicler of the Red Army's contribution to the collective movement, a farm chairman, Comrade Morozov, took to his new assignment with enthusiasm and love. "Our discipline," he told a visitor, "is just like it was in the Red Army. . . . We work in strict accordance with directives from the agronomist." The visitor predicted, "We shall send thousands of Morozovs to the villages and farmsteads. Through them we shall plant flowering corners of socialism—new collective farms and communes."[77]

Not all the forays of Red Army personnel during the collectivization campaign were so positive. On several occasions in 1930, troops were called out to "liquidate kulak demonstrations." Now the army took special care to designate only party members to exercise the coercive measures and relieved rank-and-file Red Army men

---

74. Agafonov, "Kommunisticheskaia partiia," p. 14. Agafonov's figures come from the Ukrainian Military District and Ukrainian party archives. He claims that in May 1931 the proportion of discharged soldiers who joined collective farms climbed to 90 percent.

75. All the letters were part of a political intelligence report to PUR (no. 21, 2 April 1930), cited in Bedzhanian, "Kommunisticheskaia partiia," p. 580.

76. G. Kardash, *Kommuna Lenina v Primor'e* (Khabarovsk, 1932), pp. 27, 30.

77. Ritman, *Pylaiushchie budni*, pp. 41–42.

from punitive raids.[78] When the Central Committee announced a grain requisitioning drive at the end of July 1930, PUR's assistant director, Anton Bulin, categorically forbade any political workers or Red Army brigades to take part in it. Any pressure that soldiers might bring to bear on their families to fulfill the new quotas was to be exerted exclusively through letters or in talks before village assemblies on their visits home.[79] Bulin's ban marked the first time in three years that the army had not participated in the annual grain collection drives.

One army commentator summarized the year-long campaign to train collective farmers largely as a failure, especially in the area of training personnel with any genuine technical qualifications. He confessed that the army simply did not have the resources for proper training programs, and he also leveled the predictable charge that the civilian organizations that should have been most interested in the training programs failed to cooperate with the army's political staff. The one area he judged a success was the training of tractor drivers. He recommended that PUR limit its future training efforts to conveying "general knowledge in the sphere of socialist reconstruction of agriculture in the countryside and the organizational and economic structure of collective and state farms and machine tractor stations.[80] PUR adopted a scaled-down plan for 1931 which hewed closely to his recommendations. In November PUR canceled all courses except those for tractor drivers. Any discussions of collectivization were limited strictly to regular political classes. PUR recommended that political departments compensate for the curtailment in training programs by organizing more excursions to collective and state farms and to machine tractor stations. For 1931, instead of the 100,000 collective farm workers that the Red Army graduated in the previous year, PUR promised to provide only 29,500 tractor drivers.[81] Many soldiers were trained in tractor-driving skills as part of their routine education, so the new goals involved no disruption in military training whatsoever. Henceforth, the army prepared the

---

78. Bedzhanian, "Kommunisticheskaia partiia," pp. 586–87. Bedzhanian reports armed confrontations in the Ukraine in March, May, and September 1930. Davies gives an account of Red Army units called to suppress a peasant uprising in the North Caucasus, in *Socialist Offensive*, pp. 258–59.

79. "Direktiva PU RKKA o razvertyvanii massovoi raboty v chastiakh v sviazi s provedeniem kampanii khlebozagotovok," 31 July 1930, in *PPR* IV, p. 60.

80. "Itogi i zadachi podgotovki massovykh kadrov dlia sotsialisticheskogo sektora sel'skogo khoziaistva," *Voennyi vestnik* 33 (1930): 51–53.

81. *Krasnaia zvezda*, 1 December 1930. A later directive allocated the numbers to be prepared in each military district. See "Direktiva Narkomzema SSSR i PU RKKA o podgotovke iz chisla uvol'niaemykh krasnoarmeitsev kadrov traktoristov," 12/15 February 1931, in *PPR* IV, p. 139.

largest component of the machine tractor station personnel.[82] Because the machine tractor stations became the crucial agency through which the state exerted its control over the peasantry, the army continued to perform a valuable state-building function, but in succeeding years PUR devoted increasingly less attention to programs that might divert resources and troop time from purely military training tasks.

82. For a discussion of the machine tractor stations, see R. W. Davies, *The Industrialization of Soviet Russia*, vol. 2: *The Soviet Collective Farm, 1929–1930* (Cambridge: Harvard University Press, 1980), chap. 2. During 1930 the central administration governing tractors, Traktotsentr, trained no more than 20,000 to 25,000 drivers (p. 29).

Conclusion

The peasant who completes the communist school of the Red Army already has a certain seed of proletarian education, of socialist education. [In our country] the broadest masses are involved in state work, and these masses reshape the state apparatus. This process unmakes our fundamental classes, depeasantizes the peasantry, and deproletarianizes the proletariat.
—Nikolai Bukharin, 1927

By the end of the 1920s the Red Army was a fundamentally different institution from the units of Red Guards and former imperial soldiers improvised in late 1917. Despite the high command's fears and the occasional soldiers' protests, the Red Army survived collectivization. That it did so surely was a tribute to the success of the national leadership in winning the cooperation of soldiers and officers during the social upheaval at the end of 1929 and throughout 1930. The center benefited from a combination of relatively favorable living standards for career military men, the considerable apparatus of political instruction, and selective use of coercion against defiant soldiers. Partly as a consequence of the military command's persistent efforts to secure a respectable place for the army in postrevolutionary society, the future of their institution was no longer in question, as it had been in the early years after the Civil War. The army's hard-won legitimacy was the product of a realignment in the civil–military relationship over the first dozen years of the Soviet state.

That relationship, which shaped political culture in fundamental ways, was marked by two very different conflicts during the early years of the Red Army's history.[1] The first, lasting from early 1918 until late 1923, pitted civilian revolutionaries against military professionals over the principles of organizing defense for a socialist state. The revolutionaries defended the commune ideal of the mili-

1. For a broad survey of civil–military relations in the Soviet state, see Timothy J. Colton, *Commissars, Commanders, and Civilian Authority: The Structure of Soviet Military Politics* (Cambridge: Harvard University Press, 1979).

tia, with its democratic ethos and provisional character. Civilians feared a Bonapartist coup if defense were left to the officers, many of whom came from the Imperial Army. To forestall such a coup, the revolutionaries introduced the system of dual command and the institution of the commissar, the most important legacies of this first struggle for control over the instruments of armed coercion. The military professionals resisted these encroachments on what they felt to be their professional expertise and argued that only a traditional standing army founded on strict discipline and barracks regimen could safeguard the gains of the Revolution against modern armies. Finally in 1924 the civilians suffered defeat, even as the military reluctantly accepted the compromise of a mixed system of territorial militia and regular cadre army, because the militia that survived the struggle was declared to be provisional until a genuine regular army could supplant it; furthermore, the organizational principles of this compromised militia force differed little from those of the Red Army.

During the second conflict, which lasted very briefly, from late 1929 through 1930, the civilians no longer wanted to introduce their methods and styles into army life; on the contrary, they hoped to harness the discipline and loyalty of soliders to their ambitious scheme of rural transformation. Now the military professionals fought the diversion of soldiers' energies to civilian campaigns on the grounds that the collectivization drive undermined combat readiness by sacrificing troop training and seriously impaired morale when soldiers' relatives in the countryside suffered from the excesses of local activists. An influential group in the high command vigorously opposed collectivization and favored a less coercive and more moderately paced transformation of the economy. In the short run, the military men who opposed collectivization lost out to other military men allied to powerful political leaders who were intent on taking advantage of the considerable manpower resources of the largely peasant army to further the building of socialism in the countryside. Eventually, however, the anticollectivization professionals won the Stalin leadership over to a less disruptive policy and the army was spared from further extensive service in the collectivization drive. Officers who opposed collectivization argued the special interests of the military, particularly the crucial importance of military training and combat morale during a time of heightened international tensions.[2] The outcome of the second conflict made it clear that the civilian leadership no longer questioned the value of an army in the Soviet state; rather, they wanted to take

2. Nearly all the men identified as having disputed the wisdom of collectivization fell during the Great Terror. The most notable included Bliukher, Iakir, and Uborevich.

advantage of the exceptional discipline and "political literacy" of soldiers and junior officers to further their own domestic political campaigns. The experience of 1929–1930 also demonstrated that militia units were not nearly so attractive or reliable to the proponents of collectivization as the regular Red Army men proved to be, notwithstanding the mixed results that soldiers' participation brought to the campaign.

The high command lobbied for the army's cause persistently, both at the level of the party elite and among the mass volunteer organizations that were enlisted to assist in pre-induction training. Their efforts certainly played a major role in establishing a considerable measure of legitimacy for military institutions and values; however, the improvement in the military's fortunes also stemmed from the high command's success in transforming the Red Army into a professional institution. The Red Army made considerable strides toward a high level of professionalism after the Frunze reforms.[3] The reformers phased out the practice of dual command and thereby eliminated much of the organizational chaos that had plagued all attempts to bolster troop discipline in the early 1920s. By the end of the 1920s most officers had advanced training in military subjects; the high command was resolutely committed to upgrading standards of performance. The Red Army's quick victories in the skirmishes with Japan became a source of pride and esprit de corps. And a firm annual military budget, together with relatively good salaries, pensions, and other benefits, allowed the army to attract more than adequate numbers of young men to careers as officers.

Despite the apparent triumph of the values and interests of the military elite, however, the military men never got their way altogether. One essential component of military professionalism was lacking: autonomy in regard to admission to the officer corps and promotion within it. The Bolshevik leadership deemed such matters too important to leave to the officers. As a result, military expertise was not the only standard by which men were judged; political attitude and family background often were decisive in the Workers'-Peasants' Red Army. Officers were vividly reminded of these limits on their freedom when their ranks were thinned during the Great Terror of the 1930s. A constant constraint on the military elite was the competition of a paramilitary force of growing importance, the OGPU, successor to the Cheka. The relations between army and OGPU were never without friction because the police interfered in military affairs, despite all protestations from the military command. When Red Army units proved unreliable in suppressing

3. I borrow the criteria for military professionalism from Fuller, *Civil–Military Conflict*, pp. 5–6. See also Amos Perlmutter, *The Military and Politics in Modern Times* (New Haven: Yale University Press, 1977), pp. 1–6, 30–35, 281–88.

peasant protests during the collectivization drive, the center called in OGPU troops to restore order. Their numbers were large enough to enable OGPU chiefs to challenge the army's claim to monopoly on the instruments of armed coercion.

These limits notwithstanding, the army's institutional stability and prominence were reflected in an increase in the prestige attached to military careers and a concomitant increase in loyalty to the Red Army. Whereas the Imperial Army had been plagued by widespread draft evasion, by the mid-1920s large numbers of peasant and worker conscripts looked on military service as an avenue of upward mobility and especially as a way out of rural poverty. Memoirs and other evidence suggest that officers and soldiers had developed a strong sense of group identity and loyalty to the army. The suicide Parsh so pinned his hopes on a long career in the army that when his hopes were dashed, he could see no other course than to end his life. Military men were loyal to the army even when they disagreed with central state policy. Though military men opposed collectivization and the ruthless state leadership that imposed it, for example, they remained dedicated to the army as an honorable career and to their fellow soldiers and officers.[4] Bliukher and the men at the top of the military chain of command who joined him in opposing collectivization continued to serve in the Stalin state. Despite years of loyal service, they later paid for their political opinions with their lives.

The rise of the army to a prominent place in Soviet politics and society by the end of the 1920s, together with the fact that the Soviet leadership commingled military obligation and citizenship in the new state, shaped the evolution of soldiers' status in postrevolutionary Soviet society. Only citizens had the right and obligation to serve in the Red Army; the large numbers of disfranchised kulaks and former elites were forbidden to bear arms and thereby deprived of a whole range of benefits and opportunities. Beginning with the Civil War, army service also became a major vehicle for admission both to the nation's most important political institution, the Communist Party, and to the burgeoning urban and rural bureaucracies.

Because the Bolsheviks' version of class analysis often was grounded in prerevolutionary realities, the postrevolutionary status of soldiers befuddled most of the analysts. Even before the Revolution soldiers had not fitted neatly into the available categories of social analysis. In some sense, soldiers resembled factory workers and so shared some characteristics of what Marxist analysts would label a class; still, soldiers kept one foot in the countryside and mani-

4. See the account by a refugee and career military man, "The Life of a Soviet Soldier," in *Thirteen Who Fled*, ed. Louis Fischer (New York: Harper, 1949), pp. 25–39.

fested many traits that Bolsheviks and other social democrats had always associated with the peasantry, a social formation that failed to qualify as a class but retained important features of its former estate status under the old regime. The officers and political officers, for their part, came to resemble a new caste and often were so branded during the 1920s, primarily by civilian critics who resented what they felt to be the disproportionate importance assigned to military men and institutions during peacetime.

The overwhelming majority of soldiers came from the peasantry, yet the special treatment that the state reserved for these peasants in uniform set them and their families sharply apart from their fellow villagers back home. Again the categories of analysis were ill-fitted to the fluid social and economic world of early-twentieth-century Russia; the revolution that put in place a self-proclaimed dictatorship of the proletariat rendered their usefulness even more problematic. Not surprisingly, a certain ambiguity clouded soldiers' place in the social and political structure. Indeed, most rank-and-file soldiers found themselves midway between the proletariat, in whose name the Soviet leadership ruled, and the peasantry, which the leaders and many peasant servicemen considered backward and in need of reshaping. Generally the proletarian dictatorship—in its policies and practice, if never officially—virtually included soldiers and veterans in the politically all-important category of the proletariat, treating them as nearly equal to factory workers. Yet their origins in the peasantry were never quite forgotten.

Peasant conscripts obeyed officers who usually came from working-class or peasant backgrounds but viewed themselves primarily in light of their career status; thus peasant soldiers resembled peasant citizens in their decidedly inferior position in the proletarian dictatorship, in the one case in relation to the officers, in the other in relation to proletarians and the white-collar bureaucrats. Frunze, in his very revealing remarks on discipline in the army, drew an analogy between the officer corps and the rank-and-file troops, on the one hand, and the vanguard Communist Party and the rest of society, on the other hand. In other words, by virtue of soldiers' relative lack of political maturity and wisdom, they were expected to obey officers in the same way that the mass of Soviet society should follow the lead of the Communist Party. Political instructors in the army repeated the formula of proletarian hegemony in the worker-peasant alliance to convey another truth of political life in Soviet Russia: that in a proletarian dictatorship, proletarians outranked peasants. Thus the soldiers shared the ambiguous status of the peasantry, whose uncertain future was at the heart of the Soviet leaders' dilemmas as they pondered alternative paths to an urban, industrial, socialist society. Still, wherever in the social structure they might be located, soldiers were clearly the beneficiaries of a special social contract according to which they traded their loyalty and service to the regime for material and status benefits in Soviet society at large. And it was to predominantly peasant soldiers that the Soviet state looked to extend its hegemony over the rest of society by inducing their fellow citizens to make great sacrifices toward the goal of a socialist order.

As army service became a key component of citizenship and political careers in the new state, so army service helped shape the state's own self-identity in crucial ways by contributing to the militarization of both the political elite and their ideology. Army veterans took home and into state institutions practices and attitudes that they had learned either in combat or in peacetime army service. When Trotsky lamented that the hundreds of thousands of military men who left the army after the Civil War "persistently introduced everywhere that regime which had ensured success in the Civil War,"[5] he meant that former soldiers would rather obey and issue orders in the name of unity than submit to democratic debate, election procedures, and tolerance of dissenting opinions. He also meant that after their army experience, these men were far more likely to resort to coercion and threat of armed force if problems arose. These former soldiers had received their basic ideas about the Revolution and socialism from their political instructors, but even more important, their fundamental familiarity with the new Soviet regime and its key institutions came by way of their military service. In their eyes, the methods and attitudes they learned in the army were no less revolutionary or socialist than those of the civilians in the party and state; in fact, veterans were very likely to view their version of socialism as more legitimate than any platform defended by one or another opposition group in the early years of the Soviet state. As a result, key postrevolutionary institutions bore the imprint of the Civil War circumstances, most notably the party organization, rural government, and non-Russian administration.

The militarization of Bolshevik political culture also had an ideological component. The militarized socialism that took shape in Soviet political culture was the result of an interpenetration of militarist and socialist values, and among its elements were a bellicist world view and the predominance of national security values and military interests in the economic and cultural life of the country. The militarization of political culture persisted beyond the Civil War years into the 1920s; it was present well before the "second rev-

5. Trotsky, *Revolution Betrayed*, pp. 89–90.

olution" of the first five-year plan.[6] During the Communist Party debates that followed the inauguration of the New Economic Policy,
when civilian critics branded the state's Civil War–era policies as
"war communism," the more militant Communists took up this
would-be term of opprobrium and praised the often harsh policies of
those years as the "heroic period of the Russian Revolution." For
these men and women, increasingly impatient with the halfhearted
compromise policies of the NEP retreat, socialist and military values
were inextricably interwoven; they saw no need to fear the values
that had given the proletarian dictatorship a military victory over its
earliest enemies.[7] Their critics among the Bolshevik civilian political elite considered militarism incompatible with socialist ideals.
The militarizers insisted that they were as sincere in their socialist
convictions as any civilian. They defended the militarization of civilian society with arguments of realpolitik buttressed by citations
from Marx, Engels, and Lenin, as well as the lessons learned in
nearly seven years of protracted warfare (1914–1921) on the territory
of the former Russian empire.

The transformation of Soviet socialism into its militarized or
Stalinist variant was not a matter of the army imposing its will on
an unwilling civilian political elite. Military or martial values could
not have come to occupy so prominent a place if they had not found
substantial resonance in the larger political culture of the Bolshevik
party and the state bureaucracy. If the early antisocialists were correct in identifying potentially authoritarian components in socialist
schemes for centralized economic planning and in the privileging
of "proletarian" consciousness, then the militarizers capitalized
precisely on those features of the socialist legacy to press their demands upon largely sympathetic party and state bureaucracies. For
nineteenth-century socialists, including and perhaps especially the
Bolsheviks, people who lived by exploiting others' labor for profit
were "bourgeois" or "petit bourgeois," or, in the countryside, "kulaks." To revolutionaries, by contrast, sacrifice of a comfortable personal life for the sacred socialist cause was a point of honor that set
them off from the philistines of liberal society. For their part, traditional military elites have, as a corollary of their own self-

6. For an example of the readiness to justify harsh coercive measures in the name
of socialism, see Trotsky's *Terrorism and Communism* (London: New Park, 1975; first
published in 1920 as *Terrorizm i kommunizm*), esp. chap. 8. In the 1920s the writings
and speeches of key military men stand out, esp. those of Mikhail Frunze, Mikhail
Tukhachevsky, and Kliment Voroshilov; but industrial administrators such as Valerian Kuibyshev and educational leaders such as Anatoly Lunacharsky also joined in
the campaign for militarization, as we saw in chaps. 5 and 6.

7. For an influential version of this defense of Civil War policies and values, see
Lev Kritsman, *Geroicheskii period velikoi russkoi revoliutsii (Opyt analiza t. n.
'voennogo kommunizma')* (Moscow, 1924).

legitimating ideology, looked at the civilian world of commerce, the profit motive, and individualism with contempt in what William Fuller calls "negative corporatism."[8] Most soldiers view the risk they take for the greater national good as a point of honor that distinguishes them from moneygrubbing civilians. Soviet public political culture in the 1920s shared much of this contempt. Even before the Revolution, Russian military and socialist cultures had shared a profound disdain for commercial activity, the profit motive, and the market economy. But during the Revolution and Civil War, Bolshevik socialism and Red Army military culture were fused in a new set of political attitudes and behavior that persisted throughout the 1920s.[9] Part of the new political culture appealed to military men; part appealed to many nonmilitary Bolshevik leaders.

Beyond matters of honor and self-image, the army had a very practical and considerable stake in the state's taking control over ever-larger parts of the national economy because it had to rely too often on unstable markets for many of its supplies. Here, too, the military's institutional interests overlapped with a certain kind of socialist world view that identified progress with central control over large-scale industrial enterprises and equated backwardness with the anarchy of market forces in an economy dominated by petty traders and workers. The industrialization debates of the 1920s were not only a struggle between advocates of moderate industrialization and those who were eager for a more "revolutionary" tempo. They were also competitions between the militarizers and the spokesmen for more civilian and consumer-oriented strategies.[10] After the center announced the successful completion of the second five-year plan of industrialization, the military got its reward. Great quantities of new hardware were diverted to the army to bring it up to world technical standards; the territorial militia units were phased out; by 1939 the regular army had grown to 1.3 million men and women, finally approaching the size of the Imperial Army on the eve of the Great War. In short, military professionals favored some aspects of the militarization of economic and political institutions, but certainly not all the schemes of the leadership, most notably those, such as collectiv-

8. Fuller, Civil–Military Conflict, pp. 26–29. Fuller applies "negative corporatism" to the last decades of the Imperial Army, but it also can describe those features of the Red Army that its critics identified as components of a restored caste mentality.

9. See Robert V. Daniels, "The Militarization of Socialism in Russia, 1902–1946," Occasional Paper no. 200 (Washington, D.C.: Kennan Institute for Advanced Russian Studies, 1985).

10. See Alexander Erlich, The Soviet Industrialization Debate, 1924–1928 (Cambridge: Harvard University Press, 1960), pp. 28–29, 37, 51, 68, 167–68, 180. Erlich's account gives only slight importance to issues of military preparedness in the debates.

ization, which threatened to undermine the effectiveness of their organization by pitting large parts of the civilian populace against
each other.

This discussion of militarized socialism is not meant to suggest
that military men were to blame for the mass repressions and other
horrors of the Stalin period, especially since so many military men
themselves suffered in the nationwide purges and terror. Nor is there
a simple causal relationship between military service and the stands
soldiers took on particular political issues. Among both the military
command and rank-and-file soldiers disagreements flared over the
nature of socialism and the correct methods for building it.[11] Those
disagreements very often replicated disputes in civilian political circles; moreover, many politically articulate actors in Soviet politics
outside the army shared the fundamental tenets of the national security consensus and the militarized socialism I have described. After all, the Stalin leadership justified the severe regime it pursued
during the 1930s, including the mass repressions, in the name of a
national security consensus. At the purge trials, charges of spying
for foreign powers and undermining the security of the Soviet state
were always near the top of the trumped-up accusations brought
against people tried and sentenced. The discourse of the show trials
of the 1930s is one example of the fundamental reorientation of political culture that had been occurring at least since the mid-1920s,
and arguably since 1917. Clearly not all sectors of society shared the
values of militarized socialism and the national security consensus,
nor did they share such values with equal degrees of enthusiasm;
nevertheless, those values did set the parameters of political debate
and the discussion of alternatives in broad areas of public life. It
is in this sense that I argue that Soviet socialism was a militarized
socialism.

One of the most important conclusions to emerge from this study
is that the militarization of Soviet society was the conscious aim of a
political leadership that is difficult to characterize as either purely
civilian or strictly military. Most of Stalin's closest allies from the
mid-1920s had held joint political and military authority during the
Civil War.[12] These Civil War veterans learned their statesmen's skills

11. For example, several high commanders objected both to collectivization as it
was implemented in the early 1930s and to the involvement of soldiers and veterans
in the collectivization campaign, while other military leaders demanded higher plan
targets and more army participation.
12. Among the full members of the Politburo through 1951, thirteen had held important positions during the Civil War. See George K. Schueller, "The Politburo," in
World Revolutionary Elites: Studies in Coercive Ideological Movements, ed. Harold D.
Lasswell and David Lerner (Cambridge: MIT Press, 1965), pp. 123–25. The members

under fire and frequently invoked national security issues in their speeches and writings. When these men were called upon to resolve the many social, economic, and political dilemmas that faced the regime, their rhetoric and solutions, not surprisingly, resembled those of military campaigns. The militarization of the new political elite was replicated throughout the Soviet state and party hierarchies and explains in great measure why a man such as Nikolai Bukharin stood little chance of playing a prominent role after the first years of Soviet power. Though Bukharin's politics and personality had their attractive aspects, he and his allies clearly stood for a party experience more civilian in tone than the Stalin cohort thought advisable.[13] His gradualism and reformism placed him at sharp odds with the authoritarian and voluntaristic inclinations of the rising new elite that looked to Stalin for leadership. Stalin, in breaking with Bukharin's prescriptions for Soviet Russia's ills, appealed to these men with simple slogans of direct action.

Any definition of the type of militarized socialism that characterized Soviet society and politics from at least the mid-1920s must take a complex of features into account. First, Soviet political and military elites shared a view of war and struggle as the norm for international and domestic relations at the current stage of historical development. Their views resembled and were related to the social Darwinist consensus about the inevitability of struggle which competed for primacy with liberalism in the European political and military culture at the turn of the century. And the Soviet world view, unlike the liberal world views that shaped discourse in such countries as Britain and the United States, according to which war was an aberration or a mistake, repudiated liberal pacifism as a dangerous illusion.

In contrast to the social Darwinists, however, the Soviet leaders formulated their own version of what Michael Howard has called "bellicist views"[14] with the theoretical apparatus of Marxism and Leninism and the lessons they had learned from the Great War and, more important, from the Civil War. This Marxist framework fundamentally distinguishes Soviet ideology from the militarism of fascism and Nazism, with which scholars and publicists have drawn explicit parallels. Significantly, what set the social Darwinist and Nazi views apart from the Marxist-Leninist consensus was the former's grounding in ahistorical biological or racial theories of human

---

of the reform commissions in 1923 and 1924 also formed a substantial core of the Stalin leadership: Andreev, Bubnov, Ordzhonikidze, Kuibyshev, Gusev, Unshlikht, Shvernik, and Voroshilov.

13. For the most compelling argument in favor of Bukharin's politics and personality, see Cohen, *Bukharin*.

14. Michael Howard, *Causes of Wars*, pp. 10–11, 157.

behavior and the latter's historical theory of class struggle. Like the social Darwinists, the Nazis believed that struggle was inevitable and desirable; they did not expect there would come a time when peace would triumph over war. The Bolsheviks, and Communists in general, believed that the victory of communism would mark the end of war and struggle, establishing the true brotherhood of the workers of the world. In other words, war was not a permanent end in itself, as it was for the Nazis and social Darwinists.

The prominence of these bellicist views among the Soviet leadership served as the basis for the consensus on national security values expressed in the contemporary term "capitalist encirclement." The Soviet leadership constantly appealed to society to make sacrifices for the defense of the socialist homeland. The bellicist component of nearly all major party and state spokesmen focused on the dangers of capitalist encirclement and reflected genuine fear that the unstable postwar settlement in Europe might break down. The interwar years witnessed the rise of militarist and fascist regimes in Central and Eastern Europe and Japan. Many of the new regimes came to power or sustained their rule with overtly anti-Bolshevik and anticommunist platforms.[15] The center knew all too well that if new hostilities erupted, the Red Army would not be able to repulse the invading forces of a major European power. Nor was Moscow confident in the support of its own populace in the event of a foreign invasion. Beyond the genuine threats posed by many of the nations that bordered the Soviet Union, the Soviet leadership had an ideological disposition, based on their Marxian perspective on international politics and affirmed in practice by the behavior of major European powers during the Civil War, to expect both new outbreaks of worldwide armed conflict and attempts to invade or overthrow the only socialist state in the world. The themes of army programs for political education clearly indicate the new leadership's confidence that it had won no small measure of legitimacy in the eyes of its populace by defeating the forces of international capital in the Civil War. The Soviet state was born out of protest against a major worldwide conflict and tempered in the fires of a civil war that drew in the forces of foreign belligerents. Finally, the political and military leadership often had been able to mobilize popular support and cooperation during the Civil War by appealing to patriotism. In short, the theme of national security, or capitalist encirclement, held

15. Besides the Soviet leaders' preoccupations with France and Britain, occasionally they also feared hostilities with Rumania, Poland, Japan, China, and Bulgaria. The Baltic states and Finland also harbored considerable resentment against the Soviet Republic and revanchist politicians in those states fared well in national contests.

a firm place in the center's appeals for popular support of its policies to militarize civilian life.

The national security culture legitimized near-universal conscription of male citizens for fixed terms of military service and high
rates of taxation to support the armed services and defense economy. Society was permanently mobilized for war, and all institutions of socialization and education were geared toward inculcating
military-patriotic virtues. The Soviet militarizers defended a political culture that placed very high value on personal sacrifice and
obedience. Whereas other societies could afford to indulge their citizens' material self-interest and to tolerate personal or family claims
on loyalty, the Soviet state had emerged from years of war as an
alarmingly vulnerable pawn in the international arena; only collective self-sacrifice could ensure the nation's survival in the wake of
the devastation of human and material resources.

Despite the militarizers' success in transforming Soviet political
culture, however, they never achieved a full-fledged militarism; that
had never been their aim. Rather, their achievement was a distinctive interpenetration of militarist and socialist values. To clarify the
specific features of Soviet militarized socialism, let us compare
civil–military relations in the Soviet Union with those in other regimes that historians and political scientists have characterized as
militarist.[16] First, the experience of the Red Army has much in common with that of armies in the non-European, nonindustrialized
world, where revolutionary elites have often embarked on ambitious
programs of political change and social transformation.[17] Outside of
Europe, national liberation movements have struggled against the
political domination of the imperial powers and often proclaimed
new political orders based on or borrowed from the teachings of
Marx and Lenin. The victory of the new orders depends heavily on
armed insurrection of the lower classes against other political elites
who advocate bourgeois or liberal constitutional settlements. In
most cases, the armies are called upon to play important roles in
nation and state building; furthermore, military service becomes
a crucial element in one's standing in the new political elite. The
Red Army, too, played a large role in shaping the character of the

16. A considerable and rich literature on civil–military relations began to appear in
the 1950s, including Samuel P. Huntington, *The Soldier and the State: The Theory
and Politics of Civil–Military Relations* (Cambridge: Harvard University Press, 1954);
S. E. Finer, *The Man on Horseback: The Role of the Military in Politics* (London: Pall
Mall, 1962); Morris Janowitz, *The Professional Soldier* (Chicago: Free Press, 1960);
Perlmutter, *Military and Politics*; and Stanislaw Andreski, *Military Organization and
Society* (Berkeley: University of California Press, 1971).

17. See Lucian W. Pye, "Armies in the Process of Political Modernization," in *The
Role of the Military in Underdeveloped Countries*, ed. John J. Johnson (Princeton:
Princeton University Press, 1962), pp. 69–90; and Finer, *Man on Horseback*.

Russian Revolution, which marked a transition from the European revolutions that overthrew the old regimes to the non-European revolutions of the twentieth century.[18] Many of the new states that have emerged from these twentieth-century revolutions share striking features with the Soviet state of the Stalin period, including one-party authoritarian political cultures and extensive state intervention for social and economic reform. The new states also typically assign very high priority to national security values in order to justify the maintenance of large standing armies and internal police forces.

One notable exception to this generalization has been the experience of most Latin American military regimes, which offer some instructive contrasts that highlight key aspects of the Soviet case. After all, many militarist regimes have been content with attaining hegemony in the political life of the country, justifying their authoritarian or repressive orders by appealing to patriotism and arguments of national security but still permitting markets to function in economic and some cultural spheres. During much of modern Latin American history, when the military has seized power for itself, it has done so after political and economic crisis has undermined the fragile balance of civil–military relations which had buttressed civilian rule; military juntas typically have taken over civilian functions but backed old national elites and their conservative agendas, leaving economic decision making and social structures largely intact. Military regimes have presided over conservative authoritarian orders and limited their ideologies, when they formulated ideologies at all, to preservation of the status quo.[19]

The Soviet leadership, by contrast, pursued an unprecedentedly thoroughgoing militarization of the national economy and culture by combining features of military ethos and organization with certain features of socialism, as well as a new Soviet patriotism that borrowed heavily from imperial Russian political culture. In the second half of the 1920s, when influential groups in the political leadership increasingly came to characterize the economic, social, and political situation as a crisis, the military per se never stepped in to assume power to resolve the crisis. Instead, a group of militarized political leaders who had coalesced around Stalin pursued a ruthless program of economic modernization and state building in the name of national defense and socialism. The political leaders did not rely on the political, military, and economic elites of imperial Russia, but to a large extent created their own power base by promoting loyal

18. For a statement about the transitional nature of the Russian Revolution, see Martin Malia, *Comprendre la Révolution russe* (Paris: Seuil, 1980), pp. 32–33.

19. See Alfred Stepan, *The Military in Politics: Changing Patterns in Brazil* (Princeton: Princeton University Press, 1971); and his *Rethinking Military Politics: Brazil and the Southern Cone* (Princeton: Princeton University Press, 1988).

workers, peasants, and soldiers into a new hybrid political class, which included some managerial personnel from the old regime. The original ideology of the new elite was authoritarian but not conservative, at least not in the sense of resurrecting or preserving the political and social power of the former elites. Later, by the mid-1930s, the new elite acquiesced in a more conservative political culture, but only because political, social, and economic power had already been radically transformed.

The regime most frequently said to parallel the Soviet state has been Hitler's Third Reich. Here, too, however, the differences are more striking than the similarities. When the Nazis came to power in Germany, they did not systemically destroy the professional army; rather the Nazis preserved most of the officer corps and many of the traditions of the Reichswehr. As the army's professionalism and esprit de corps limited the Nazis' ability to penetrate its elite, Hitler set about to co-opt the military along with other German social and economic elites. Military men did not take over civilian political and economic roles, but performed traditional tasks of national defense. Moreover, Nazi bellicism differed from the Soviet variant not only in its appeals to racialist and biological arguments, but also in its openly expansionist and imperialist aims. Large numbers of German officers did not share the ideological proclivities of the party leadership, but nevertheless continued to serve the German Reich as loyal soldiers. Neither did the Nazis have to create a whole network of institutions to socialize their population in the values of the political elite. Instead, through the process of *Gleichschaltung*, new paramilitary organizations—such as the Gestapo and the SS—succeeded in diverting previously autonomous labor organizations, schools, and youth movements to the service of the party and state.[20]

Despite the prominent role that former imperial officers and NCOs played in the early years, the Bolsheviks did not try to preserve the structure, traditions, or personnel of the Imperial Army after the first confused weeks in power. In any event, the professional cohesion of the Imperial Army broke under the strains of the Great War and the Civil War. Large numbers of former officers joined the White movement; many others joined the Bolsheviks very soon after 1917; still others cast their lot with the revolutionary elite later in the Civil War. As a result, the former Russian military elite could not withstand the Communist Party's encroachments on their professional autonomy in the same way that the Reichswehr officer corps

20. For a discussion of Nazi techniques of cooptation and subversion of existing social and cultural organizations, see William Sheridan Allen, *The Nazi Seizure of Power: The Experience of a Single German Town, 1930–1935* (New York: New Viewpoints, 1973), esp. pp. 213–26.

was able to do. The Red Army was genuinely an army of a new type that reflected the new social and political structures of postrevolutionary Soviet Russia. Once the army had attained a measure of legitimacy in the Soviet political and social orders, the old military elite that survived in a much expanded Soviet officer corps was able to exert greater influence in shaping Red Army traditions. They succeeded in, say, reviving Russian nationalism and Great Power ideology only to the extent that their attitudes and practices found a resonance in the political culture of the army and party elites. The army in which they played an important but not decisive role differed greatly from the Imperial Army. For all their purported and genuine similarities, the Red Army was not the Imperial Army, just as the Soviet state was not the imperial bureaucracy and the social structure of the proletarian dictatorship was not that of the imperial autocracy.

In the Soviet Union, the peculiar mixture of deference to military needs, promotion of military values, and distinct constraints on military professionalism stemmed from the novel form of civil–military relations that the Bolshevik leadership devised with the creation of the Red Army. That relationship was grounded in the attitude of the political leadership toward the army as a favored helpmate in their ambitious schemes for state building. The role of the army in building a new state structure was not new in either Russian or European history. On the contrary, some early modern European states, most notably in Prussia and among the condottieri in Italy, were often little more than military organizations with tax-collecting bureaucracies. Later the *levée en masse* of the French Revolution and the victories of Napoleon linked universal military conscription and citizenship in ways that challenged all the European monarchies and eventually the rest of the world as well.[21] In Russia, too, every major transformation in the political and social structures was inextricably bound up with changes in military affairs, especially in the sphere of service requirements. The process of enserfment, Peter the Great's reforms, and the Great Reforms of the second half of the nineteenth century all bore the imprint of military exigencies, and each of them redefined the obligations of military service and, by extension, of social status in fundamental ways.[22]

21. Otto Hintze, "Military Organization and State Organization," in *The Historical Essays of Otto Hintze*, ed. Felix Gilbert (New York: Oxford University Press, 1975), pp. 180–215; and Howard, "War and the Nation State" and "War in the Making and Unmaking of Europe," both in *Causes of Wars*.

22. See Richard Hellie, *Enserfment and Military Change in Muscovy* (Chicago: University of Chicago Press, 1971), esp. pts. I and III; V. O. Kliuchevskii, *Peter the Great*, trans. L. Archibald (New York: Vintage, 1961); Pavel Miliukov, *Gosudarstvennoe khoziaistvo v Rossii v pervoi chetverti XVIII stoletiia i reforma Petra Velikogo* (St. Petersburg, 1892); Elise Kimerling, "Soldiers' Children, 1719–1856: A Study of Social

After 1917 the Bolsheviks faced a problem very similar to one that had vexed imperial bureaucrats before them, the "underinstitutionalization" or "undergovernment" of the country, especially the countryside.[23] Throughout the 1920s the party remained weak and the soviet administrative network ineffective. As a result, the center relied on the trade unions, Komsomol, the party, and, of course, the army to provide the loyal cadres needed to fill its national and local bureaucracies. The army played a fundamental role in state building and nation building as a working environment that brought together representatives of all social groups entitled to Soviet citizenship, as well as many of the diverse national groups that made up the Soviet Union. Stalin described the army as "the only nationwide [vserossiiskii] and statewide [vsefederativnyi] place of assembly, where people of various provinces and regions come together, study, and accustom themselves to political life"; furthermore, the army was "a school" and "a great apparatus linking the party with the workers and the poor peasantry."[24] Stalin was not alone in recognizing the soldiers' role in disseminating the state's agenda and executing its will across the country; spokesmen across the political spectrum praised the army as a "school of socialism." Soldiers learned the rhetoric of the new elite; they learned the ropes of party and soviet administrative bodies; they became acquainted with urban and industrial lifestyles. If they were ambitious, they could use their skills and knowledge to advance their careers and rise to positions of authority. Even if they had little interest in furthering the state's goals and simply wanted to improve their material situation at home, the army's political staff instructed them in the essential bureaucratic skills.

Active-duty soldiers, veterans, and the militarized political elite were the key actors in the process of the interpenetration of militarist and socialist values; they also articulated the intricately intertwined interests of the Red Army and the Soviet state and its many political institutions and organizations. The central leadership, in pursuit of its program of militarized socialism, placed military needs at the top of its list of economic priorities by the end of the first five-year plan. Patriotic and military virtues came to dominate

Engineering in Imperial Russia," Forschungen zur Osteuropäischen Geschichte 30 (1982): 61–136; Keep, Soldiers of the Tsar. Interestingly, Trotsky saw a direct link between his work in the army and Peter the Great's reforms; see "Stroitel'stvo krasnoi vooruzhennoi sily," 28 November 1920, in KVR, vol. 2, pt. 1, p. 122.

23. See S. Frederick Starr, Decentralization and Self-Government in Russia, 1830–1870 (Princeton: Princeton University Press, 1972). Bolshevik rhetoric renders state building as "soviet building" or "soviet construction" (sovetskoe stroitel'stvo).

24. Stalin, "Organizatsionnyi otchet Tsentral'nogo Komiteta RKP (b)," 17 April 1923 in Sochineniia, 5:205.

education and culture.[25] In a symbolically important move, Andrei Bubnov left his job as director of PUR to replace Anatoly Lunacharsky as commissar of enlightenment in 1929.[26] And the military benefited in more direct ways from the center's attentions. Against the backdrop of a series of new titles and honorary awards, military and naval ranks for officers were restored, as well as several privileges for officers, including immunity from prosecution by civilian judicial organs.

But just as the economy and social structure of the Soviet state in the 1920s posed limits to the ambitious plans of the army high command, so the much-transformed Red Army of the late 1920s opened opportunities for certain kinds of state-building activities while setting clear limits on others, such as collectivization. Recall that the military professionals had upheld the special interests of the army in opposing the compromise between a territorial militia and a regular army. The provisional resolution of the question of military organization was very much a part of the unstable political, social, and economic compromises that grew out of the NEP settlement. Just as the center tried to preserve a healthy balance between the state and private economic sectors, all the while unhappy with the arrangement and looking forward to the day when the state sector would triumph definitively over the capitalist market, so the military leadership was saddled with a compromise it resented—the mixed system of territorial militia and regular army. And the political leadership in turn defended the mixed system by arguing that the weak national economy was unable to support a full-size regular army. As long as the Soviet economy was based on small-scale peasant agriculture and a narrow industrial sector, the military command had to postpone its dreams of a genuine army.

The collectivization campaign offers other lessons for both army and state. The army did more than just survive the ordeal, for soldiers, political staff, and officers played an active and crucial role in the campaign to transform the countryside. In early 1930 Bukharin condemned the system of collectivized agriculture as a new version of "the military-feudal exploitation of the peasantry."[27] Despite Stalin's insistence that collectivization was the only means to guarantee the cities and army adequate food supplies at a time of heightened

25. In 1934 treason against the motherland (*rodina*) became a capital offense for the first time; a newspaper editorial announcing the new law declared that every Soviet citizen ought to love the motherland. For more on changes in culture and education during the 1930s, see Nicholas S. Timasheff, *The Great Retreat* (New York: Dutton, 1946).

26. Vladimir Zatonskii made a similar move out of military-political work to become commissar of enlightenment in the Ukraine.

27. Cohen cites Molotov, "Na dva fronta," *Bol'shevik* 2 (31 January 1930): 14, as the source for Bukharin's charges, in *Bukharin*, p. 452, n. 158.

international tensions,[28] the role of demobilized soldiers gave more than a kernel of truth to the Right Opposition's critique. Where farmers had once engaged in small-scale private or cooperative enterprises and sold their surpluses on the free market, soldier-farmers obeyed, or were meant to obey, directives from planners in large rural administrative agencies. The participation of soldiers accounted for the short-term success of the collectivization campaign in breaking the resistance of the peasantry, but their resort to "administrative methods" in agriculture also contributed to the long-term failure of the center to create a productive rural economic sector. Moreover, the mobilization of tens of thousands of soldiers for the collectivization drive diverted precious resources from regular training activities and threatened to undermine the Red Army's combat readiness and troop morale at a time when an attack from Poland appeared imminent. The threat provoked a strongly worded and widespread demand among the top military command that collectivization be halted before it ruined the country.

In summary, the Red Army, by virtue of its institutional and professional imperatives, decisively limited this ultimate project of the state. At the same time, the army opened up opportunities for radical state intervention in society; from its earliest days it had played an important role, as a "school of socialism," in sociopolitical training and cadre formation. In collectivization as in nearly every major political undertaking in the 1920s, soldiers provided crucial aid to the proletarian dictatorship in its "primitive accumulation of legitimacy." They helped build the state's institutional structure and shaped the political culture that would usher in the era of Soviet socialism.

---

28. See Stalin's answer to the Right Opposition in "O pravom uklone v VKP (b)," in *Sochineniia,* 12:51–56. In the mid-1920s writers on the defense economy linked the collectivization of agriculture to preparations for a future war. See Checinski, "Economics of Defense," p. 74. Checinski cites the following articles as evidence for his claim: A. Karpushin-Zorin, "Podgotovka sel'skogo khoziaistva k obespecheniiu armii i naseleniia vo vremia voiny," *Voina i revoliutsiia* 7–8 (1925): 114–21, and "Mirovaia voina i prodovol'stvennyi vopros," *Voina i revoliutsiia* 8 (1926): 80–92; and S. Ventsov, *Narodnoe khoziaistvo i oborona SSSR* (Moscow/Leningrad, 1928), pp. 66ff.

Bibliography

Archival Sources

Smolensk Archives: The records of the Western Regional Committee of the Communist Party of the Soviet Union; see the guide *Records of the Smolensk Oblast of the All-Union Communist Party of the Soviet Union, 1917–41.* Washington, D.C.: National Archives and Records Service, 1980.

Newspapers and Periodicals

Bednota. Moscow.
Biulleten' Politicheskogo upravleniia Revvoensoveta Respubliki: Prikazy, tsirkuliary i instruktsii. Moscow.
Biulleten' Vserossiiskogo biuro voennykh komissarov. Moscow.
Izvestiia. Moscow.
Kommunisticheskoe prosveshchenie. Moscow.
Krasnaia armiia. Samara.
Krasnaia prisiaga. Smolensk.
Krasnaia rota. Kharkov.
Krasnaia zvezda. Moscow.
Krasnoarmeets. Moscow.
Krasnoarmeiskaia pechat'. Moscow.
Krasnoarmeiskii bibliotekar'. Moscow.
Krasnoarmeiskii spravochnik. Moscow.
Krasnyi boets. Tiflis.
Krasnyi kursant. Petrograd.
Krasnyi strelok. Smolensk.
Na strazhe. Leningrad.
Politrabotnik. Moscow.
Politrabotnik Sibiri. Omsk.
Politvestnik. Moscow.

Pravda. Moscow.
Put' politrabotnika. Kharkov.
Revoliutsionnaia voina. Petrograd.
Sputnik politrabotnika. Moscow.
Statisticheskoe obozrenie. Moscow.
Tolmachevets. Leningrad.
Vestnik statistiki. Moscow.
Voennoe znanie. Moscow.
Voennyi vestnik. Moscow.
Vooruzhennyi narod. Petrograd/Moscow.
Zhurnalist. Moscow.

Official Publications

Dekrety Sovetskoi vlasti. 12 vols. Moscow, 1957–1986.
Desiat' let Krasnoi Armii: Al'bom diagramm. Moscow, 1928.
Desiatyi s''ezd RKP (b), mart 1921 goda: Stenograficheskii otchet. Moscow, 1963.
Deviataia konferentsiia RKP (b), sentiabr' 1920 goda: Protokoly. Moscow, 1972.
Deviatyi s''ezd RKP (b), mart–aprel' 1920 goda: Protokoly. Moscow, 1960.
Direktivy komandovaniia frontov Krasnoi Armii, 1917–1922 gg. 4 vols. Moscow, 1971–1978.
Distsiplinarnyi ustav Raboche-Krest'ianskoi Krasnoi Armii. Petrograd, 1922.
Dvenadtsatyi s''ezd RKP (b), 17–25 aprelia 1923 goda: Stenograficheskii otchet. Moscow, 1968.
Dvukhletniaia programma politzaniatii s krasnoarmeitsami: Sbornik prikazov i tsirkuliarov Politicheskogo Upravleniia RKKA SSSR. Moscow, 1928.
Iz istorii grazhdanskoi voiny v SSSR. 3 vols. Moscow, 1960–1961.
KPSS i stroitel'stvo vooruzhennykh sil SSSR. Moscow, 1959.
KPSS o vooruzhennykh silakh Sovetskogo Soiuza: Dokumenty, 1917–1968. Moscow, 1969.
KPSS o vooruzhennykh silakh Sovetskogo Soiuza: Dokumenty, 1917–1981. Moscow, 1981.
KPSS v rezoliutsiiakh i resheniiakh s''ezdov, konferentsii i plenumov TsK. Vols. 2, 3, 5. Moscow, 1970.
Materialy soveshchaniia po vneshkol'noi rabote v RKKA. Moscow, 1927.
Odinnadtsatyi s''ezd RKP (b), mart–aprel' 1922 goda: Stenograficheskii otchet. Moscow, 1961.
Oktiabr'skaia revoliutsiia i armiia: Sbornik dokumentov. Moscow, 1973.
Otchet Narkomvoenmora za 1922/23 g. Moscow, 1925.
Otchet Narkomvoenmora za 1924/25 g. Moscow, 1926.
Otchet o deiatel'nosti Otdela voennoi literatury pri RVSR i Vysshego voennogo redaktsionnogo soveta: S 1 ianv. 1921 g. po 31 dek. 1922 g. Moscow, 1923.
Otchet o deiatel'nosti Politicheskogo otdela RVS 6-i armii s 1 ianv. po 1 apr. 1921 g. Kherson, 1921.
Otchet Politicheskogo upravleniia Leningradskogo voennogo okruga: Mai 1923 g.–mai 1924 g. Leningrad, 1924.
Partiino-politicheskaia rabota v Krasnoi Armii (aprel' 1918–fevral' 1919): Dokumenty. Moscow, 1961.

Partiino-politicheskaia rabota v Krasnoi Armii (mart 1919–1920 gg.): Dokumenty. Moscow, 1964.

Partiino-politicheskaia rabota v Krasnoi Armii: Dokumenty, 1921–1929. Moscow, 1981.

Partiino-politicheskaia rabota v Krasnoi Armii: Dokumenty, iiul' 1929 g.– mai 1941 g. Moscow, 1985.

Perepiska sekretariata TsK RKP (b) s mestnymi partiinymi organizatsiiami. Moscow, 1957–1972.

Perevybory v sovety RSFSR v 1925–1926 gg. Moscow, 1926.

Piatnadtsatyi s"ezd VKP (b), dekabr' 1927 goda: Stenograficheskii otchet. Moscow, 1962.

Plamennoe slovo: Listovki grazhdanskoi voiny (1918–1922 gg.). Moscow, 1967.

Politicheskii ustav Krasnoi Armii i Flota. 2d ed. Petrograd, n.d.

Rezoliutsii partkonferentsii chastei Petrukraiona i spetschastei P. V. O. proiskhodivshei s 15–18 dek. 1921 g. Petrograd, 1922.

Sbornik materialov III Vsesoiuznogo soveshchaniia po politrabote v Krasnoi Armii i Flote. Moscow, 1924.

Sbornik prikazov i tsirkuliarov PU RKKA SSSR no. 15: Dvukhletniaia programma politzaniatii s krasnoarmeitsami. Moscow, 1927.

Sbornik prikazov i tsirkuliarov PU RKKA SSSR no. 21: Dvukhletniaia programma politzaniatii s krasnoarmeitsami s ob"iasnitel'noi zapiskoi. Moscow, 1925.

Sbornik prikazov RVS SSSR. Moscow, 1924.

Sbornik statei po partiinoi i politprosvetrabote v Krasnoi Armii i Flote v mirnoe vremia (k 3-mu soveshchaniiu politrabotnikov Krasnoi Armii i Flota SSSR). Moscow, 1923.

S"ezdy sovetov Soiuza SSR, soiuznykh i avtonomnykh sovetskikh sotsalisticheskikh respublik: Sbornik dokumentov, 1917–1937 gg. 7 vols. Moscow, 1959–1965.

Shestoi s"ezd Leninskogo kommunisticheskogo soiuza molodezhi: Stenograficheskii otchet, 12–18 iiulia 1924 g. Moscow/Leningrad, 1924.

Soveshchanie sekretarei iacheek pri PURe: Stenograficheskii otchet. Moscow, 1925.

Trinadtsatyi s"ezd RKP (b), mai 1924 goda: Stenograficheskii otchet. Moscow, 1963.

Tsirkuliary i instruktsii Politupravleniia Turkestanskogo Fronta. Tashkent, 1921.

V. I. Lenin i VChK: Sbornik dokumentov, 1917–1922 gg. Moscow, 1975.

VLKSM v rezoliutsiiakh ego s"ezdov i konferentsii, 1918–1928. Moscow, 1929.

Vos'moi s"ezd RKP (b), mart 1919 goda: Protokoly. Moscow, 1959.

Vremennyi ustav vnutrennei sluzhby RKKA (1924). Moscow, 1935.

Vsearmeiskie soveshchaniia politrabotnikov, 1918–1940 (rezoliutsii). Moscow, 1984.

Vserossiiskoe soveshchanie po agitrabote v Krasnoi Armii i Flote. Moscow, 1922.

Vsesoiuznoe soveshchanie nachpuokrov, nachpuflotov, voenkomkorov, voenkomdivov i nachpodivov, 17–22 noiabria 1924 g.: Stenograficheskii otchet. Moscow, 1924.

Contemporary Russian-Language Sources

Belitskii, S., V. Popov, and N. Beliaev, eds. *Besedy o voennom dele i Krasnoi armii: Sbornik dlia kruzhkov voennykh znanii na fabrikakh, zavodakh, pri klubakh i shkolakh.* 2d ed. Moscow, 1928.

Bol'shakov, A. M. *Derevnia, 1917–1927.* Moscow, 1927.

Bronin, Iakov G. *Politgramota komsomol'tsa: Uchebnik dlia komsomol'-skikh politshkol pervoi stupeni.* Moscow/Leningrad, 1927.

Brykin, N. *V novoi derevne: Ocherki derevenskogo byta.* Leningrad, 1925.

Burov, Ia. I. *Derevnia na perelome.* Moscow/Leningrad, 1926.

Danishevskii, Karl. *Revoliutsionnye voennye tribunaly.* Moscow, 1920.

Degtiarev, Leonid S. *Politrabota v Krasnoi Armii.* Leningrad, 1925.

Denikin, Anton. *Ocherki russkoi smuty.* 5 vols. Paris, n.d.

Dobrovol'skii, A., N. Sokolov, and A. Speranskii. *Organizatsiia i tekhnika protsessa priema novobrantsev v otdel'noi voiskovoi chasti.* Moscow, 1925.

Dushak, Andrei I. *Metodika i organizatsiia partiinogo prosveshcheniia.* Moscow, 1927.

Evdokimov, E. L. *Politicheskie zaniatiia v Krasnoi Armii.* Leningrad, 1933.

Frunze, Mikhail V. *Na novykh putiakh.* Moscow, 1925.

——. *Sobranie sochinenii.* 3 vols. Moscow/Leningrad, 1926–1929.

Geller, Iosif I. *Krasnaia armiia na fronte kollektivizatsii.* Samara, 1930.

Grigorov, G. *Otpuskniki v derevne.* Leningrad, 1926.

Gurvich, G. S. *Istoriia Sovetskoi Konstitutsii.* Moscow, 1923.

Gusev, Sergei I. *Uroki grazhdanskoi voiny.* Moscow, 1921.

Iakovlev, Iakov. *Derevnia, kak ona est'.* Moscow, 1923.

Ivanovich, S. (V. I. Talin). *Krasnaia armiia.* Paris: Sovremennye zapiski, 1931.

Karatygin, P. *Obshchie osnovy mobilizatsii promyshlennosti dlia nuzhd voiny.* Moscow, 1925.

Kardash, G. *Kommuna Lenina v Primor'e.* Khabarovsk, 1932.

Kartsevskii, S. I. *Iazyk, voina i revoliutsiia.* Berlin: Russkoe universal'noe izdatel'stvo, 1923.

Kiriukhin, N. I. *Iz dnevnika voennogo komissara.* Moscow, 1928.

Kokorin, M. A. *Voennaia rabota partiinoi iacheiki.* Moscow/Leningrad, 1929.

Korol', M. *Voprosy voenno-politicheskogo vospitaniia v Krasnoi Armii.* Moscow/Leningrad, 1927.

Kosmin, E. *Politicheskaia rabota v territorial'nykh chastiakh.* Moscow/Leningrad, 1928.

Krasnaia armiia i oborona Sovetskogo soiuza. Moscow, 1925.

Krasnaia Armiia v 1924 g. i "Krasnaia zvezda." Moscow, 1925.

Kratkii ocherk kul'turno-politicheskoi raboty v Krasnoi Armii za 1918 god. Moscow, 1919.

Kritsman, Lev. *Geroicheskii period velikoi russkoi revoliutsii (Opyt analiza t. n. 'voennogo kommunizma').* Moscow, 1924.

Kudrin, N. *Sovetskoe stroitel'stvo na sele i zadachi krasnoarmeitsa-otpusknika.* Moscow, 1925.

Kuznetsov, I. *Metodika politzaniatii v Krasnoi Armii.* Moscow, 1927.

Libedinskii, Iurii. *Komissary.* Moscow/Leningrad, 1927.

Machajski, Jan Waclaw. *Bankrotstvo sotsializma XIX stoletiia.* N.p., 1905.

——. *Umstvennyi rabochii.* Geneva, 1904.

Mikhailov, Semen. *Brigadnaia roshcha*. 2d ed. Leningrad, 1930.
Mikula, M., ed. *Demobilizovannye na derevenskoi rabote: Krasnoarmeiskie pis'ma*. Moscow, 1926.
Miliukov, Pavel. *Gosudarstvennoe khoziaistvo v Rossii v pervoi chetverti XVIII stoletiia i reforma Petra Velikogo*. St. Petersburg, 1892.
Movchin, M. *Komplektovanie Krasnoi Armii*. Moscow, 1928.
Movetskii, M. *Krasnaia armiia i MOPR*. Moscow, 1926.
Narodnoe khoziaistvo Soiuza SSR v tsifrakh: Statisticheskii spravochnik. Moscow, 1925.
Nashi raznoglasiia v voennom dele. Moscow, 1925.
Oborona strany i grazhdanskaia shkola. Ed. L. S. Degtiarev and N. F. Artemenko. Moscow/Leningrad, 1927.
Olikov, S. *Dezertirstvo v Krasnoi Armii i bor'ba s nim*. Leningrad, 1926.
Petrovskii, David A. *Voennaia shkola v gody revoliutsii*. Moscow, 1924.
Podvoiskii, Nikolai, and M. Pavlovich, eds. *Revoliutsionnaia voina*. Moscow, 1919.
Pod znakom revoliutsii. Harbin, 1927.
Polev, N. *Komandnyi sostav RKKA i inostrannykh armii*. Leningrad, 1927.
Ritman, M. *Pylaiushchie budni krasnoarmeiskoi agitkolonny v sotsialisticheskom pereustroistve derevni*. Moscow, 1930.
Selishchev, A. *Iazyk revoliutsionnoi epokhi: Iz nabliudenii nad russkim iazykom poslednikh let, 1917–1926*. Moscow, 1926.
Shafir, Ia. *Gazeta i derevnia*. Moscow, 1923.
Shaposhnikov, Boris M. *Mozg armii*. 3 vols. Moscow, 1927–1929.
Shaposhnikov, R. *Osnovy politicheskoi raboty v RKKA*. Leningrad, 1927.
Shpil'rein, I. N., D. I. Reitynbarg, and G. O. Netskii. *Iazyk krasnoarmeitsa*. Moscow/Leningrad, 1928.
Smena vekh. Prague, 1921.
Sovetskaia azbuka. Moscow, 1919.
Sputnik molodogo komandira. Moscow, 1927.
Sumskoi, N. *Komsomol'skaia rabota v Krasnoi Armii*. Moscow/Leningrad, 1929.
Suzdal'tseva, V. I. (Tagunova). *Partiinaia rabota na Severnom Fronte*. Archangel, 1926.
Svechin, Aleksandr A. *Strategiia*. 2d ed. Moscow, 1927.
Tal', V. *Istoriia Krasnoi armii*. Moscow/Leningrad, 1929.
Tishchenko, I. P. *Istoriia organizatsii i praktiki voennoi kooperatsii Sibiri*. Novonikolaevsk, 1922.
Triandafillov, Vladimir K. *Kharakter operatsii sovremennykh armii*. Moscow, 1929.
Trotskii, Lev D. *Kak vooruzhalas' revoliutsiia*. 3 vols. Moscow, 1923–1925.
——. *Literatura i revoliutsiia*. Moscow, 1923.
——. *Novyi kurs*. Moscow, 1924.
——. *Ob "Urokakh Oktiabria."* Leningrad, 1924.
——. *Voprosy byta*. Moscow, 1923.
——. *Za Leninizm*. Leningrad, 1925.
Tukhachevskii, Mikhail N. *Voprosy sovremennoi strategii*. Moscow, 1926.
Voennaia rabota komsomola: Sbornik statei. Moscow/Leningrad, 1927.
Voroshilov, Kliment E. *Oborona SSSR: Izbrannye stat'i, rechi i pis'ma*. Moscow, 1937.
——. *Stat'i i rechi*. Moscow, 1937.
Vyrvich, A. *Krasnaia armiia v bor'be s negramotnost'iu*. Moscow, 1925.

Za chto borolis': Rasskazy krasnoarmeitsev-otpusknikov i ikh druzei o nashei bor'be za sotsializm i ob uchastii krasnoarmeitsev-otpusknikov v bor'be za sotsialisticheskoe pereustroistvo derevni. Moscow/Leningrad, 1928.
Zorin, B. P. *Krasnaia Armiia i oborona SSSR.* Moscow/Leningrad, 1926.

Dissertations

Agafonov, Georgii S. "Kommunisticheskaia partiia—organizator aktivnogo uchastiia Krasnoi Armii v sotsialisticheskom preobrazovanii derevni v 1926–1932 gg. (na materialakh Ukrainy)." Candidate's dissertation, Lenin Military Political Academy, Moscow, 1976.
Bedzhanian, R. M. "Kommunisticheskaia partiia—organizator aktivnogo uchastiia Krasnoi Armii v sotsialisticheskom stroitel'stve (1918–1932)." Doctoral dissertation, Lenin Military Political Academy, Moscow, 1969.
Chausov, P. Kh. "Rol' Krasnoi armii v kolkhoznom stroitel'stve na Dal'nem Vostoke v 1927–1932 gg." Candidate's dissertation, Irkutsk State University, 1966.
Khripunov, Vil' K. "Kul'turnaia rabota v Krasnoi Armii v 20-e gody (po materialam Sibirskogo voennogo okruga)." Doctoral dissertation, Novosibirsk State University, 1977.
McDonald, David MacLaren. "Autocracy, Bureaucracy, and Change in the Formation of Russian Foreign Policy (1895–1914): 'United Government' and Russian Diplomacy during the 'Crisis of Autocracy.' " Ph. D. dissertation, Columbia University, 1987.
Makeikina, R. P. "Kul'turnoe stroitel'stvo v Novgorodskoi gubernii v 1921–1927 gg." Candidate's dissertation, Hertsen Pedagogical Institute, Leningrad, 1972.
Pikha, Dmitrii. "Bor'ba Kommunisticheskoi partii za ukreplenie Sovetskikh Vooruzhennykh Sil v 1924–1928 godakh (na materialakh Ukrainskogo voennogo okruga i partiinykh organizatsii Ukrainy)." Candidate's dissertation, Kiev State University, 1964.
Shevchenko, Ivan. "Ideino-politicheskoe vospitanie lichogo sostava Leningradskogo voennogo okruga v gody voennoi reformy (1924–1925 gg)." Candidate's dissertation, Leningrad Higher Party School, 1979.

Russian-Language Sources Published since 1945

Alferov, V. N. *Vozniknovenie i razvitie rabsel'korovskogo dvizheniia v SSSR.* Moscow, 1970.
Andreev, V. M. *Pod znamenem proletariata.* Moscow, 1981.
Aralov, Semen I. *V. I. Lenin i Krasnaia Armiia.* Moscow, 1969.
Berkhin, Il'ia B. *Voennaia reforma v SSSR, 1924–1925.* Moscow, 1958.
Bonch-Bruevich, Mikhail D. *Vsia vlast' sovetam.* Moscow, 1957.
Bugai, N. F. *Revkomy.* Moscow, 1981.
Chkhikvadze, V. M. *Sovetskoe voenno-ugolovnoe pravo.* Moscow, 1948.
Chmyga, A. F. *Ocherki po istorii kolkhoznogo dvizheniia na Ukraine (1921–1925).* Moscow, 1959.
Elagin, Iurii. *Temnyi genii (Vsevolod Meierkhol'd).* 2d ed. London: Overseas Publications Interchange, 1982.

El'kina, Dora Iu. "Likvidatsiia negramotnosti v Krasnoi Armii na frontakh grazhdanskoi voiny." *Narodnoe obrazovanie* 12 (1957): 52–56.

Fediukin, S. A. *Bor'ba s burzhuaznoi ideologiei v usloviiakh perekhoda k NEPu.* Moscow, 1977.

——. *Sovetskaia vlast' i burzhuaznye spetsialisty.* Moscow, 1965.

——. *Velikii Oktiabr' i intelligentsiia.* Moscow, 1972.

Fevral'skii, Aleksandr. *Zapiski rovesnika veka.* Moscow, 1976.

Frenkin, Mikhail. *Russkaia armiia i revoliutsiia.* Munich, 1978.

——. *Zakhvat vlasti bol'shevikami v Rossii i rol' tylovykh garnizonov armii.* Jerusalem: Stav, 1982.

Frunze, Mikhail V. *Izbrannye proizvedeniia.* Moscow, 1940, 1957 (2 vols.), 1965, 1977.

——. "Ob itogakh reorganizatsii Krasnoi Armii." *Voenno-istoricheskii zhurnal* (1966): 66–75 and 8 (1966): 64–72.

Gimpel'son, Efim G. *Sovety v gody interventsii i grazhdanskoi voiny.* Moscow, 1968.

Gorodetskii, Efim N. "Demobilizatsiia armii v 1917–1918 gg." *Istoriia SSSR* 1 (1958): 3–31.

——. *Rozhdenie Sovetskogo gosudarstva.* Moscow, 1965.

Grazhdanskaia voina v SSSR v dvukh tomakh. Moscow, 1980.

Gromakov, A., "Deiatel'nost' Kommunisticheskoi partii po ukrepleniiu Krasnoi Armii v 1921–1923 gg." *Voenno-istoricheskii zhurnal* 2 (1973): 84–88.

Gusev, Sergei I. *Grazhdanskaia voina i Krasnaia Armiia: Sbornik statei.* Moscow, 1958.

Istoriia sovetskogo krest'ianstva. 3 vols. Moscow, 1986–1987.

Iurkov, Ivan A. *Ekonomicheskaia politika partii v derevne, 1917–1920.* Moscow, 1980.

Iz istorii grazhdanskoi voiny i interventsii, 1917–1922. Moscow, 1974.

Iz istorii rabochego klassa i revoliutsionnogo dvizheniia. Moscow, 1958.

Kardashov, Vladislav. *Voroshilov.* Moscow, 1976.

Kavtaradze, A. G. *Voennye spetsialisty na sluzhbe Respubliki Sovetov, 1917–1920 gg.* Moscow, 1988.

Kizilov, N. I. *NKVD RSFSR, 1917–1930 gg.* Moscow, 1969.

Kliatskin, Saul M. *Na zashchite Oktiabria: Organizatsiia reguliarnoi armii i militsionnoe stroitel'stvo v Sovetskoi Respublike, 1917–1920.* Moscow, 1965.

Klochkov, V. F. "Rol' Krasnoi Armii v likvidatsii negramotnosti i podgotovki kadrov dlia sela v gody sotsialisticheskogo stroitel'stva." *Istoriia SSSR* 3 (1980): 94–103.

Kolesnichenko, I. "K voprosu o konflikte v RVS Iuzhnogo fronta (sent.–okt. 1918 g.)." *Voenno-istoricheskii zhurnal* 2 (1962): 39–47.

Kolychev, Vasilii G. *Partiino-politicheskaia rabota v Krasnoi Armii v gody grazhdanskoi voiny.* Moscow, 1978.

Korablev, Iurii I. *V. I. Lenin i zashchita zavoevanii Velikogo Oktiabria.* Moscow, 1979.

"Kruglyi stol: Istoricheskaia nauka v usloviiakh perestroiki," *Voprosy istorii* 3 (1988): 3–57.

Kuchkin, A. P. *V boiakh i pokhodakh ot Volgi do Eniseia: Zapiski voennogo komissara.* Moscow, 1969.

Kuibysheva, G. V., N. V. Nelidov, and A. V. Khavin. *Valerian Vladimirovich Kuibyshev.* Moscow, 1966.

Kulish-Amirkhanova, A. S. *Rol' Krasnoi Armii v khoziaistvennom i kul'-turnom stroitel'stve v Dagestane (1920–1923 gg.).* Makhachkala, 1964.

Kuz'min, Nikolai F. *Na strazhe mirnogo truda (1921–1940 gg.).* Moscow, 1959.

Lenin, Vladimir Il'ich. *Polnoe sobranie sochinenii.* 40 vols. 5th ed. Moscow, 1958–1965.

Leninskii sbornik. 38 vols. Moscow, 1924–1975.

Lisenkov, M. M. *Kul'turnaia revoliutsiia v SSSR i armiia.* Moscow, 1977.

Lomov, N., and T. Kin. "Dobrovol'nye voenno-nauchnye obshchestva (Iz istorii sozdaniia)." *Voenno-istoricheskii zhurnal* 5 (1975): 122–26.

Mikoian, Anastas. *V nachale dvadtsatykh . . .* Moscow, 1975.

Molodtsygin, M. A. "Krasnaia gvardiia posle Oktiabria." *Voprosy istorii* 10 (1980): 25–43.

Ostriakov, S. *Voennye chekisty.* Moscow, 1979.

Petrov, Iurii P. "Deiatel'nost' Kommunisticheskoi partii po provedeniiu edinonachaliia v Vooruzhennykh Silakh (1925–1931 gody)." *Voenno-istoricheskii zhurnal* 5 (1963): 12–23.

———. *Stroitel'stvo politorganov, partiinykh i komsomol'skikh organizatsii armii i flota (1918–1968).* Moscow, 1968.

Portnov, Viktor P., and Mark M. Slavin. *Pravovye osnovy stroitel'stva Krasnoi Armii, 1918–1920 gg.* Moscow, 1985.

Revoliutsiia nas v boi zovet. Moscow, 1967.

Rudakov, M., I. Kolesnichenko, and V. Lunin. "Nekotorye voprosy raboty politorganov v gody inostrannoi voennoi interventsii i grazhdanskoi voiny." *Voenno-istoricheskii zhurnal* 8 (1962): 3–12.

Sovetskie vooruzhennye sily: Istoriia stroitel'stva. Moscow, 1978.

Stalin, Iosif V. *Sochineniia.* 13 vols. Moscow, 1946–1951.

Suvenirov, Oleg F. *Kommunisticheskaia partiia—organizator politicheskogo vospitaniia Krasnoi Armii i Flota, 1921–1928.* Moscow, 1976.

Tolstoi, Aleksei N. *Sobranie sochinenii.* 10 vols. Moscow, 1958–1961.

Tsvetaev, N. *Voennye voprosy v resheniiakh VIII s''ezda RKP (b).* Moscow, 1960.

Tyl Sovetskoi Armii za 40 let. Moscow, 1958.

Ushakov, M. I. "Iz istorii deiatel'nosti partii po organizatsii vsevobucha." *Voprosy istorii KPSS* 5 (1978): 102–12.

Valentinov (Vol'skii), N. *Novaia ekonomicheskaia politika i krizis partii posle smerti Lenina: Vospominaniia.* Stanford, Calif.: Hoover Institution Press, 1971.

Varenov, Vasilii I. *Pomoshch' Krasnoi Armii v razvitii kolkhoznogo stroitel'stva 1929–1933 gg.: Po materialam Sibirskogo voennogo okruga.* Moscow, 1978.

Vatsetis, Ioakim. "Vospominaniia." In *Pamiat'*, vol. 2. Moscow, 1977; Paris, 1979.

Vospominaniia o V. I. Lenine. 3 vols. Moscow, 1956–1960.

Zaionchkovskii, Petr A. *Samoderzhavie i russkaia armiia na rubezhe XIX–XX stoletii.* Moscow, 1973.

Zolotnitskii, David. *Zori teatral'nogo Oktiabria.* Leningrad, 1976.

Sources in Languages Other than Russian

Abramovitch, Raphael R. *The Soviet Revolution.* New York: International Universities Press, 1962.

Abramsky, Chimen, ed. *Essays in Honour of E. H. Carr.* London: Archon, 1974.

Adamson, Walter L. *Hegemony and Revolution: A Study of Antonio Gramsci's Political and Cultural Theory.* Berkeley: University of California Press, 1980.

Allen, William Sheridan. *The Nazi Seizure of Power: The Experience of a Single German Town, 1930–1935.* New York: New Viewpoints, 1973.

Andreski, Stanislaw. *Military Organization and Society.* Berkeley: University of California Press, 1971.

Antonov-Ovseenko, Anton. *The Time of Stalin: Portrait of a Tyranny.* Trans. George Saunders. New York: Harper & Row, 1981.

Anweiler, Oskar. *The Soviets: The Russian Workers, Peasants, and Soldiers Councils, 1905–1921.* New York: Pantheon, 1974.

Arian, Asher, Ilan Talmud, and Tamar Hermann. *National Security and Public Opinion in Israel.* Boulder, Colo.: Westview, 1988.

Bailes, Kendall. "Alexei Gastev and the Controversy over Taylorism, 1918–1924." *Soviet Studies* 29 (July 1977): 373–94.

Berger, Martin. *Engels, Armies, and Revolution.* Hamden, Conn.: Archon, 1977.

Berghahn, Volker. *Militarism: The History of an International Debate, 1861–1979.* New York: St. Martin's, 1982.

Bertaud, Jean-Paul. *La Révolution armée.* Paris: Laffont, 1979.

Beyrau, D. *Militär und Gesellschaft im vorrevolutionären Russland.* Cologne: Boehlau, 1984.

Black, Cyril E., ed. *The Transformation of Russian Society.* Cambridge: Harvard University Press, 1969.

Brooks, Jeffrey. "Popular and Public Values in the Soviet Press, 1921–1928." Paper presented at Conference on Popular Culture—East and West, Bloomington, Ind., 1 May 1986.

——. *When Russia Learned to Read.* Princeton: Princeton University Press, 1985.

Brovkin, Vladimir. "Politics, Not Economics, Was the Key." *Slavic Review* 44 (Summer 1985): 244–250.

Bukharin, Nikolai, and Evgenii Preobrazhenskii. *The ABC of Communism.* Trans. Eden Paul and Cedar Paul. London: Communist Party of Great Britain, 1927.

Bushnell, John. *Mutiny amid Repression: Russian Soldiers in the Revolution of 1905–1906.* Bloomington: Indiana University Press, 1985.

——. "The Tsarist Officer Corps, 1881–1914: Customs, Duties, Inefficiency." *American Historical Review* 86 (October 1981): 753–80.

Carr, E. H. *The Bolshevik Revolution.* 3 vols. New York: Macmillan, 1951–1953.

——. *The Interregnum, 1923–1924.* New York: Macmillan, 1954.

——. *Socialism in One Country, 1924–26.* 3 vols. New York: Macmillan, 1958–1964.

—— and R. W. Davies. *Foundations of a Planned Economy, 1926–1929.* 2 vols. in 3. New York: Macmillan, 1969–1971.

Checinski, Michael. "The Economics of Defence in the USSR." *Survey* 29 (Spring 1985): 59–78.

Chekhov, Anton. *The Portable Chekhov.* Trans. and ed. A. Yarmolinsky. New York: Viking, 1968.

Cohen, Stephen. *Bukharin and the Bolshevik Revolution: A Political Biography, 1888–1938.* New York: Knopf, 1973.

Colton, Timothy J. *Commissars, Commanders, and Civilian Authority: The Structure of Soviet Military Politics.* Cambridge: Harvard University Press, 1979.

Daniels, Robert V. *The Conscience of the Revolution: Communist Opposition in Soviet Russia.* Cambridge: Harvard University Press, 1960.

——. "The Militarization of Socialism in Russia, 1902–1946." Occasional Paper no. 200. Washington, D.C.: Kennan Institute for Advanced Russian Studies, 1985.

Davies, R. W. *The Development of the Soviet Budgetary System.* Cambridge: Cambridge University Press, 1958.

——. *The Industrialization of Soviet Russia.* 2 vols. Cambridge: Harvard University Press, 1980.

Deutscher, Isaac. *The Prophet Armed: Trotsky, 1879–1921.* New York: Oxford University Press, 1954.

——. *The Prophet Unarmed: Trotsky, 1921–1929.* New York: Oxford University Press, 1959.

——. *Stalin: A Political Biography.* New York: Oxford University Press, 1966.

Dewar, Margaret. *Labour Policy in the USSR, 1917–1928.* London: Royal Institute of International Affairs, 1956.

Dotsenko, Paul. *The Struggle for Democracy in Siberia, 1917–1920.* Stanford: Hoover Institution Press, 1983.

Eklof, A. Benoit. "Peasant Sloth Reconsidered: Strategies of Education and Learning in Rural Russia before the Revolution." *Journal of Social History* 14 (Spring 1981): 355–85.

Emmons, Terence, and Wayne S. Vucinich, eds. *The Zemstvo in Russia.* Cambridge: Cambridge University Press, 1982.

Erickson, John. *The Soviet High Command: A Military-Political History 1918–1941.* New York: St. Martin's Press, 1962.

Erlich, Alexander. *The Soviet Industrialization Debate, 1924–1928.* Cambridge: Harvard University Press, 1960.

Fainsod, Merle. *How Russia Is Ruled.* Cambridge: Harvard University Press, 1962.

——. *Smolensk under Soviet Rule.* New York: Vintage, 1963.

Ferro, Marc. *The Russian Revolution of February 1917.* Trans. J. L. Richards and Nicole Stone. Englewood Cliffs, N.J.: Prentice-Hall, 1972.

——. *October 1917: A Social History of the Russian Revolution.* Trans. Norman Stone. London: Routledge & Kegan Paul, 1980.

Field, Daniel. "From the Editor: Controversy." *Russian Review* 45 (October 1986): v–vi.

Finer, S. E. *The Man on Horseback: The Role of the Military in Politics.* London: Pall Mall, 1962.

Fischer, Louis, ed. *Thirteen Who Fled.* New York: Harper, 1949.

Fitzpatrick, Sheila. "The Bolsheviks' Dilemma: Class, Culture, and Politics in Early Soviet Years." *Slavic Review* 47 (Winter 1988): 599–613.

——. *The Commissariat of Enlightenment: Soviet Organization of Education and the Arts under Lunacharsky, October 1917–1921.* New York: Cambridge University Press, 1970.

——. *Education and Social Mobility in the Soviet Union, 1922–1934.* New York: Cambridge University Press, 1979.

Foucault, Michel. *Power/Knowledge. Selected Interviews and Other Writings, 1972–1977.* Ed. Conlin Gordon. New York: Pantheon, 1980.

Fuller, William C., Jr. *Civil-Military Conflict in Imperial Russia, 1881–1914.* Princeton: Princeton University Press, 1985.

Furmanov, Dmitrii. *Chapaev.* Moscow: Foreign Language Publishing House, 1959.

Gallie, W. B. *Philosophers of Peace and War: Kant, Clausewitz, Marx, Engels, and Tolstoy.* New York: Cambridge University Press, 1978.

Gerson, Lennard. *The Secret Police in Lenin's Russia.* Philadelphia: Temple University Press, 1976.

Goldman, Emma. *My Disillusionment in Russia.* Gloucester, Mass.: Peter Smith, 1983.

Gorer, Geoffrey, and John Rickman. *The People of Great Russia: A Psychological Study.* New York: Chanticleer, 1950.

Gramsci, Antonio. *Selections from the Prison Notebooks of Antonio Gramsci.* Trans. and ed. Quinton Hoare and Geoffrey Nowell Smith. New York: International Publishers, 1985.

Harding, Neil. *Lenin's Political Thought.* 2 vols. New York: St. Martin's, vol 1: 1977, vol 2: 1981.

——, ed. *The State in Socialist Society.* Albany: State University of New York Press, 1984.

Harper, Samuel. *Making Bolsheviks.* Chicago: University of Chicago Press, 1931.

Haslam, Jonathan. *Soviet Foreign Policy, 1930–1933: The Impact of the Depression.* London: Macmillan, 1983.

Heller, Mikhail, and Aleksandr M. Nekrich. *Utopia in Power: The History of the Soviet Union from 1917 to the Present.* Trans. Phyllis B. Carlos. New York: Summit, 1986.

Hellie, Richard. *Enserfment and Military Change in Muscovy.* Chicago: University of Chicago Press, 1971.

Hintze, Otto. *The Historical Essays of Otto Hintze.* Ed. Felix Gilbert. New York: Oxford University Press, 1975.

Howard, Michael. *The Causes of Wars.* London: Unwin, 1983.

Huntington, Samuel P. *The Soldier and the State: The Theory and Politics of Civil–Military Relations.* Cambridge: Harvard University Press, 1954.

Jacobs, Walter Darnell. *Frunze: The Soviet Clausewitz, 1885–1925.* The Hague: Martinus Nijhoff, 1969.

Janowitz, Morris. *The Professional Soldier.* Glenview, Ill.: Free Press, 1960.

Jasny, Naum. *Soviet Economists of the Twenties.* Cambridge: Cambridge University Press, 1972.

Jaurès, Jean. *L'Armée nouvelle.* Paris: Editions Sociales, 1911.

Johnson, John J., ed. *The Role of the Military in Underdeveloped Countries.* Princeton: Princeton University Press, 1962.

Kautsky, Karl. *The Social Revolution.* Trans. A. M. Simons and May Wood Simons. Chicago: C. H. Kerr, 1916.

——. *Terrorism and Communism.* Westport, Conn.: Hyperion, 1973. First English ed. London, 1920.

Keep, John L. H. *The Russian Revolution: A Study in Mass Mobilization.* New York: Norton, 1976.

——. *Soldiers of the Tsar.* Oxford: Clarendon, 1985.

Kenez, Peter. "A Profile of the Pre-Revolutionary Officer Corps." *California Slavic Studies* 7 (1973): 121–58.

Kimerling, Elise. "Civil Rights and Social Policy in Soviet Russia, 1918–1936." *Russian Review* 41 (January 1982): 24–46.

——. "Soldiers' Children, 1719–1856: A Study of Social Engineering in Imperial Russia." *Forschungen zur Osteuropäischen Geschichte* 30 (1982): 61–136.

Kingston-Mann, Esther. *Lenin and the Problem of Marxist Peasant Revolution.* New York: Oxford University Press, 1985.

Kirshon, Vladimir. *Red Rust.* New York: Brentano's, 1930.

Kliuchevskii, Vasilii O. *Peter the Great.* Trans. L. Archibald. New York: Vintage, 1961.

Kopelev, Lev. *The Education of a True Believer.* Trans. Gary Kern. New York: Harper & Row, 1980.

Lasswell, Harold D. *Propaganda Technique in World War I.* Cambridge: MIT Press, 1971.

—— and David Lerner, eds. *World Revolutionary Elites: Studies in Coercive Ideological Movements.* Cambridge: MIT Press, 1965.

Leggett, George. *The Cheka: Lenin's Political Police.* Oxford: Clarendon, 1981.

Lewin, Moshe. *The Making of the Soviet System.* New York: Pantheon, 1985.

——. "More than One Piece Is Missing in the Puzzle." *Slavic Review* 44 (Summer 1985): 239–43.

——. *Russian Peasants and Soviet Power: A Study of Collectivization.* New York: Norton, 1968.

Lih, Lars. *Bread and Authority in Russia.* Berkeley: University of California Press, forthcoming.

Lynn, John A. *The Bayonets of the Republic.* Urbana : University of Illinois Press, 1984.

Malia, Martin. *Comprendre la Révolution russe.* Paris: Seuil, 1980.

Malle, Sylvana. *The Economic Organization of War Communism, 1918–1921.* Cambridge: Cambridge University Press, 1985.

Mally, Lynn. *Culture of the Future: The Proletkult Movement in Revolutionary Russia.* Berkeley: University of California Press, forthcoming.

Marx, Karl. *The Eighteenth Brumaire of Louis Bonaparte.* New York: International Publishers, 1983.

Mawdsley, Evan. *The Russian Civil War.* Boston: Allen & Unwin, 1987.

Meyer, Alfred G. "The Functions of Ideology in the Soviet Political System." *Soviet Studies* 17 (January 1966): 273–85.

Odom, William E. *The Soviet Volunteers: Modernization and Bureaucracy in a Public Mass Organization.* Princeton: Princeton University Press, 1973.

Orlovsky, Daniel. *Russia's Democratic Revolution: The Provisional Government of 1917 and the Origin of the Soviet State.* Berkeley: University of California Press, forthcoming.

Paret, Peter ed. *Makers of Modern Strategy from Machiavelli to the Nuclear Age.* Princeton: Princeton University Press, 1986.

Perlmutter, Amos. *The Military and Politics in Modern Times.* New Haven: Yale University Press, 1977.

Pethybridge, Roger. "Concern for Bolshevik Ideological Predominance at the Start of the NEP." *Russian Review* 41 (October 1982): 445–53.
——. *The Social Prelude to Stalinism.* New York: St. Martin's, 1974.
Radkey, Oliver H. *Russia Goes to the Polls: The Election to the All-Russian Constituent Assembly, 1917.* Ithaca: Cornell University Press, 1989.
Remington, Thomas. *Building Socialism in Bolshevik Russia: Ideology and Industrial Organization, 1917–1921.* Pittsburgh: University of Pittsburgh Press, 1984.
Rigby, T. H. *Communist Party Membership in the USSR, 1917–1967.* Princeton: Princeton University Press, 1968.
Riordan, James. *Sport in Soviet Society.* Cambridge: Cambridge University Press, 1977.
Ritter, Gerhard. *Das Kommunemodell und die Begründung der Roten Armee im Jahre 1918.* Berlin: Osteuropa-Institut, 1965.
Rosenberg, William G. "Russian Labor and Bolshevik Power after October." *Slavic Review* 44 (Summer 1985): 213–38.
——. "The Zemstvo in 1917 and under Bolshevik Rule." In *The Zemstvo in Russia,* ed. Terence Emmons and Wayne S. Vucinich, pp. 410–16. Cambridge: Cambridge University Press, 1982.
Rudnitsky, Konstantin. *Meyerhold the Director.* Trans. George Petrov. Ed. Sydney Schultze. Ann Arbor, Mich.: Ardis, 1981.
Schapiro, Leonard. *The Communist Party of the Soviet Union.* New York: Vintage, 1971.
Serrigny, Bertaud. *Reflexions sur l'art de guerre.* Paris: Charles–La Vauzelle, 1921.
Service, Robert. *The Bolshevik Party in Revolution: A Study in Organizational Change, 1917–1923.* New York: Macmillan, 1979.
Sholokhov, Mikhail. *Seeds of Tomorrow.* Trans. Stephen Garry. New York: Knopf, 1935.
Siegelbaum, Lewis. *The Politics of Industrial Mobilization in Russia.* New York: St. Martin's, 1983.
Sorlin, Pierre. *The Soviet People and Their Society.* Trans. Daniel Weissbart. New York: Praeger, 1968.
Starr, S. Frederick. *Decentralization and Self-Government in Russia, 1830–1870.* Princeton: Princeton University Press, 1972.
Stepan, Alfred. *The Military in Politics: Changing Patterns in Brazil.* Princeton: Princeton University Press, 1971.
——. *Rethinking Military Politics: Brazil and the Southern Cone.* Princeton: Princeton University Press, 1988.
Thomson, Boris. *Lot's Wife and the Venus of Milo.* Cambridge: Cambridge University Press, 1978.
Timasheff, Nicholas S. *The Great Retreat.* New York: Dutton, 1946.
Tirado, Isabel. *Young Guard! The Communist Youth League, Petrograd 1917–1920.* Westport, Conn.: Greenwood, 1988.
Treadgold, Donald. *Lenin and His Rivals: The Struggle for Russia's Future, 1898–1908.* New York: Praeger, 1965.
Trotsky, Leon. *My Life.* New York: Scribner's, 1930.
——. *Problems of Everyday Life, and Other Writings on Culture and Science.* New York: Monad, 1973.
——. *The Revolution Betrayed.* New York: Merit, 1965.
——. *Terrorism and Communism.* London: New Park, 1975.

——. The Trotsky Papers, 1917–1922. 2 vols. Ed. Jan M. Meijer. The Hague: Mouton, 1964–1971.

Tucker, Robert C., ed. Stalinism: Essays in Historical Interpretation. New York: Norton, 1977.

Tumarkin, Nina. Lenin Lives! The Lenin Cult in Soviet Russia. Cambridge: Harvard University Press, 1983.

Wade, Rex. Red Guards and Workers' Militias in the Russian Revolution. Stanford: Stanford University Press, 1984.

Weber, Eugen. Peasants into Frenchmen: The Modernization of Rural France, 1870–1914. Stanford: Stanford University Press, 1976.

Wildman, Allan K. The End of the Russian Imperial Army. Vol. 1, The Old Army and the Soldiers' Revolt (March–April 1917); vol. 2, The Road to Soviet Power and Peace. Princeton: Princeton University Press, 1980, 1988.

Zhukov, G. K. Zichrornot Hamarshal Zhukov. Tel Aviv: Maarachot, 1982.

Index

Studies in Soviet History and Society

edited by Joseph S. Berliner, Seweryn Bialer, *and* Sheila Fitzpatrick

STUDIES OF THE HARRIMAN INSTITUTE

Soviet National Income in 1937 by Abram Bergson (Columbia University Press, 1953).

Through the Glass of Soviet Literature: Views of Russian Society, ed. Ernest Simmons, Jr. (Columbia University Press, 1953).

Polish Postwar Economy by Thad Paul Alton (Columbia University Press, 1954).

Management of the Industrial Firm in the USSR: A Study in Soviet Economic Planning by David Granick (Columbia University Press, 1954).

Soviet Policies in China, 1917–1924 by Allen S. Whiting (Columbia University Press, 1954; paperback, Stanford University Press, 1968).

Literary Politics in the Soviet Ukraine, 1917–1934 by George S. N. Luckyj (Columbia University Press, 1956).

The Emergence of Russian Panslavism, 1856–1870 by Michael Boro Petrovich (Columbia University Press, 1956).

Lenin on Trade Unions and Revolution, 1893–1917 by Thomas Taylor Hammond (Columbia University Press, 1956).

The Last Years of the Georgian Monarchy, 1658–1832 by David Marshall Lang (Columbia University Press, 1957).

The Japanese Thrust into Siberia, 1918 by James William Morley (Columbia University Press, 1957).

Bolshevism in Turkestan, 1917–1927 by Alexander G. Park (Columbia University Press, 1957).

Soviet Marxism: A Critical Analysis by Herbert Marcuse (Columbia University Press, 1958; paperback, Columbia University Press, 1985).

Soviet Policy and the Chinese Communists, 1931–1946 by Charles B. McLane (Columbia University Press, 1958).

The Agrarian Foes of Bolshevism: Promise and Defeat of the Russian Socialist Revolutionaries, February to October 1917 by Oliver H. Radkey (Columbia University Press, 1958).

Pattern for Soviet Youth: A Study of the Congresses of the Komsomol, 1918–1954 by Ralph Talcott Fisher, Jr. (Columbia University Press, 1959).

The Emergence of Modern Lithuania by Alfred Erich Senn (Columbia University Press, 1959).

The Soviet Design for a World State by Elliot R. Goodman (Columbia University Press, 1960).

Settling Disputes in Soviet Society: The Formative Years of Legal Institutions by John N. Hazard (Columbia University Press, 1960).

Soviet Marxism and Natural Science, 1917–1932 by David Joravsky (Columbia University Press, 1961).

Russian Classics in Soviet Jackets by Maurice Friedberg (Columbia University Press, 1962).

Stalin and the French Communist Party, 1941–1947 by Alfred J. Rieber (Columbia University Press, 1962).

Sergei Witte and the Industrialization of Russia by Theodore K. Von Laue (Columbia University Press, 1962).

Ukrainian Nationalism by John H. Armstrong (Columbia University Press, 1963).

The Sickle under the Hammer: The Russian Socialist Revolutionaries in the Early Months of Soviet Rule by Oliver H. Radkey (Columbia University Press, 1963).

Comintern and World Revolution, 1928–1943: The Shaping of Doctrine by Kermit E. McKenzie (Columbia University Press, 1964).

Weimar Germany and Soviet Russia, 1926–1933: A Study in Diplomatic Instability by Harvey L. Dyck (Columbia University Press, 1966).

Financing Soviet Schools by Harold J. Noah (Teachers College Press, 1966).

Russia, Bolshevism, and the Versailles Peace by John M. Thompson (Princeton University Press, 1966).

The Russian Anarchists by Paul Avrich (Princeton University Press, 1967).

The Soviet Academy of Sciences and the Communist Party, 1927–1932 by Loren R. Graham (Princeton University Press, 1967).

Red Virgin Soil: Soviet Literature in the 1920's by Robert A. Maguire (Princeton University Press, 1968; paperback, Cornell University Press, 1987).

Communist Party Membership in the U.S.S.R., 1917–1967 by T. H. Rigby (Princeton University Press, 1968).

Soviet Ethics and Morality by Richard T. De George (University of Michigan Press, 1969; paperback, Ann Arbor Paperbacks, 1969).

Vladimir Akimov on the Dilemmas of Russian Marxism, 1895–1903 by Jonathan Frankel (Cambridge University Press, 1969).

Soviet Perspectives on International Relations, 1956–1967 by William Zimmerman (Princeton University Press, 1969).

Krondstadt, 1921 by Paul Avrich (Princeton University Press, 1970).

Class Struggle in the Pale: The Formative Years of the Jewish Workers' Movement in Tsarist Russia by Ezra Mendelsohn (Cambridge University Press, 1970).

The Proletarian Episode in Russian Literature by Edward J. Brown (Columbia University Press, 1971).

Labor and Society in Tsarist Russia: The Factory Workers of St. Petersburg, 1855–1870 by Reginald E. Zelnik (Stanford University Press, 1971).

Archives and Manuscript Repositories in the U.S.S.R.: Moscow and Leningrad by Patricia K. Grimsted (Princeton University Press, 1972).

The Baku Commune, 1917–1918 by Ronald G. Suny (Princeton University Press, 1972).

Mayakovsky: A Poet in the Revolution by Edward J. Brown (Princeton University Press, 1973).

Oblomov and His Creator: The Life and Art of Ivan Goncharov by Milton Ehre (Princeton University Press, 1973).

German Politics under Soviet Occupation by Henry Krisch (Columbia University Press, 1974).

Soviet Politics and Society in the 1970's, ed. Henry W. Morton and Rudolph L. Tokes (Free Press, 1974).

Liberals in the Russian Revolution by William G. Rosenberg (Princeton University Press, 1974).

Famine in Russia, 1891–1892 by Richard G. Robbins, Jr. (Columbia University Press, 1975).

In Stalin's Time: Middle-class Values in Soviet Fiction by Vera Dunham (Cambridge University Press, 1976).

The Road to Bloody Sunday by Walter Sablinsky (Princeton University Press, 1976; paperback, Princeton University Press, 1986).

The Familiar Letter as a Literary Genre in the Age of Pushkin by William Mills Todd III (Princeton University Press, 1976).

Russian Realist Art. The State and Society: The Peredvizhniki and Their Tradition by Elizabeth Valkenier (Ardis, 1977; paperback, Columbia University Press, 1989).

The Soviet Agrarian Debate by Susan Solomon (Westview Press, 1978).

Cultural Revolution in Russia, 1928–1931, ed. Sheila Fitzpatrick (Indiana University Press, 1978; paperback, Midland Books, 1984).

Soviet Criminologists and Criminal Policy: Specialists in Policy-Making by Peter Solomon (Columbia University Press, 1978).

Technology and Society under Lenin and Stalin: Origins of the Soviet Technical Intelligentsia by Kendall E. Bailes (Princeton University Press, 1978).

The Politics of Rural Russia, 1905–1914, ed. Leopold H. Haimson (Indiana University Press, 1979).

Political Participation in the U.S.S.R. by Theodore H. Friedgut (Princeton University Press, 1979; paperback, Princeton University Press, 1982).

Education and Social Mobility in the Soviet Union, 1921–1934 by Sheila Fitzpatrick (Cambridge University Press, 1979).

The Soviet Marriage Market: Mate-Selection in Russia and the USSR by Wesley Andrew Fisher (Praeger, 1980).

Prophecy and Politics: Socialism, Nationalism, and the Russian Jews, 1862–1917 by Jonathan Frankel (Cambridge University Press, 1981).

Dostoevsky and "The Idiot": Author, Narrator, and Reader by Robin Feuer Miller (Harvard University Press, 1981).

Moscow Workers and the 1917 Revolution by Diane Koenker (Princeton University Press, 1981; paperback, Princeton University Press, 1986).

Archives and Manuscript Repositories in the USSR: Estonia, Latvia, Lithuania, and Belorussia by Patricia K. Grimsted (Princeton University Press, 1981).

Zionism in Poland: The Formative Years, 1915–1926 by Ezra Mendelsohn (Yale University Press, 1982).

Soviet Risk-Taking and Crisis Behavior by Hannes Adomeit (George Allen & Unwin, 1982).

Russia at the Crossroads: The 26th Congress of the CPSU, ed. Seweryn Bialer and Thane Gustafson (George Allen & Unwin, 1982).

The Crisis of the Old Order in Russia: Gentry and Government by Roberta Thompson Manning (Princeton University Press, 1983; paperback, Princeton University Press, 1986).

Sergei Aksakov and Russian Pastoral by Andrew A. Durkin (Rutgers University Press, 1983).

Politics and Technology in the Soviet Union by Bruce Parrott (MIT Press, 1983).

The Soviet Union and the Third World: An Economic Bind by Elizabeth Kridl Valkenier (Praeger, 1983).

Russian Metaphysical Romanticism: The Poetry of Tiutchev and Boratynskii by Sarah Pratt (Stanford University Press, 1984).

Ruling Russia: Politics and Administration in the Age of Absolutism, 1762–1796 by John LeDonne (Princeton University Press, 1984).

Insidious Intent: A Structural Analysis of Fedor Sologub's Petty Demon by Diana Greene (Slavica, 1986).

Leo Tolstoy: Resident and Stranger by Richard Gustafson (Princeton University Press, 1986).

Workers, Society, and the State: Labor and Life in Moscow, 1918–1929 by William Chase (University of Illinois Press, 1987).

Andrey Bely: Spirit of Symbolism, ed. John Malmstad (Cornell University Press, 1987).

Government and Peasant in Russia, 1861–1906: The Prehistory of the Stolypin Reforms by David A. J. Macey (Northern Illinois University Press, 1987).

The Making of Three Russian Revolutionaries: Voices from the Menshevik Past, ed. Leopold H. Haimson in collaboration with Ziva Galili y García and Richard Wortman (Cambridge University Press, 1988).

Revolution and Culture: The Bogdanov-Lenin Controversy by Zenovia A. Sochor (Cornell University Press, 1988).

A Handbook of Russian Verbs by Frank Miller (Ardis, 1989).

Russian Literary Politics and the Pushkin Celebration of 1880 by Marcus C. Levitt (Cornell University Press, 1989).

Alien Tongues: Bilingual Russian Writers of the "First Emigration" by Elizabeth Klosty Beaujour (Cornell University Press, 1989).

Soldiers in the Proletarian Dictatorship: The Red Army and the Soviet Socialist State, 1917–1930 by Mark von Hagen (Cornell University Press, 1990).

Library of Congress Cataloging-in-Publication Data

Von Hagen, Mark, 1954–
  Soldiers in the proletarian dictatorship : the Red Army and the
Soviet socialist state, 1917–1930 / Mark von Hagen.
      p.   cm.—(Studies in Soviet history and society) (Studies of the Harriman In-
stitute)
  Bibliography: p.
  Includes index.
  ISBN 0-8014-2420-8 (alk. paper)
    1. Civil-military relations—Soviet Union—History—20th century.   2. Soviet
Union. Raboche-Krest'ianskaia Krasnaia Armiia—History.   3. Soviet Union—
Politics and government—1917–1936.   4. Socialism—Soviet Union—History—20th
century.   5. Kommunisticheskaia partiia Sovetskogo Soiuza—Party work—
History—20th century.   I. Title.   II. Series.   III. Series: Studies in Soviet history
and society (Ithaca, N.Y.)
UA770.V5492   1990
322'.5'0947—dc20   89-36148